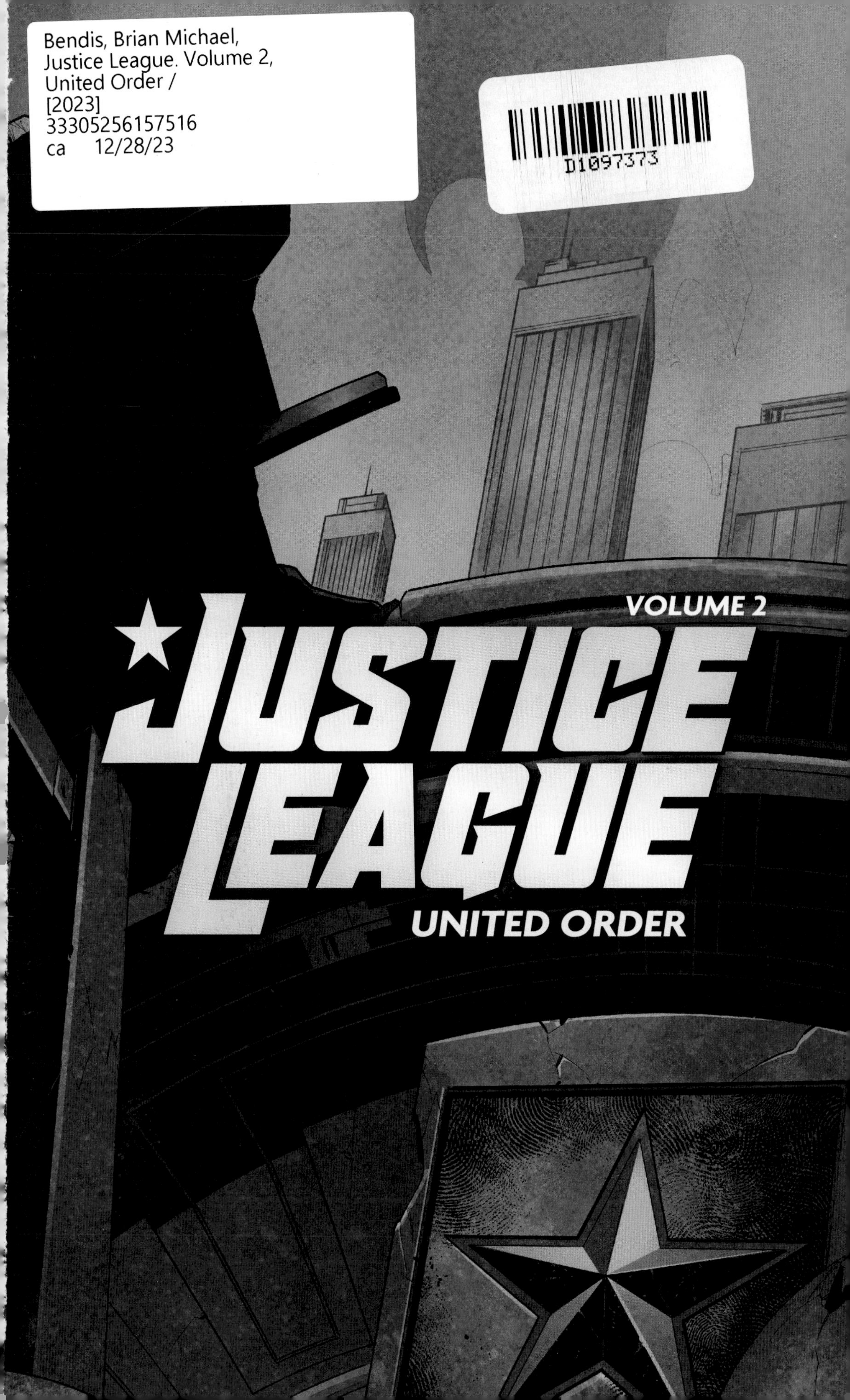
VOLUME 2
JUSTICE LEAGUE
UNITED ORDER

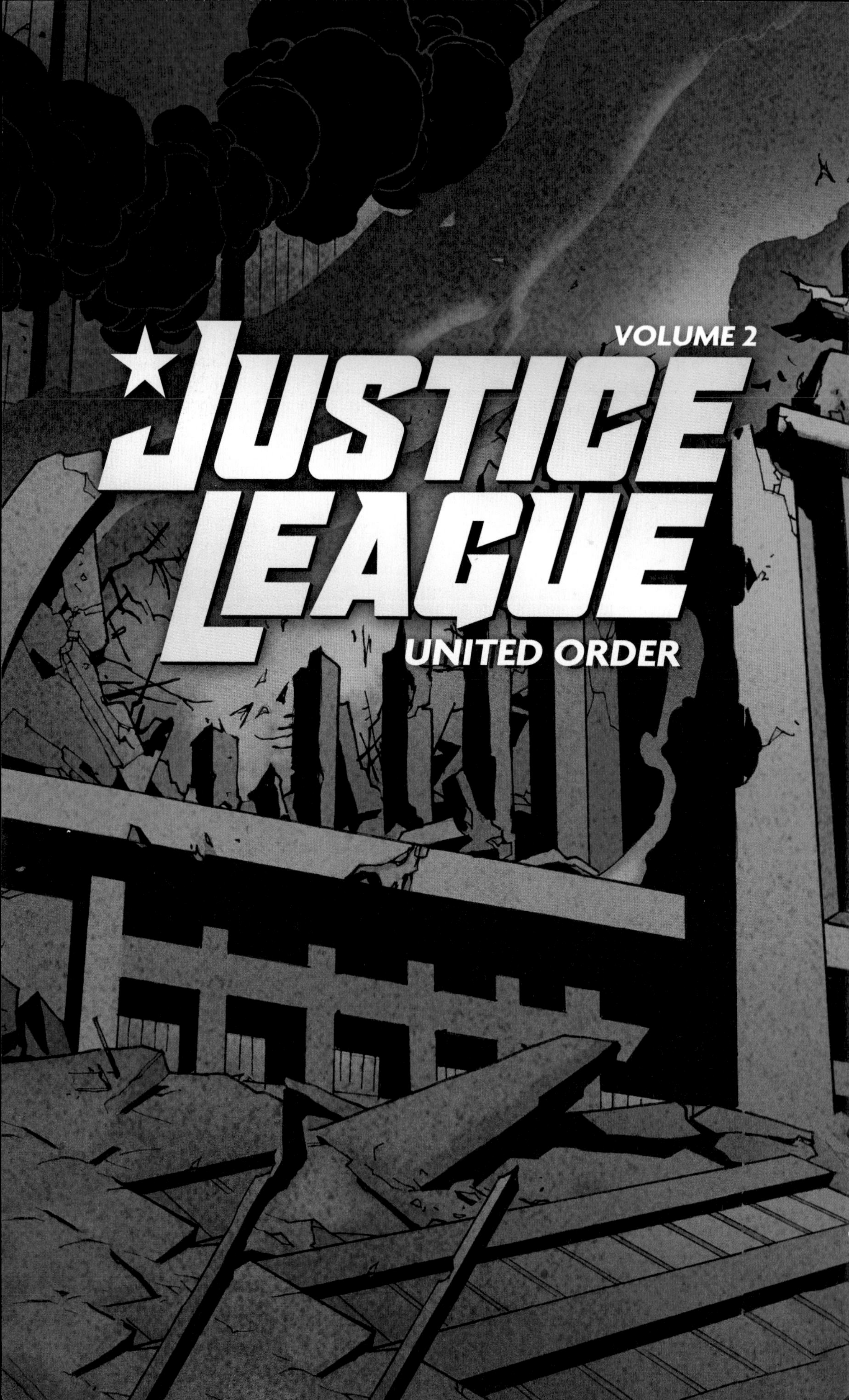
VOLUME 2
JUSTICE LEAGUE
UNITED ORDER

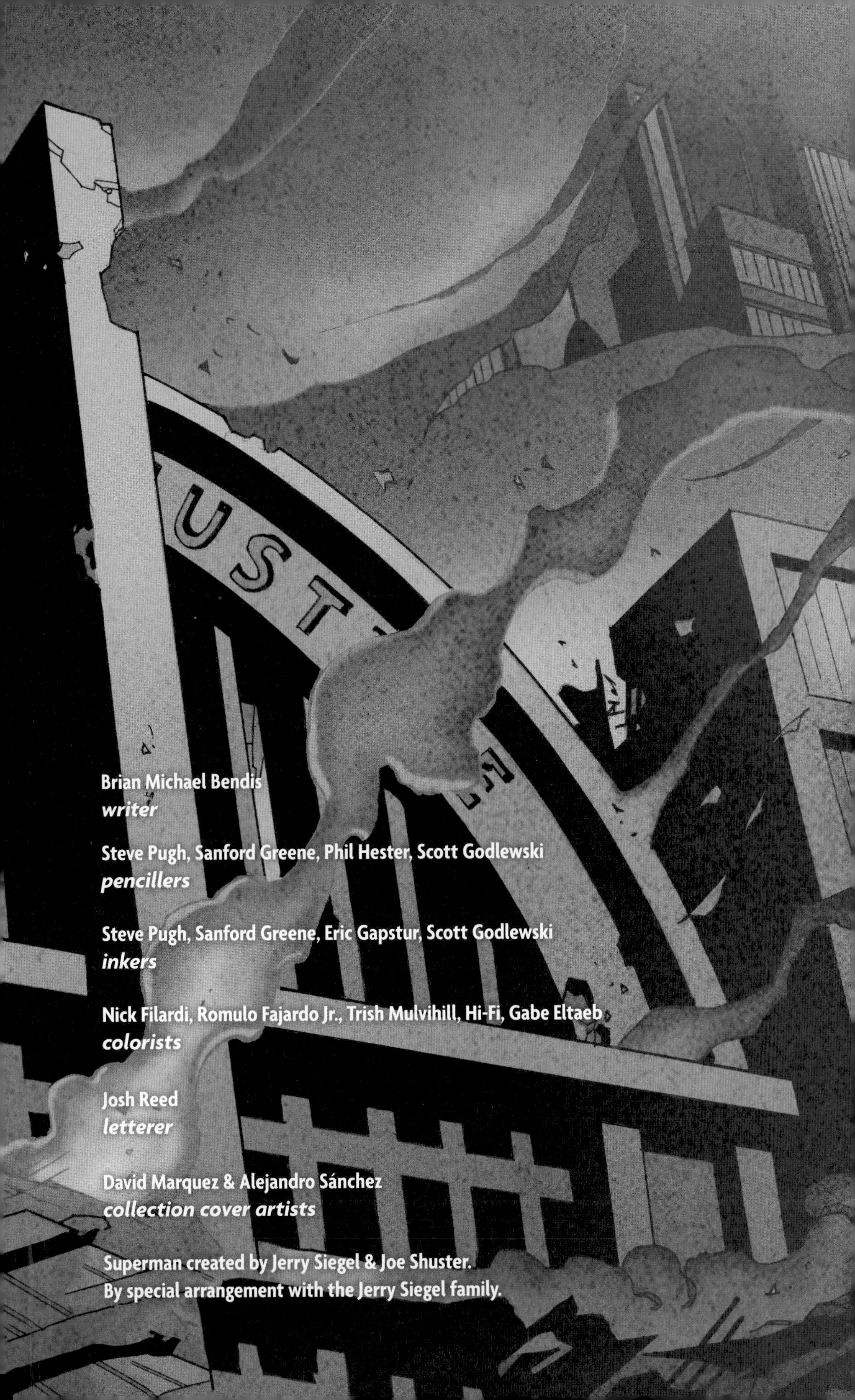

Brian Michael Bendis
writer

Steve Pugh, Sanford Greene, Phil Hester, Scott Godlewski
pencillers

Steve Pugh, Sanford Greene, Eric Gapstur, Scott Godlewski
inkers

Nick Filardi, Romulo Fajardo Jr., Trish Mulvihill, Hi-Fi, Gabe Eltaeb
colorists

Josh Reed
letterer

David Marquez & Alejandro Sánchez
collection cover artists

Superman created by Jerry Siegel & Joe Shuster.
By special arrangement with the Jerry Siegel family.

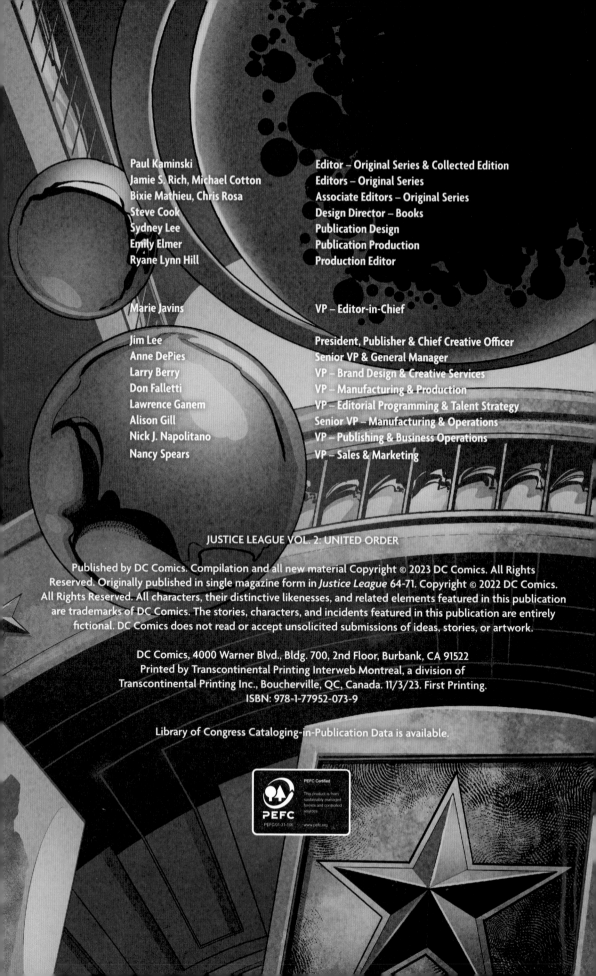

Paul Kaminski	Editor – Original Series & Collected Edition
Jamie S. Rich, Michael Cotton	Editors – Original Series
Bixie Mathieu, Chris Rosa	Associate Editors – Original Series
Steve Cook	Design Director – Books
Sydney Lee	Publication Design
Emily Elmer	Publication Production
Ryane Lynn Hill	Production Editor
Marie Javins	VP – Editor-in-Chief
Jim Lee	President, Publisher & Chief Creative Officer
Anne DePies	Senior VP & General Manager
Larry Berry	VP – Brand Design & Creative Services
Don Falletti	VP – Manufacturing & Production
Lawrence Ganem	VP – Editorial Programming & Talent Strategy
Alison Gill	Senior VP – Manufacturing & Operations
Nick J. Napolitano	VP – Publishing & Business Operations
Nancy Spears	VP – Sales & Marketing

JUSTICE LEAGUE VOL. 2: UNITED ORDER

DC Comics, 4000 Warner Blvd., Bldg. 700, 2nd Floor, Burbank, CA 91522
Printed by Transcontinental Printing Interweb Montreal, a division of Transcontinental Printing Inc., Boucherville, QC, Canada. 11/3/23. First Printing.
ISBN: 978-1-77952-073-9

Library of Congress Cataloging-in-Publication Data is available.

PEFC Certified
This product is from sustainably managed forests and controlled sources
PEFC
PEFC/01-31-106
www.pefc.org

Justice League #64 cover art by
David Marquez & Alejandro Sánchez

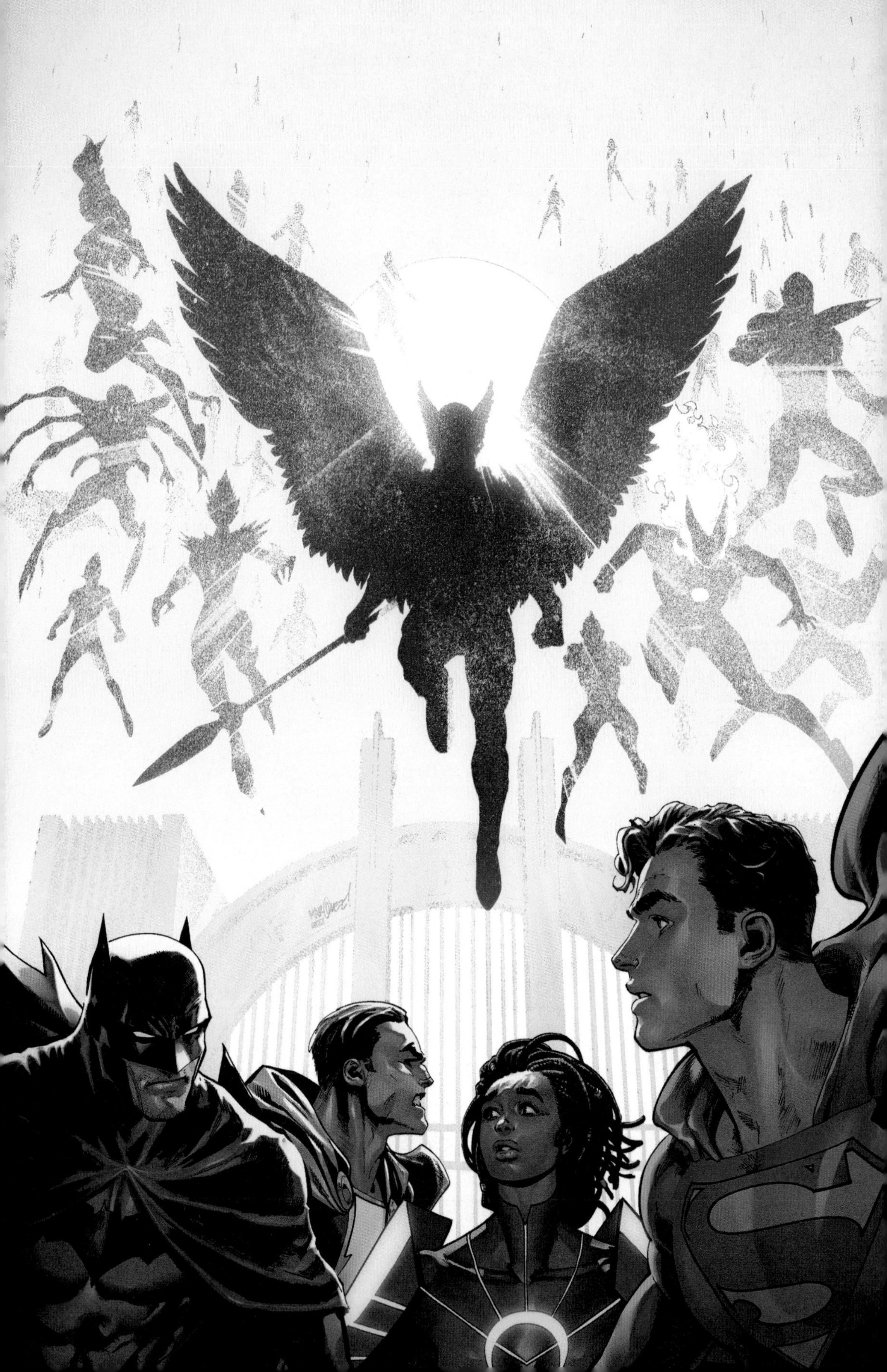

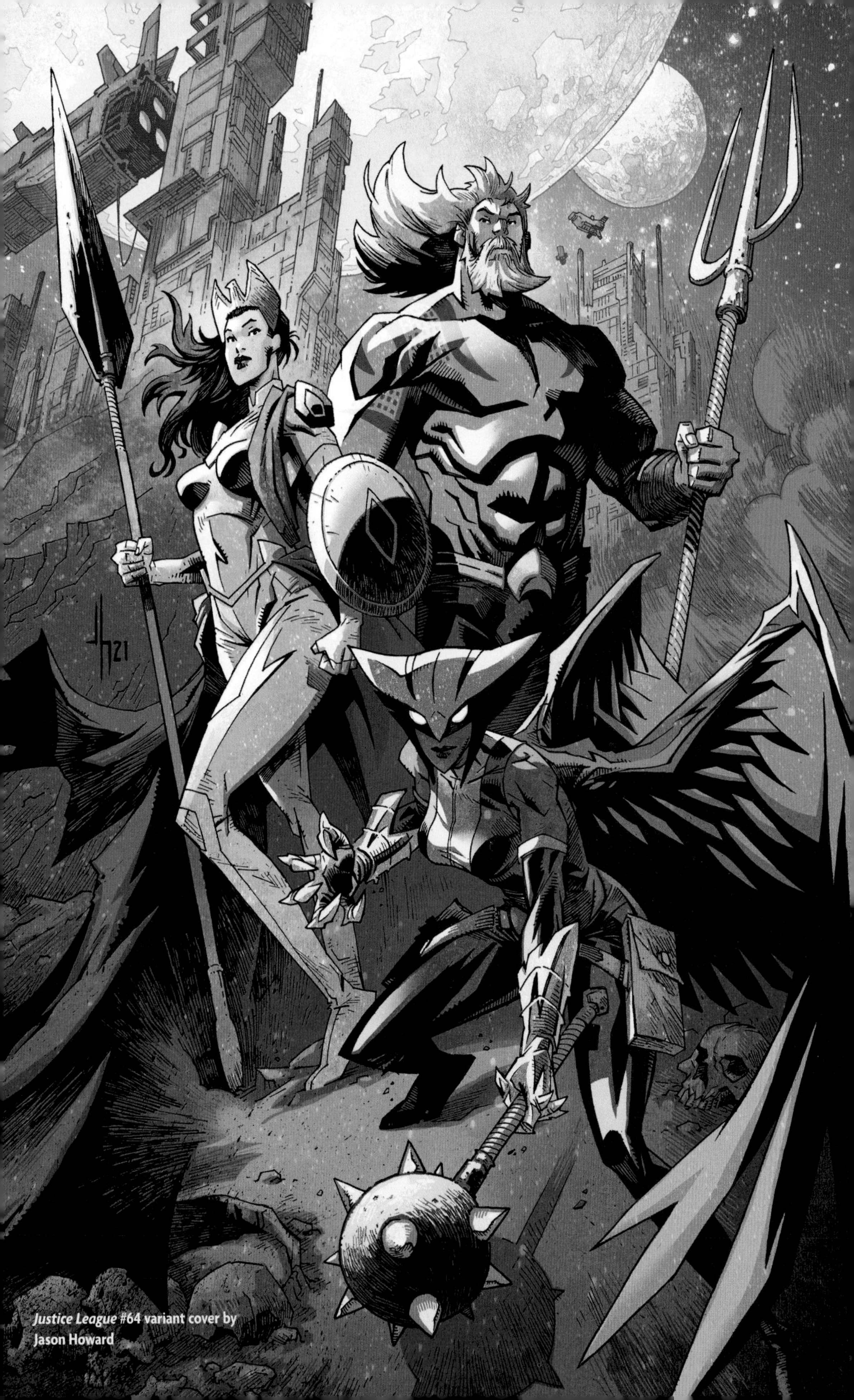
JH21

Justice League #64 variant cover by
Jason Howard

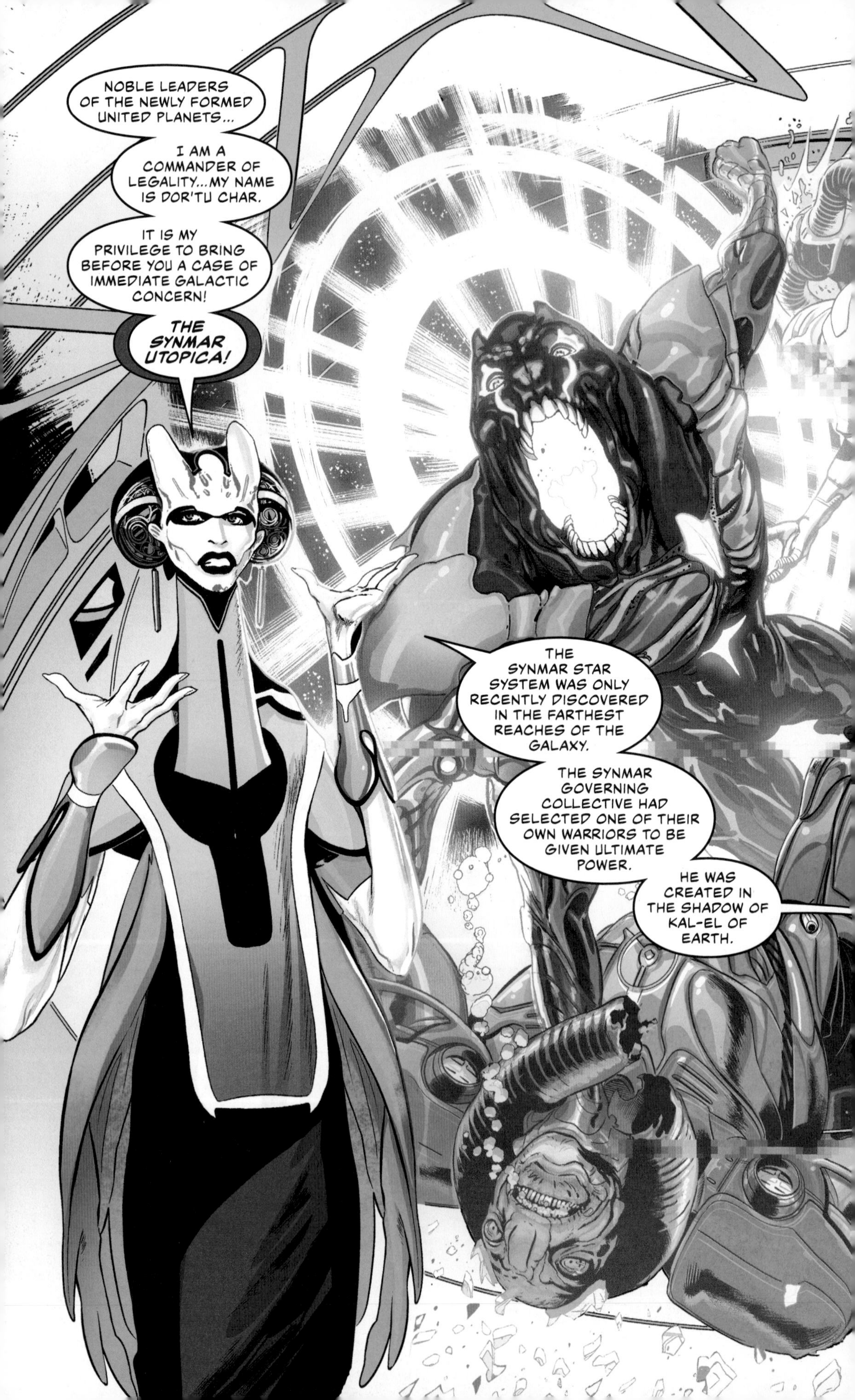
NOBLE LEADERS OF THE NEWLY FORMED UNITED PLANETS...
I AM A COMMANDER OF LEGALITY...MY NAME IS DOR'TU CHAR.
IT IS MY PRIVILEGE TO BRING BEFORE YOU A CASE OF IMMEDIATE GALACTIC CONCERN!
THE SYNMAR UTOPICA!
THE SYNMAR STAR SYSTEM WAS ONLY RECENTLY DISCOVERED IN THE FARTHEST REACHES OF THE GALAXY.
THE SYNMAR GOVERNING COLLECTIVE HAD SELECTED ONE OF THEIR OWN WARRIORS TO BE GIVEN ULTIMATE POWER.
HE WAS CREATED IN THE SHADOW OF KAL-EL OF EARTH.

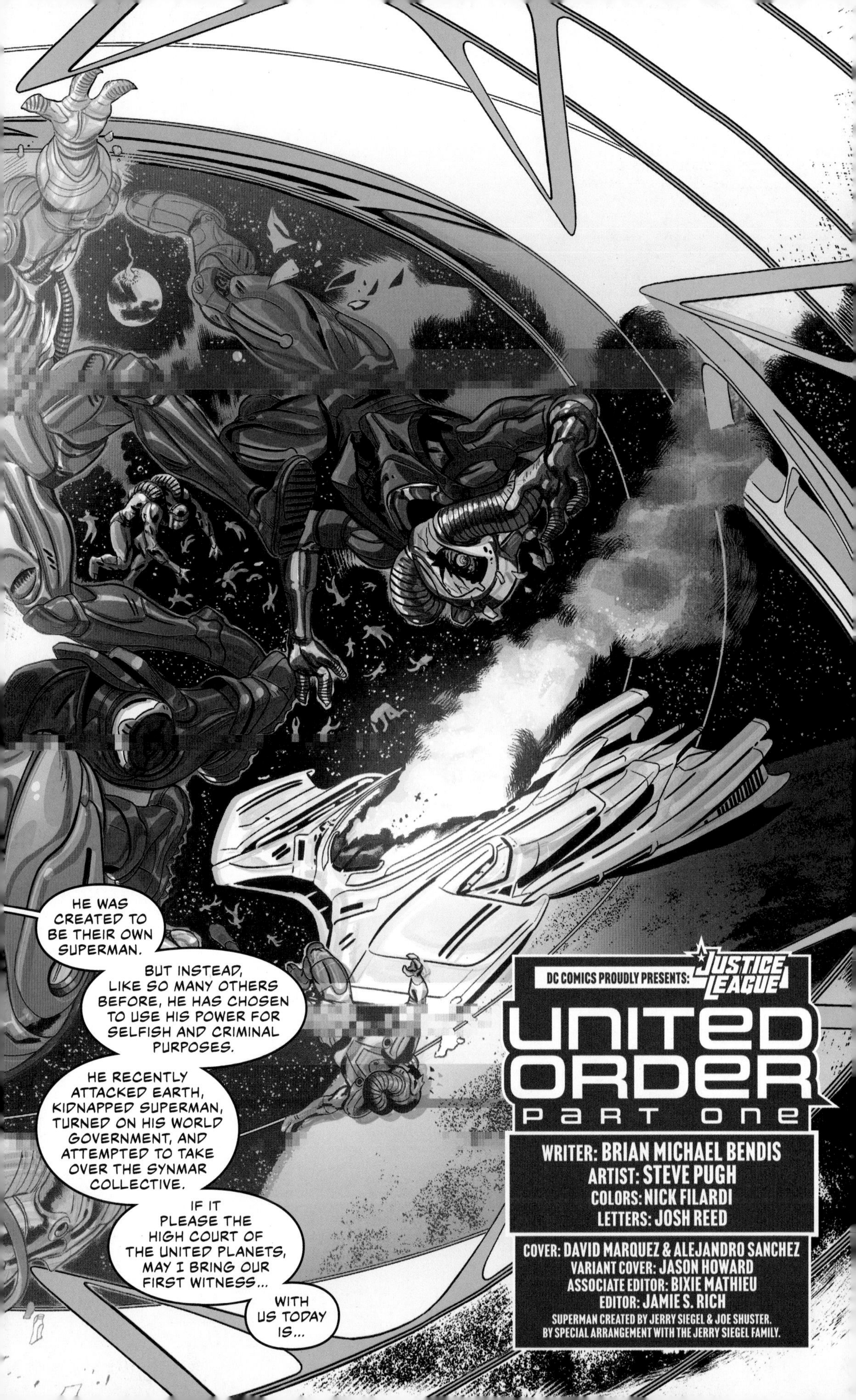

HE WAS CREATED TO BE THEIR OWN SUPERMAN.
BUT INSTEAD, LIKE SO MANY OTHERS BEFORE, HE HAS CHOSEN TO USE HIS POWER FOR SELFISH AND CRIMINAL PURPOSES.
HE RECENTLY ATTACKED EARTH, KIDNAPPED SUPERMAN, TURNED ON HIS WORLD GOVERNMENT, AND ATTEMPTED TO TAKE OVER THE SYNMAR COLLECTIVE.
IF IT PLEASE THE HIGH COURT OF THE UNITED PLANETS, MAY I BRING OUR FIRST WITNESS...
WITH US TODAY IS...
DC COMICS PROUDLY PRESENTS: JUSTICE LEAGUE
UNITED ORDER
PART ONE
WRITER: BRIAN MICHAEL BENDIS
ARTIST: STEVE PUGH
COLORS: NICK FILARDI
LETTERS: JOSH REED
COVER: DAVID MARQUEZ & ALEJANDRO SANCHEZ
VARIANT COVER: JASON HOWARD
ASSOCIATE EDITOR: BIXIE MATHIEU
EDITOR: JAMIE S. RICH
SUPERMAN CREATED BY JERRY SIEGEL & JOE SHUSTER.
BY SPECIAL ARRANGEMENT WITH THE JERRY SIEGEL FAMILY.

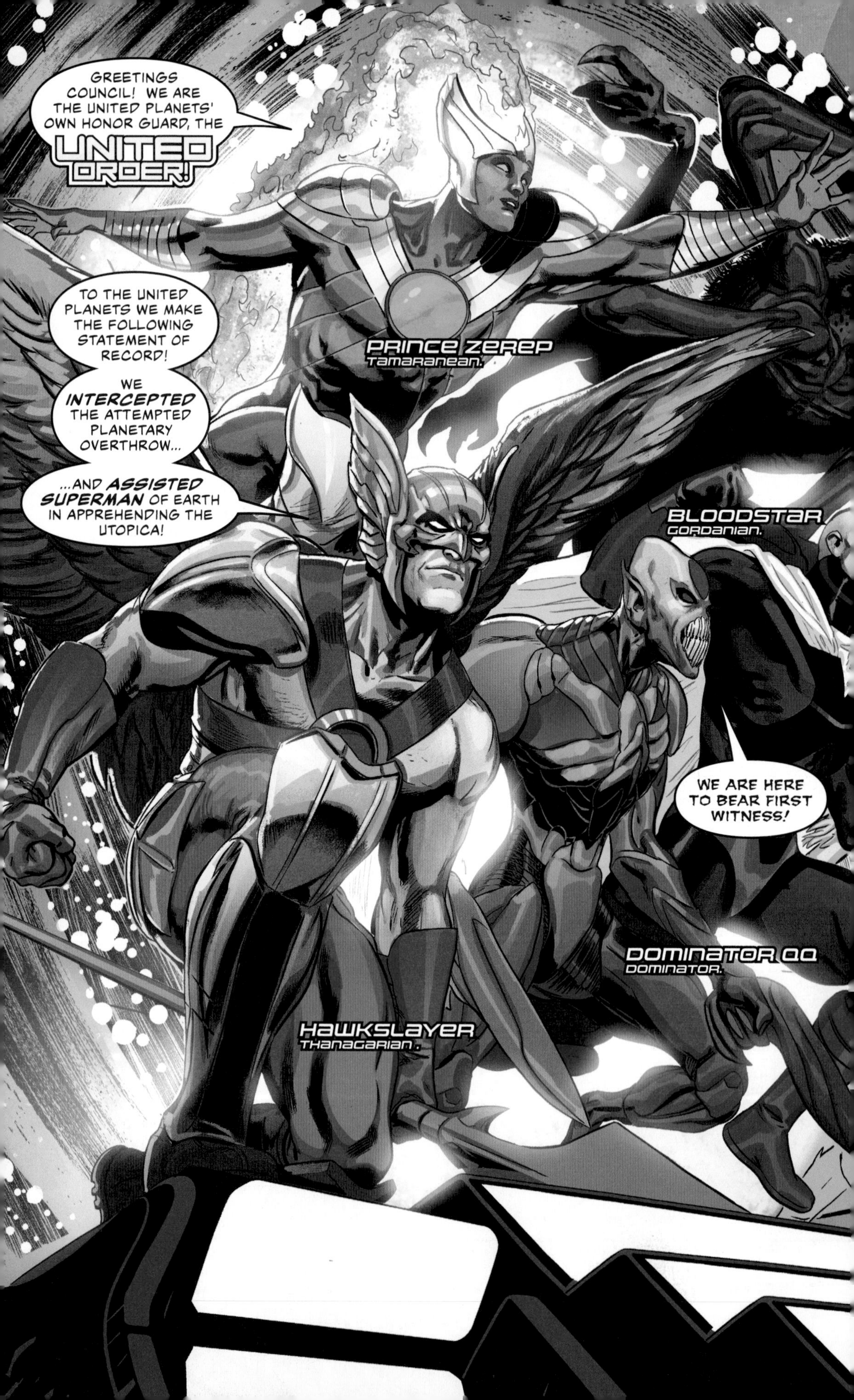
GREETINGS COUNCIL! WE ARE THE UNITED PLANETS' OWN HONOR GUARD, THE
UNITED ORDER!
TO THE UNITED PLANETS WE MAKE THE FOLLOWING STATEMENT OF RECORD!
WE INTERCEPTED THE ATTEMPTED PLANETARY OVERTHROW...
...AND ASSISTED SUPERMAN OF EARTH IN APPREHENDING THE UTOPICA!
PRINCE ZEREP
TAMARANEAN.
BLOODSTAR
GORDANIAN.
WE ARE HERE TO BEAR FIRST WITNESS!
DOMINATOR QQ
DOMINATOR.
HAWKSLAYER
THANAGARIAN.

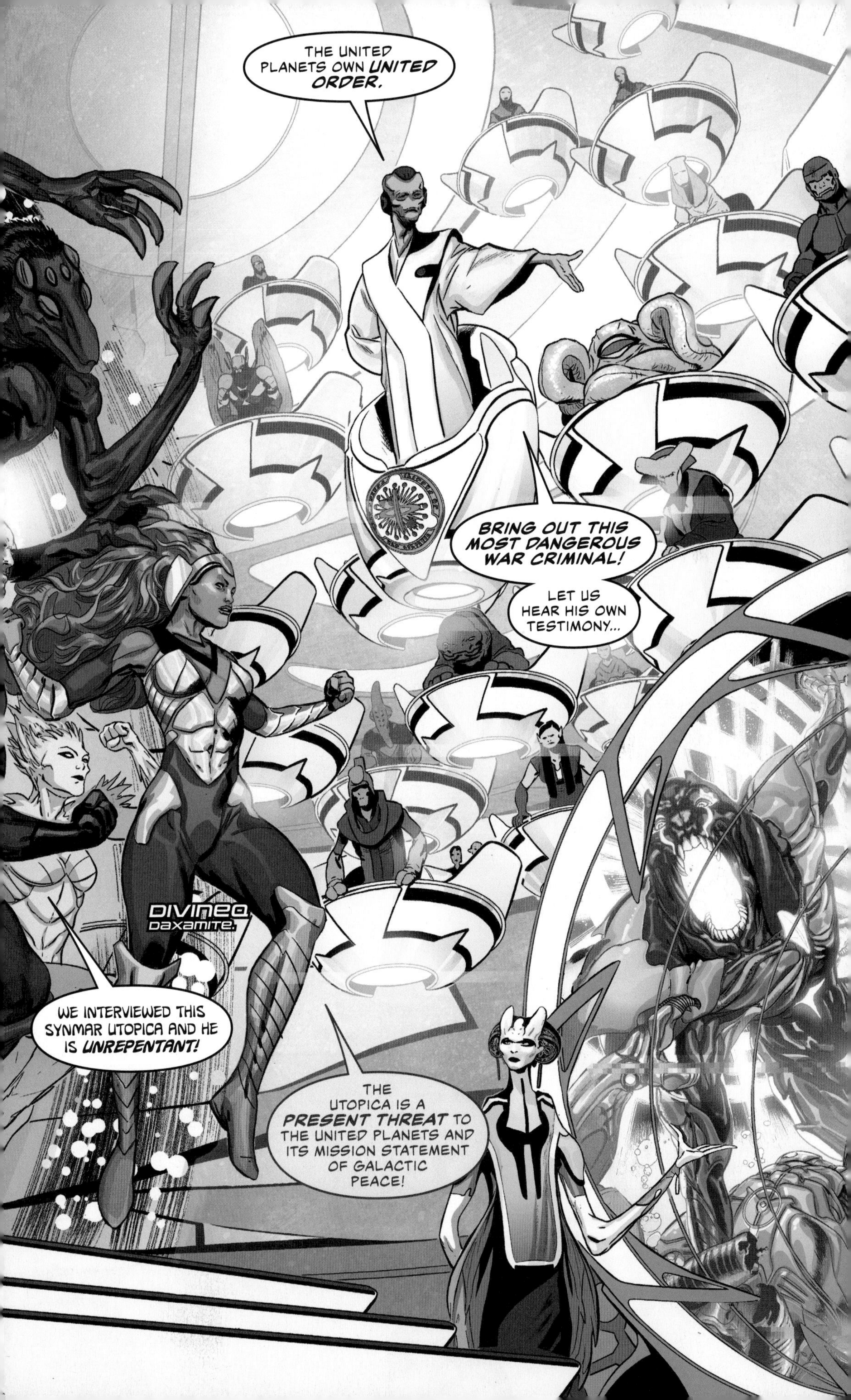
THE UNITED PLANETS OWN UNITED ORDER.
BRING OUT THIS MOST DANGEROUS WAR CRIMINAL!
LET US HEAR HIS OWN TESTIMONY...
DIVINEA DAXAMITE.
WE INTERVIEWED THIS SYNMAR UTOPICA AND HE IS UNREPENTANT!
THE UTOPICA IS A PRESENT THREAT TO THE UNITED PLANETS AND ITS MISSION STATEMENT OF GALACTIC PEACE!

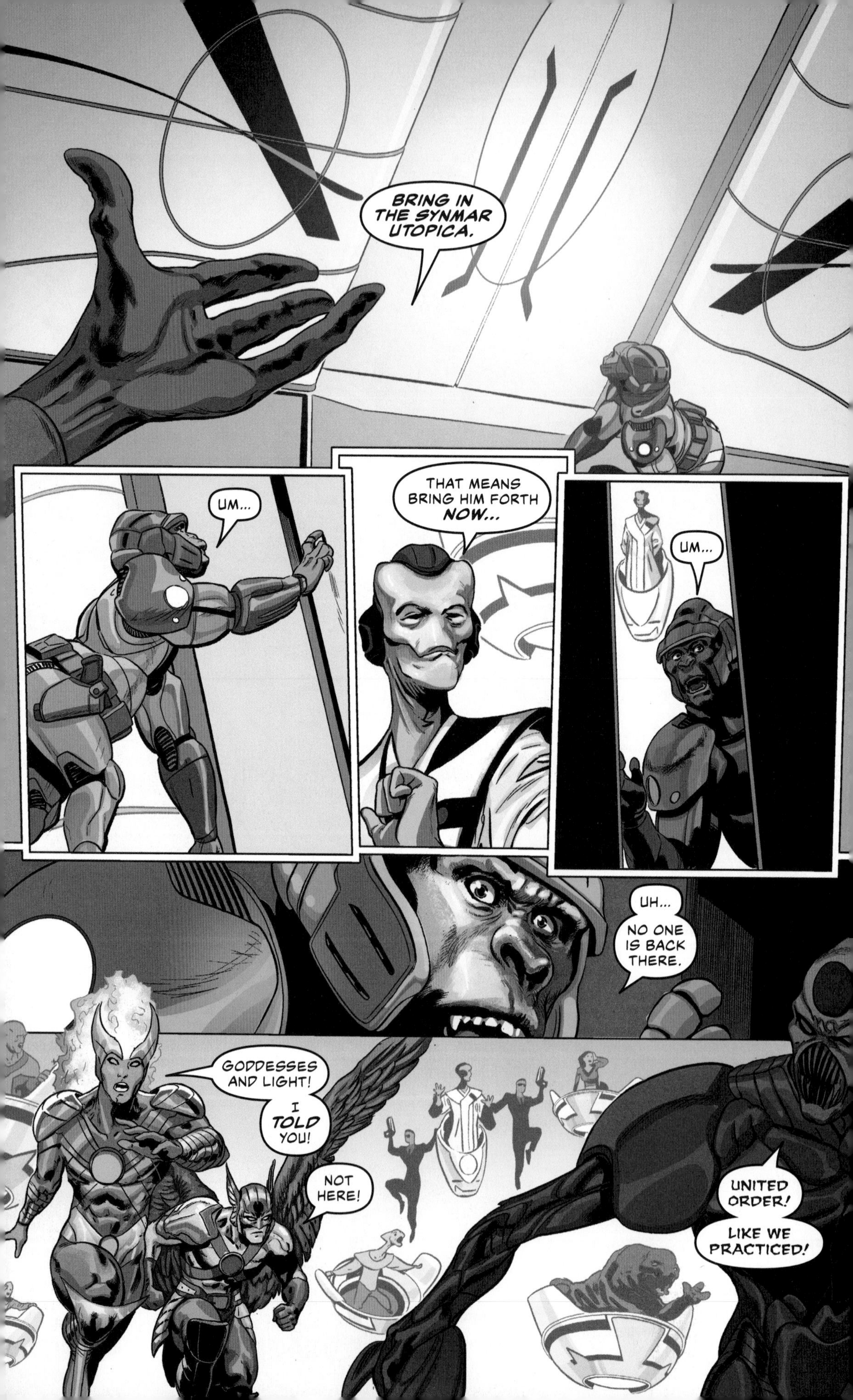
BRING IN THE SYNMAR UTOPICA.
UM...
THAT MEANS BRING HIM FORTH NOW...
UM...
UH...
NO ONE IS BACK THERE.
GODDESSES AND LIGHT!
I TOLD YOU!
NOT HERE!
UNITED ORDER!
LIKE WE PRACTICED!

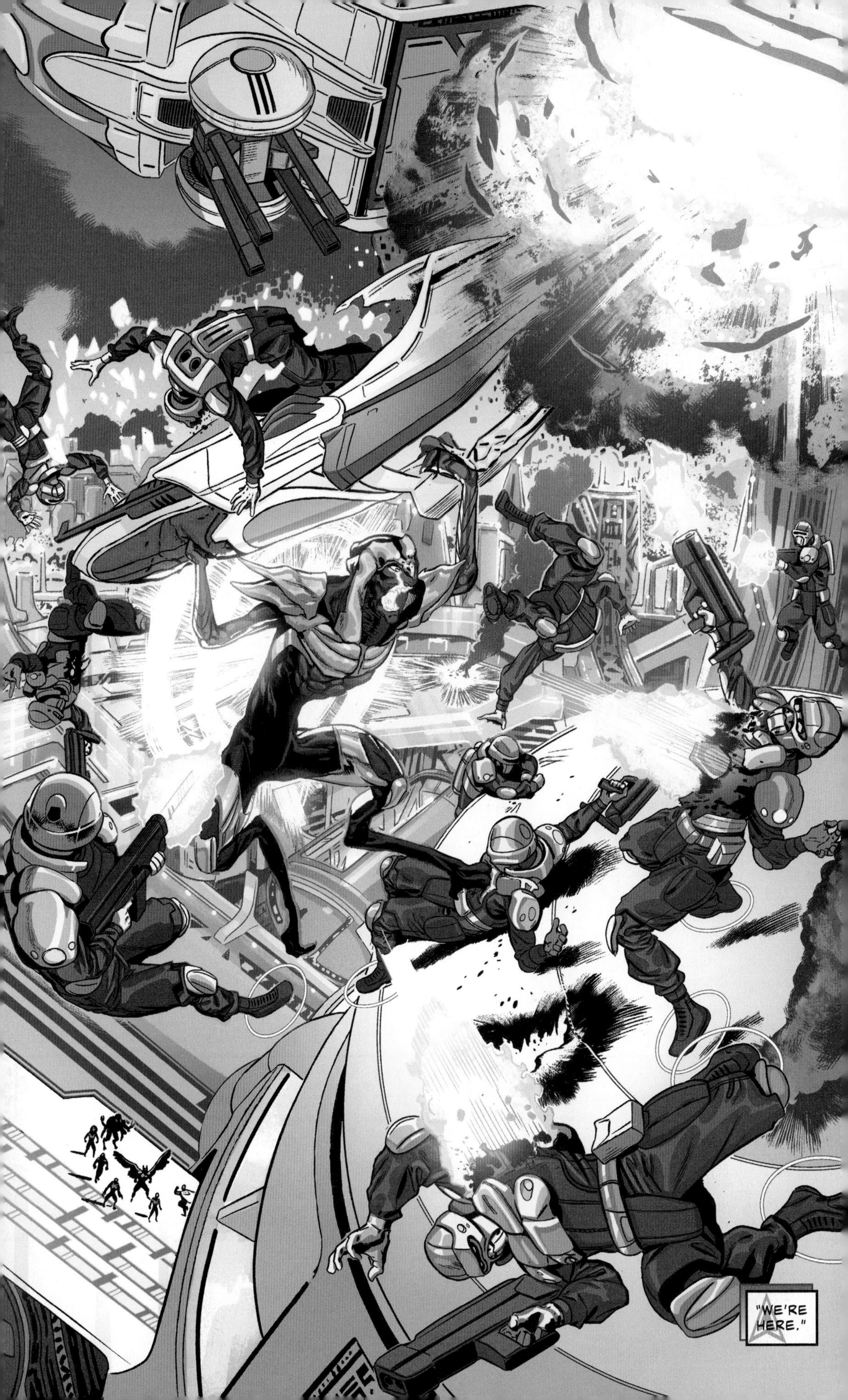
"WE'RE HERE."

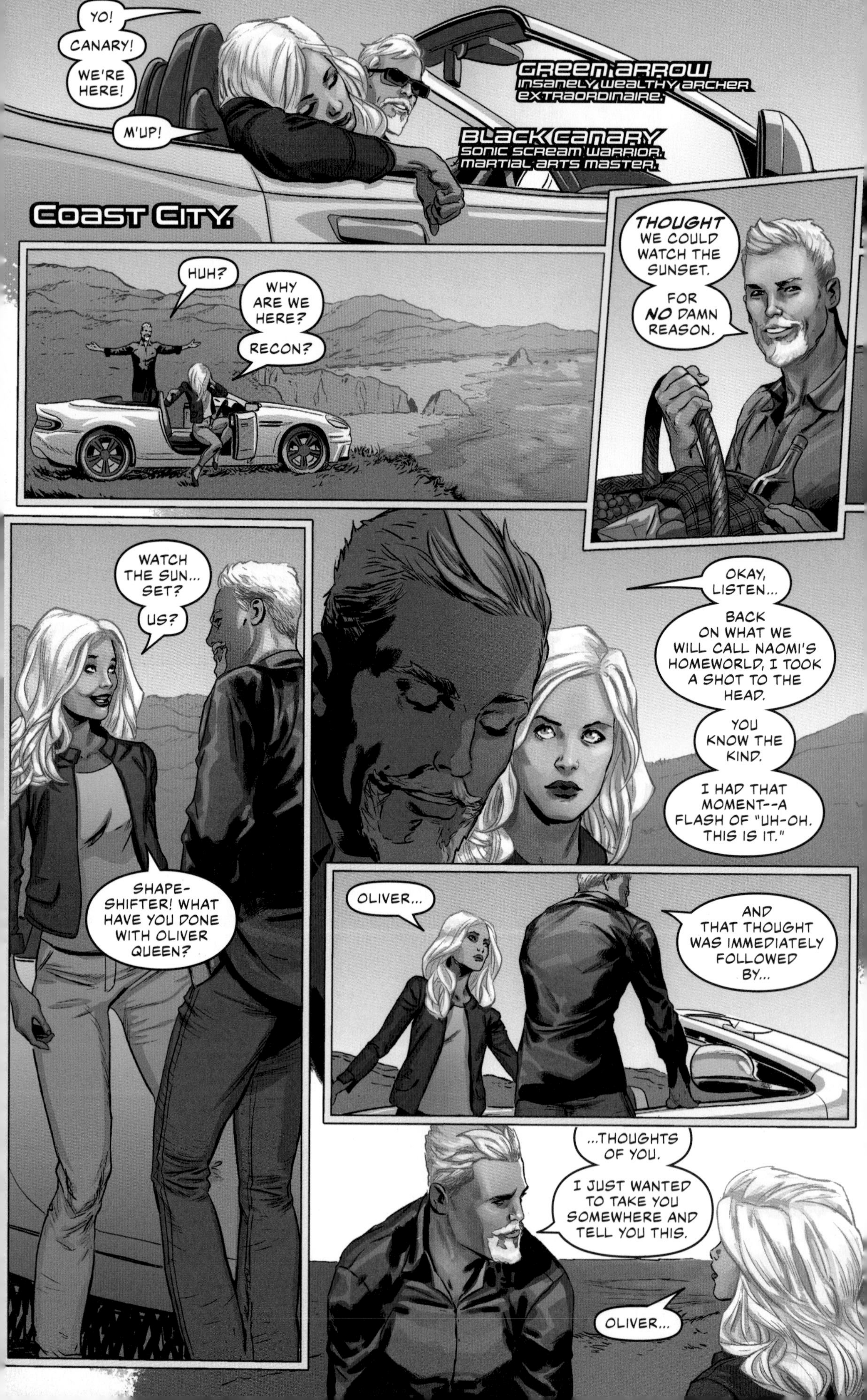
YO!
CANARY!
WE'RE HERE!
M'UP!
GREEN ARROW
INSANELY WEALTHY ARCHER EXTRAORDINAIRE.
BLACK CANARY
SONIC SCREAM WARRIOR. MARTIAL ARTS MASTER.
COAST CITY.
HUH?
WHY ARE WE HERE?
RECON?
THOUGHT WE COULD WATCH THE SUNSET.
FOR NO DAMN REASON.
WATCH THE SUN... SET?
US?
SHAPE-SHIFTER! WHAT HAVE YOU DONE WITH OLIVER QUEEN?
OKAY, LISTEN...
BACK ON WHAT WE WILL CALL NAOMI'S HOMEWORLD, I TOOK A SHOT TO THE HEAD.
YOU KNOW THE KIND.
I HAD THAT MOMENT--A FLASH OF "UH-OH. THIS IS IT."
OLIVER...
AND THAT THOUGHT WAS IMMEDIATELY FOLLOWED BY...
...THOUGHTS OF YOU.
I JUST WANTED TO TAKE YOU SOMEWHERE AND TELL YOU THIS.
OLIVER...

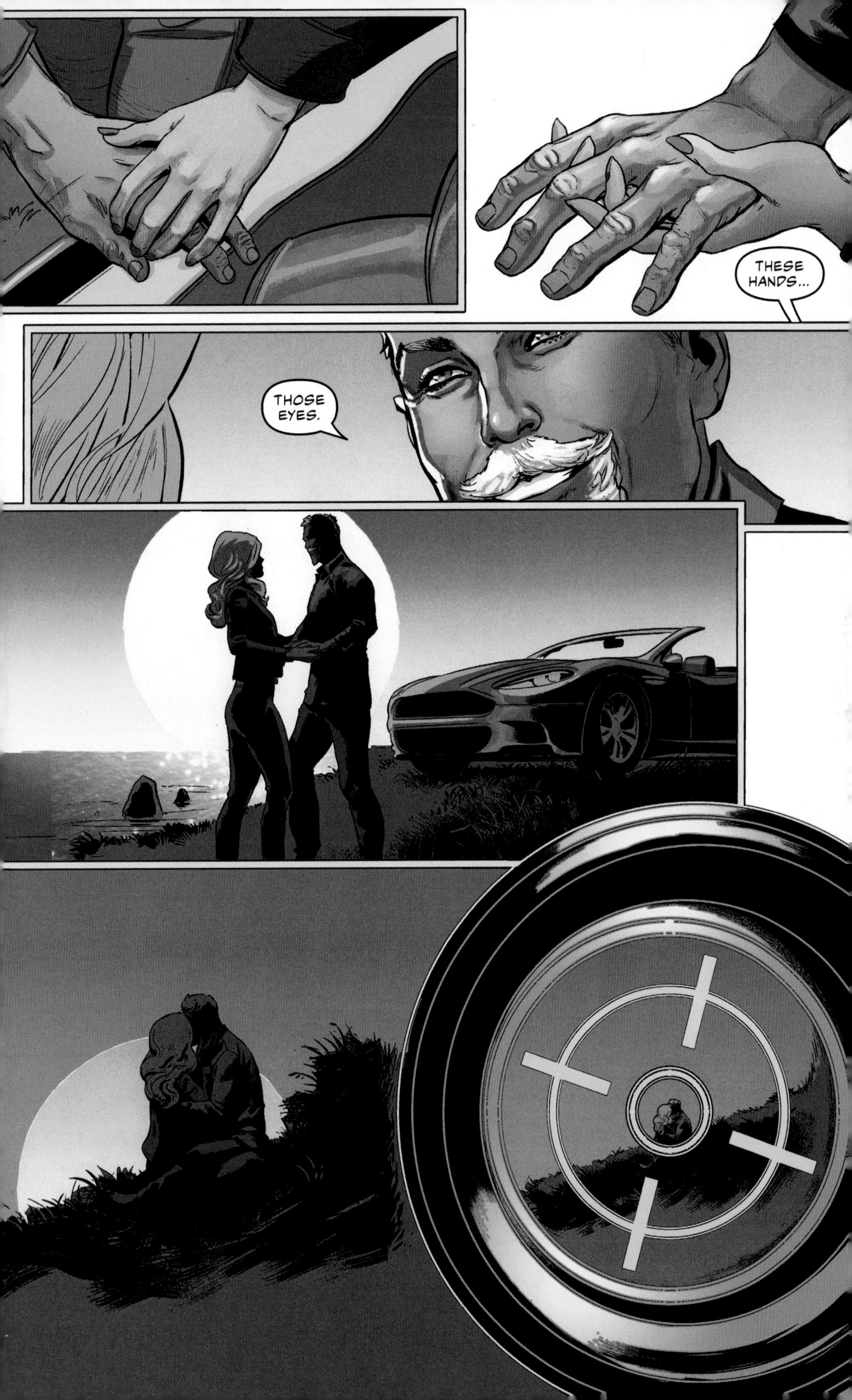
THESE HANDS...
THOSE EYES.

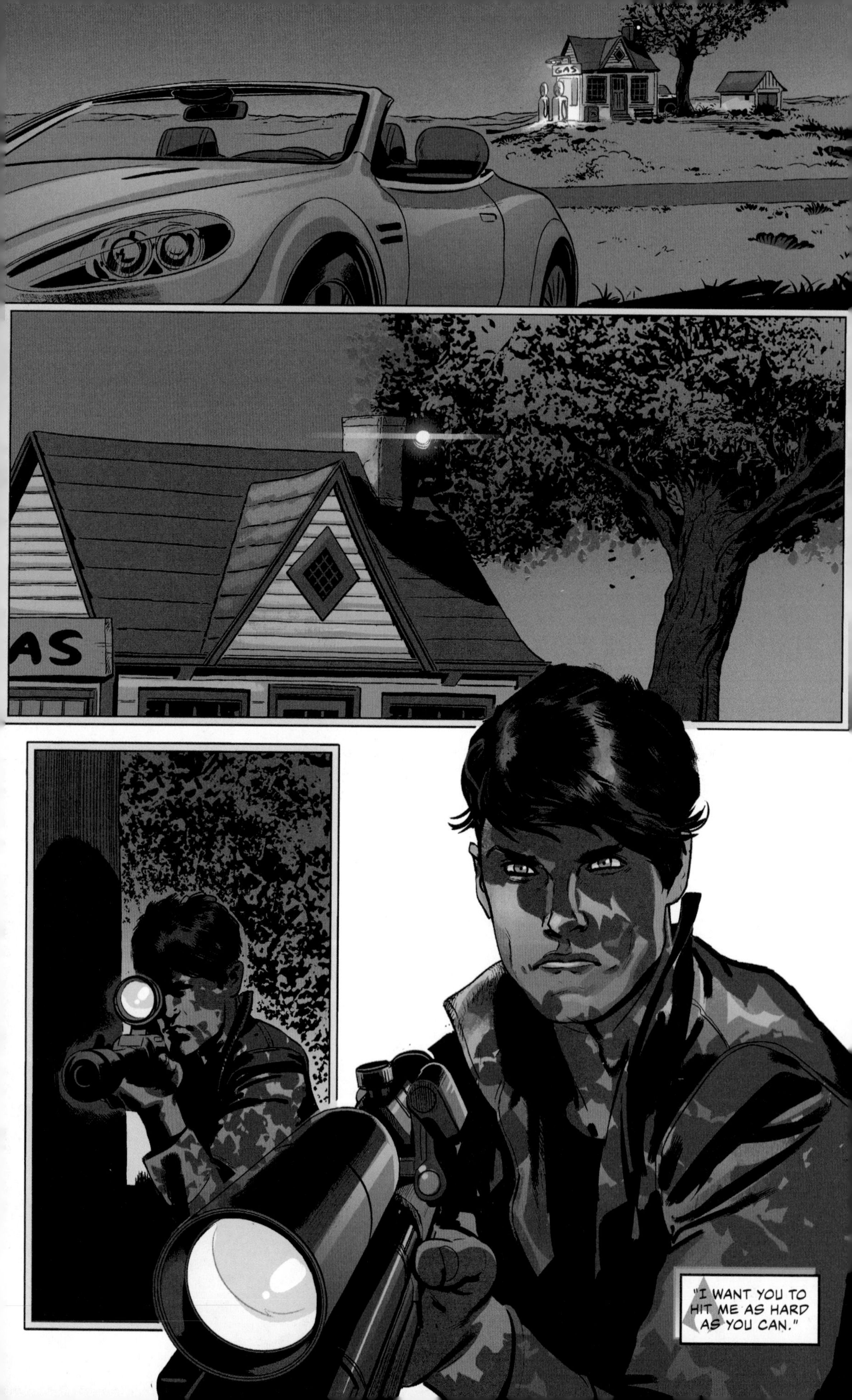
GAS
AS
"I WANT YOU TO HIT ME AS HARD AS YOU CAN."

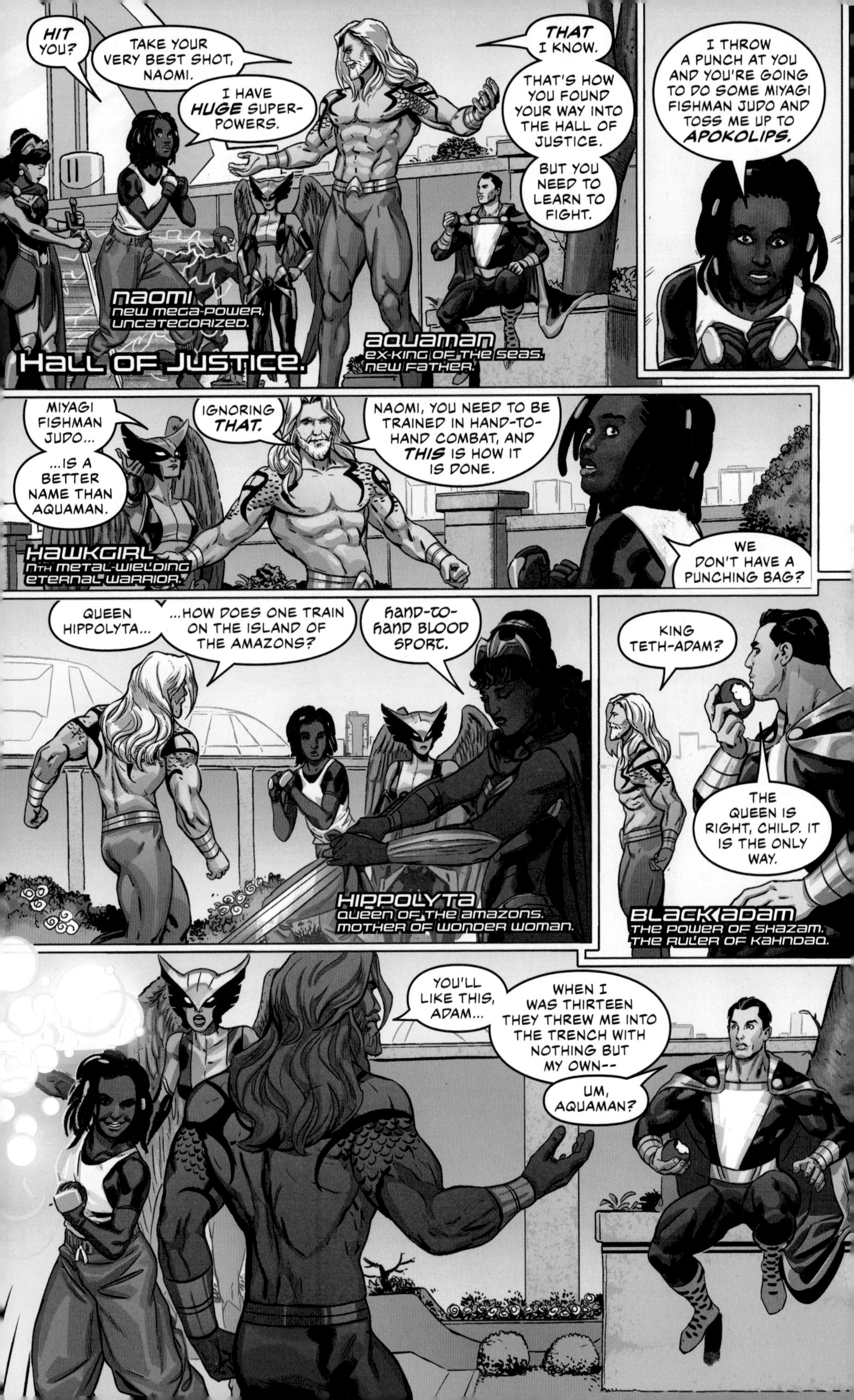
HIT YOU?
TAKE YOUR VERY BEST SHOT, NAOMI.
I HAVE HUGE SUPER-POWERS.
THAT I KNOW.
THAT'S HOW YOU FOUND YOUR WAY INTO THE HALL OF JUSTICE.
BUT YOU NEED TO LEARN TO FIGHT.
NAOMI
NEW MEGA-POWER, UNCATEGORIZED.
HALL OF JUSTICE.
AQUAMAN
EX-KING OF THE SEAS. NEW FATHER.
I THROW A PUNCH AT YOU AND YOU'RE GOING TO DO SOME MIYAGI FISHMAN JUDO AND TOSS ME UP TO APOKOLIPS.
MIYAGI FISHMAN JUDO...
...IS A BETTER NAME THAN AQUAMAN.
IGNORING THAT.
NAOMI, YOU NEED TO BE TRAINED IN HAND-TO-HAND COMBAT, AND THIS IS HOW IT IS DONE.
HAWKGIRL
NTH METAL-WIELDING ETERNAL WARRIOR.
WE DON'T HAVE A PUNCHING BAG?
QUEEN HIPPOLYTA...
...HOW DOES ONE TRAIN ON THE ISLAND OF THE AMAZONS?
HAND-TO-HAND BLOOD SPORT.
HIPPOLYTA
QUEEN OF THE AMAZONS. MOTHER OF WONDER WOMAN.
KING TETH-ADAM?
THE QUEEN IS RIGHT, CHILD. IT IS THE ONLY WAY.
BLACK ADAM
THE POWER OF SHAZAM. THE RULER OF KAHNDAQ.
YOU'LL LIKE THIS, ADAM...
WHEN I WAS THIRTEEN THEY THREW ME INTO THE TRENCH WITH NOTHING BUT MY OWN--
UM, AQUAMAN?

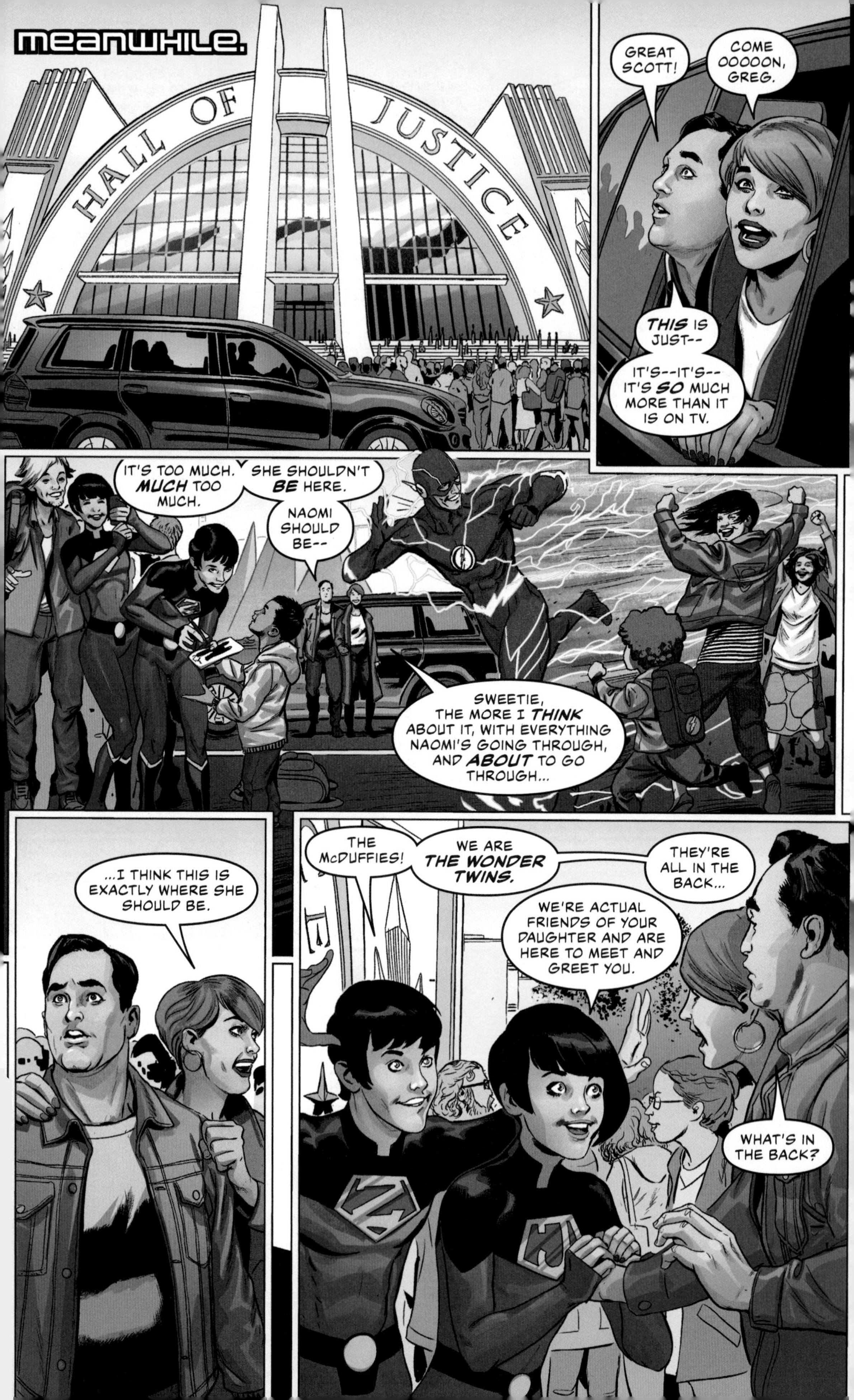
MEANWHILE.
HALL OF JUSTICE
GREAT SCOTT!
COME OOOOON, GREG.
THIS IS JUST--
IT'S--IT'S--IT'S SO MUCH MORE THAN IT IS ON TV.
IT'S TOO MUCH. MUCH TOO MUCH.
SHE SHOULDN'T BE HERE.
NAOMI SHOULD BE--
SWEETIE, THE MORE I THINK ABOUT IT, WITH EVERYTHING NAOMI'S GOING THROUGH, AND ABOUT TO GO THROUGH...
...I THINK THIS IS EXACTLY WHERE SHE SHOULD BE.
THE McDUFFIES!
WE ARE THE WONDER TWINS.
THEY'RE ALL IN THE BACK...
WE'RE ACTUAL FRIENDS OF YOUR DAUGHTER AND ARE HERE TO MEET AND GREET YOU.
WHAT'S IN THE BACK?

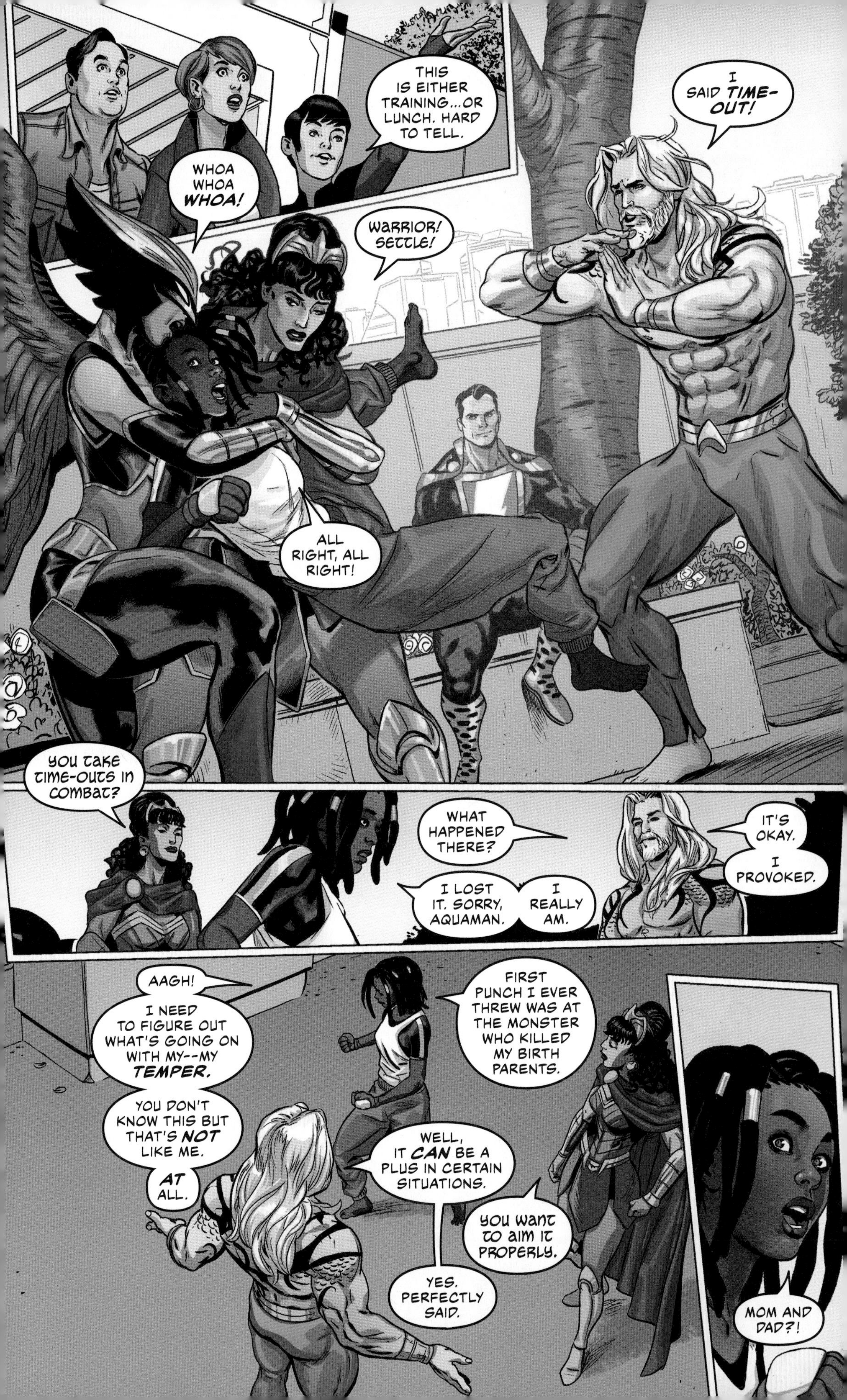
THIS IS EITHER TRAINING...OR LUNCH. HARD TO TELL.
WHOA WHOA WHOA!
I SAID TIME-OUT!
WARRIOR! SETTLE!
ALL RIGHT, ALL RIGHT!
YOU TAKE TIME-OUTS IN COMBAT?
WHAT HAPPENED THERE?
I LOST IT. SORRY, AQUAMAN.
I REALLY AM.
IT'S OKAY.
I PROVOKED.
AAGH!
I NEED TO FIGURE OUT WHAT'S GOING ON WITH MY--MY TEMPER.
YOU DON'T KNOW THIS BUT THAT'S NOT LIKE ME.
AT ALL.
FIRST PUNCH I EVER THREW WAS AT THE MONSTER WHO KILLED MY BIRTH PARENTS.
WELL, IT CAN BE A PLUS IN CERTAIN SITUATIONS.
YOU WANT TO AIM IT PROPERLY.
YES. PERFECTLY SAID.
MOM AND DAD?!

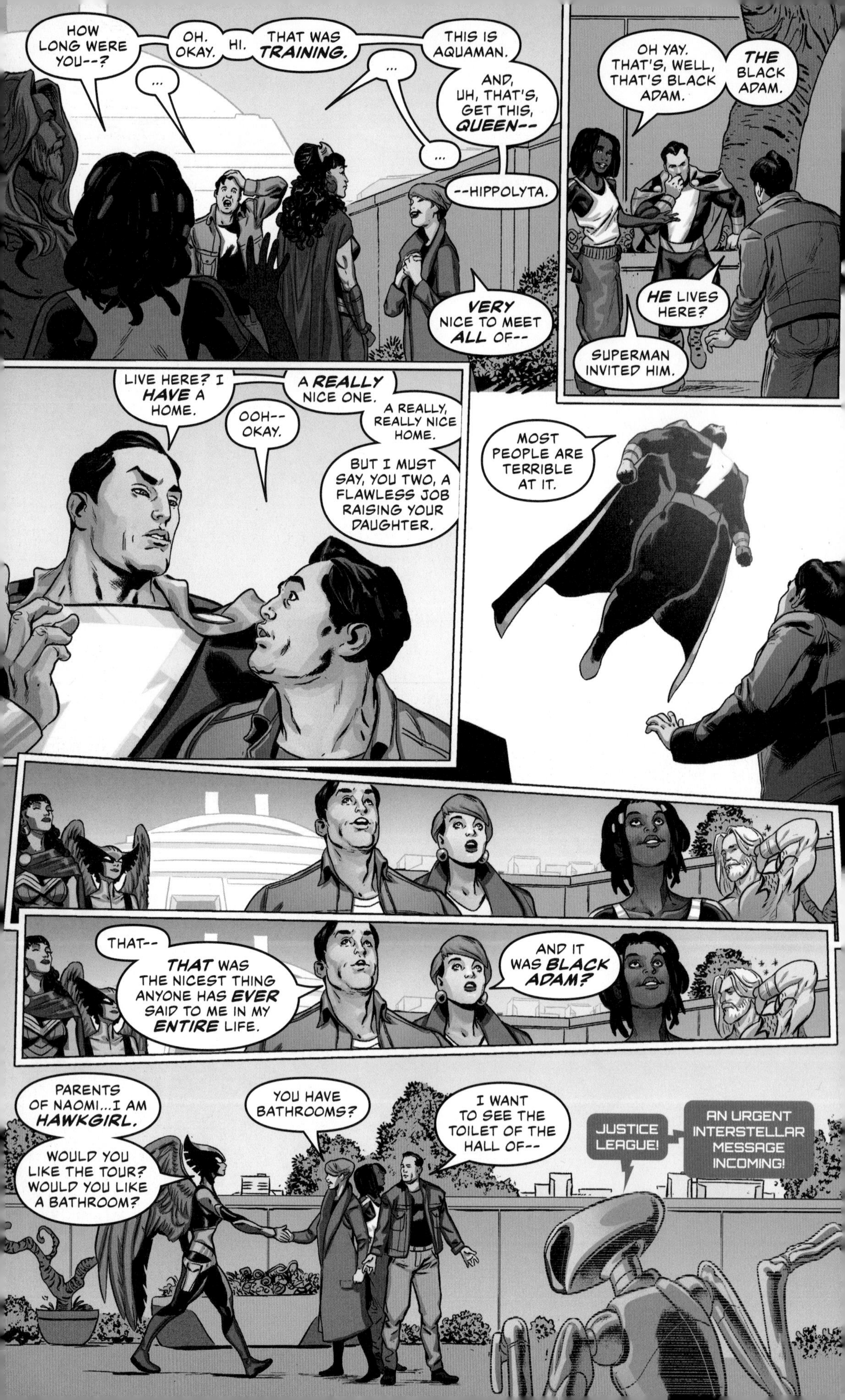
HOW LONG WERE YOU--?
OH. OKAY.
HI.
THAT WAS TRAINING.
THIS IS AQUAMAN.
...
...
AND, UH, THAT'S, GET THIS, QUEEN--
...
--HIPPOLYTA.
VERY NICE TO MEET ALL OF--
OH YAY. THAT'S, WELL, THAT'S BLACK ADAM.
THE BLACK ADAM.
HE LIVES HERE?
SUPERMAN INVITED HIM.
LIVE HERE? I HAVE A HOME.
A REALLY NICE ONE.
OOH-- OKAY.
A REALLY, REALLY NICE HOME.
BUT I MUST SAY, YOU TWO, A FLAWLESS JOB RAISING YOUR DAUGHTER.
MOST PEOPLE ARE TERRIBLE AT IT.
THAT--
THAT WAS THE NICEST THING ANYONE HAS EVER SAID TO ME IN MY ENTIRE LIFE.
AND IT WAS BLACK ADAM?
PARENTS OF NAOMI...I AM HAWKGIRL.
WOULD YOU LIKE THE TOUR? WOULD YOU LIKE A BATHROOM?
YOU HAVE BATHROOMS?
I WANT TO SEE THE TOILET OF THE HALL OF--
JUSTICE LEAGUE!
AN URGENT INTERSTELLAR MESSAGE INCOMING!

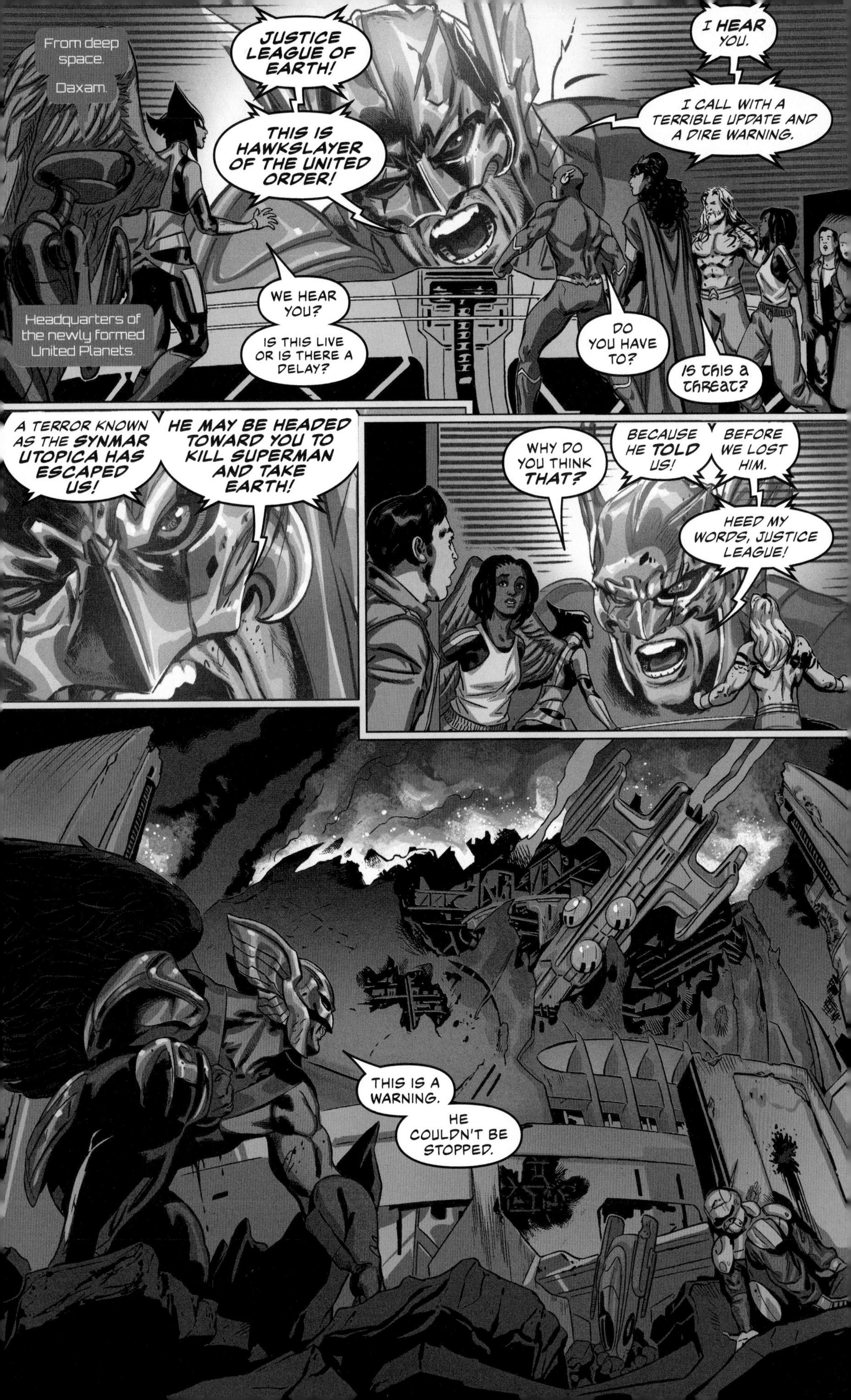
From deep space.
Daxam.
JUSTICE LEAGUE OF EARTH!
THIS IS HAWKSLAYER OF THE UNITED ORDER!
I HEAR YOU.
I CALL WITH A TERRIBLE UPDATE AND A DIRE WARNING.
Headquarters of the newly formed United Planets.
WE HEAR YOU?
IS THIS LIVE OR IS THERE A DELAY?
DO YOU HAVE TO?
IS THIS A THREAT?
A TERROR KNOWN AS THE SYNMAR UTOPICA HAS ESCAPED US!
HE MAY BE HEADED TOWARD YOU TO KILL SUPERMAN AND TAKE EARTH!
WHY DO YOU THINK THAT?
BECAUSE HE TOLD US!
BEFORE WE LOST HIM.
HEED MY WORDS, JUSTICE LEAGUE!
THIS IS A WARNING.
HE COULDN'T BE STOPPED.

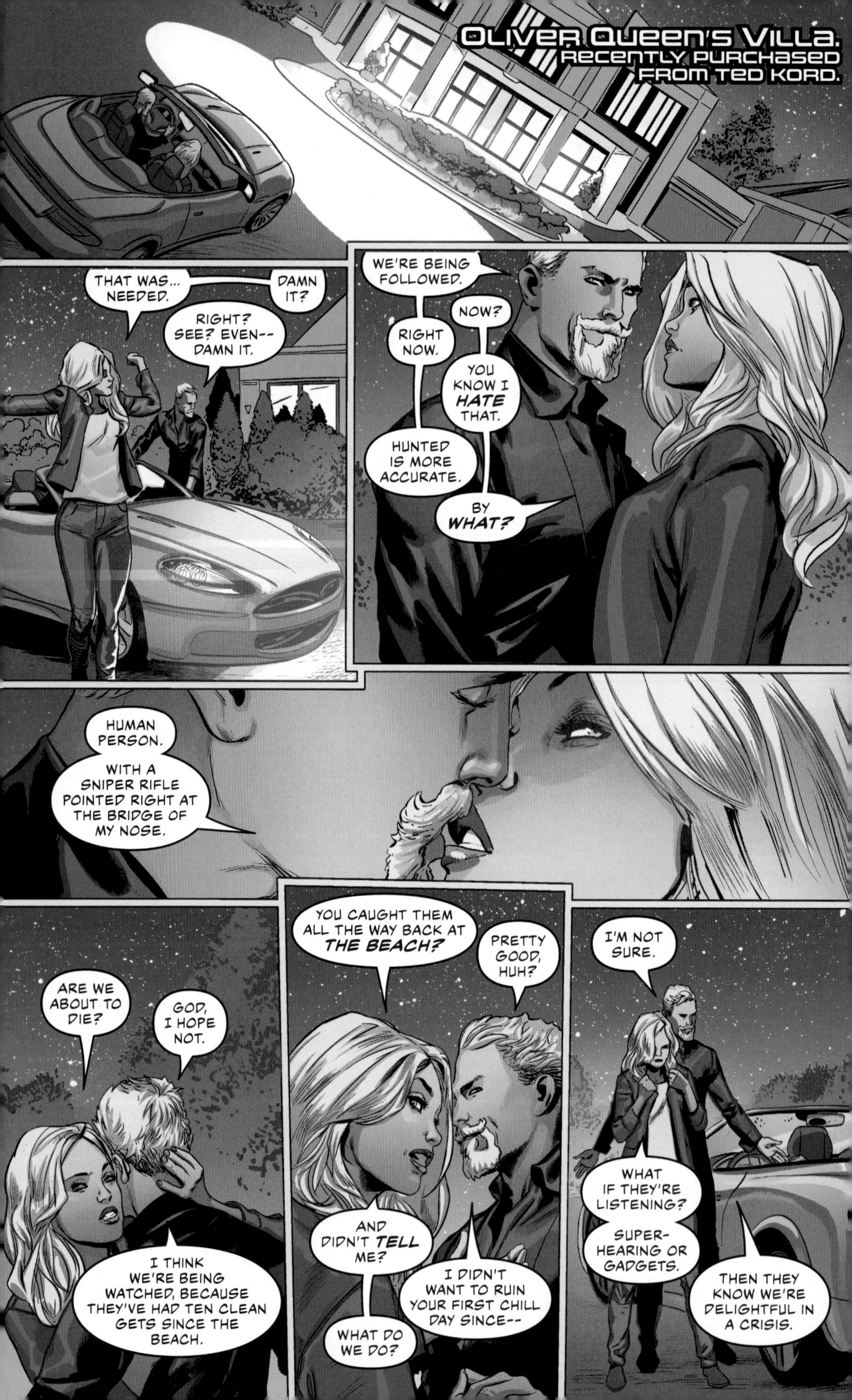

OLIVER QUEEN'S VILLA.
RECENTLY PURCHASED FROM TED KORD.
THAT WAS... NEEDED.
DAMN IT?
RIGHT? SEE? EVEN-- DAMN IT.
WE'RE BEING FOLLOWED.
NOW?
RIGHT NOW.
YOU KNOW I HATE THAT.
HUNTED IS MORE ACCURATE.
BY WHAT?
HUMAN PERSON.
WITH A SNIPER RIFLE POINTED RIGHT AT THE BRIDGE OF MY NOSE.
ARE WE ABOUT TO DIE?
GOD, I HOPE NOT.
I THINK WE'RE BEING WATCHED, BECAUSE THEY'VE HAD TEN CLEAN GETS SINCE THE BEACH.
YOU CAUGHT THEM ALL THE WAY BACK AT THE BEACH?
PRETTY GOOD, HUH?
AND DIDN'T TELL ME?
I DIDN'T WANT TO RUIN YOUR FIRST CHILL DAY SINCE--
WHAT DO WE DO?
I'M NOT SURE.
WHAT IF THEY'RE LISTENING?
SUPER-HEARING OR GADGETS.
THEN THEY KNOW WE'RE DELIGHTFUL IN A CRISIS.

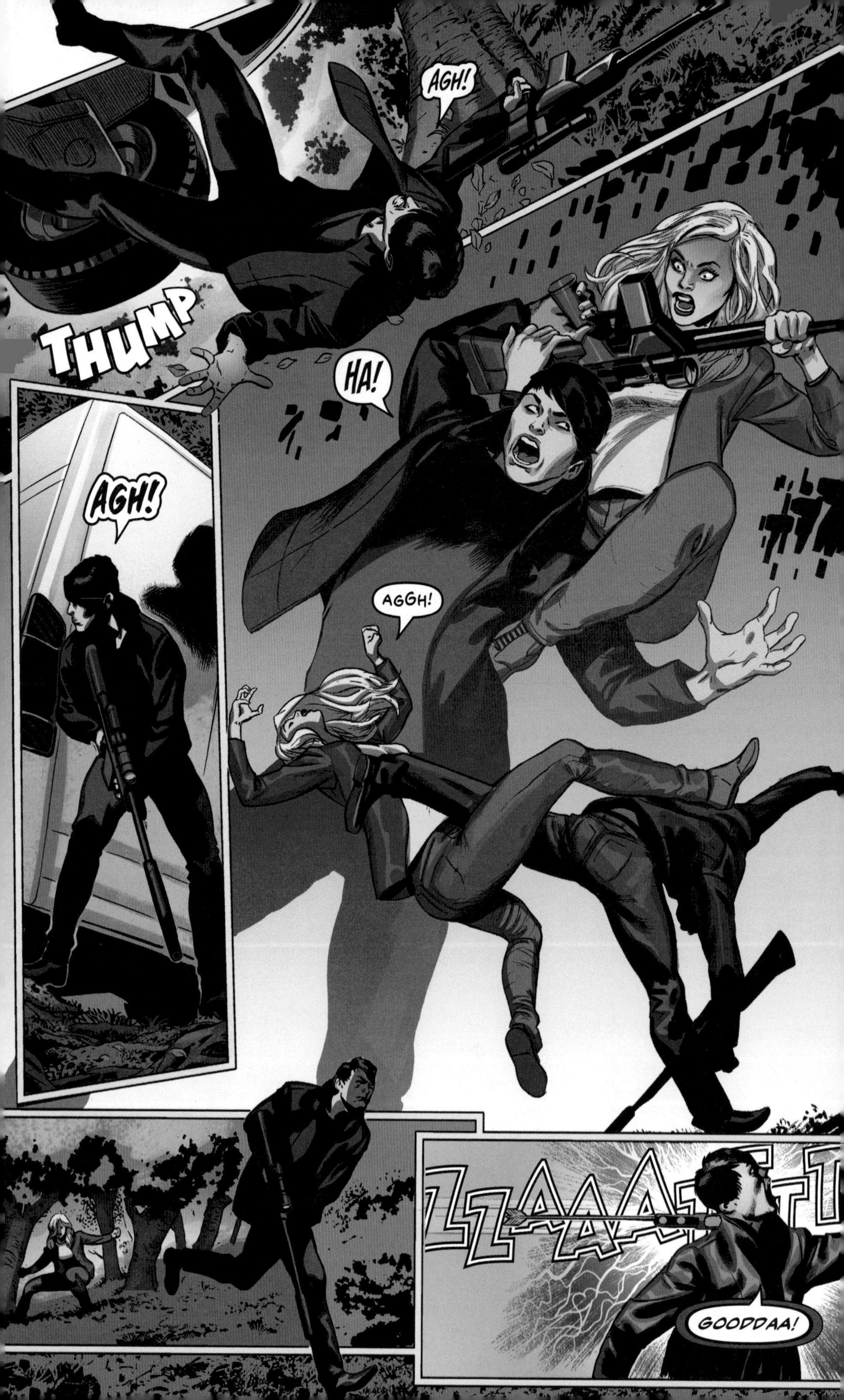
AGH!
THUMP
HA!
AGH!
AGGH!
GOODDAA!

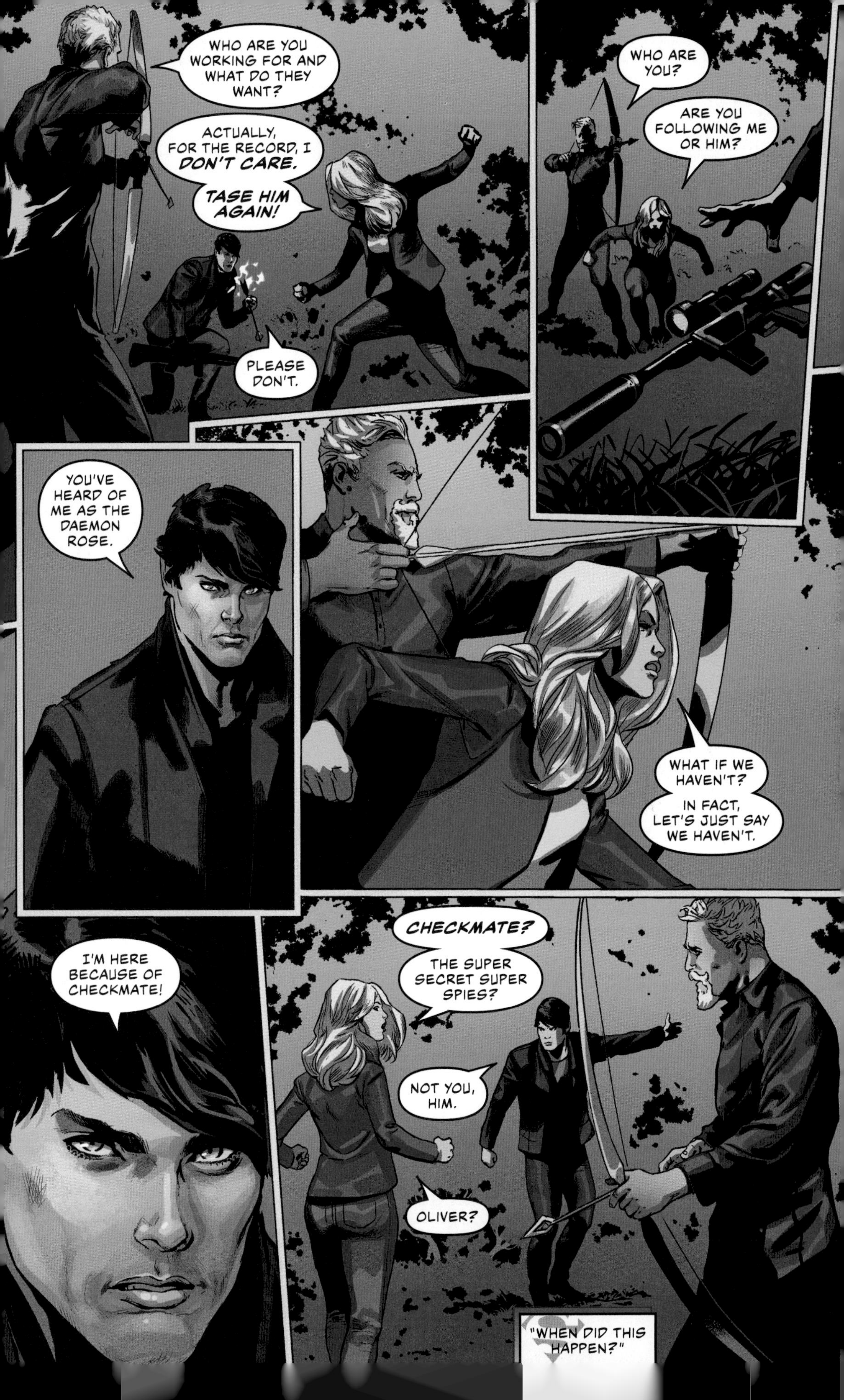
WHO ARE YOU WORKING FOR AND WHAT DO THEY WANT?
ACTUALLY, FOR THE RECORD, I *DON'T CARE.*
TASE HIM AGAIN!
PLEASE DON'T.
WHO ARE YOU?
ARE YOU FOLLOWING ME OR HIM?
YOU'VE HEARD OF ME AS THE DAEMON ROSE.
WHAT IF WE HAVEN'T?
IN FACT, LET'S JUST SAY WE HAVEN'T.
I'M HERE BECAUSE OF CHECKMATE!
CHECKMATE?
THE SUPER SECRET SUPER SPIES?
NOT YOU, HIM.
OLIVER?
"WHEN DID THIS HAPPEN?"

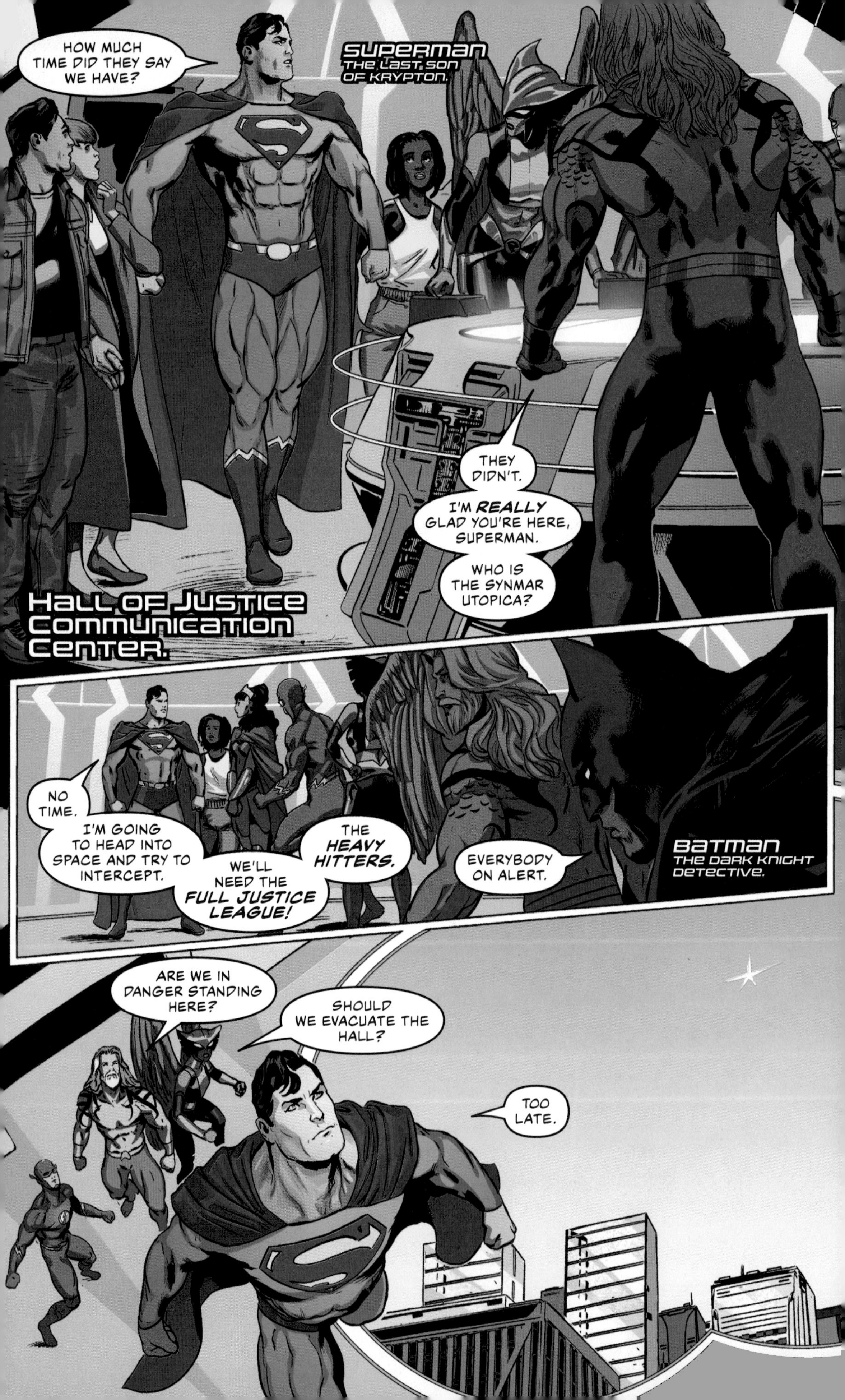
HOW MUCH TIME DID THEY SAY WE HAVE?
SUPERMAN THE LAST SON OF KRYPTON.
THEY DIDN'T.
I'M REALLY GLAD YOU'RE HERE, SUPERMAN.
WHO IS THE SYNMAR UTOPICA?
HALL OF JUSTICE COMMUNICATION CENTER.
NO TIME.
I'M GOING TO HEAD INTO SPACE AND TRY TO INTERCEPT.
WE'LL NEED THE FULL JUSTICE LEAGUE!
THE HEAVY HITTERS.
EVERYBODY ON ALERT.
BATMAN THE DARK KNIGHT DETECTIVE.
ARE WE IN DANGER STANDING HERE?
SHOULD WE EVACUATE THE HALL?
TOO LATE.

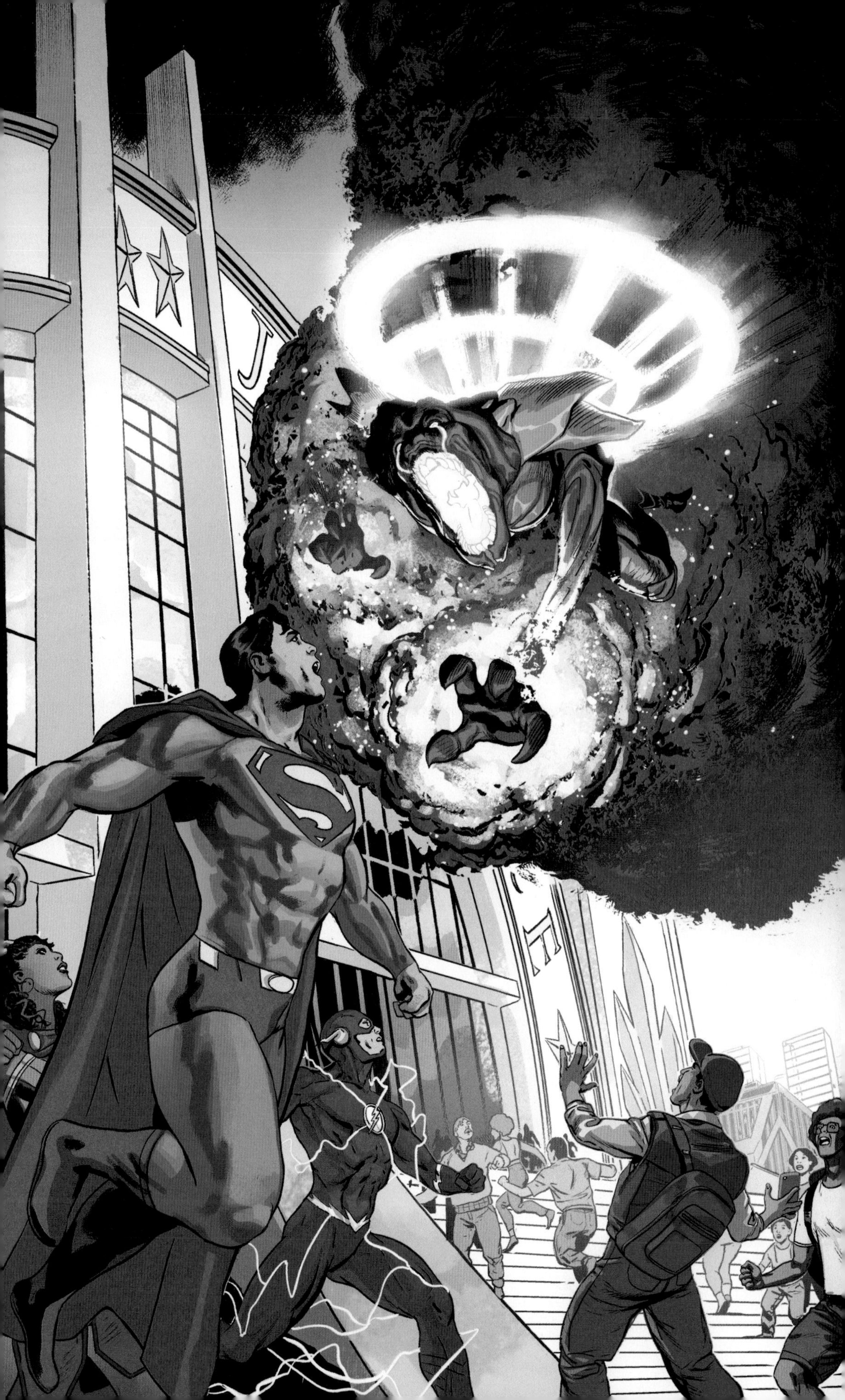

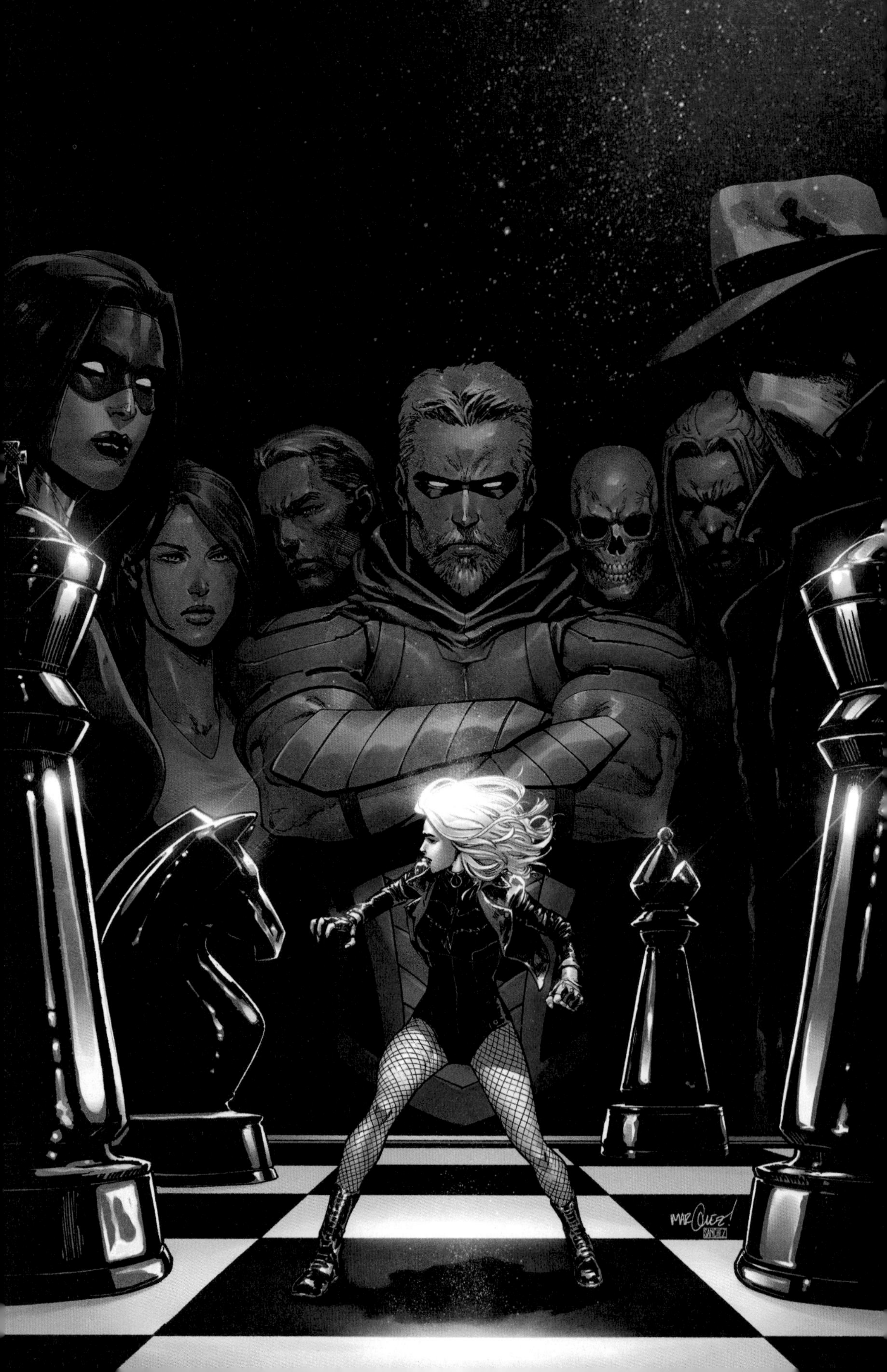

Justice League #65 cover art by
David Marquez & Alejandro Sánchez

Justice League #65 variant cover art by
David Talaski

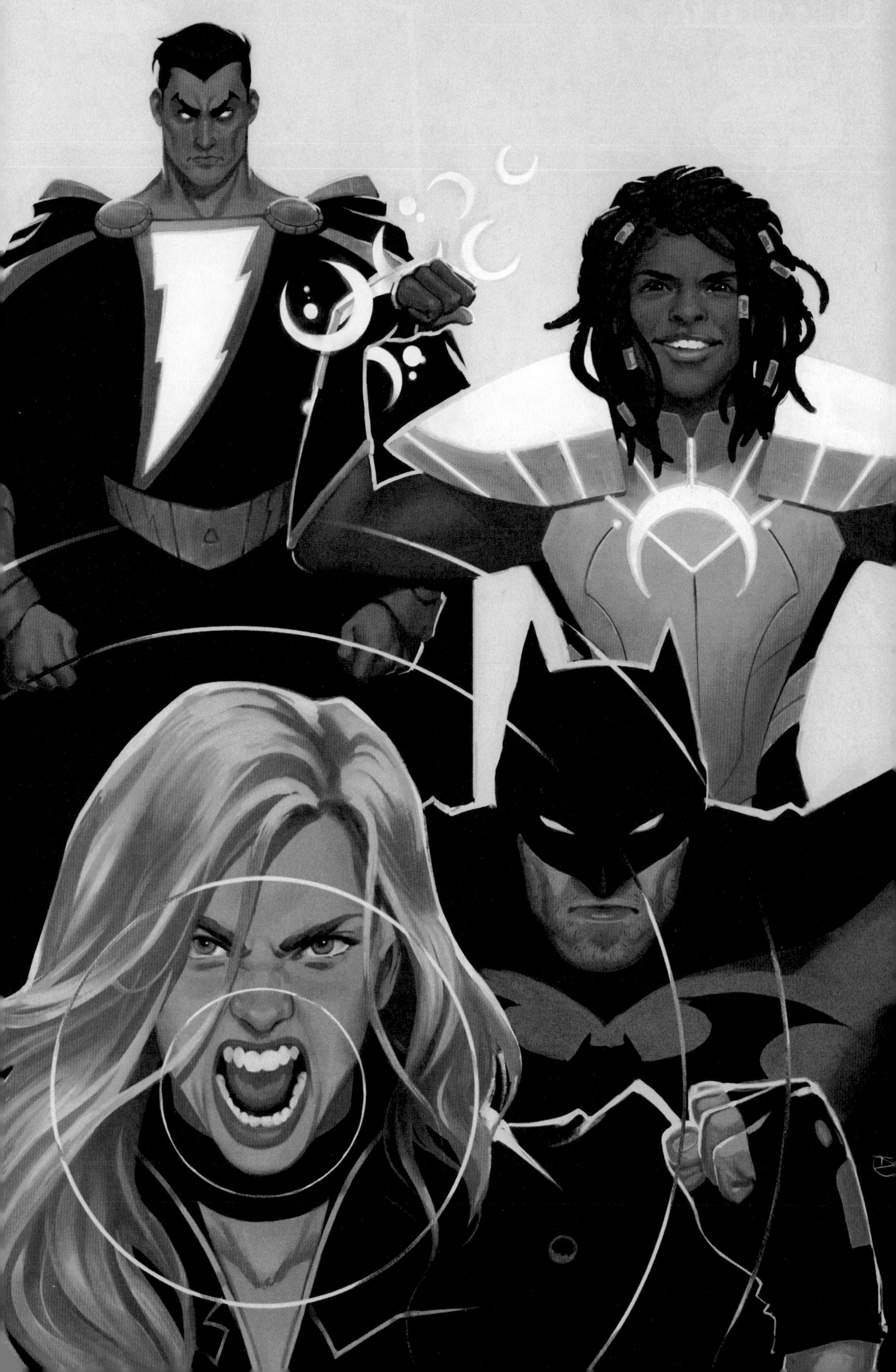

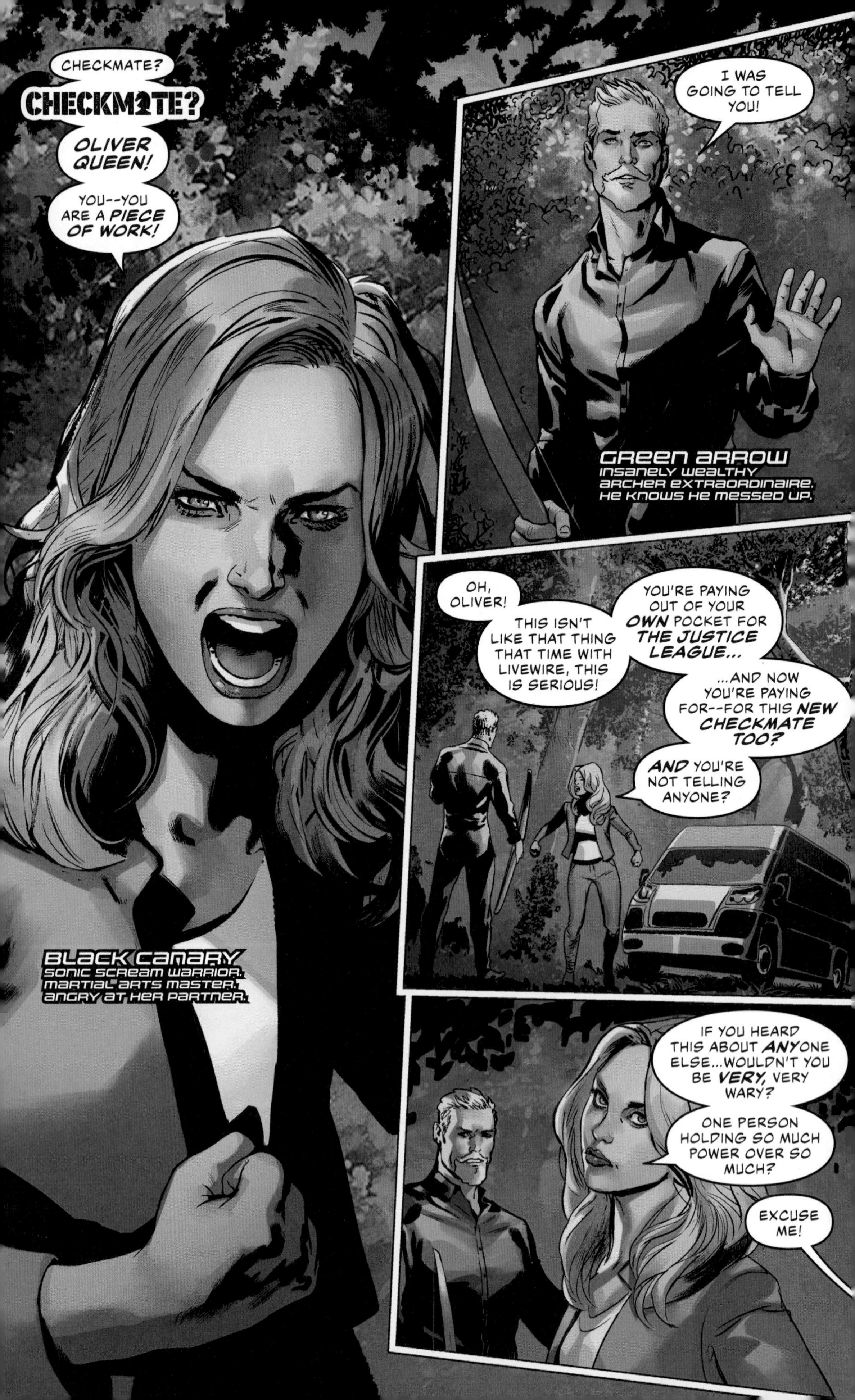
CHECKMATE?
CHECKMATE?
OLIVER QUEEN!
YOU--YOU ARE A PIECE OF WORK!
BLACK CANARY
SONIC SCREAM WARRIOR. MARTIAL ARTS MASTER. ANGRY AT HER PARTNER.
I WAS GOING TO TELL YOU!
GREEN ARROW
INSANELY WEALTHY ARCHER EXTRAORDINAIRE. HE KNOWS HE MESSED UP.
OH, OLIVER!
THIS ISN'T LIKE THAT THING THAT TIME WITH LIVEWIRE, THIS IS SERIOUS!
YOU'RE PAYING OUT OF YOUR OWN POCKET FOR THE JUSTICE LEAGUE...
...AND NOW YOU'RE PAYING FOR--FOR THIS NEW CHECKMATE TOO?
AND YOU'RE NOT TELLING ANYONE?
IF YOU HEARD THIS ABOUT ANYONE ELSE...WOULDN'T YOU BE VERY, VERY WARY?
ONE PERSON HOLDING SO MUCH POWER OVER SO MUCH?
EXCUSE ME!

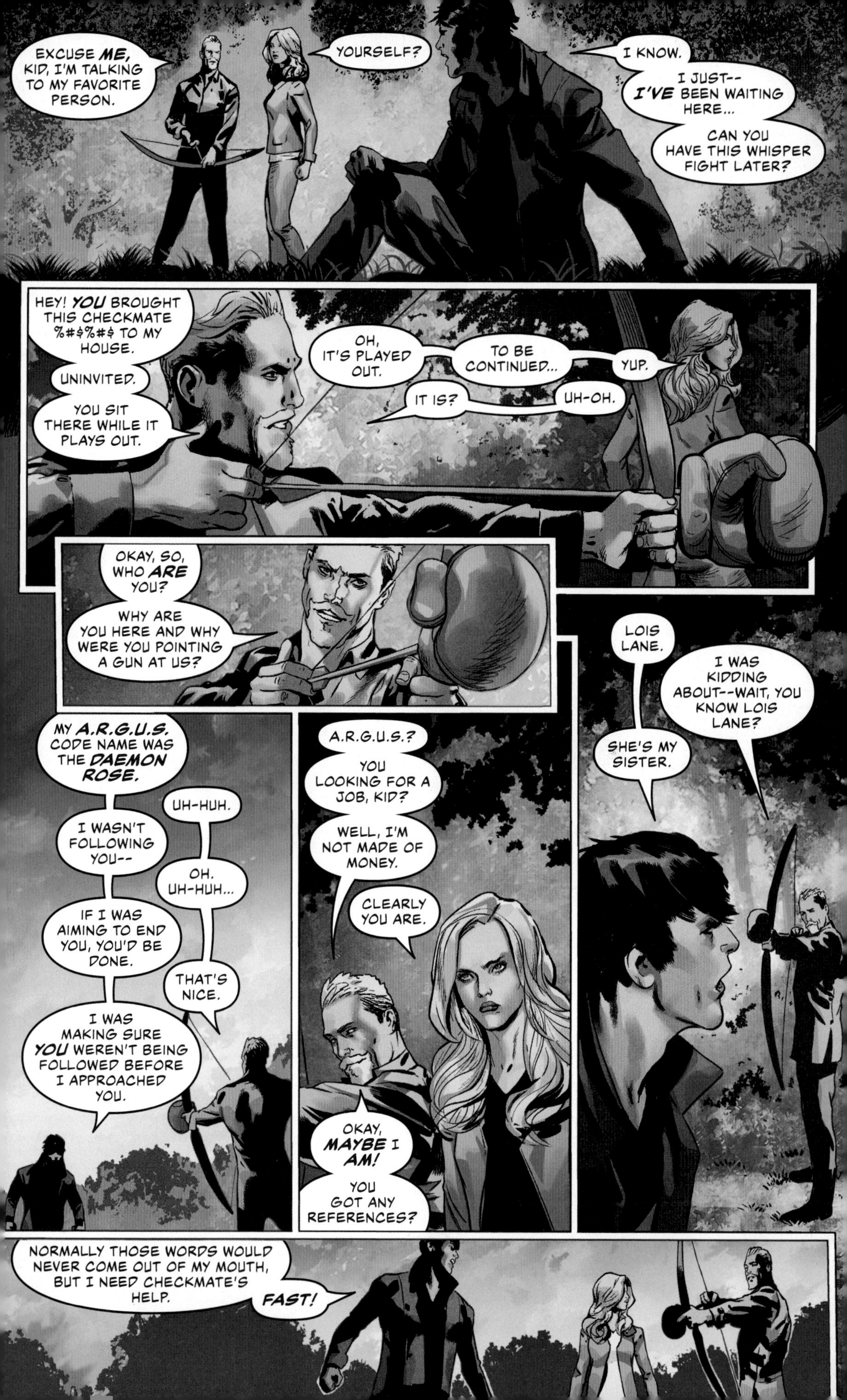
EXCUSE ME, KID, I'M TALKING TO MY FAVORITE PERSON.
YOURSELF?
I KNOW.
I JUST-- I'VE BEEN WAITING HERE...
CAN YOU HAVE THIS WHISPER FIGHT LATER?
HEY! YOU BROUGHT THIS CHECKMATE %#$%#$ TO MY HOUSE.
UNINVITED.
YOU SIT THERE WHILE IT PLAYS OUT.
OH, IT'S PLAYED OUT.
TO BE CONTINUED...
YUP.
IT IS?
UH-OH.
OKAY, SO, WHO ARE YOU?
WHY ARE YOU HERE AND WHY WERE YOU POINTING A GUN AT US?
LOIS LANE.
I WAS KIDDING ABOUT--WAIT, YOU KNOW LOIS LANE?
SHE'S MY SISTER.
MY A.R.G.U.S. CODE NAME WAS THE DAEMON ROSE.
UH-HUH.
I WASN'T FOLLOWING YOU--
OH. UH-HUH...
IF I WAS AIMING TO END YOU, YOU'D BE DONE.
THAT'S NICE.
I WAS MAKING SURE YOU WEREN'T BEING FOLLOWED BEFORE I APPROACHED YOU.
A.R.G.U.S.?
YOU LOOKING FOR A JOB, KID?
WELL, I'M NOT MADE OF MONEY.
CLEARLY YOU ARE.
OKAY, MAYBE I AM!
YOU GOT ANY REFERENCES?
NORMALLY THOSE WORDS WOULD NEVER COME OUT OF MY MOUTH, BUT I NEED CHECKMATE'S HELP.
FAST!

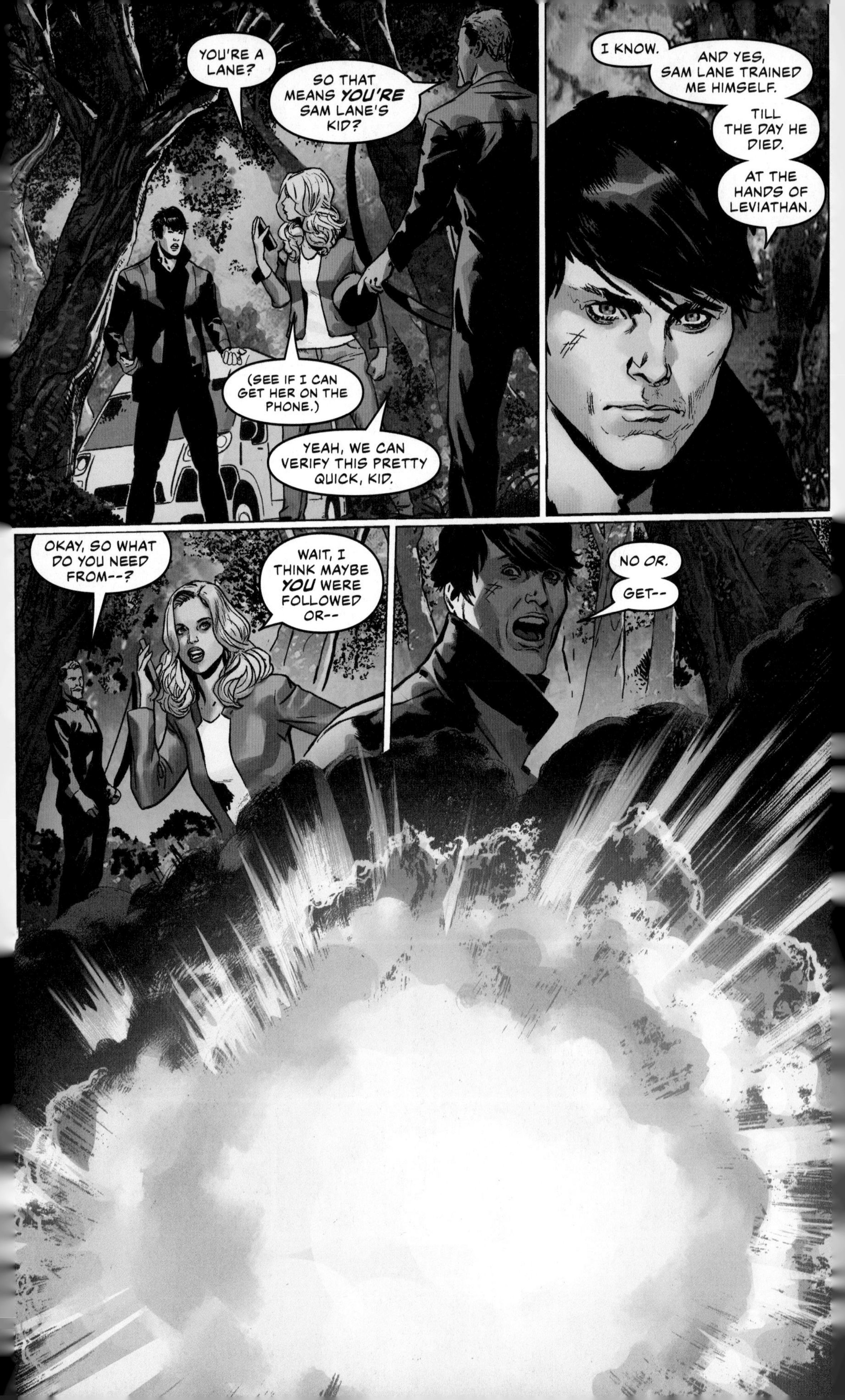

YOU'RE A LANE?
SO THAT MEANS YOU'RE SAM LANE'S KID?
(SEE IF I CAN GET HER ON THE PHONE.)
YEAH, WE CAN VERIFY THIS PRETTY QUICK, KID.
I KNOW.
AND YES, SAM LANE TRAINED ME HIMSELF.
TILL THE DAY HE DIED.
AT THE HANDS OF LEVIATHAN.
OKAY, SO WHAT DO YOU NEED FROM--?
WAIT, I THINK MAYBE YOU WERE FOLLOWED OR--
NO OR.
GET--

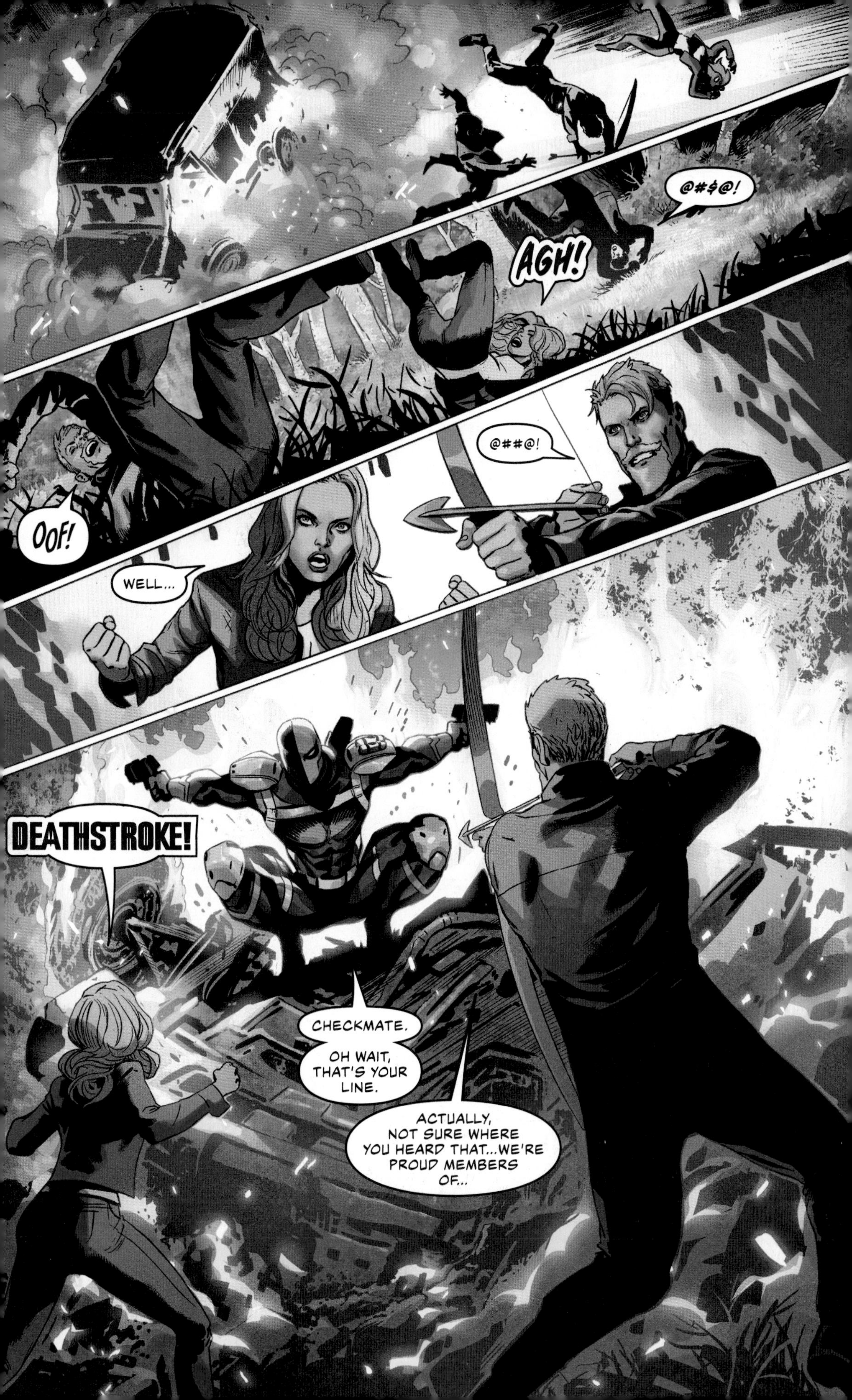
@#$@!
AGH!
OOF!
@##@!
WELL...
DEATHSTROKE!
CHECKMATE.
OH WAIT, THAT'S YOUR LINE.
ACTUALLY, NOT SURE WHERE YOU HEARD THAT...WE'RE PROUD MEMBERS OF...

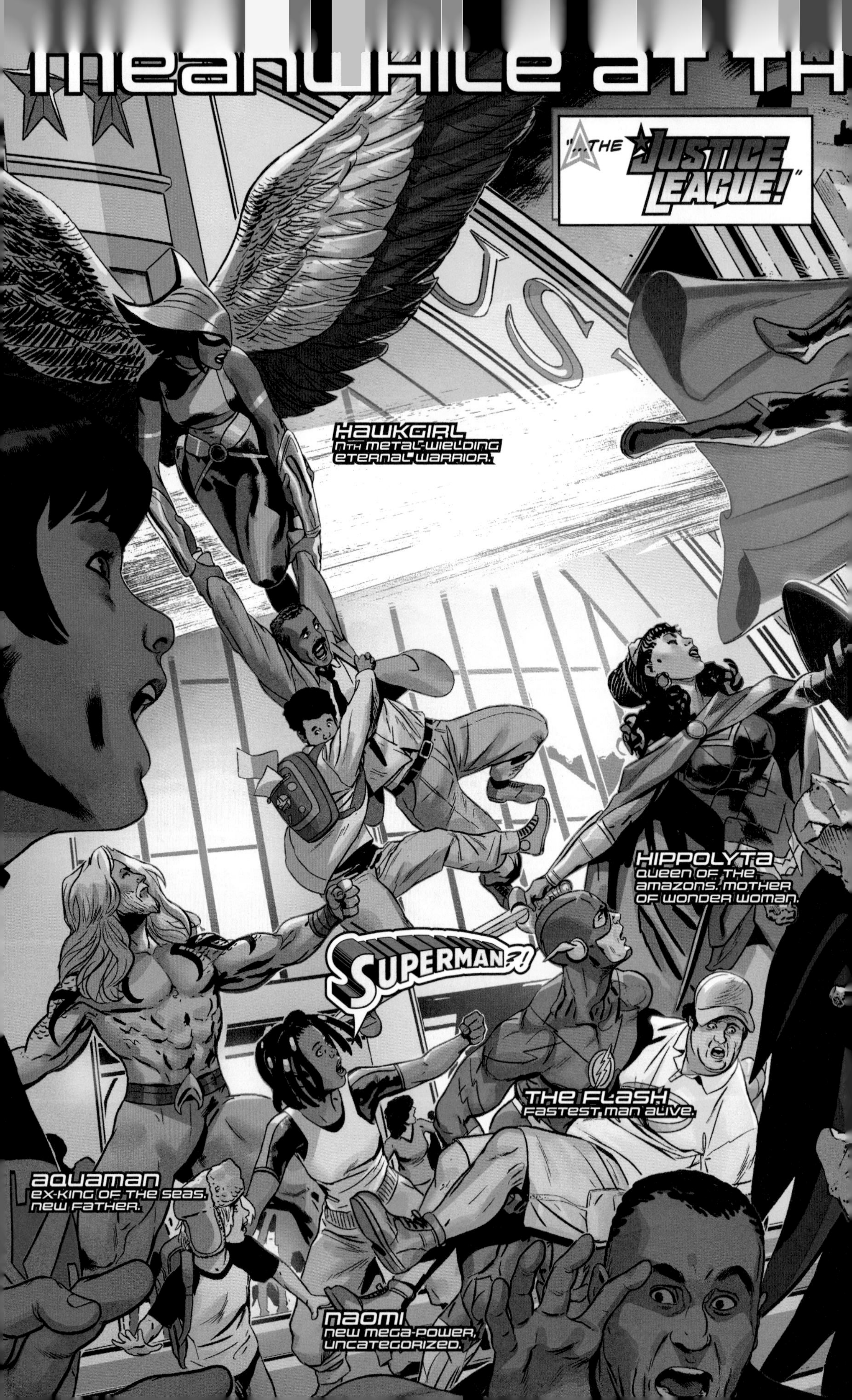
MEANWHILE AT TH
"...THE JUSTICE LEAGUE!"
HAWKGIRL
NTH METAL-WIELDING ETERNAL WARRIOR.
HIPPOLYTA
QUEEN OF THE AMAZONS, MOTHER OF WONDER WOMAN.
SUPERMAN?!
THE FLASH
FASTEST MAN ALIVE.
AQUAMAN
EX-KING OF THE SEAS, NEW FATHER.
NAOMI
NEW MEGA-POWER, UNCATEGORIZED.

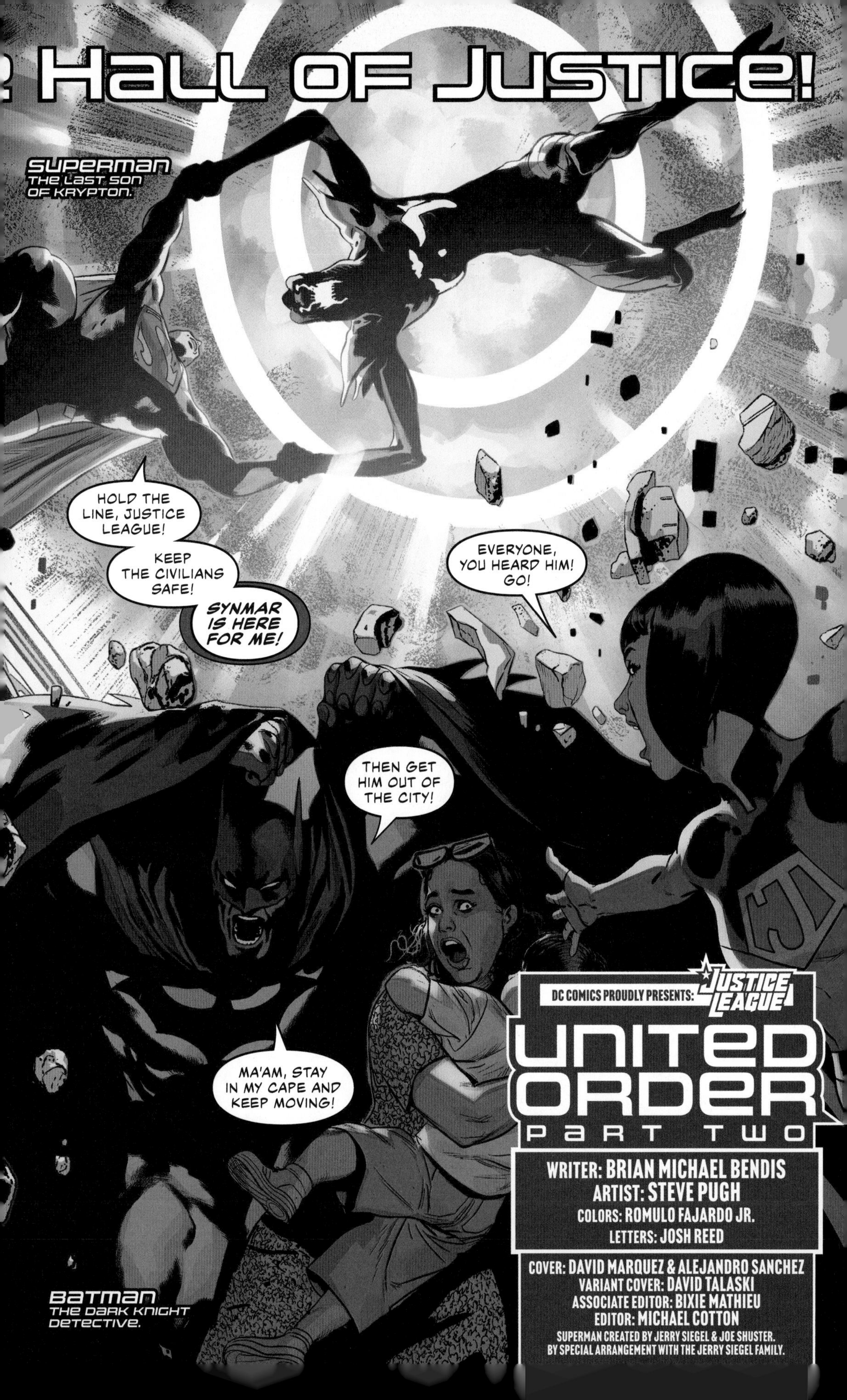

HALL OF JUSTICE!
SUPERMAN THE LAST SON OF KRYPTON.
HOLD THE LINE, JUSTICE LEAGUE!
KEEP THE CIVILIANS SAFE!
SYNMAR IS HERE FOR ME!
EVERYONE, YOU HEARD HIM! GO!
THEN GET HIM OUT OF THE CITY!
MA'AM, STAY IN MY CAPE AND KEEP MOVING!
BATMAN THE DARK KNIGHT DETECTIVE.
DC COMICS PROUDLY PRESENTS: JUSTICE LEAGUE
UNITED ORDER
PART TWO
WRITER: BRIAN MICHAEL BENDIS
ARTIST: STEVE PUGH
COLORS: ROMULO FAJARDO JR.
LETTERS: JOSH REED
COVER: DAVID MARQUEZ & ALEJANDRO SANCHEZ
VARIANT COVER: DAVID TALASKI
ASSOCIATE EDITOR: BIXIE MATHIEU
EDITOR: MICHAEL COTTON
SUPERMAN CREATED BY JERRY SIEGEL & JOE SHUSTER.
BY SPECIAL ARRANGEMENT WITH THE JERRY SIEGEL FAMILY.

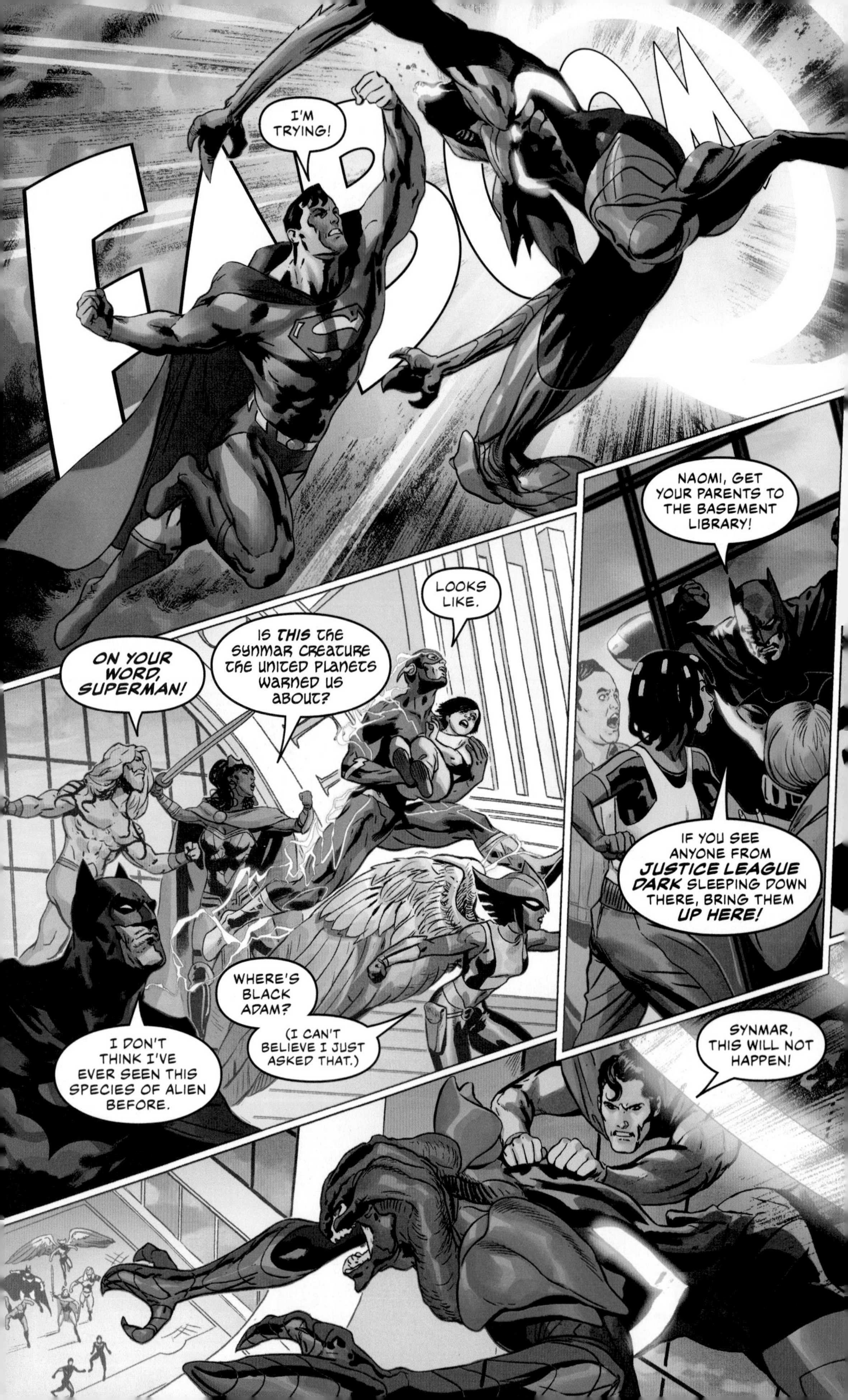
I'M TRYING!
FABOOM
ON YOUR WORD, SUPERMAN!
IS THIS THE SYNMAR CREATURE THE UNITED PLANETS WARNED US ABOUT?
LOOKS LIKE.
WHERE'S BLACK ADAM?
(I CAN'T BELIEVE I JUST ASKED THAT.)
I DON'T THINK I'VE EVER SEEN THIS SPECIES OF ALIEN BEFORE.
NAOMI, GET YOUR PARENTS TO THE BASEMENT LIBRARY!
IF YOU SEE ANYONE FROM JUSTICE LEAGUE DARK SLEEPING DOWN THERE, BRING THEM UP HERE!
SYNMAR, THIS WILL NOT HAPPEN!

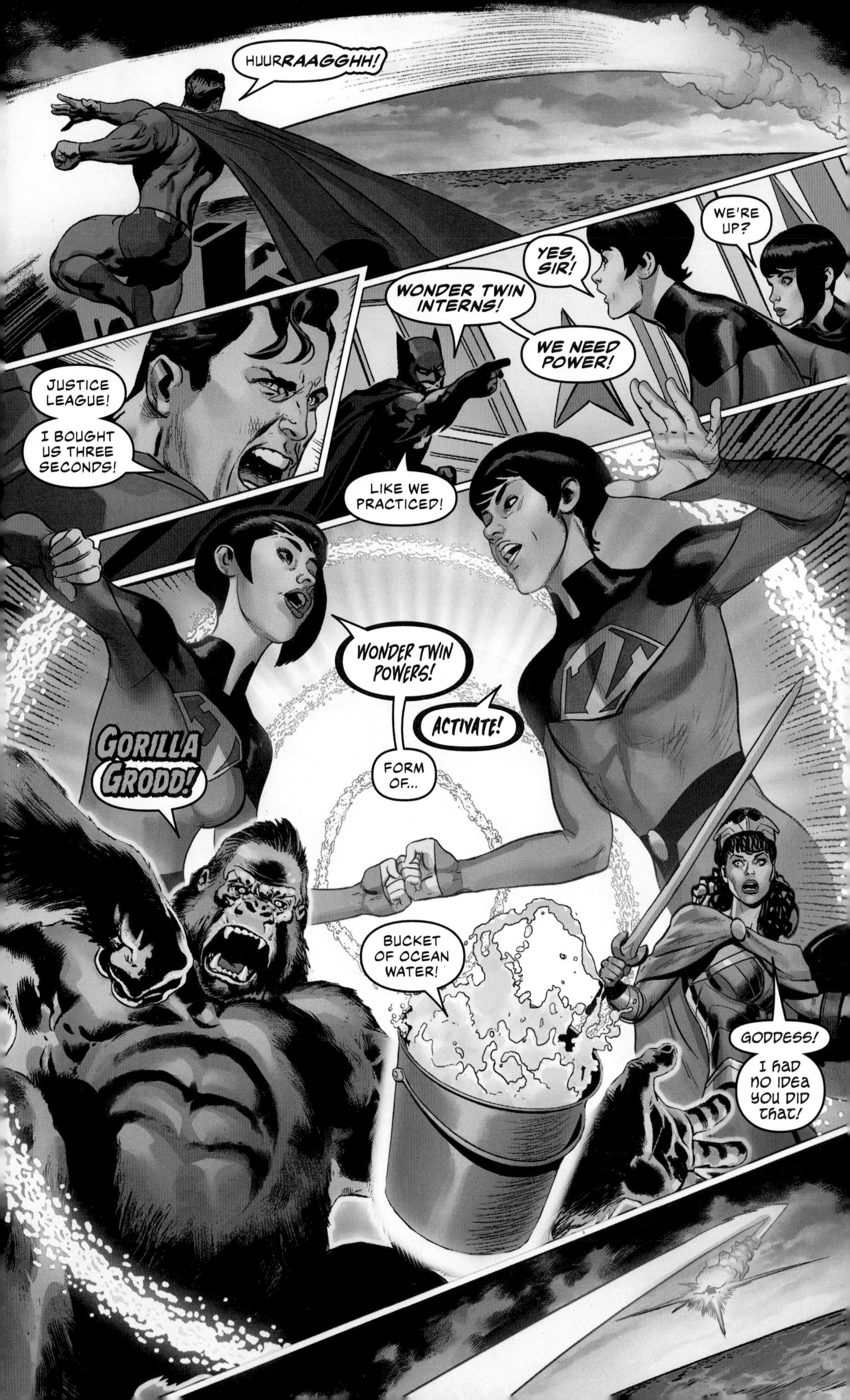
HUURRAAGGHH!
JUSTICE LEAGUE!
I BOUGHT US THREE SECONDS!
WONDER TWIN INTERNS!
WE NEED POWER!
YES, SIR!
WE'RE UP?
LIKE WE PRACTICED!
WONDER TWIN POWERS!
ACTIVATE!
FORM OF...
GORILLA GRODD!
BUCKET OF OCEAN WATER!
GODDESS!
I HAD NO IDEA YOU DID THAT!

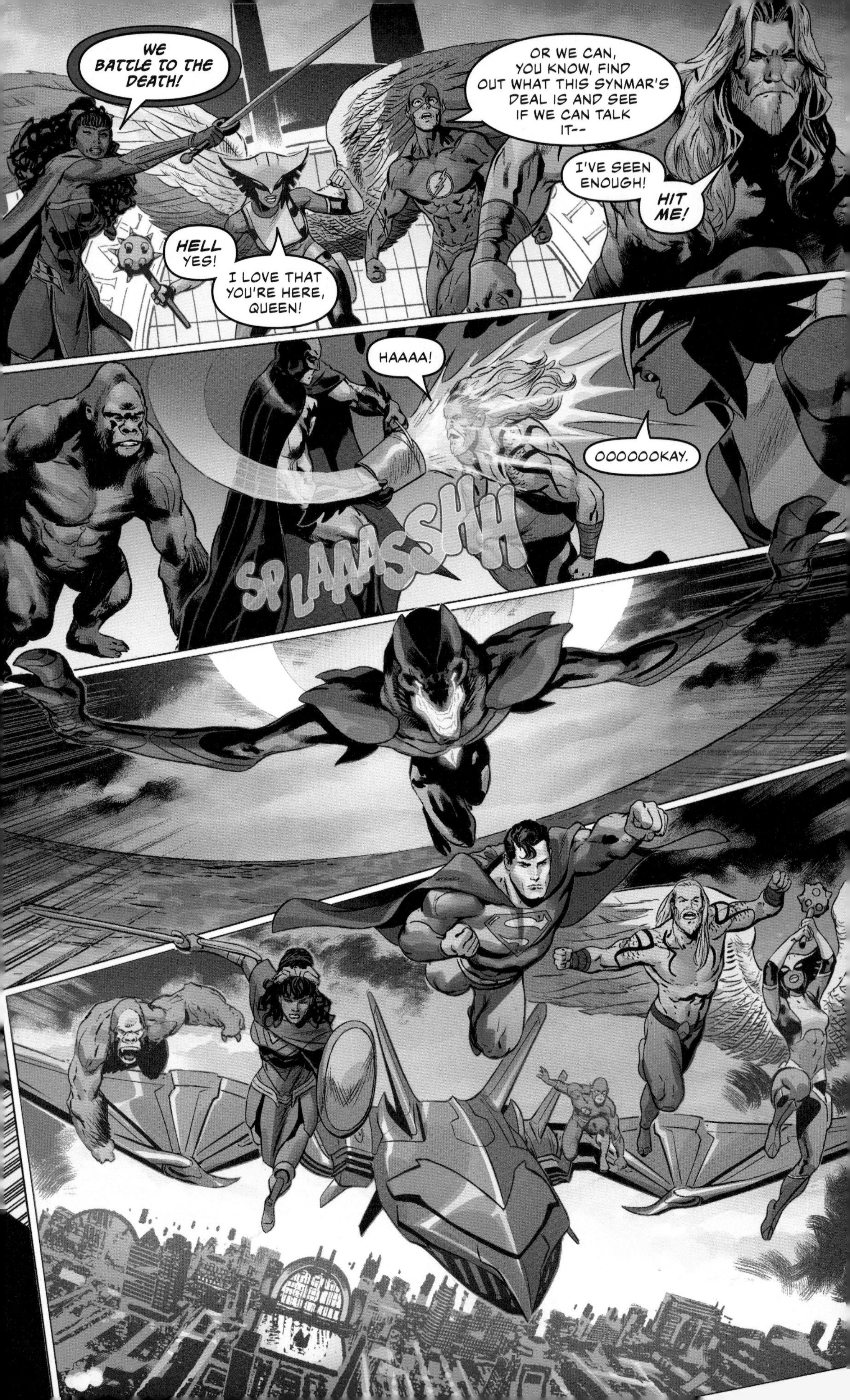
WE BATTLE TO THE DEATH!
OR WE CAN, YOU KNOW, FIND OUT WHAT THIS SYNMAR'S DEAL IS AND SEE IF WE CAN TALK IT--
I'VE SEEN ENOUGH! HIT ME!
HELL YES!
I LOVE THAT YOU'RE HERE, QUEEN!
HAAAA!
OOOOOOKAY.
SPLAAASSHH

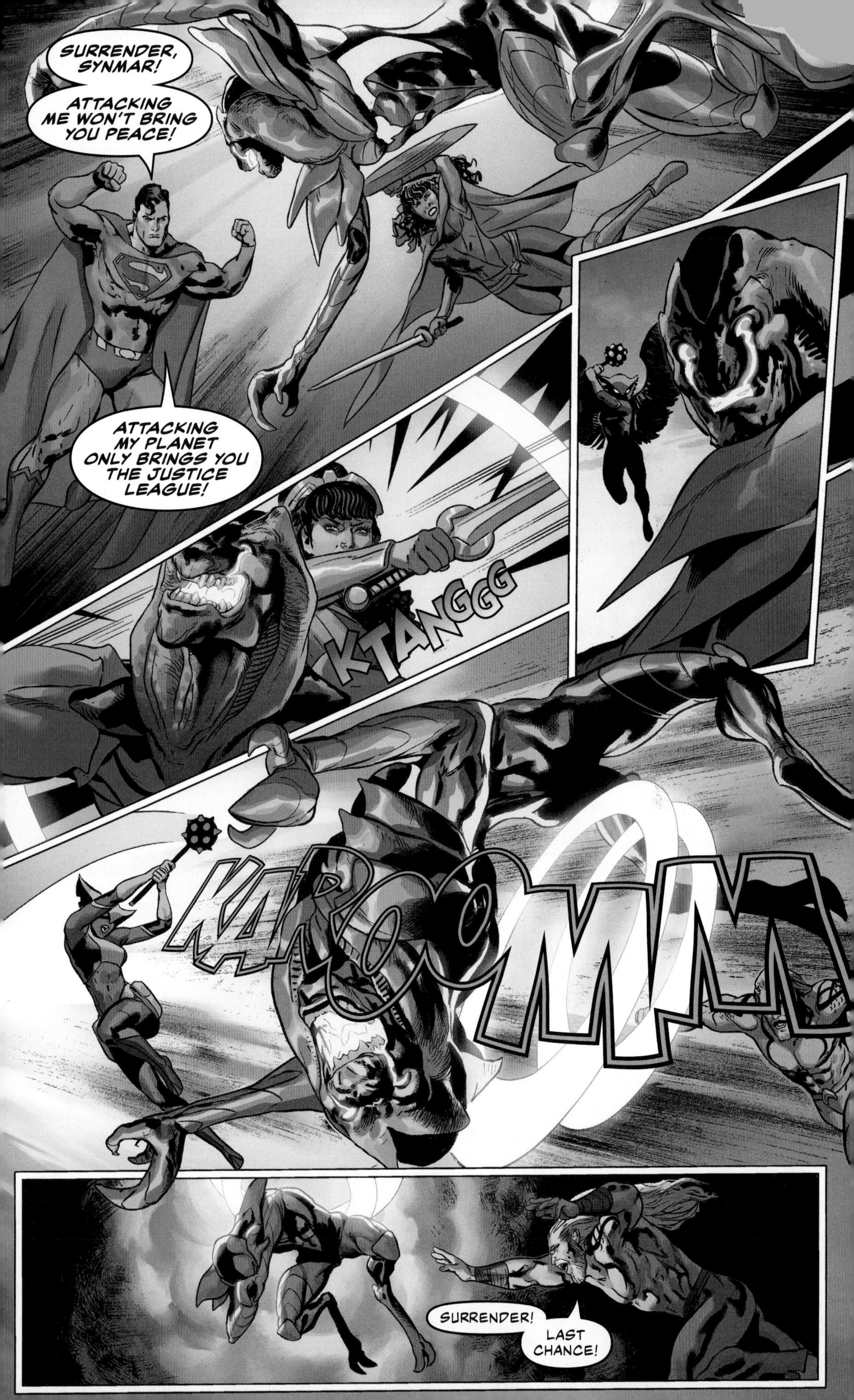
SURRENDER, SYNMAR!
ATTACKING ME WON'T BRING YOU PEACE!
ATTACKING MY PLANET ONLY BRINGS YOU THE JUSTICE LEAGUE!
KTANGGG
KAROOOMM
SURRENDER!
LAST CHANCE!

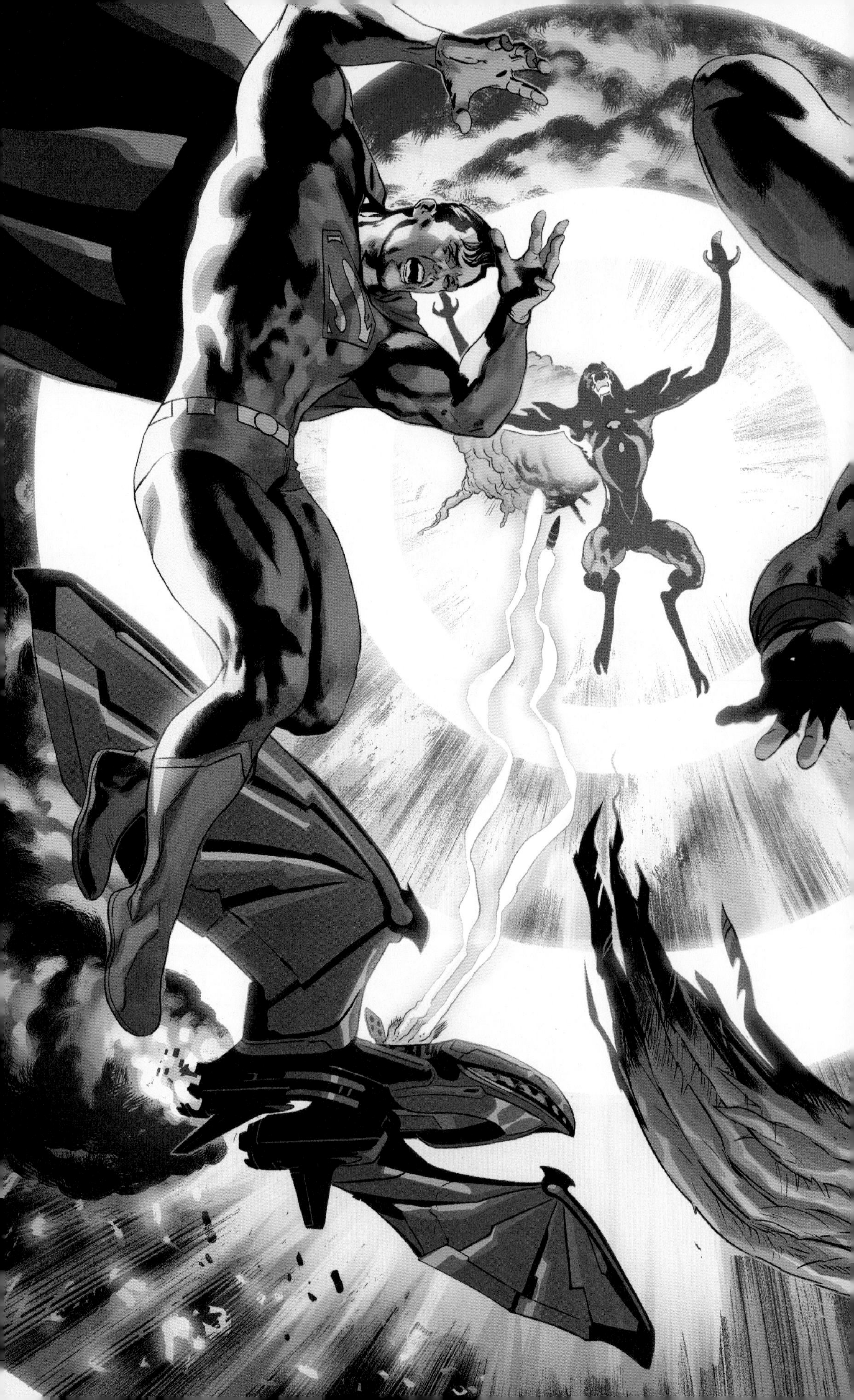

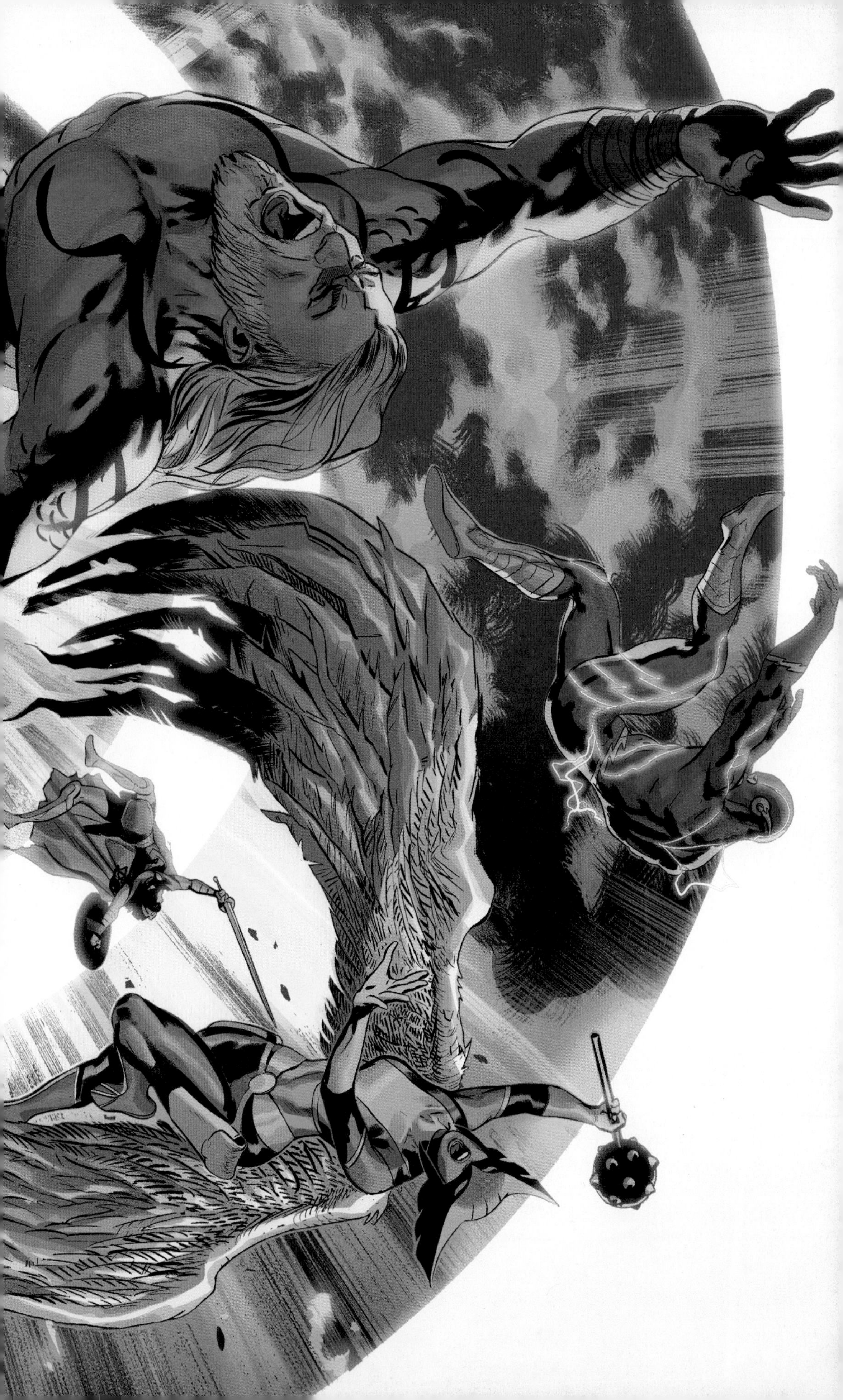

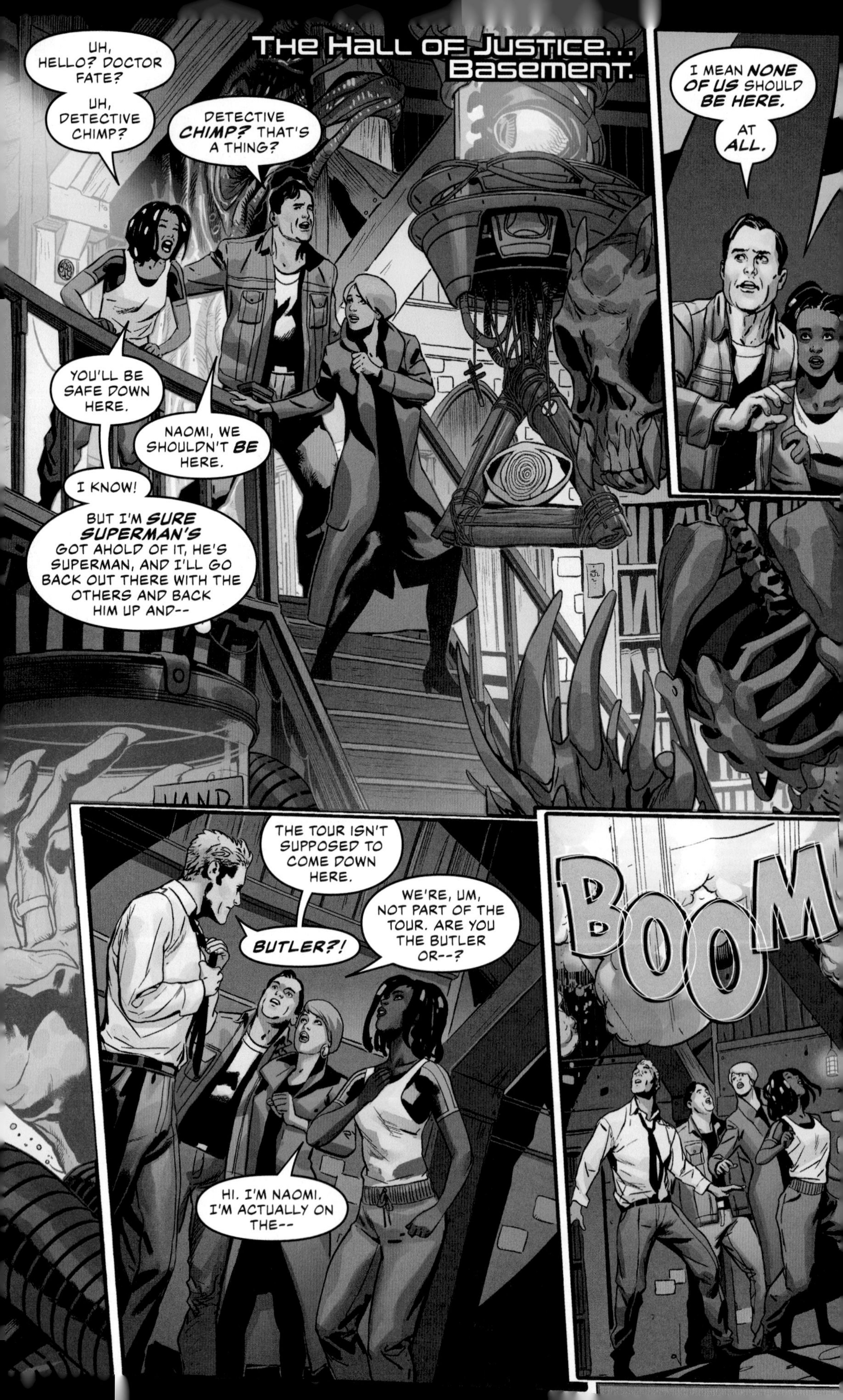
THE HALL OF JUSTICE... BASEMENT.
UH, HELLO? DOCTOR FATE?
UH, DETECTIVE CHIMP?
DETECTIVE CHIMP? THAT'S A THING?
YOU'LL BE SAFE DOWN HERE.
NAOMI, WE SHOULDN'T BE HERE.
I KNOW!
BUT I'M SURE SUPERMAN'S GOT AHOLD OF IT, HE'S SUPERMAN, AND I'LL GO BACK OUT THERE WITH THE OTHERS AND BACK HIM UP AND--
I MEAN NONE OF US SHOULD BE HERE.
AT ALL.
THE TOUR ISN'T SUPPOSED TO COME DOWN HERE.
BUTLER?!
WE'RE, UM, NOT PART OF THE TOUR. ARE YOU THE BUTLER OR--?
HI. I'M NAOMI. I'M ACTUALLY ON THE--
BOOM

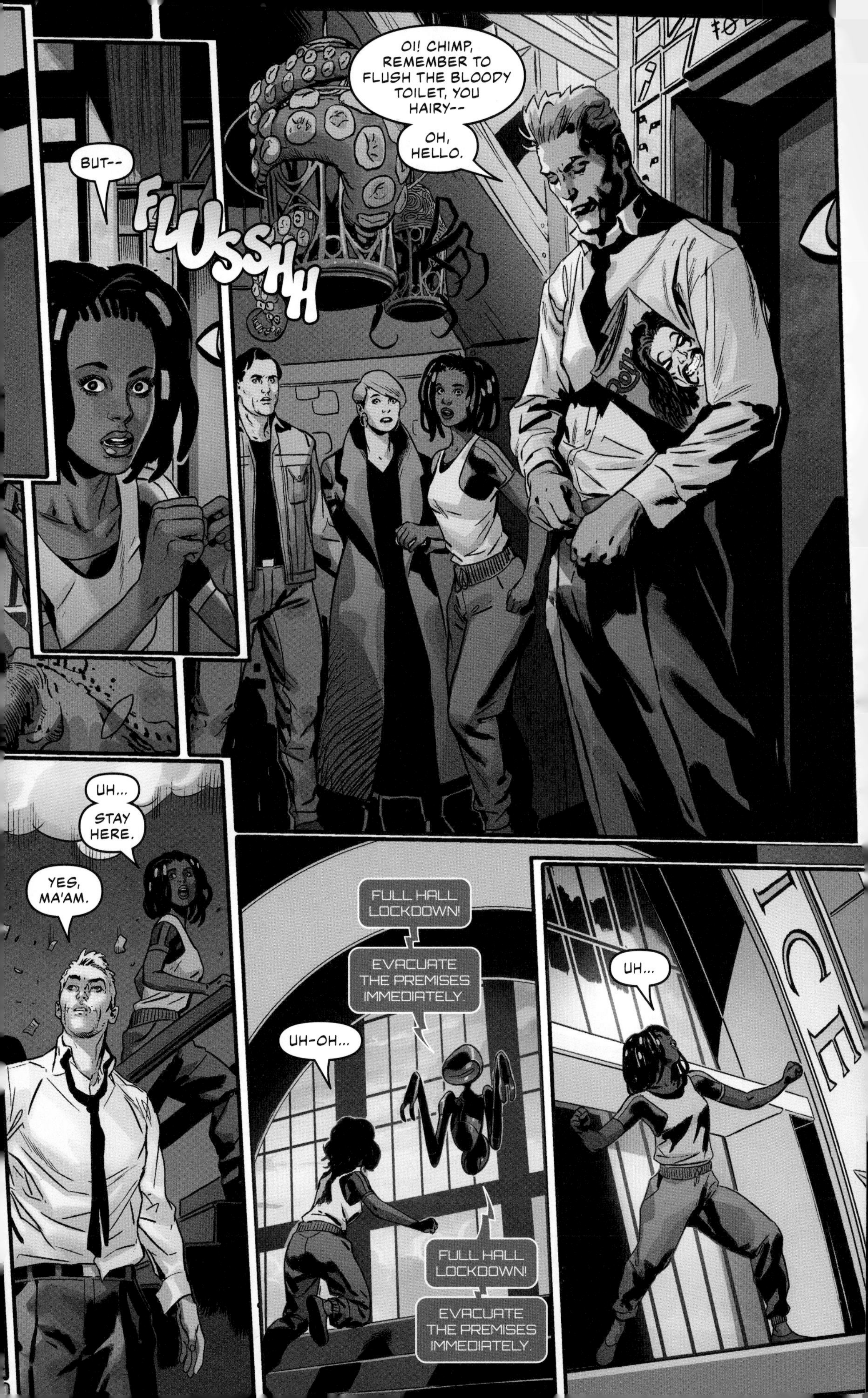
BUT--
FLUSSHH
OI! CHIMP, REMEMBER TO FLUSH THE BLOODY TOILET, YOU HAIRY--
OH, HELLO.
UH...
STAY HERE.
YES, MA'AM.
FULL HALL LOCKDOWN!
EVACUATE THE PREMISES IMMEDIATELY.
UH-OH...
FULL HALL LOCKDOWN!
EVACUATE THE PREMISES IMMEDIATELY.
UH...

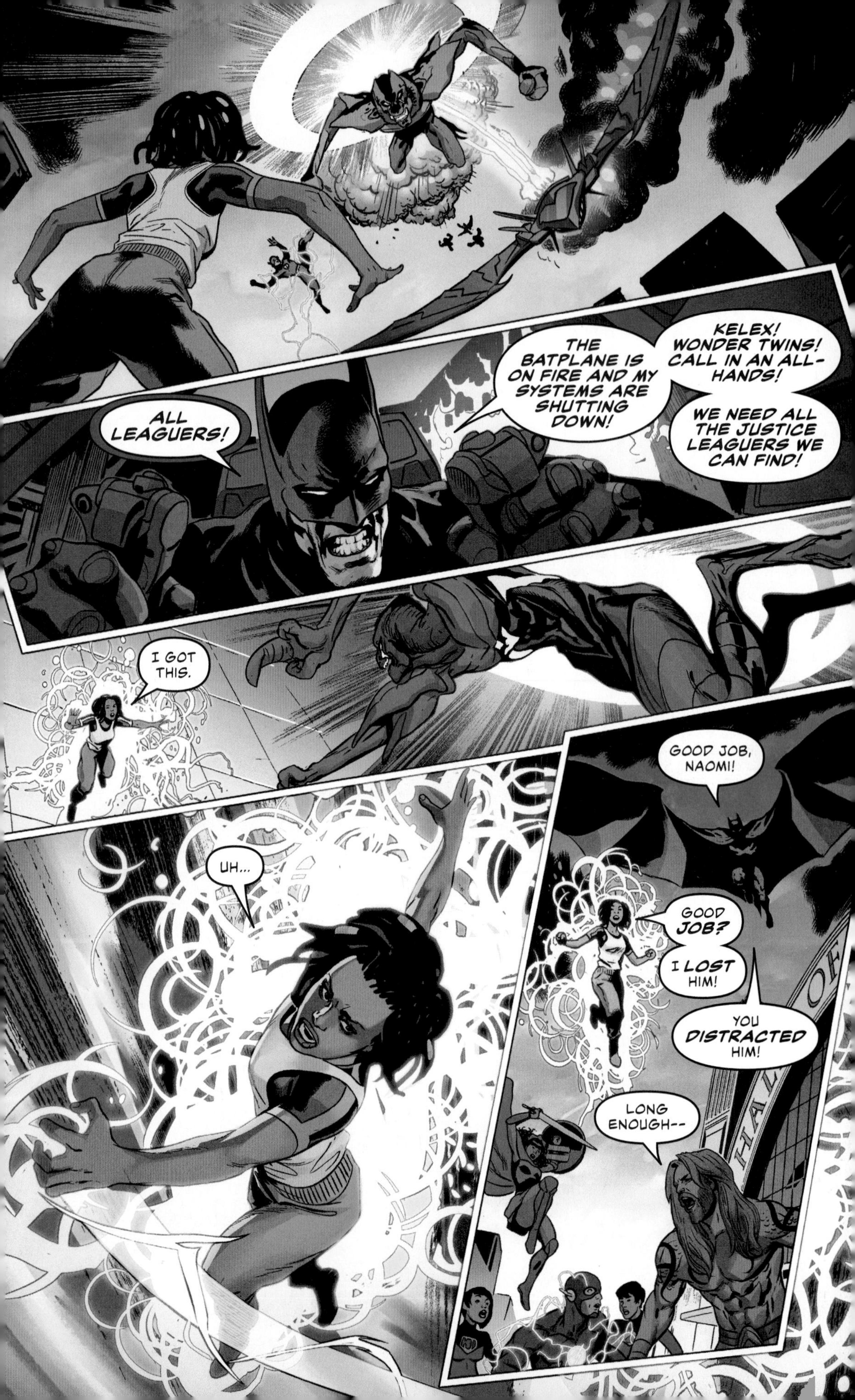
ALL LEAGUERS!
THE BATPLANE IS ON FIRE AND MY SYSTEMS ARE SHUTTING DOWN!
KELEX! WONDER TWINS! CALL IN AN ALL-HANDS!
WE NEED ALL THE JUSTICE LEAGUERS WE CAN FIND!
I GOT THIS.
UH...
GOOD JOB, NAOMI!
GOOD JOB?
I LOST HIM!
YOU DISTRACTED HIM!
LONG ENOUGH--
HAL OF

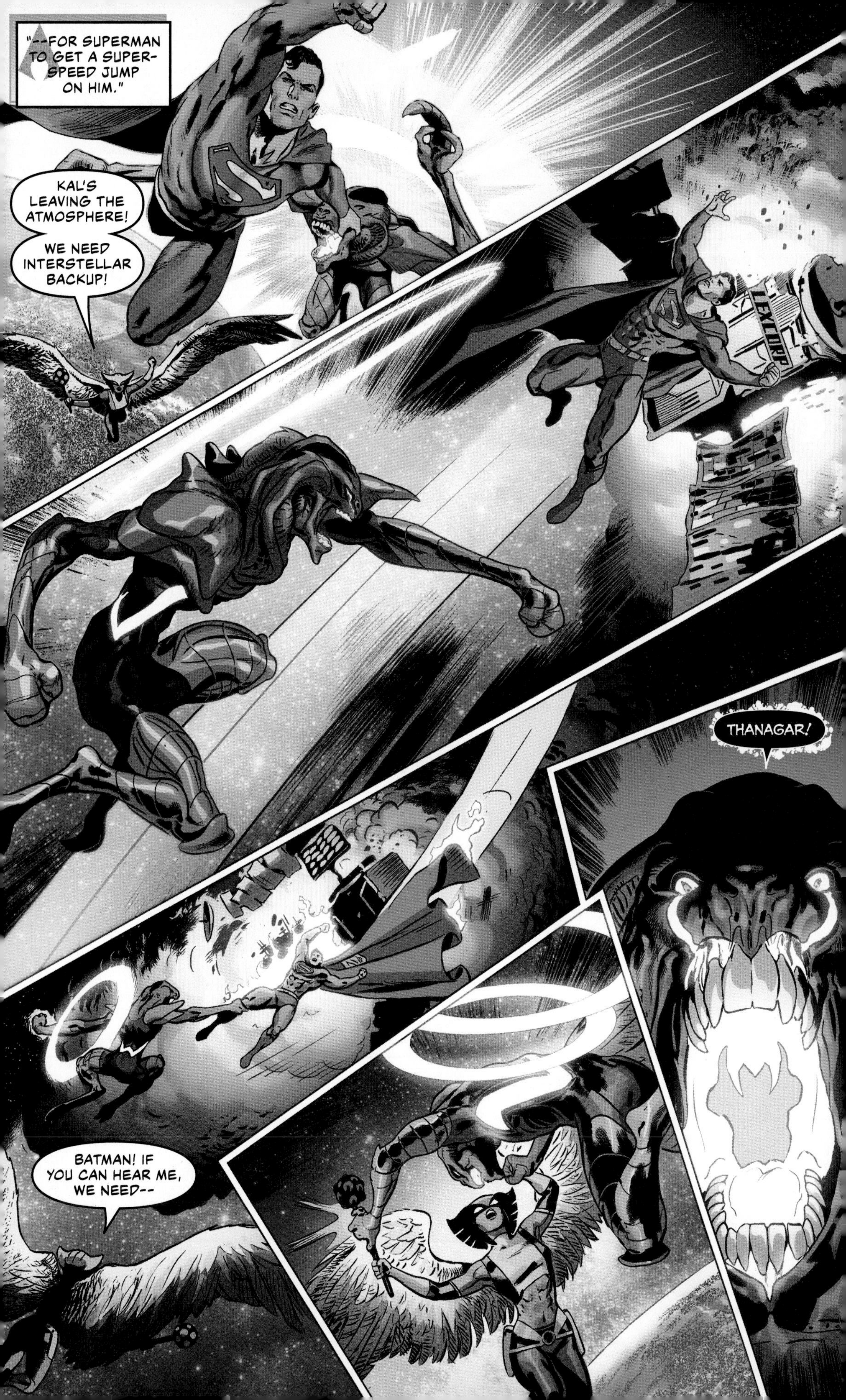
"--FOR SUPERMAN TO GET A SUPER-SPEED JUMP ON HIM."
KAL'S LEAVING THE ATMOSPHERE!
WE NEED INTERSTELLAR BACKUP!
LEXCORP
THANAGAR!
BATMAN! IF YOU CAN HEAR ME, WE NEED--

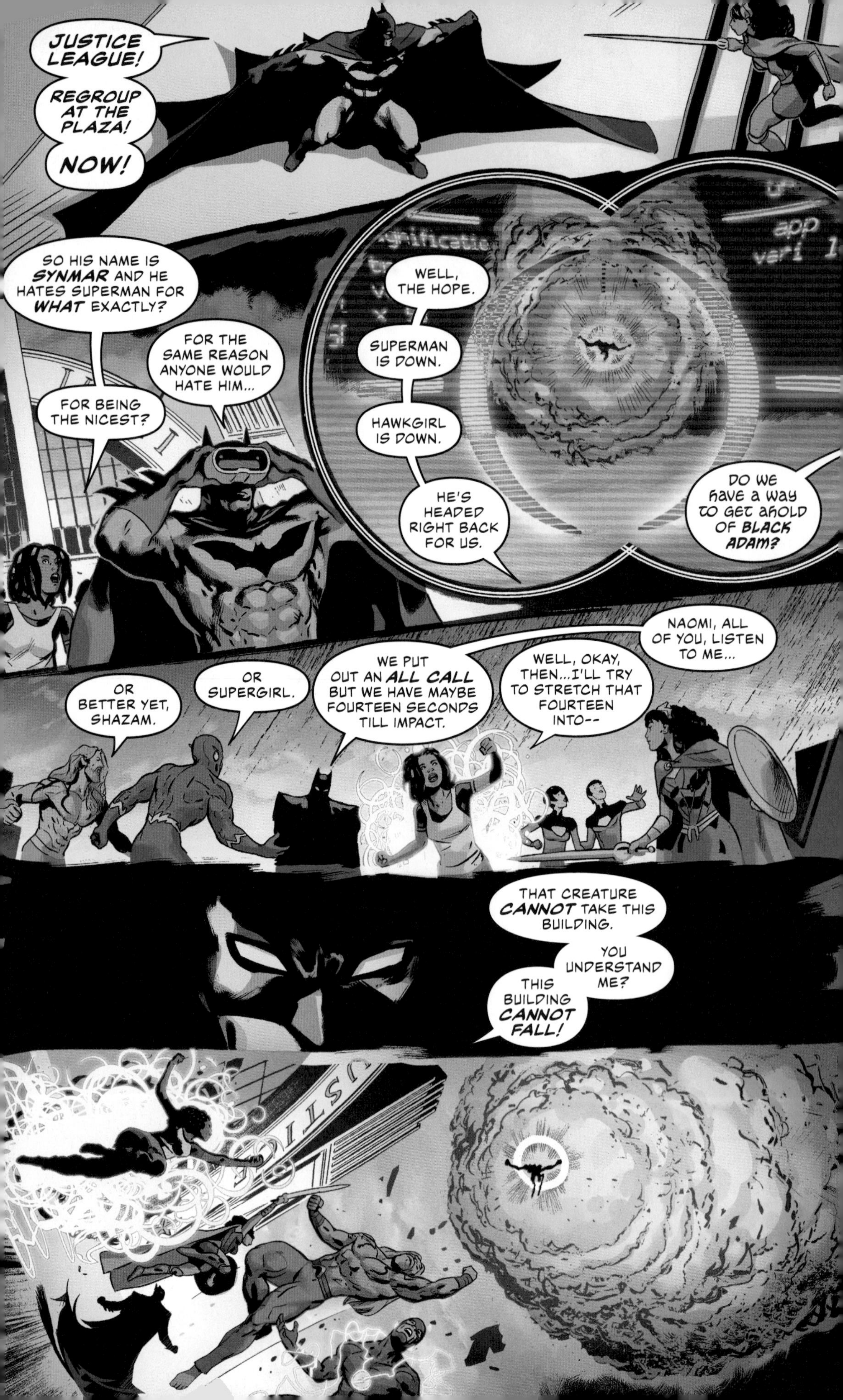
JUSTICE LEAGUE!
REGROUP AT THE PLAZA!
NOW!
SO HIS NAME IS SYNMAR AND HE HATES SUPERMAN FOR WHAT EXACTLY?
FOR BEING THE NICEST?
FOR THE SAME REASON ANYONE WOULD HATE HIM...
WELL, THE HOPE.
SUPERMAN IS DOWN.
HAWKGIRL IS DOWN.
HE'S HEADED RIGHT BACK FOR US.
DO WE HAVE A WAY TO GET AHOLD OF BLACK ADAM?
OR BETTER YET, SHAZAM.
OR SUPERGIRL.
WE PUT OUT AN ALL CALL BUT WE HAVE MAYBE FOURTEEN SECONDS TILL IMPACT.
WELL, OKAY, THEN...I'LL TRY TO STRETCH THAT FOURTEEN INTO--
NAOMI, ALL OF YOU, LISTEN TO ME...
THAT CREATURE CANNOT TAKE THIS BUILDING.
YOU UNDERSTAND ME?
THIS BUILDING CANNOT FALL!

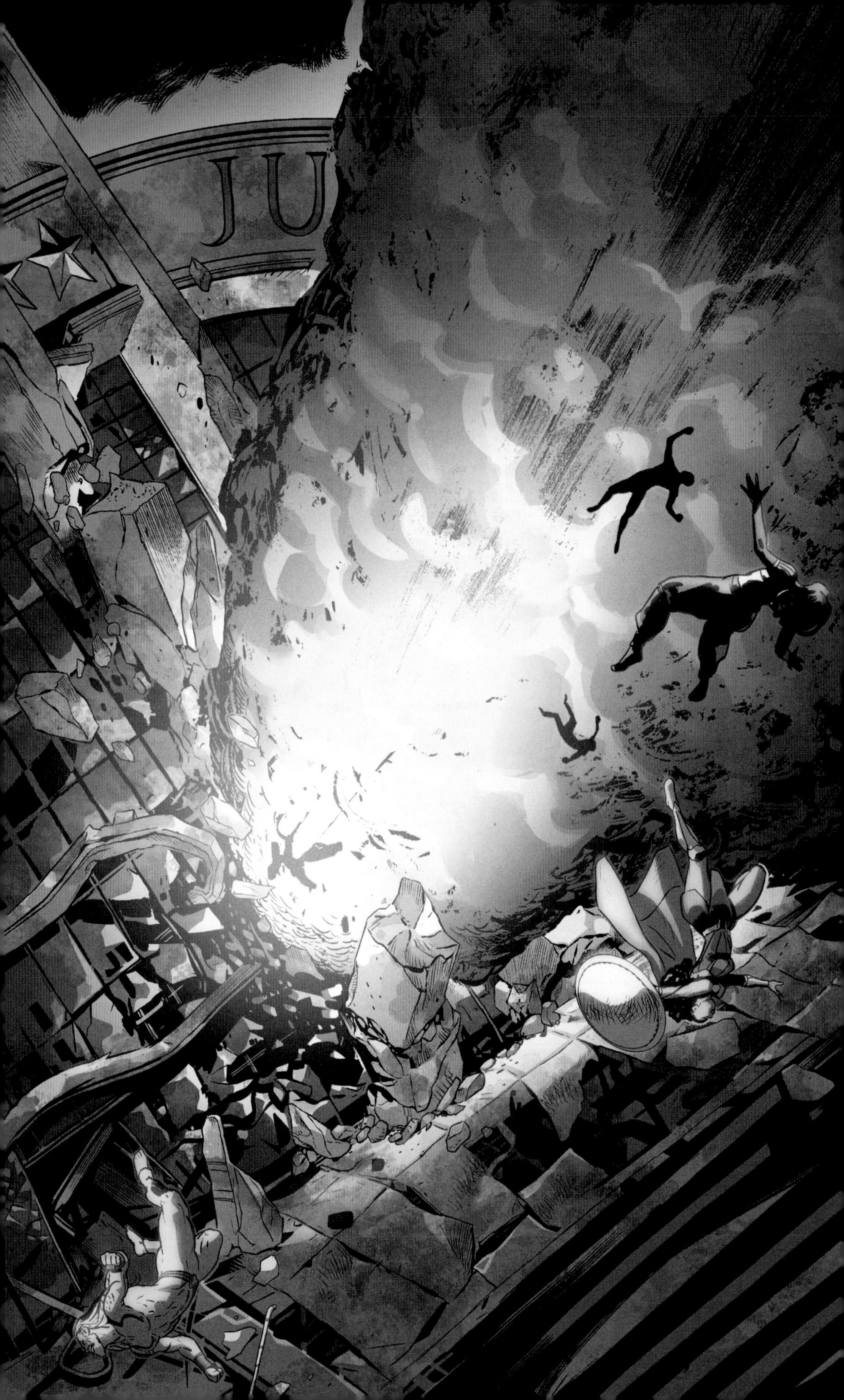
JU

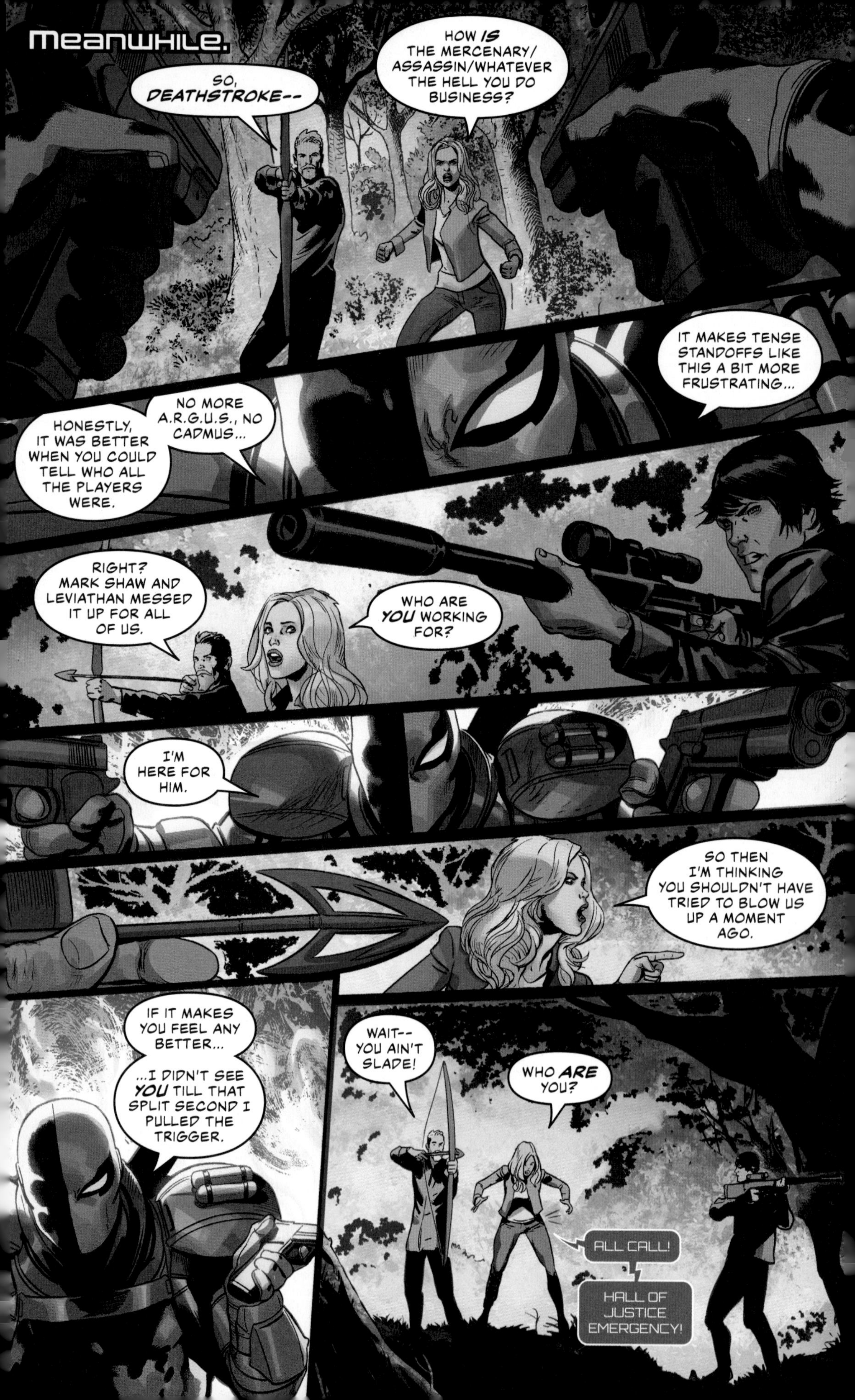
MEANWHILE.
SO, DEATHSTROKE--
HOW IS THE MERCENARY/ ASSASSIN/WHATEVER THE HELL YOU DO BUSINESS?
IT MAKES TENSE STANDOFFS LIKE THIS A BIT MORE FRUSTRATING...
NO MORE A.R.G.U.S., NO CADMUS...
HONESTLY, IT WAS BETTER WHEN YOU COULD TELL WHO ALL THE PLAYERS WERE.
RIGHT? MARK SHAW AND LEVIATHAN MESSED IT UP FOR ALL OF US.
WHO ARE YOU WORKING FOR?
I'M HERE FOR HIM.
SO THEN I'M THINKING YOU SHOULDN'T HAVE TRIED TO BLOW US UP A MOMENT AGO.
IF IT MAKES YOU FEEL ANY BETTER...
...I DIDN'T SEE YOU TILL THAT SPLIT SECOND I PULLED THE TRIGGER.
WAIT-- YOU AIN'T SLADE!
WHO ARE YOU?
ALL CALL!
HALL OF JUSTICE EMERGENCY!

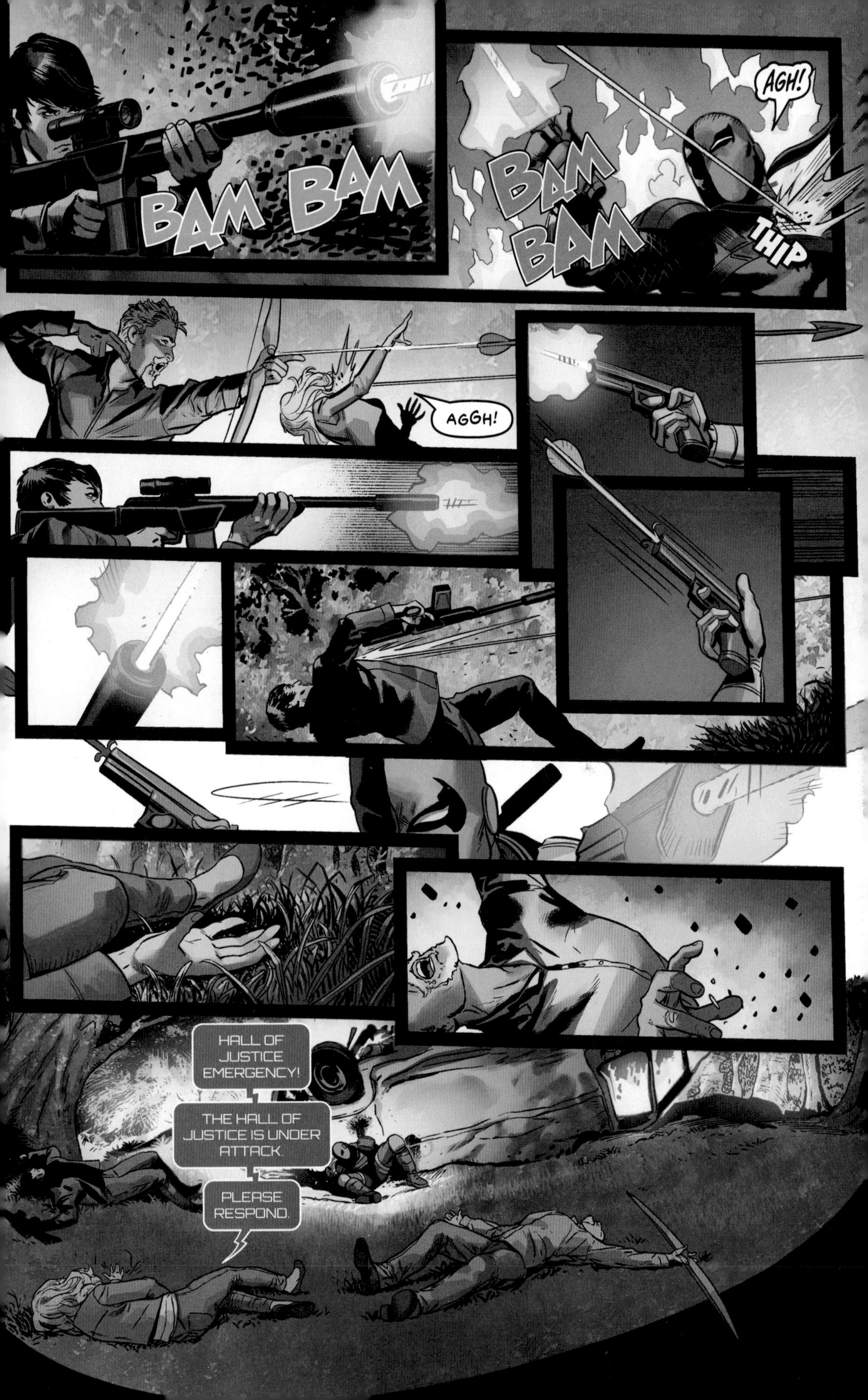
BAM BAM
AGH!
BAM BAM
THIP
AGGH!
HALL OF JUSTICE EMERGENCY!
THE HALL OF JUSTICE IS UNDER ATTACK.
PLEASE RESPOND.

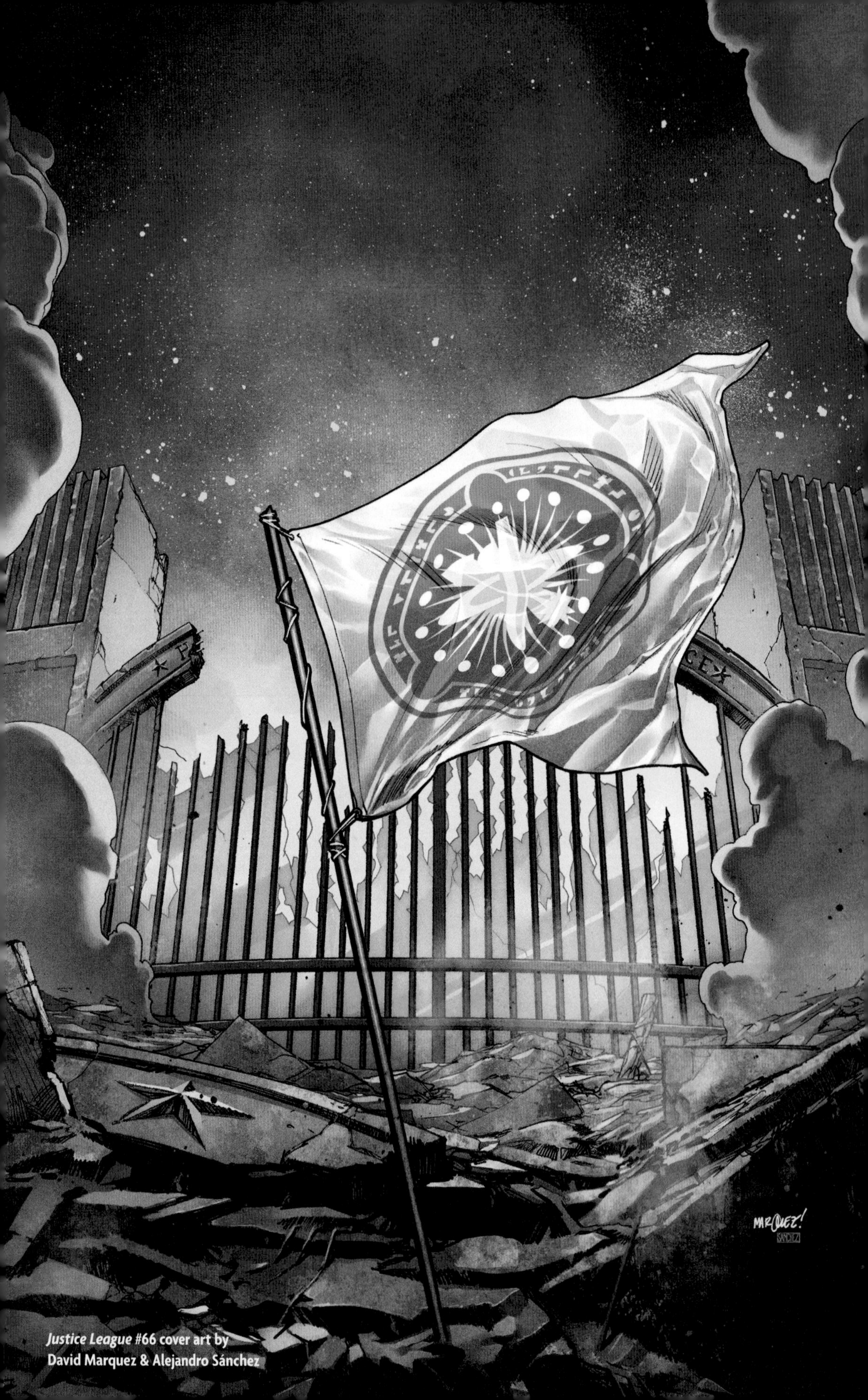

Justice League #66 cover art by
David Marquez & Alejandro Sánchez

Justice League **#66 variant cover art by**
Alexander Lozano

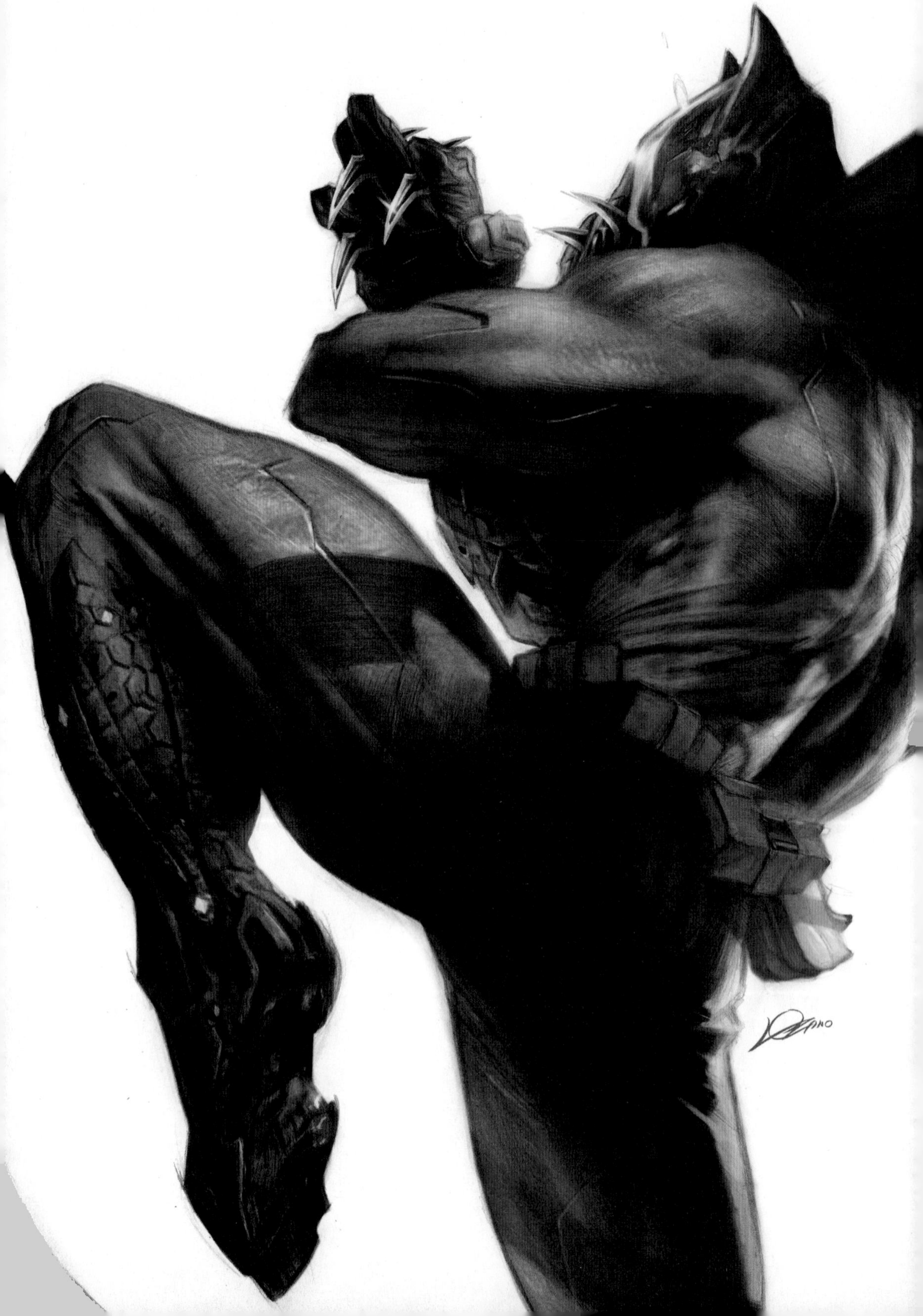

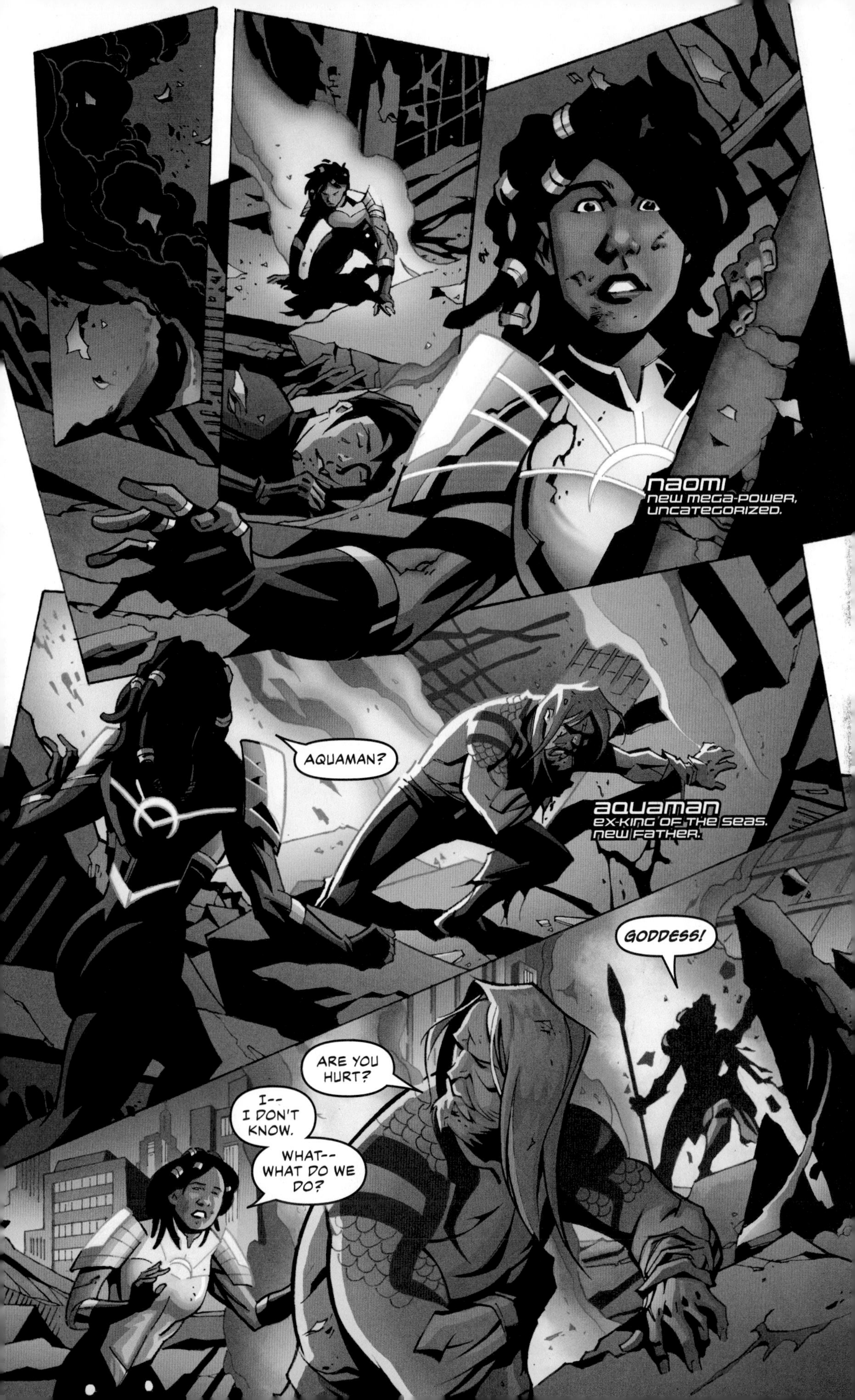
NAOMI
NEW MEGA-POWER, UNCATEGORIZED.
AQUAMAN?
AQUAMAN
EX-KING OF THE SEAS. NEW FATHER.
GODDESS!
ARE YOU HURT?
I-- I DON'T KNOW.
WHAT-- WHAT DO WE DO?

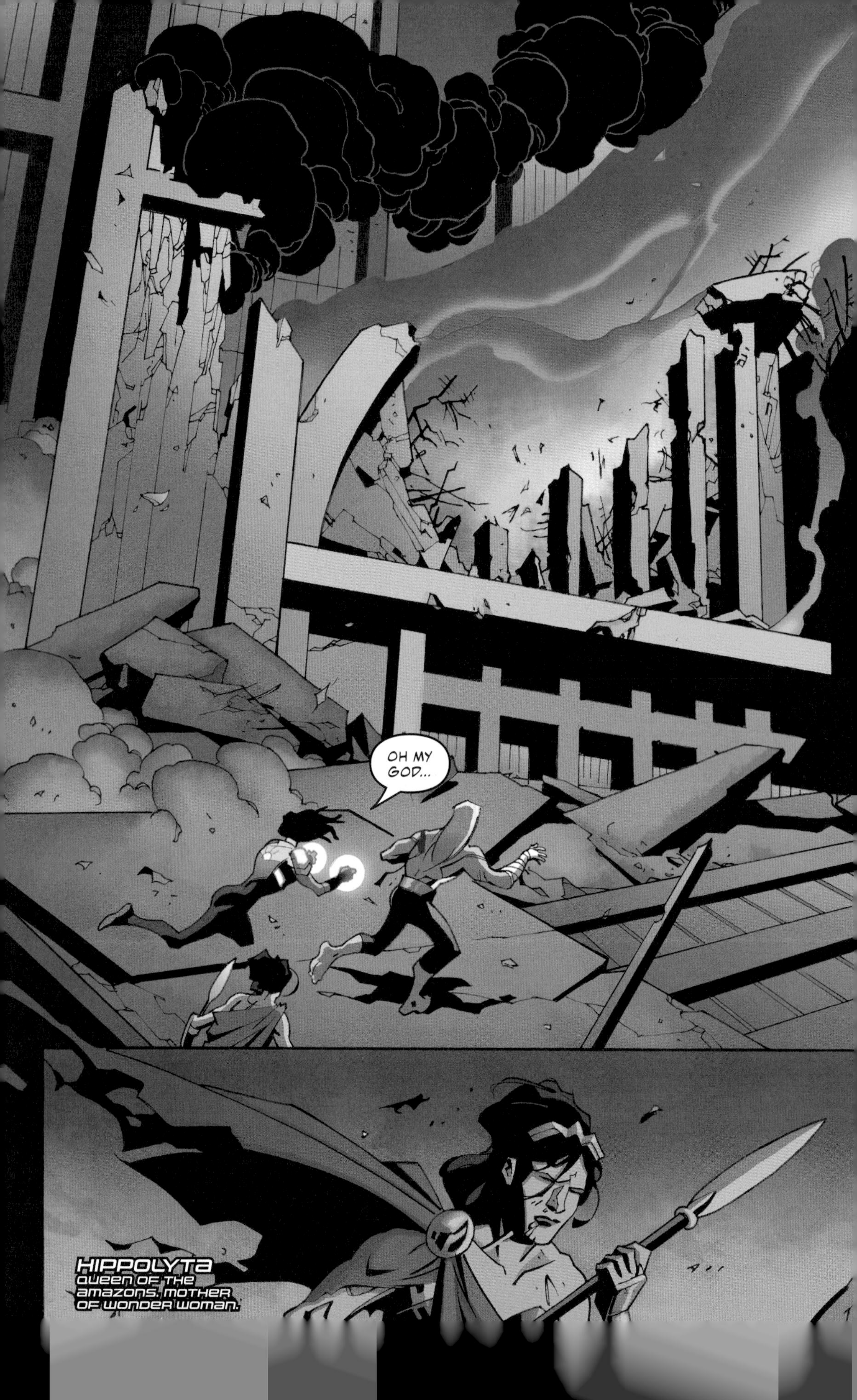
OH MY GOD...
HIPPOLYTA
QUEEN OF THE AMAZONS, MOTHER OF WONDER WOMAN.

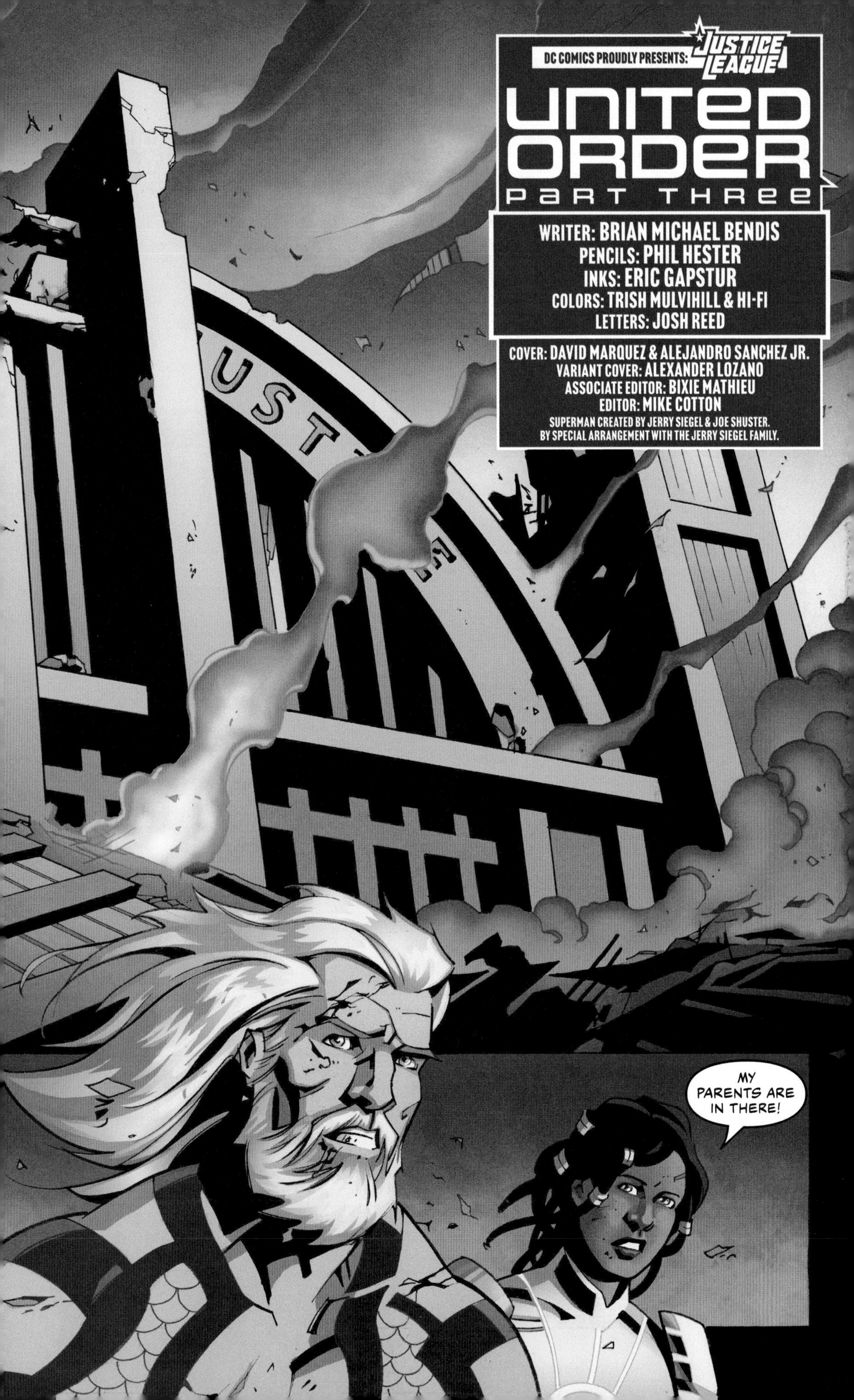
DC COMICS PROUDLY PRESENTS: JUSTICE LEAGUE
UNITED ORDER
PART THREE
WRITER: BRIAN MICHAEL BENDIS
PENCILS: PHIL HESTER
INKS: ERIC GAPSTUR
COLORS: TRISH MULVIHILL & HI-FI
LETTERS: JOSH REED
COVER: DAVID MARQUEZ & ALEJANDRO SANCHEZ JR.
VARIANT COVER: ALEXANDER LOZANO
ASSOCIATE EDITOR: BIXIE MATHIEU
EDITOR: MIKE COTTON
SUPERMAN CREATED BY JERRY SIEGEL & JOE SHUSTER.
BY SPECIAL ARRANGEMENT WITH THE JERRY SIEGEL FAMILY.
MY PARENTS ARE IN THERE!

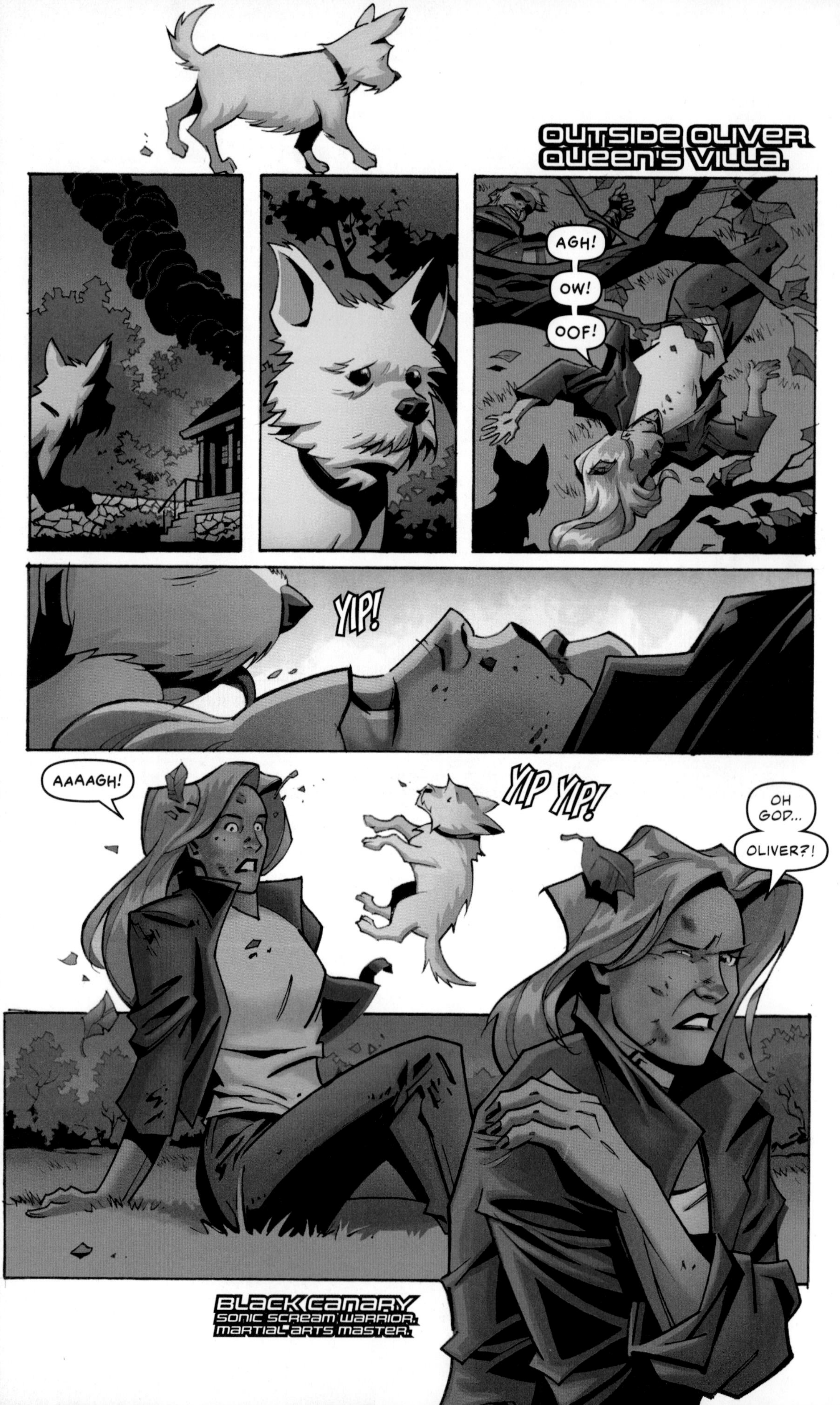
OUTSIDE OLIVER QUEEN'S VILLA.
AGH!
OW!
OOF!
YIP!
AAAAGH!
YIP YIP!
OH GOD...
OLIVER?!
BLACK CANARY
SONIC SCREAM WARRIOR.
MARTIAL ARTS MASTER.

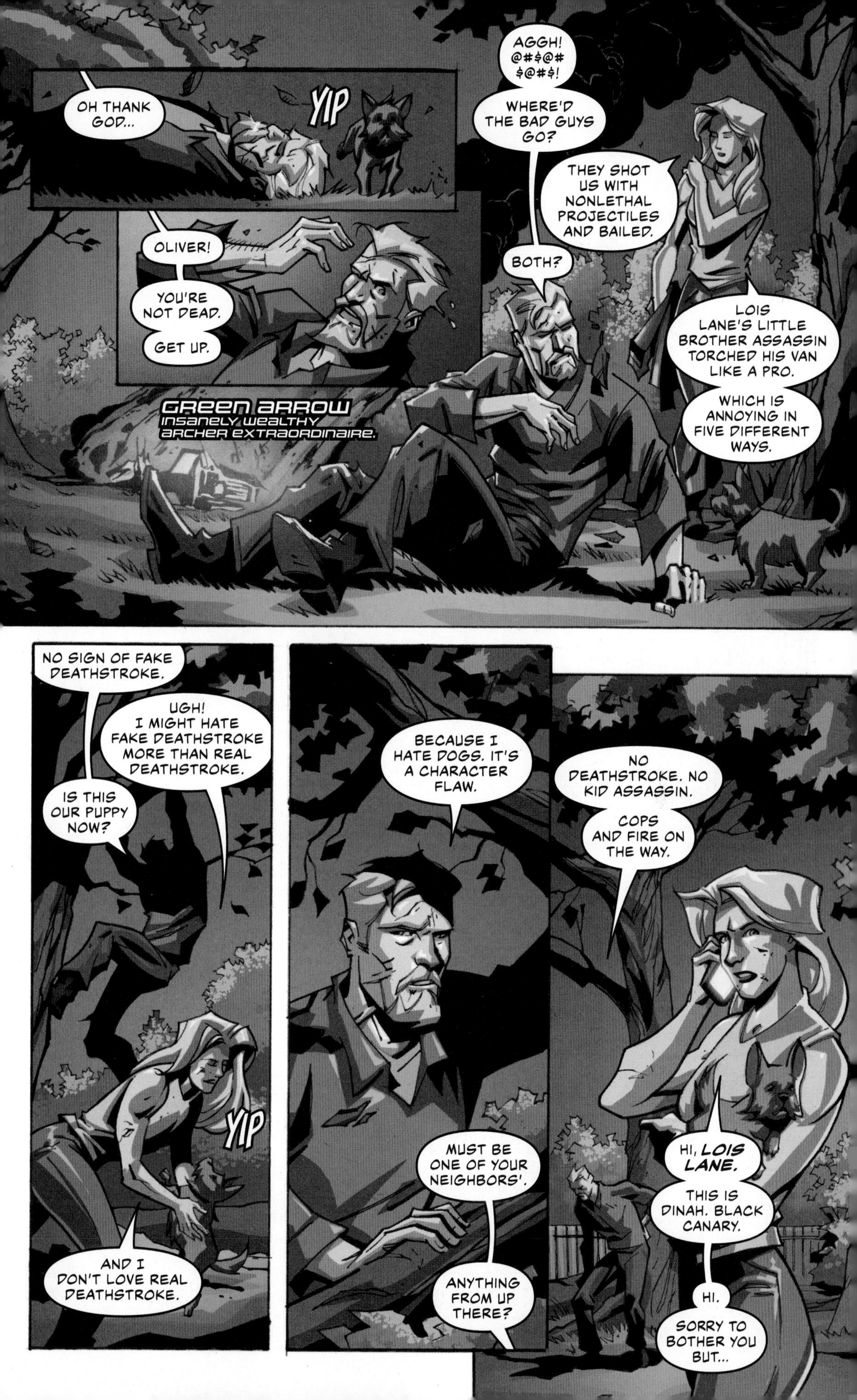
OH THANK GOD...
YIP
OLIVER!
YOU'RE NOT DEAD.
GET UP.
GREEN ARROW
INSANELY WEALTHY ARCHER EXTRAORDINAIRE.
AGGH! @#$@# $@#$!
WHERE'D THE BAD GUYS GO?
THEY SHOT US WITH NONLETHAL PROJECTILES AND BAILED.
BOTH?
LOIS LANE'S LITTLE BROTHER ASSASSIN TORCHED HIS VAN LIKE A PRO.
WHICH IS ANNOYING IN FIVE DIFFERENT WAYS.
NO SIGN OF FAKE DEATHSTROKE.
UGH! I MIGHT HATE FAKE DEATHSTROKE MORE THAN REAL DEATHSTROKE.
IS THIS OUR PUPPY NOW?
YIP
AND I DON'T LOVE REAL DEATHSTROKE.
BECAUSE I HATE DOGS. IT'S A CHARACTER FLAW.
MUST BE ONE OF YOUR NEIGHBORS'.
ANYTHING FROM UP THERE?
NO DEATHSTROKE. NO KID ASSASSIN.
COPS AND FIRE ON THE WAY.
HI, LOIS LANE.
THIS IS DINAH. BLACK CANARY.
HI.
SORRY TO BOTHER YOU BUT...

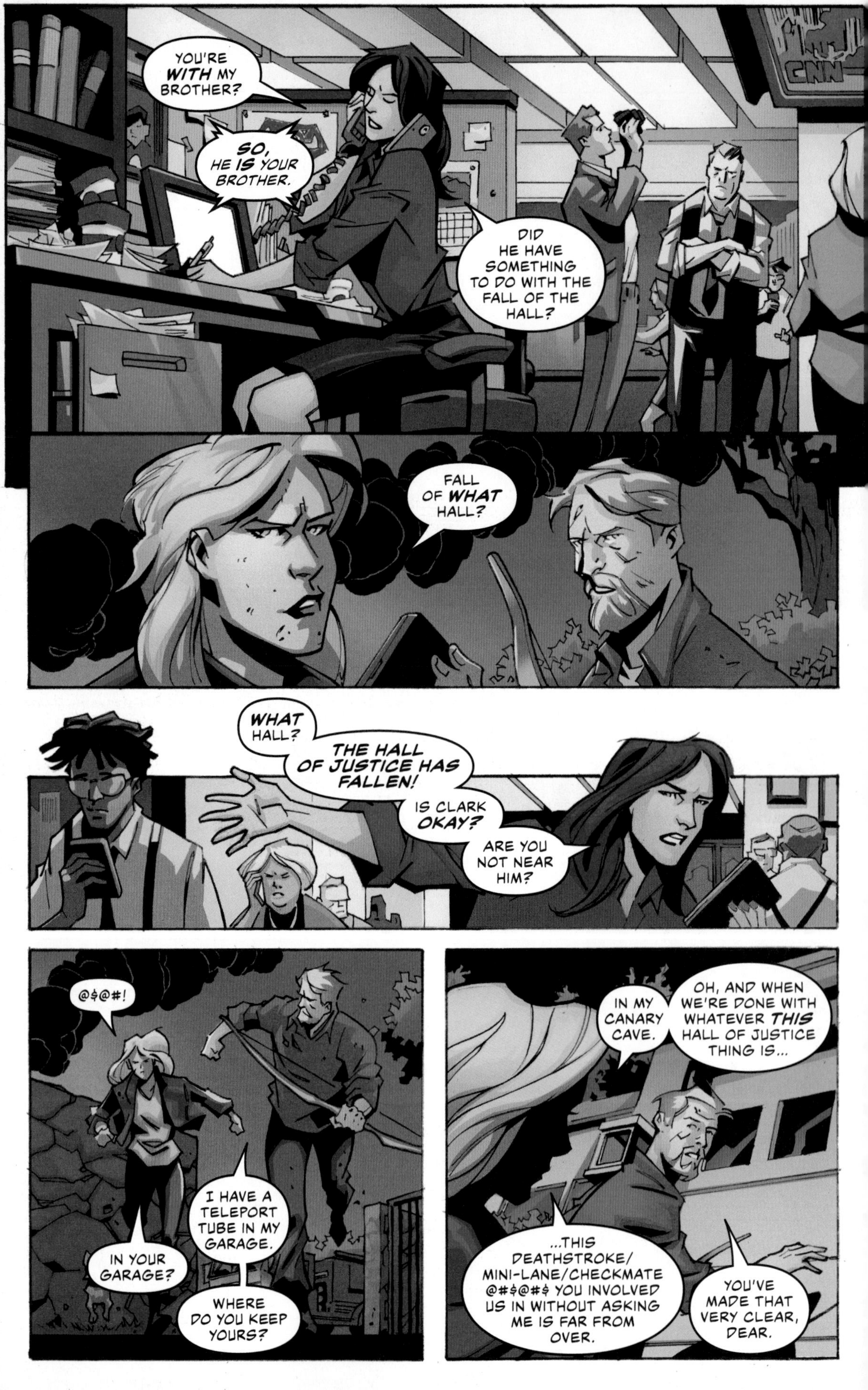
YOU'RE WITH MY BROTHER?
SO, HE IS YOUR BROTHER.
DID HE HAVE SOMETHING TO DO WITH THE FALL OF THE HALL?
CNN
FALL OF WHAT HALL?
WHAT HALL?
THE HALL OF JUSTICE HAS FALLEN!
IS CLARK OKAY?
ARE YOU NOT NEAR HIM?
@$@#!
I HAVE A TELEPORT TUBE IN MY GARAGE.
IN YOUR GARAGE?
WHERE DO YOU KEEP YOURS?
IN MY CANARY CAVE.
OH, AND WHEN WE'RE DONE WITH WHATEVER THIS HALL OF JUSTICE THING IS...
...THIS DEATHSTROKE/ MINI-LANE/CHECKMATE @#$@#$ YOU INVOLVED US IN WITHOUT ASKING ME IS FAR FROM OVER.
YOU'VE MADE THAT VERY CLEAR, DEAR.

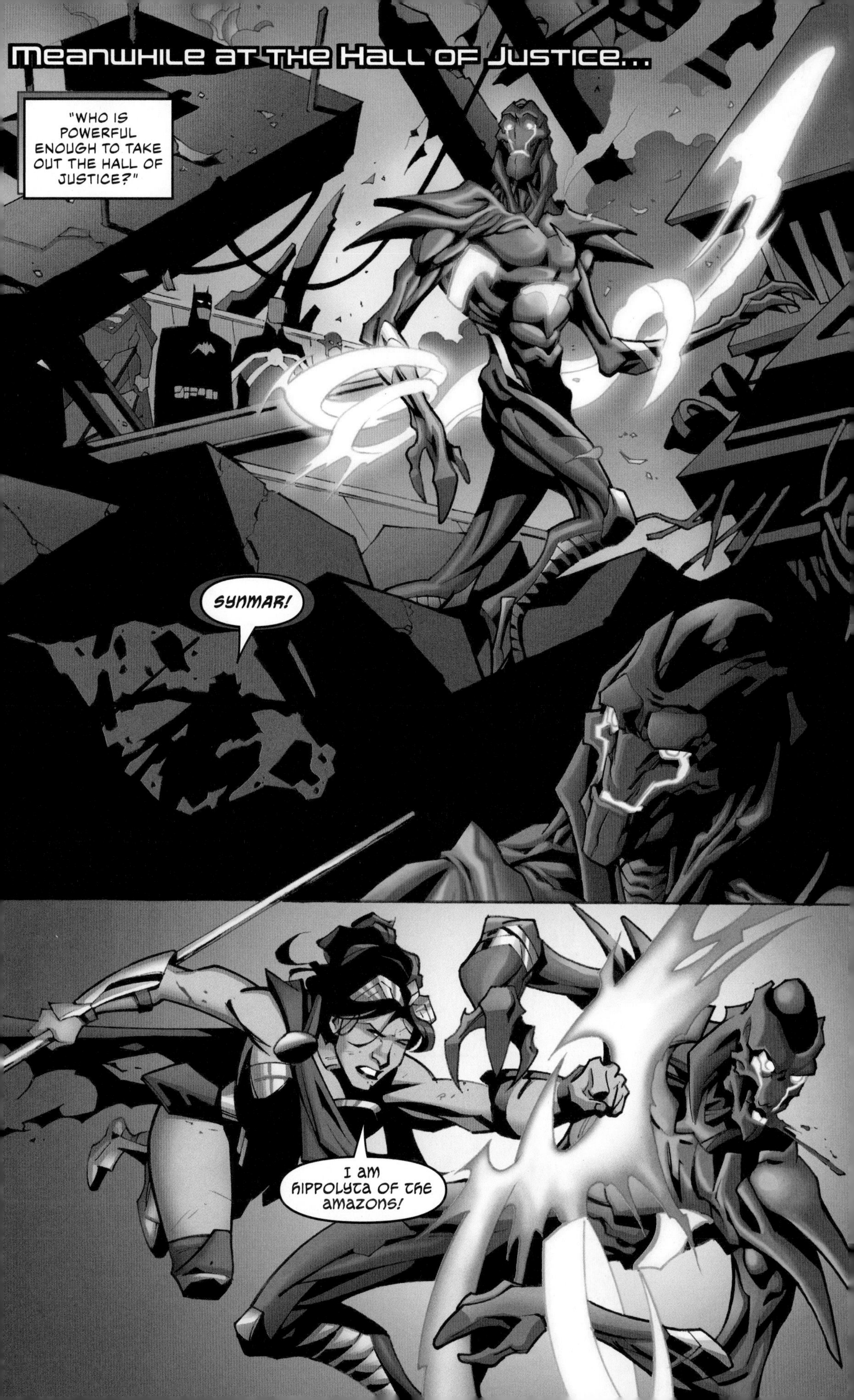
Meanwhile at the Hall of Justice...
"WHO IS POWERFUL ENOUGH TO TAKE OUT THE HALL OF JUSTICE?"
SYNMAR!
I am Hippolyta of the Amazons!

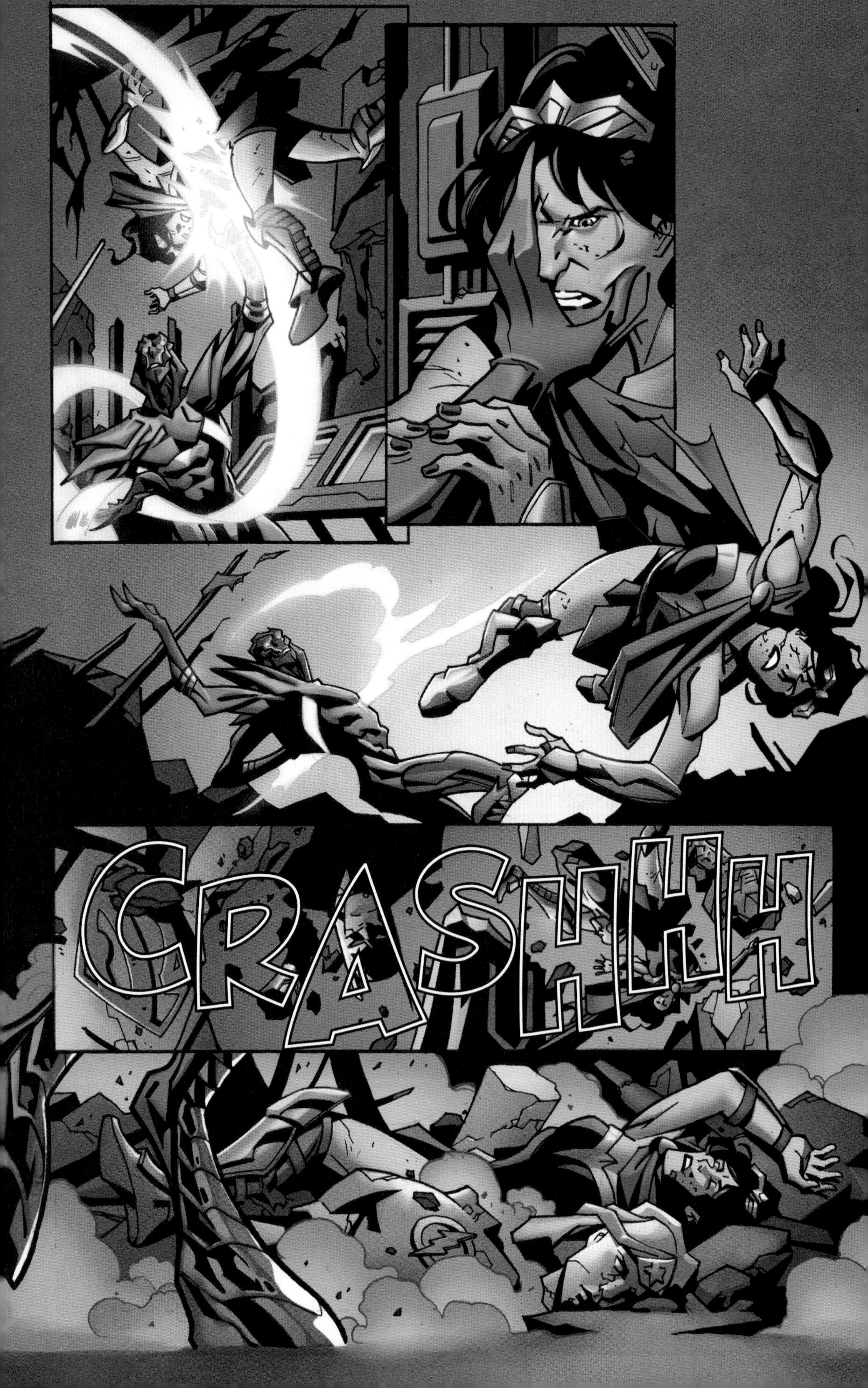
CRASHHH

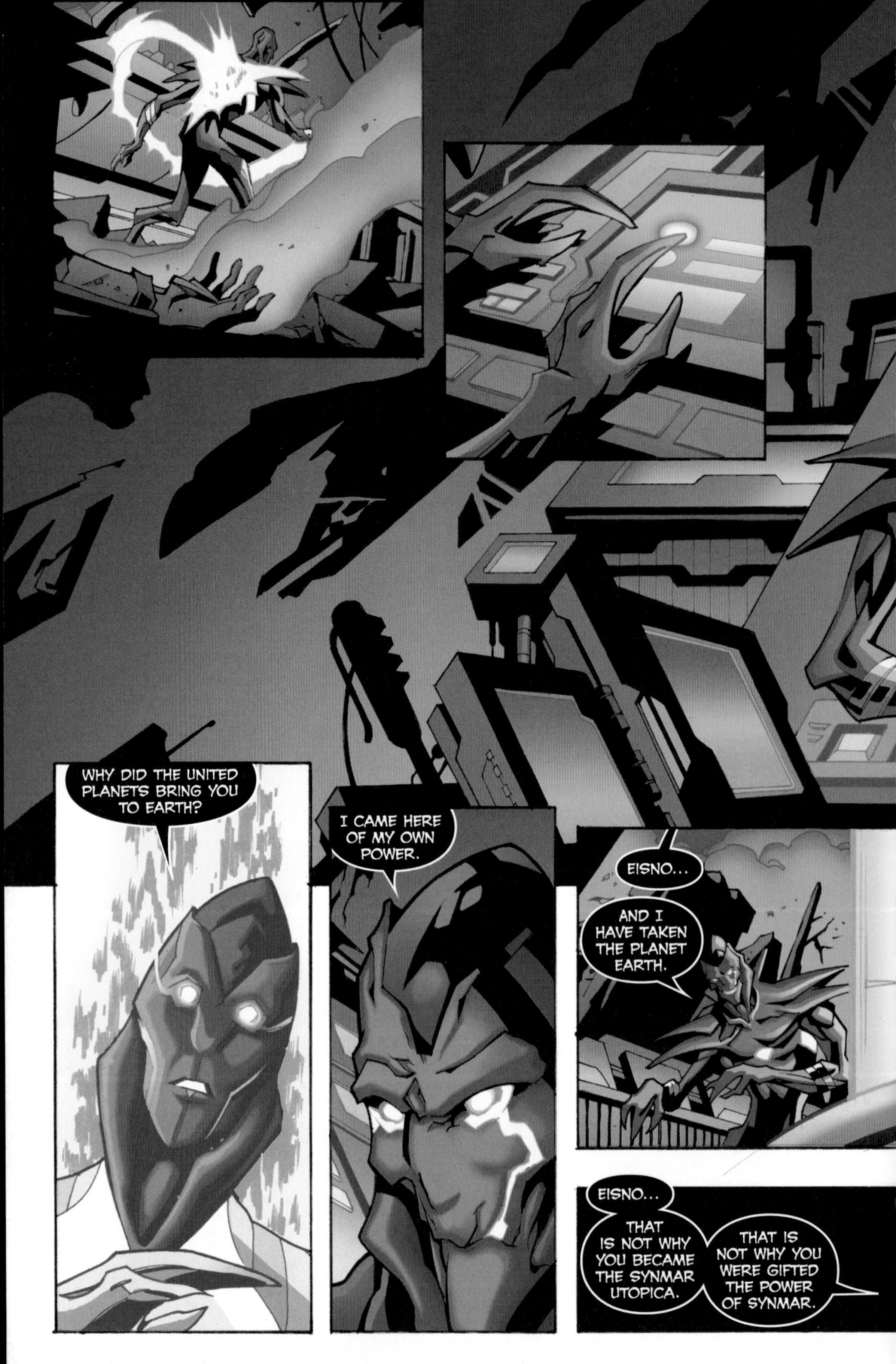
WHY DID THE UNITED PLANETS BRING YOU TO EARTH?
I CAME HERE OF MY OWN POWER.
EISNO...
AND I HAVE TAKEN THE PLANET EARTH.
EISNO...
THAT IS NOT WHY YOU BECAME THE SYNMAR UTOPICA.
THAT IS NOT WHY YOU WERE GIFTED THE POWER OF SYNMAR.

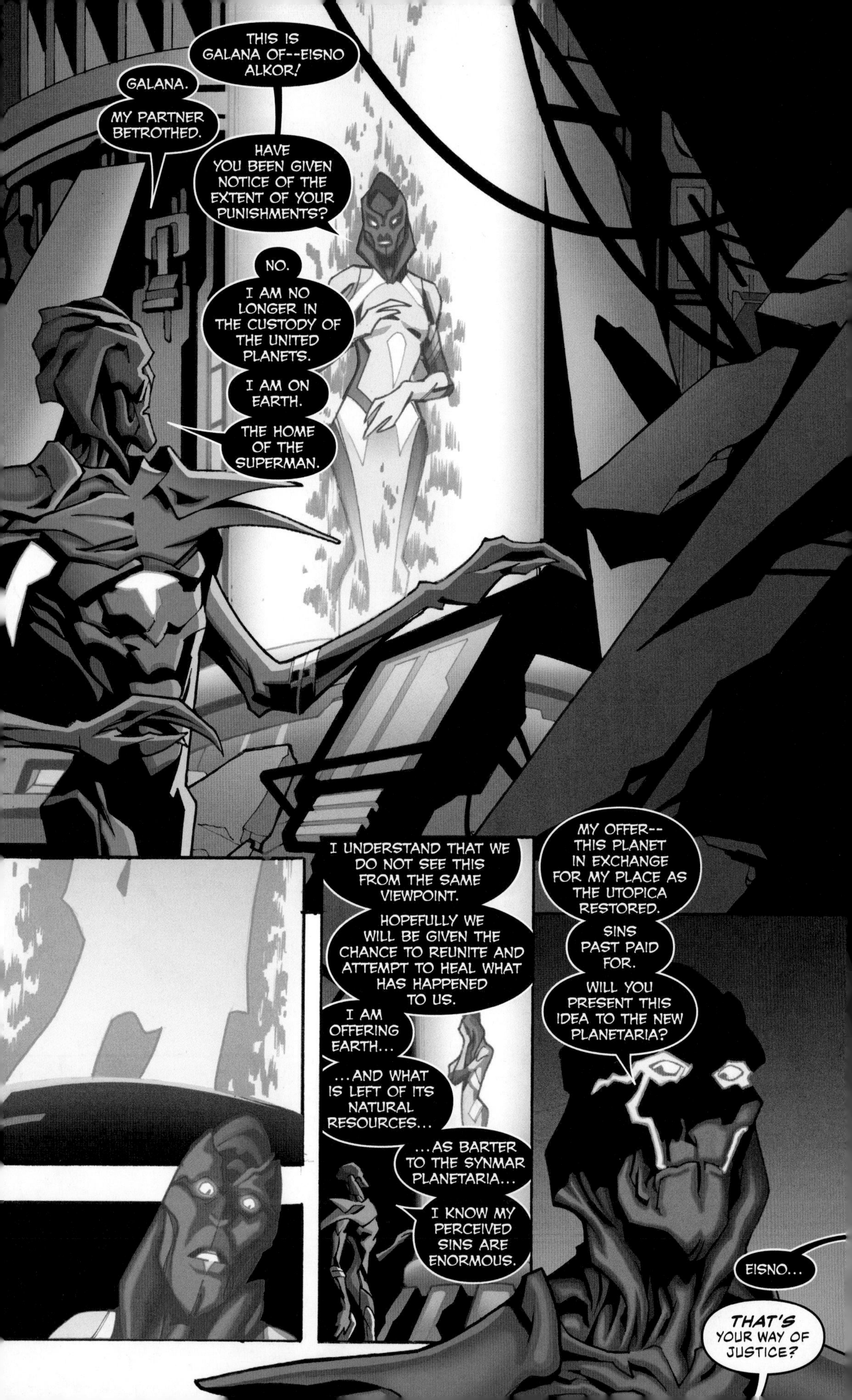
GALANA.
MY PARTNER BETROTHED.
THIS IS GALANA OF--EISNO ALKOR!
HAVE YOU BEEN GIVEN NOTICE OF THE EXTENT OF YOUR PUNISHMENTS?
NO.
I AM NO LONGER IN THE CUSTODY OF THE UNITED PLANETS.
I AM ON EARTH.
THE HOME OF THE SUPERMAN.
I UNDERSTAND THAT WE DO NOT SEE THIS FROM THE SAME VIEWPOINT.
HOPEFULLY WE WILL BE GIVEN THE CHANCE TO REUNITE AND ATTEMPT TO HEAL WHAT HAS HAPPENED TO US.
I AM OFFERING EARTH...
...AND WHAT IS LEFT OF ITS NATURAL RESOURCES...
...AS BARTER TO THE SYNMAR PLANETARIA...
I KNOW MY PERCEIVED SINS ARE ENORMOUS.
MY OFFER-- THIS PLANET IN EXCHANGE FOR MY PLACE AS THE UTOPICA RESTORED.
SINS PAST PAID FOR.
WILL YOU PRESENT THIS IDEA TO THE NEW PLANETARIA?
EISNO...
THAT'S YOUR WAY OF JUSTICE?

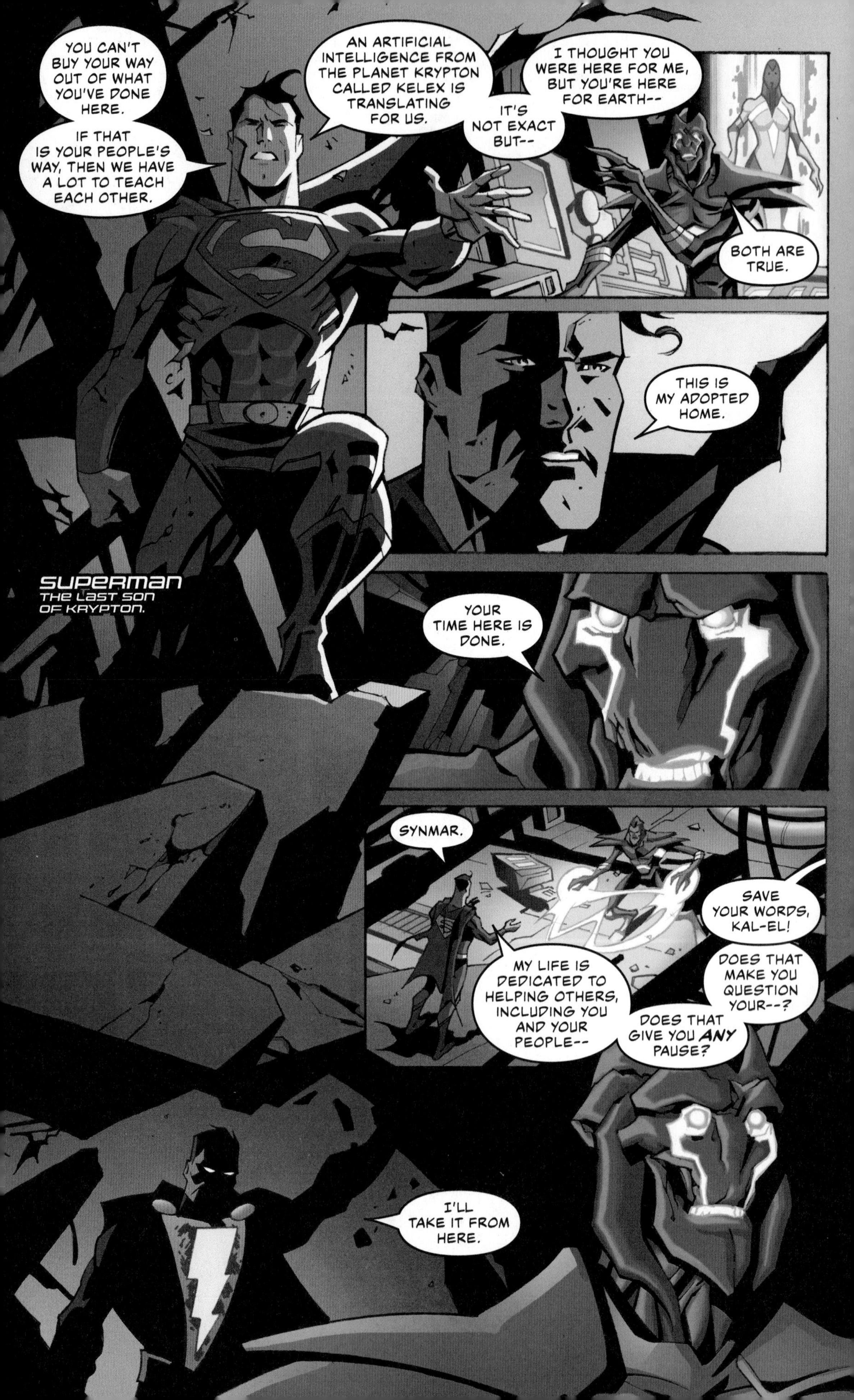
YOU CAN'T BUY YOUR WAY OUT OF WHAT YOU'VE DONE HERE.
IF THAT IS YOUR PEOPLE'S WAY, THEN WE HAVE A LOT TO TEACH EACH OTHER.
AN ARTIFICIAL INTELLIGENCE FROM THE PLANET KRYPTON CALLED KELEX IS TRANSLATING FOR US.
IT'S NOT EXACT BUT--
I THOUGHT YOU WERE HERE FOR ME, BUT YOU'RE HERE FOR EARTH--
BOTH ARE TRUE.
THIS IS MY ADOPTED HOME.
SUPERMAN
THE LAST SON OF KRYPTON.
YOUR TIME HERE IS DONE.
SYNMAR.
MY LIFE IS DEDICATED TO HELPING OTHERS, INCLUDING YOU AND YOUR PEOPLE--
SAVE YOUR WORDS, KAL-EL!
DOES THAT MAKE YOU QUESTION YOUR--?
DOES THAT GIVE YOU ANY PAUSE?
I'LL TAKE IT FROM HERE.

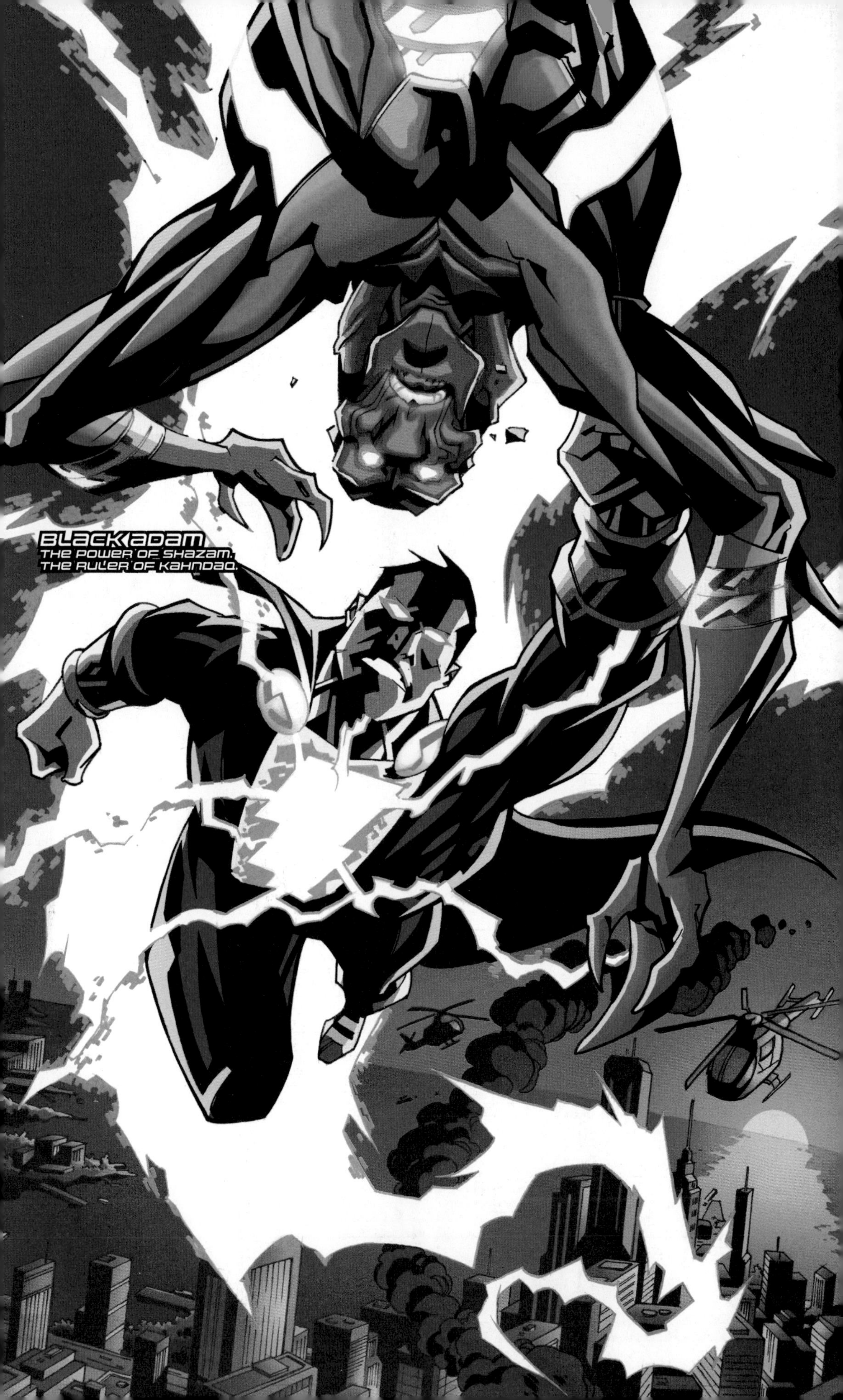
BLACK ADAM
THE POWER OF SHAZAM.
THE RULER OF KAHNDAQ.

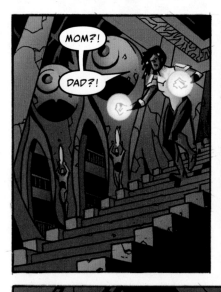

MOM?!

DAD?!

UH, MR. HELLBLAZER?

WHO I LEFT MY @#$%`& PARENTS WITH.

MOM?

SOME PEOPLE USE THE KNOCKER FOR KNOCKING.

WHERE ARE MY PARENTS?!

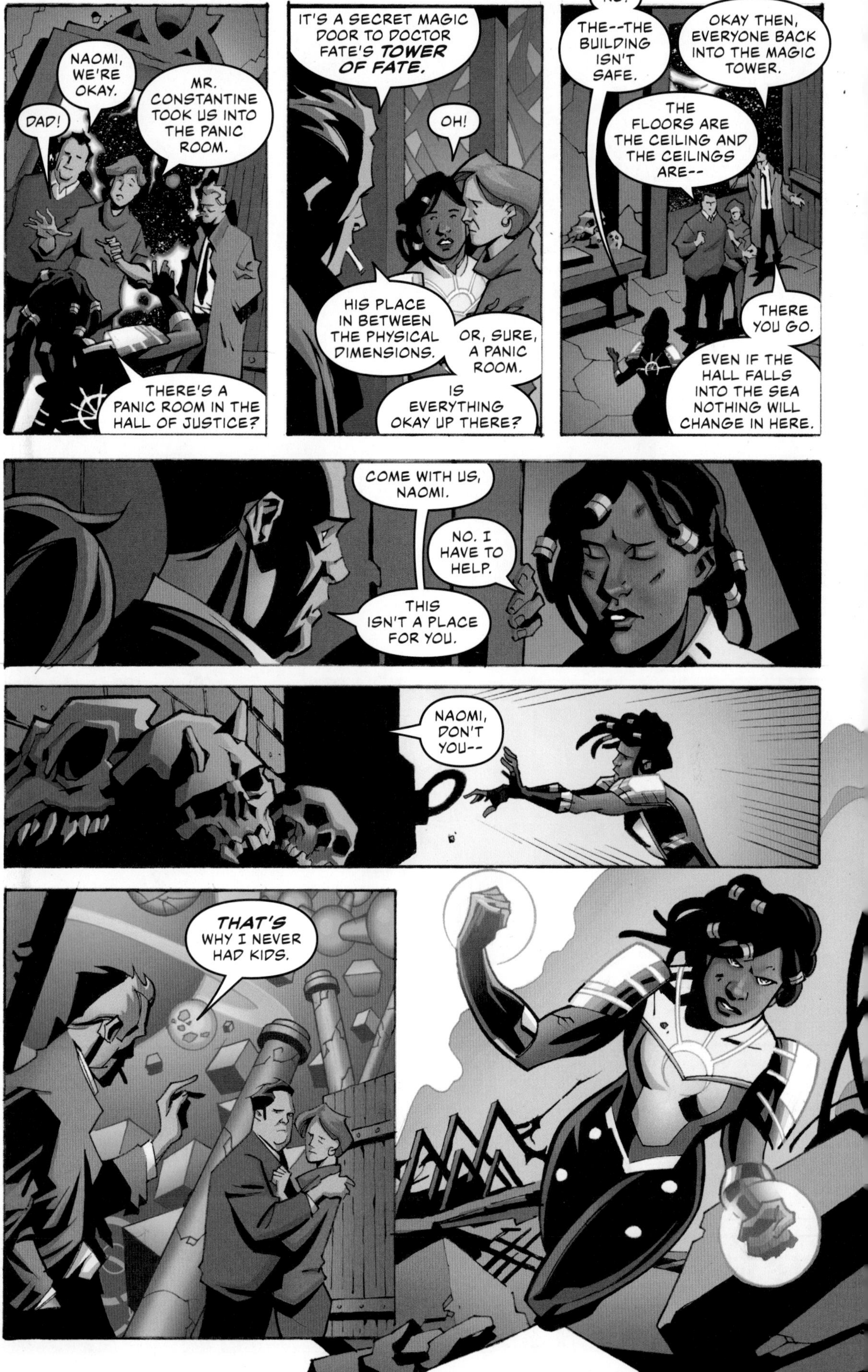

NAOMI, WE'RE OKAY.
DAD!
MR. CONSTANTINE TOOK US INTO THE PANIC ROOM.
THERE'S A PANIC ROOM IN THE HALL OF JUSTICE?
IT'S A SECRET MAGIC DOOR TO DOCTOR FATE'S TOWER OF FATE.
OH!
HIS PLACE IN BETWEEN THE PHYSICAL DIMENSIONS.
OR, SURE, A PANIC ROOM.
IS EVERYTHING OKAY UP THERE?
NO!
THE--THE BUILDING ISN'T SAFE.
OKAY THEN, EVERYONE BACK INTO THE MAGIC TOWER.
THE FLOORS ARE THE CEILING AND THE CEILINGS ARE--
THERE YOU GO.
EVEN IF THE HALL FALLS INTO THE SEA NOTHING WILL CHANGE IN HERE.
COME WITH US, NAOMI.
NO. I HAVE TO HELP.
THIS ISN'T A PLACE FOR YOU.
NAOMI, DON'T YOU--
THAT'S WHY I NEVER HAD KIDS.

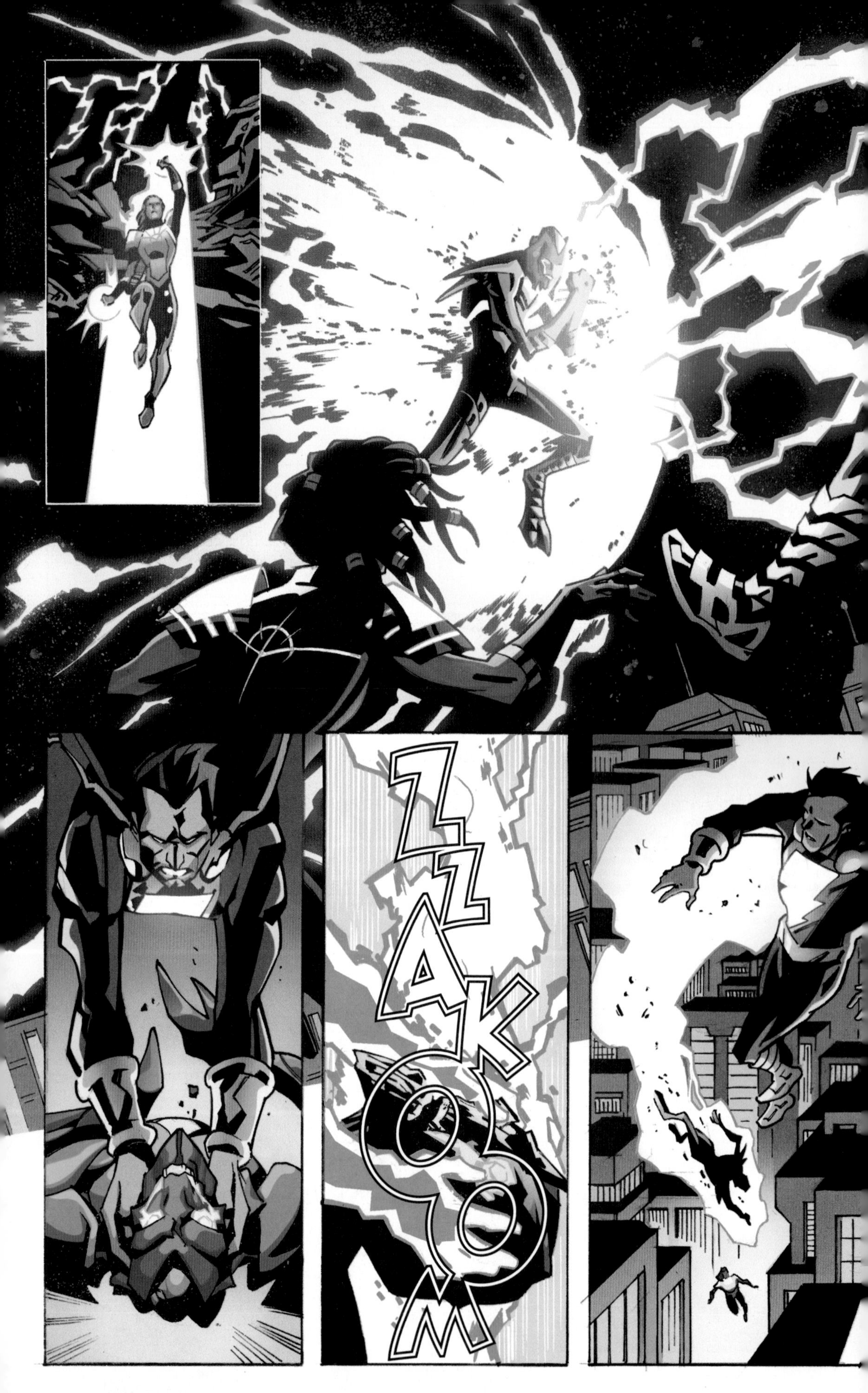
ZZZAKOOOM

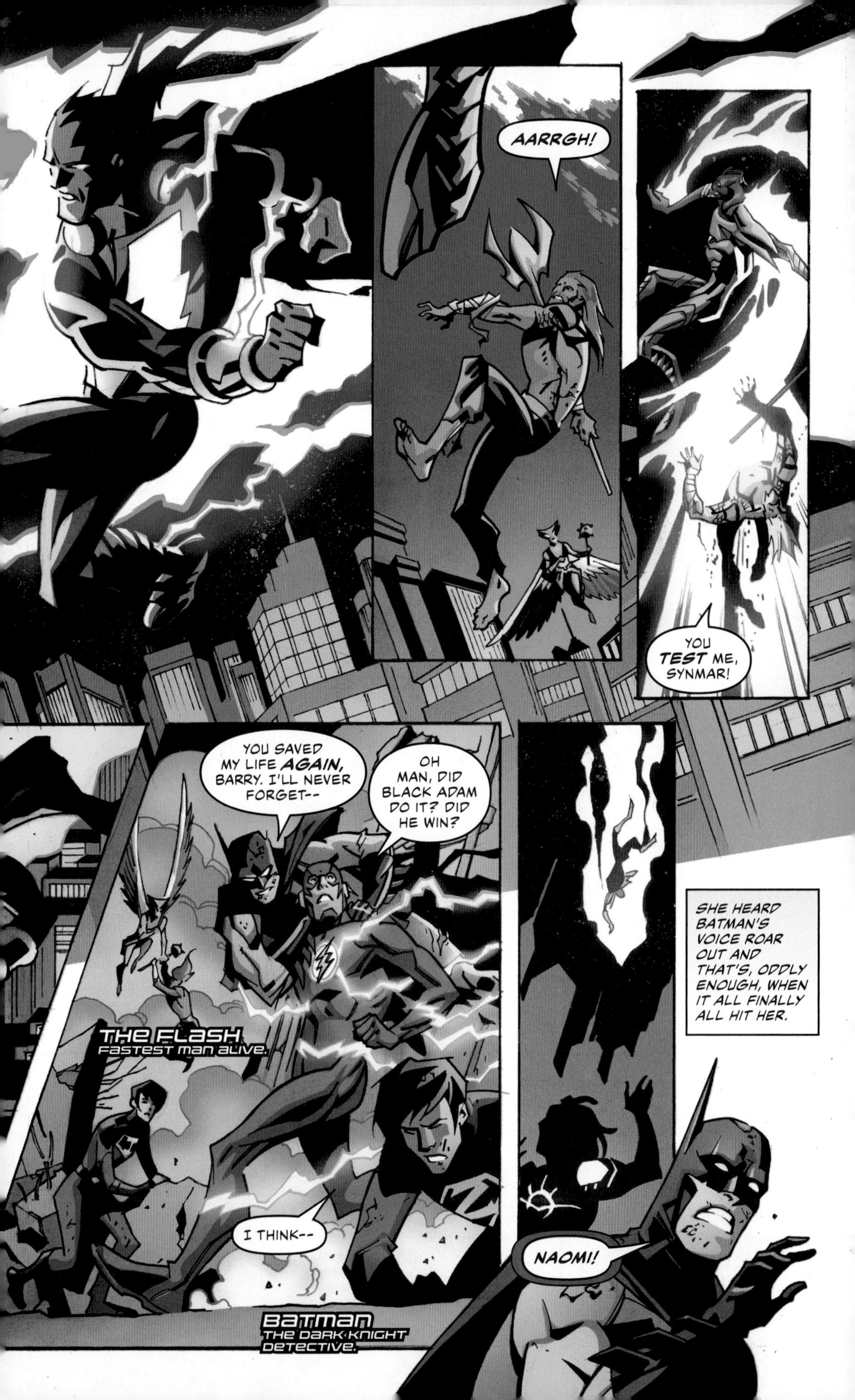

AARRGH!
YOU TEST ME, SYNMAR!
YOU SAVED MY LIFE AGAIN, BARRY. I'LL NEVER FORGET--
OH MAN, DID BLACK ADAM DO IT? DID HE WIN?
THE FLASH
FASTEST MAN ALIVE.
I THINK--
BATMAN
THE DARK KNIGHT DETECTIVE.
SHE HEARD BATMAN'S VOICE ROAR OUT AND THAT'S, ODDLY ENOUGH, WHEN IT ALL FINALLY ALL HIT HER.
NAOMI!

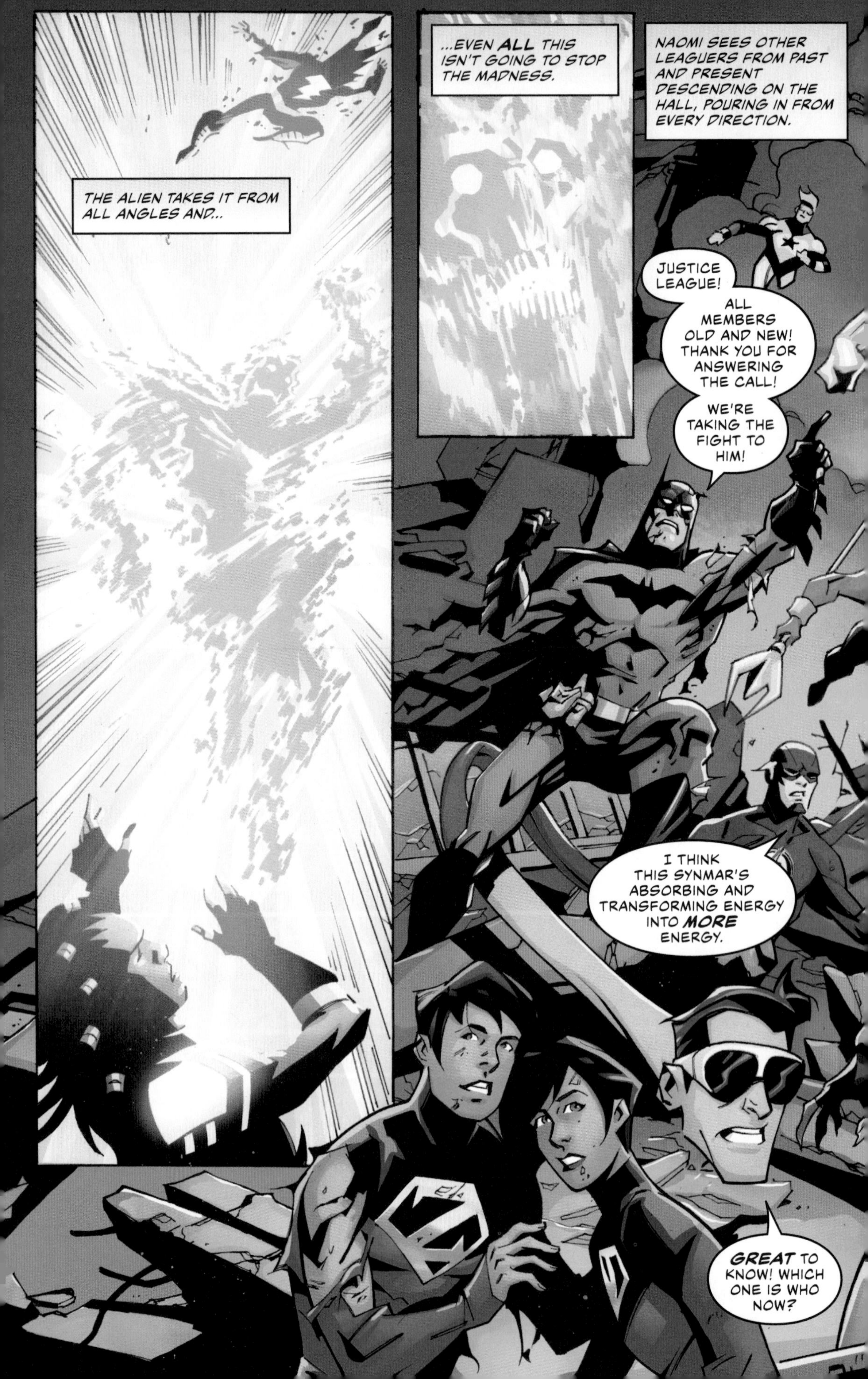

THE ALIEN TAKES IT FROM ALL ANGLES AND...
...EVEN ALL THIS ISN'T GOING TO STOP THE MADNESS.
NAOMI SEES OTHER LEAGUERS FROM PAST AND PRESENT DESCENDING ON THE HALL, POURING IN FROM EVERY DIRECTION.
JUSTICE LEAGUE!
ALL MEMBERS OLD AND NEW! THANK YOU FOR ANSWERING THE CALL!
WE'RE TAKING THE FIGHT TO HIM!
I THINK THIS SYNMAR'S ABSORBING AND TRANSFORMING ENERGY INTO MORE ENERGY.
GREAT TO KNOW! WHICH ONE IS WHO NOW?

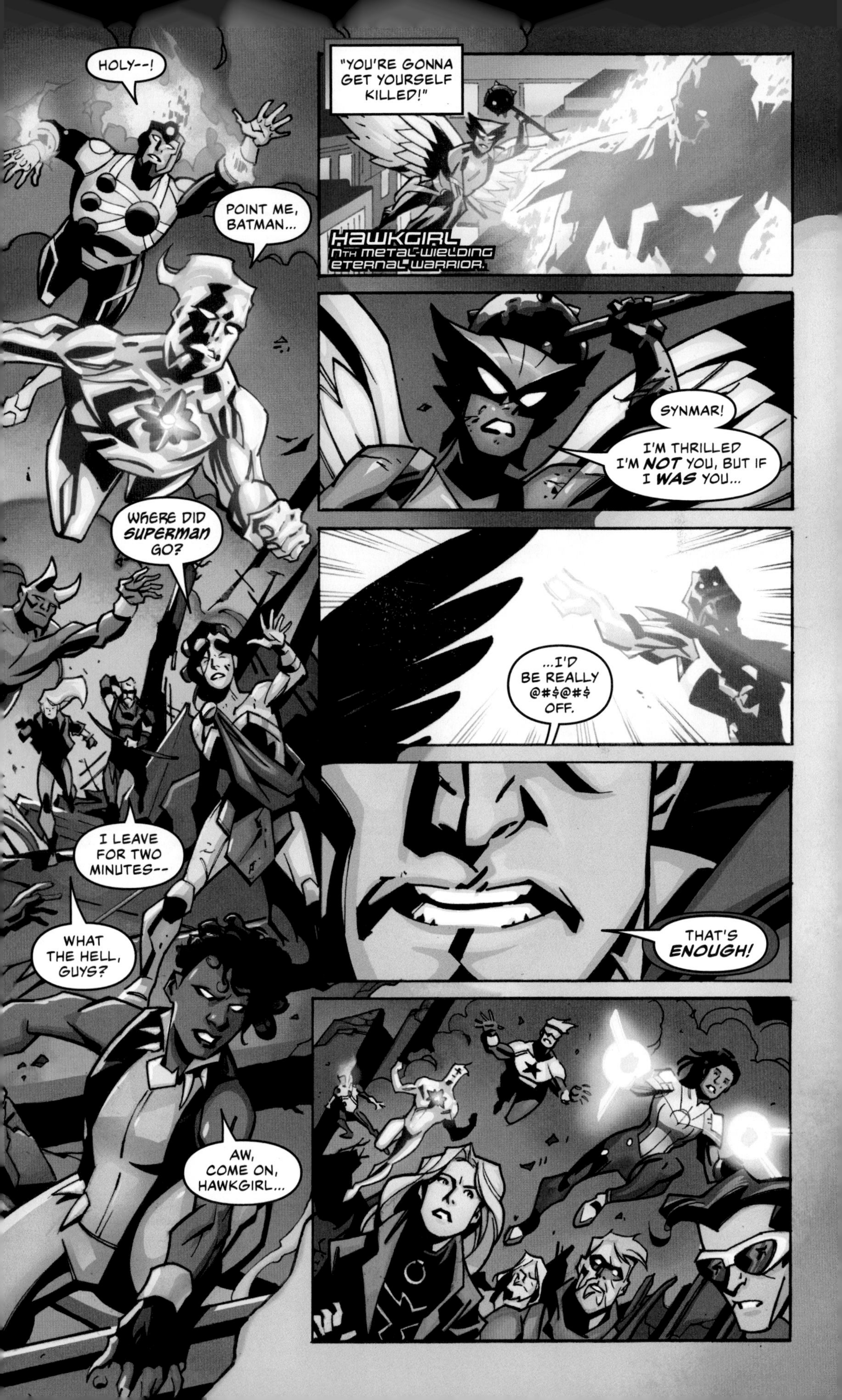
HOLY--!
POINT ME, BATMAN...
WHERE DID SUPERMAN GO?
I LEAVE FOR TWO MINUTES--
WHAT THE HELL, GUYS?
AW, COME ON, HAWKGIRL...
"YOU'RE GONNA GET YOURSELF KILLED!"
HAWKGIRL
NTH METAL-WIELDING ETERNAL WARRIOR.
SYNMAR!
I'M THRILLED I'M NOT YOU, BUT IF I WAS YOU...
...I'D BE REALLY @#$@#$ OFF.
THAT'S ENOUGH!

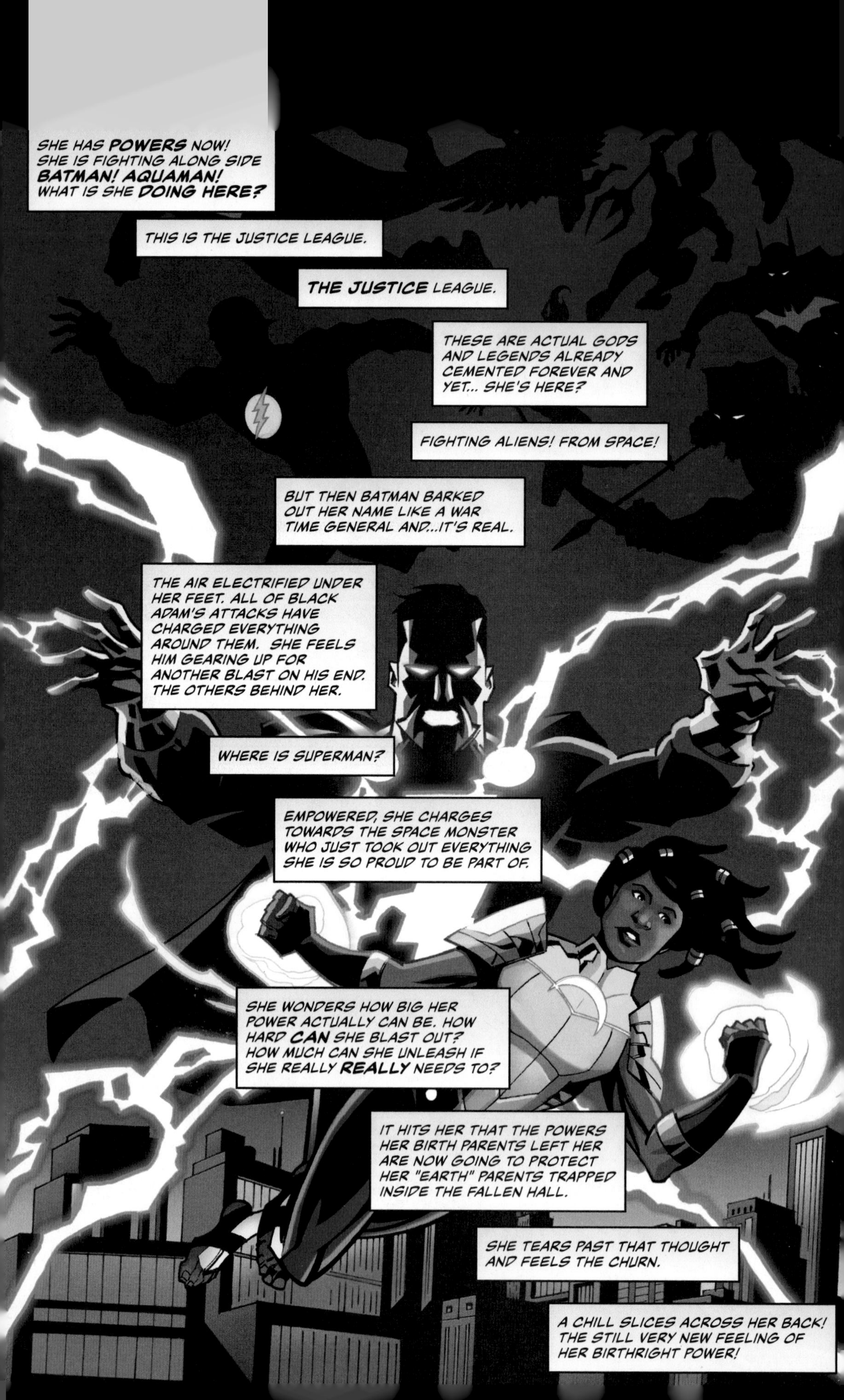
SHE HAS POWERS NOW! SHE IS FIGHTING ALONG SIDE BATMAN! AQUAMAN! WHAT IS SHE DOING HERE?
THIS IS THE JUSTICE LEAGUE.
THE JUSTICE LEAGUE.
THESE ARE ACTUAL GODS AND LEGENDS ALREADY CEMENTED FOREVER AND YET... SHE'S HERE?
FIGHTING ALIENS! FROM SPACE!
BUT THEN BATMAN BARKED OUT HER NAME LIKE A WAR TIME GENERAL AND...IT'S REAL.
THE AIR ELECTRIFIED UNDER HER FEET. ALL OF BLACK ADAM'S ATTACKS HAVE CHARGED EVERYTHING AROUND THEM. SHE FEELS HIM GEARING UP FOR ANOTHER BLAST ON HIS END. THE OTHERS BEHIND HER.
WHERE IS SUPERMAN?
EMPOWERED, SHE CHARGES TOWARDS THE SPACE MONSTER WHO JUST TOOK OUT EVERYTHING SHE IS SO PROUD TO BE PART OF.
SHE WONDERS HOW BIG HER POWER ACTUALLY CAN BE. HOW HARD CAN SHE BLAST OUT? HOW MUCH CAN SHE UNLEASH IF SHE REALLY REALLY NEEDS TO?
IT HITS HER THAT THE POWERS HER BIRTH PARENTS LEFT HER ARE NOW GOING TO PROTECT HER "EARTH" PARENTS TRAPPED INSIDE THE FALLEN HALL.
SHE TEARS PAST THAT THOUGHT AND FEELS THE CHURN.
A CHILL SLICES ACROSS HER BACK! THE STILL VERY NEW FEELING OF HER BIRTHRIGHT POWER!

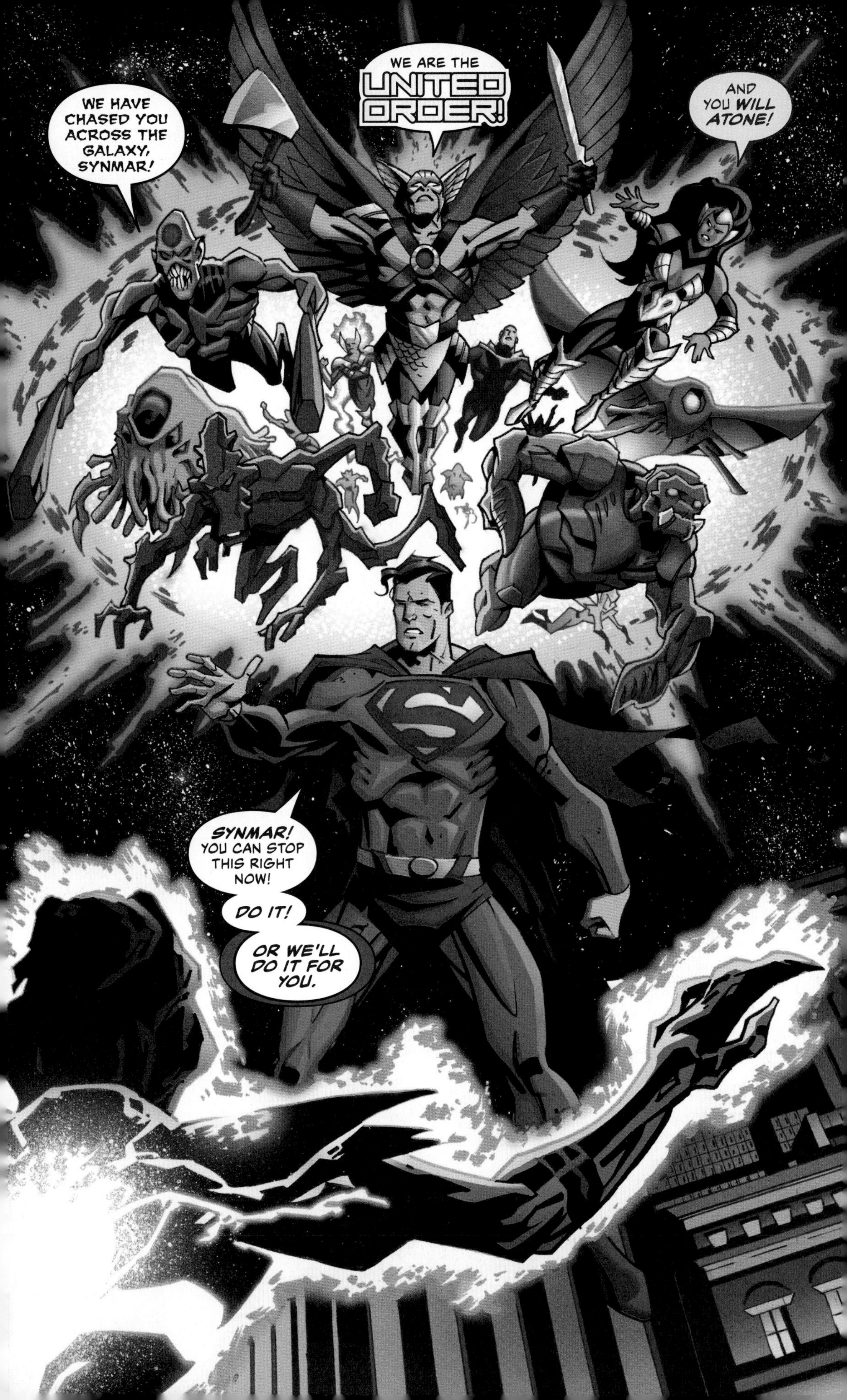
WE ARE THE UNITED ORDER!
WE HAVE CHASED YOU ACROSS THE GALAXY, SYNMAR!
AND YOU WILL ATONE!
SYNMAR! YOU CAN STOP THIS RIGHT NOW!
DO IT!
OR WE'LL DO IT FOR YOU.

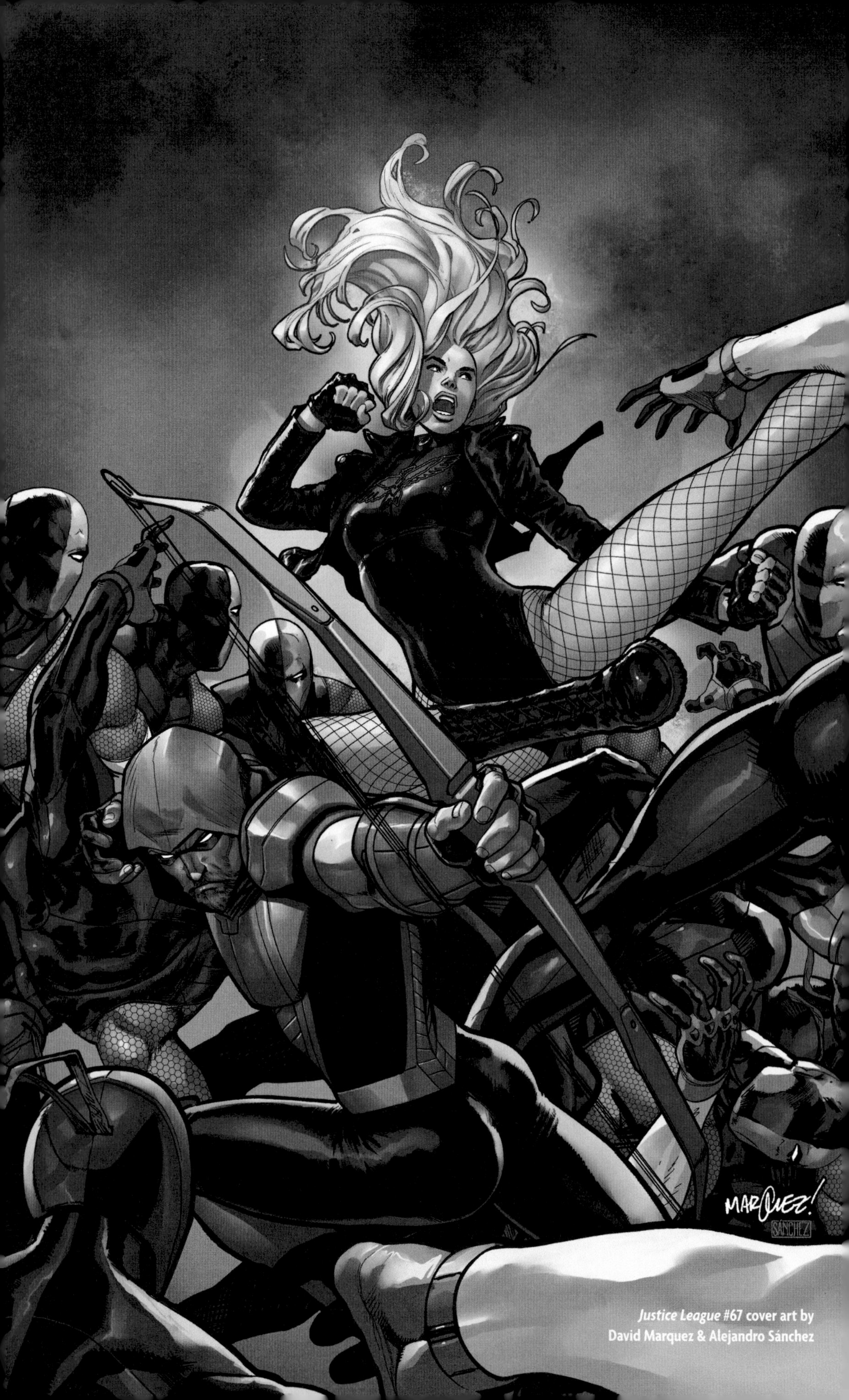
MARQUEZ!
SÁNCHEZ

Justice League #67 cover art by
David Marquez & Alejandro Sánchez

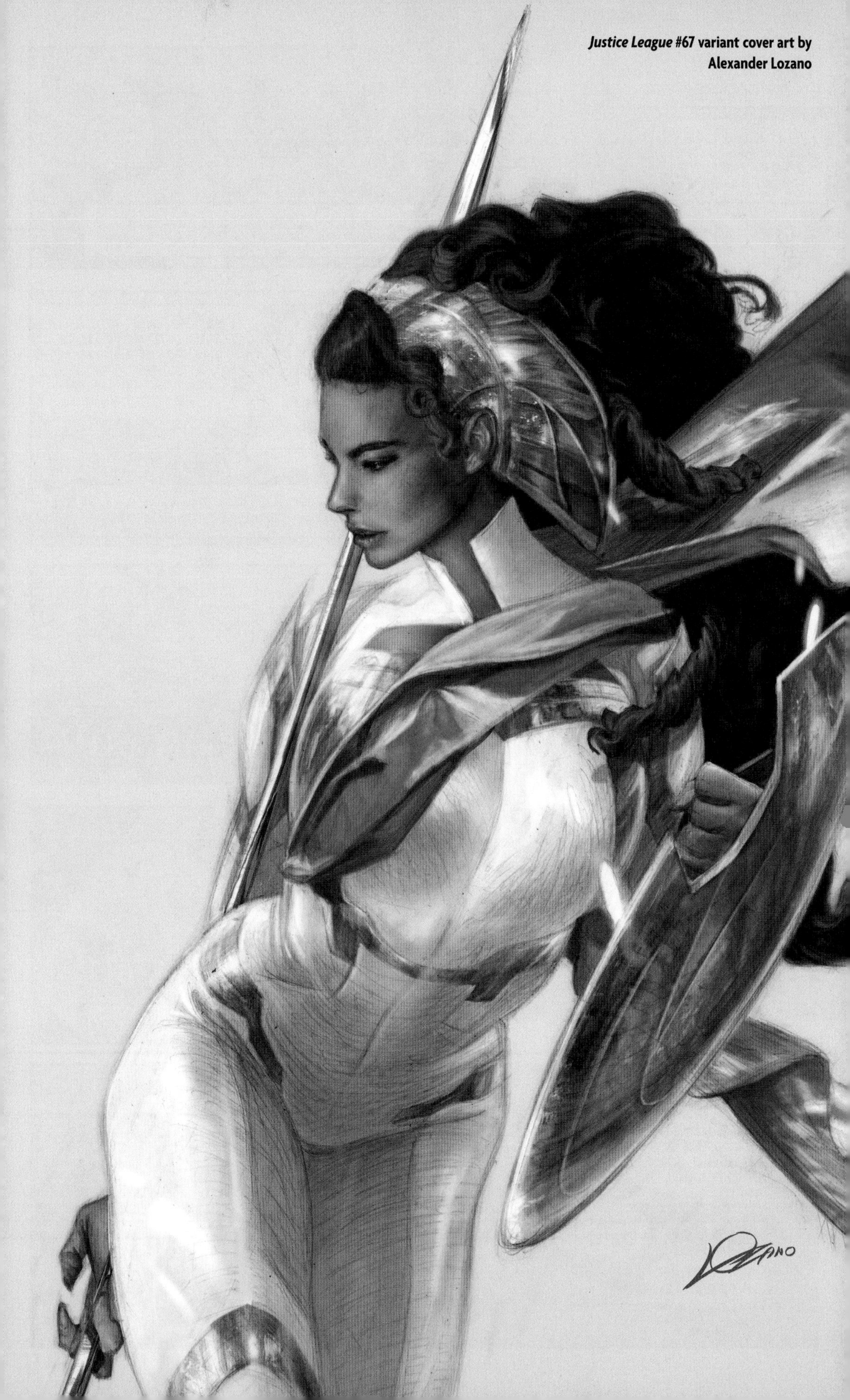

Justice League #67 variant cover art by Alexander Lozano

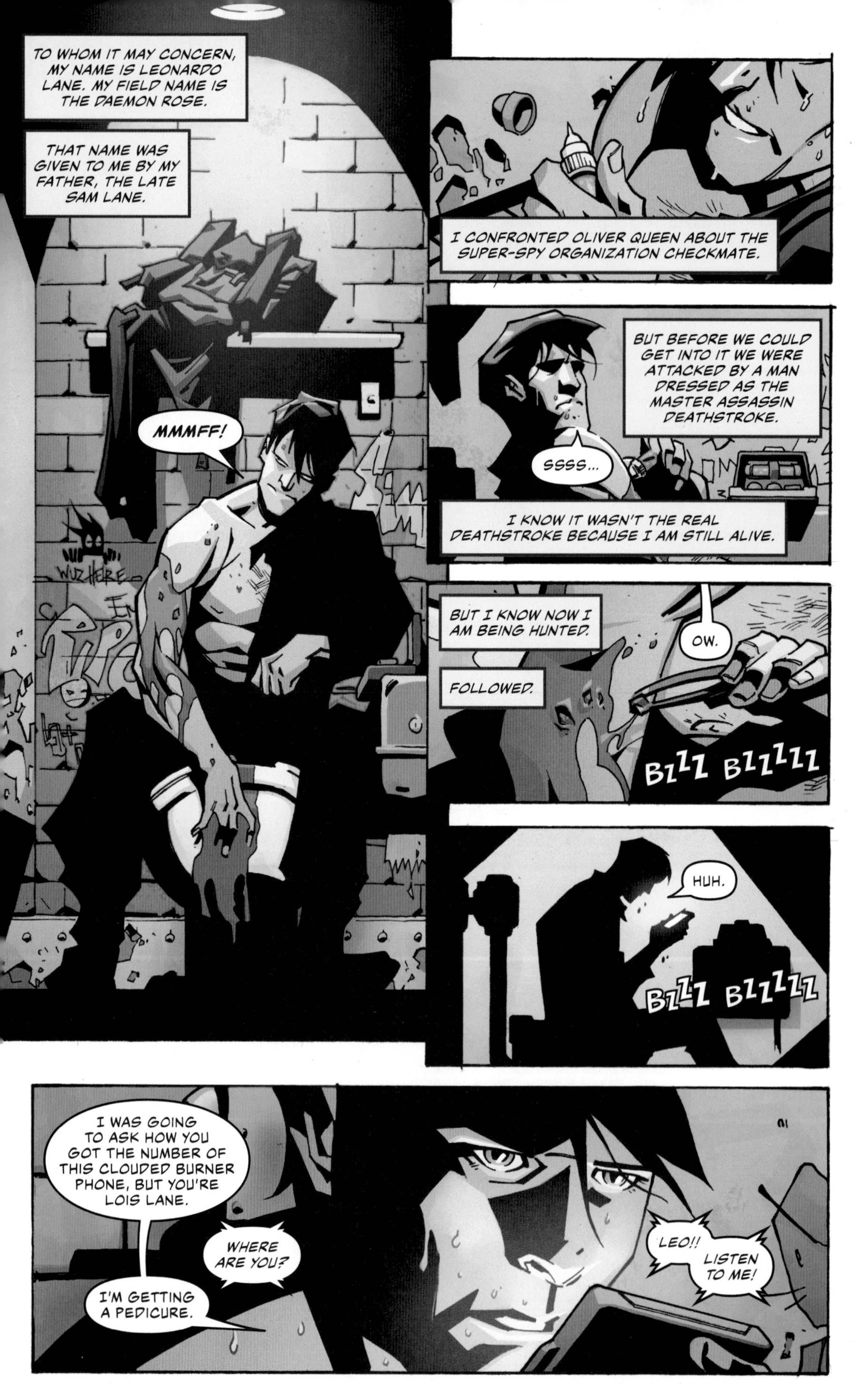
TO WHOM IT MAY CONCERN, MY NAME IS LEONARDO LANE. MY FIELD NAME IS THE DAEMON ROSE.
THAT NAME WAS GIVEN TO ME BY MY FATHER, THE LATE SAM LANE.
MMMFF!
I CONFRONTED OLIVER QUEEN ABOUT THE SUPER-SPY ORGANIZATION CHECKMATE.
BUT BEFORE WE COULD GET INTO IT WE WERE ATTACKED BY A MAN DRESSED AS THE MASTER ASSASSIN DEATHSTROKE.
SSSS...
I KNOW IT WASN'T THE REAL DEATHSTROKE BECAUSE I AM STILL ALIVE.
BUT I KNOW NOW I AM BEING HUNTED.
OW.
FOLLOWED.
BZZZ BZZZZZ
HUH.
BZZZ BZZZZZ
I WAS GOING TO ASK HOW YOU GOT THE NUMBER OF THIS CLOUDED BURNER PHONE, BUT YOU'RE LOIS LANE.
WHERE ARE YOU?
I'M GETTING A PEDICURE.
LEO!!
LISTEN TO ME!

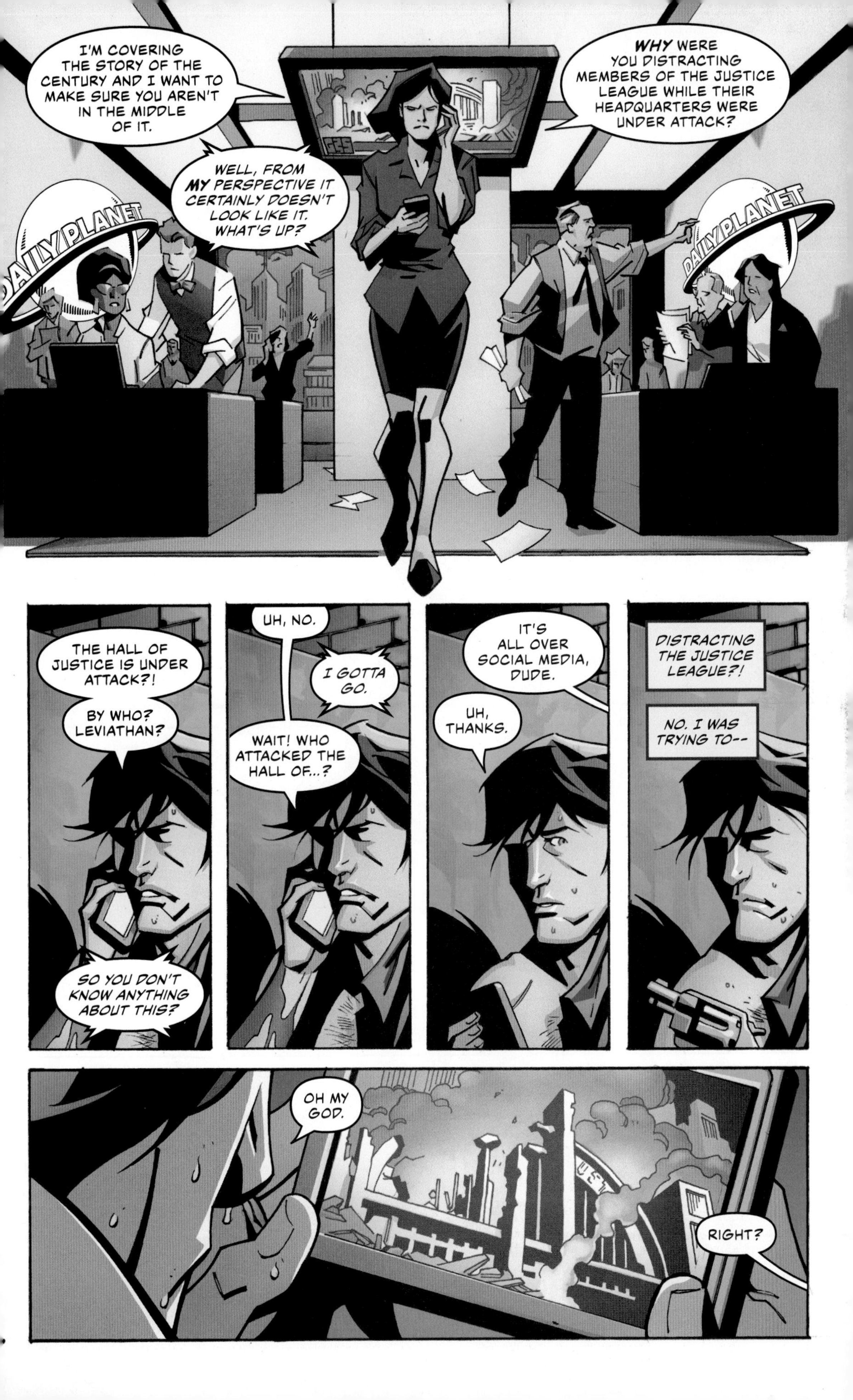
I'M COVERING THE STORY OF THE CENTURY AND I WANT TO MAKE SURE YOU AREN'T IN THE MIDDLE OF IT.
WELL, FROM MY PERSPECTIVE IT CERTAINLY DOESN'T LOOK LIKE IT. WHAT'S UP?
WHY WERE YOU DISTRACTING MEMBERS OF THE JUSTICE LEAGUE WHILE THEIR HEADQUARTERS WERE UNDER ATTACK?
DAILY PLANET
DAILY PLANET
THE HALL OF JUSTICE IS UNDER ATTACK?!
BY WHO? LEVIATHAN?
SO YOU DON'T KNOW ANYTHING ABOUT THIS?
UH, NO.
I GOTTA GO.
WAIT! WHO ATTACKED THE HALL OF...?
IT'S ALL OVER SOCIAL MEDIA, DUDE.
UH, THANKS.
DISTRACTING THE JUSTICE LEAGUE?!
NO. I WAS TRYING TO--
OH MY GOD.
RIGHT?

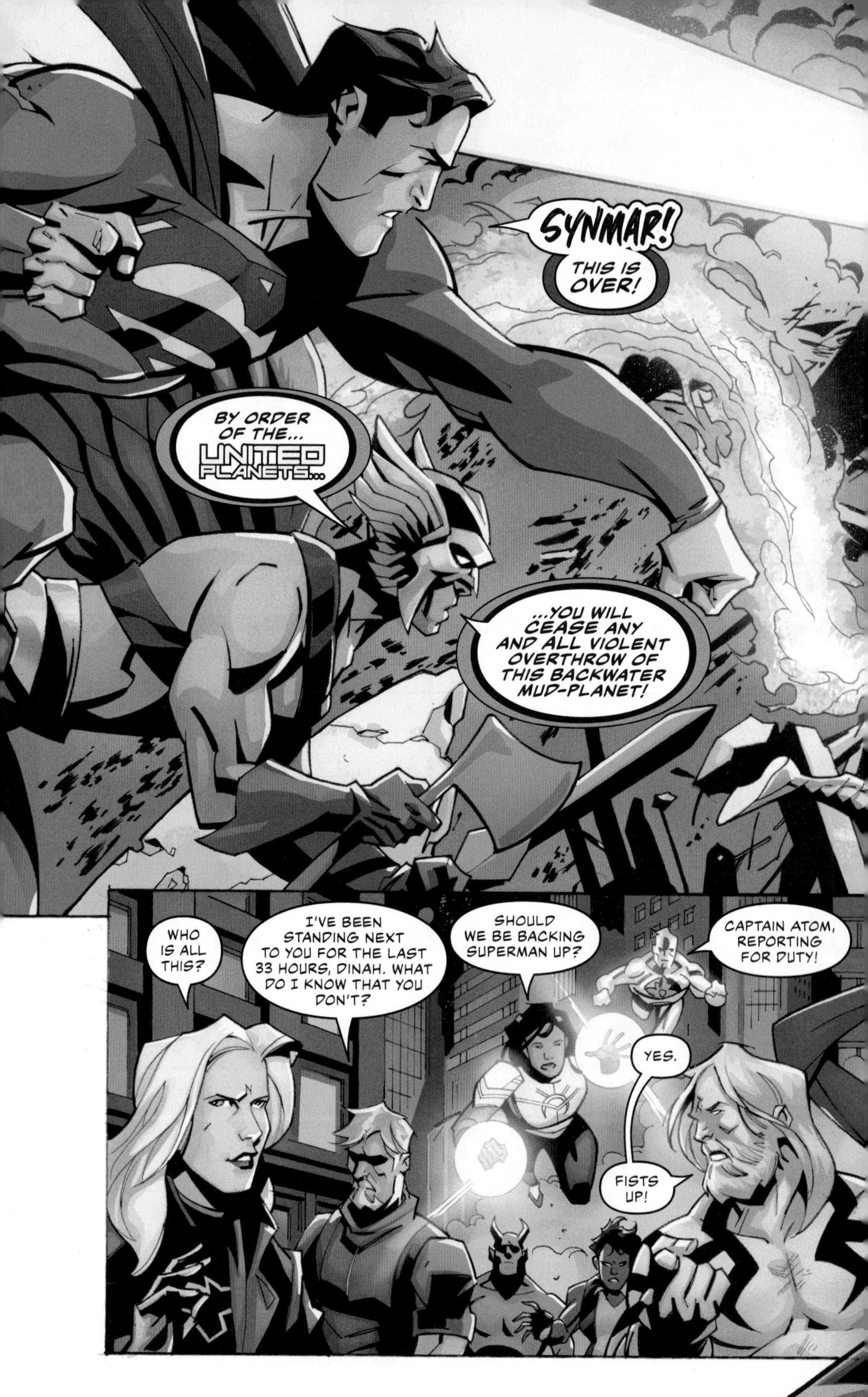
SYNMAR!
THIS IS OVER!
BY ORDER OF THE... UNITED PLANETS...
...YOU WILL CEASE ANY AND ALL VIOLENT OVERTHROW OF THIS BACKWATER MUD-PLANET!
WHO IS ALL THIS?
I'VE BEEN STANDING NEXT TO YOU FOR THE LAST 33 HOURS, DINAH. WHAT DO I KNOW THAT YOU DON'T?
SHOULD WE BE BACKING SUPERMAN UP?
CAPTAIN ATOM, REPORTING FOR DUTY!
YES.
FISTS UP!

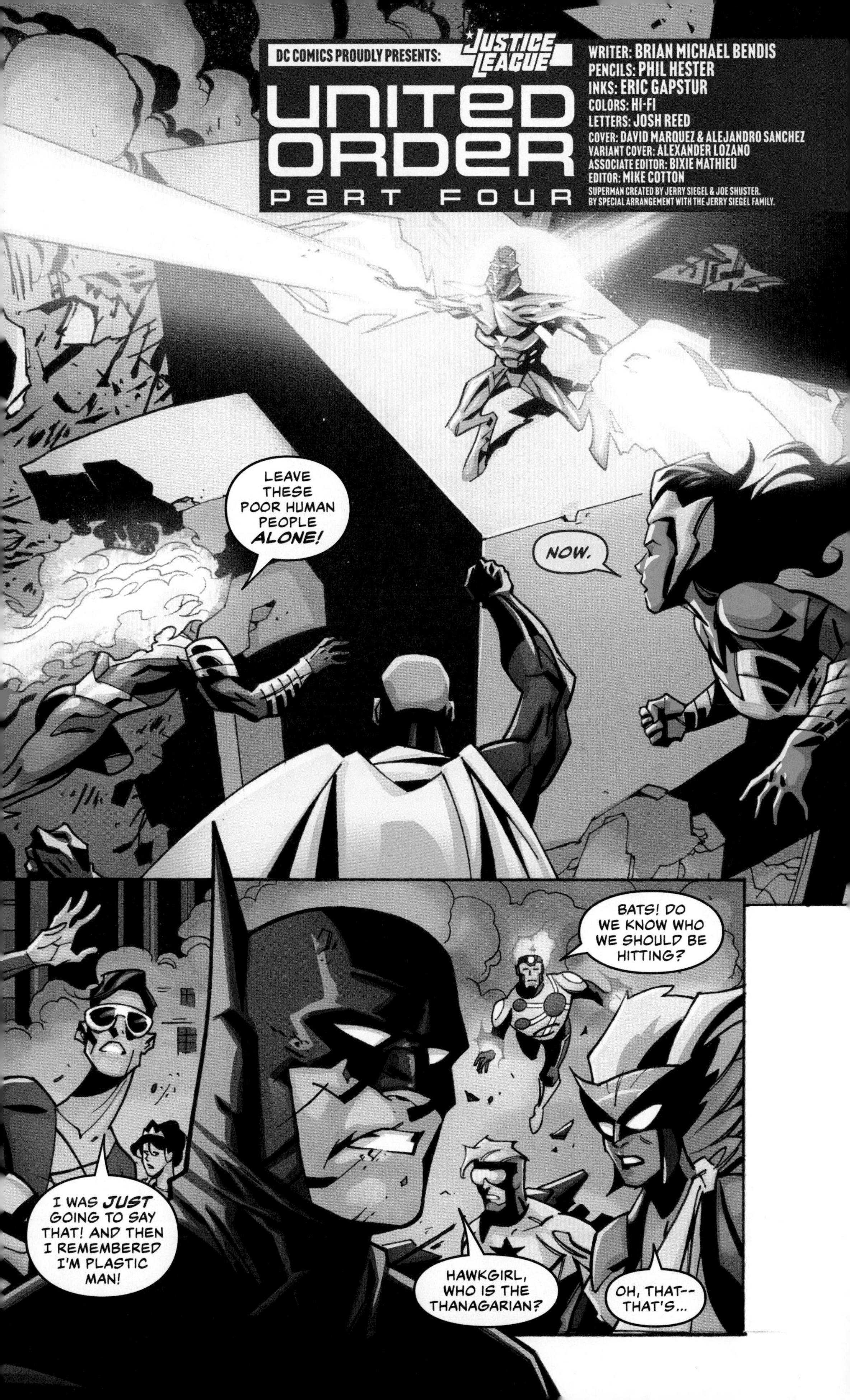
DC COMICS PROUDLY PRESENTS: JUSTICE LEAGUE
UNITED ORDER
PART FOUR
WRITER: BRIAN MICHAEL BENDIS
PENCILS: PHIL HESTER
INKS: ERIC GAPSTUR
COLORS: HI-FI
LETTERS: JOSH REED
COVER: DAVID MARQUEZ & ALEJANDRO SANCHEZ
VARIANT COVER: ALEXANDER LOZANO
ASSOCIATE EDITOR: BIXIE MATHIEU
EDITOR: MIKE COTTON
SUPERMAN CREATED BY JERRY SIEGEL & JOE SHUSTER.
BY SPECIAL ARRANGEMENT WITH THE JERRY SIEGEL FAMILY.
LEAVE THESE POOR HUMAN PEOPLE ALONE!
NOW.
BATS! DO WE KNOW WHO WE SHOULD BE HITTING?
I WAS JUST GOING TO SAY THAT! AND THEN I REMEMBERED I'M PLASTIC MAN!
HAWKGIRL, WHO IS THE THANAGARIAN?
OH, THAT-- THAT'S...

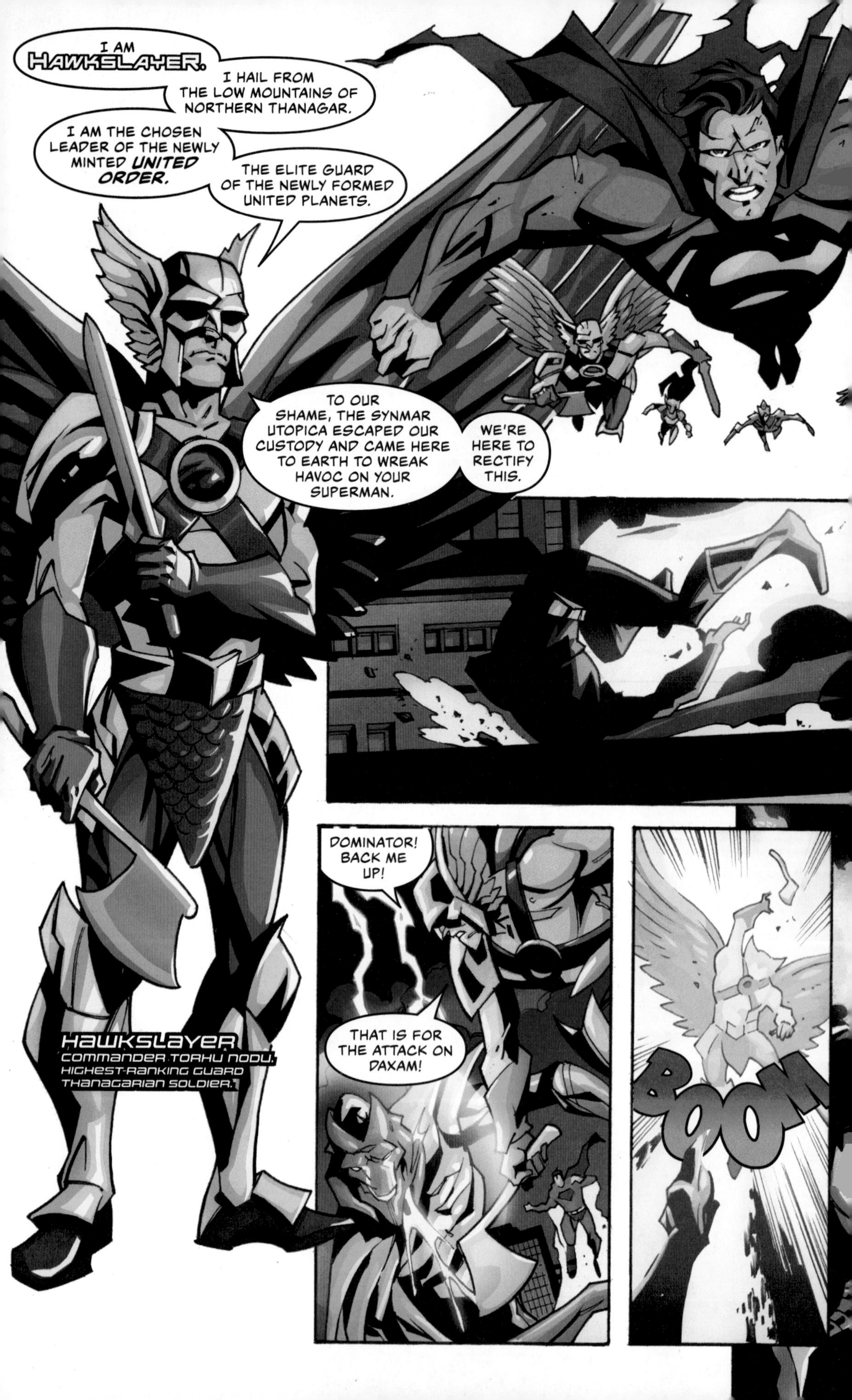
I AM HAWKSLAYER.
I HAIL FROM THE LOW MOUNTAINS OF NORTHERN THANAGAR.
I AM THE CHOSEN LEADER OF THE NEWLY MINTED UNITED ORDER.
THE ELITE GUARD OF THE NEWLY FORMED UNITED PLANETS.
TO OUR SHAME, THE SYNMAR UTOPICA ESCAPED OUR CUSTODY AND CAME HERE TO EARTH TO WREAK HAVOC ON YOUR SUPERMAN.
WE'RE HERE TO RECTIFY THIS.
HAWKSLAYER
COMMANDER TORHU NODU.
HIGHEST-RANKING GUARD
THANAGARIAN SOLDIER.
DOMINATOR! BACK ME UP!
THAT IS FOR THE ATTACK ON DAXAM!
BOOM

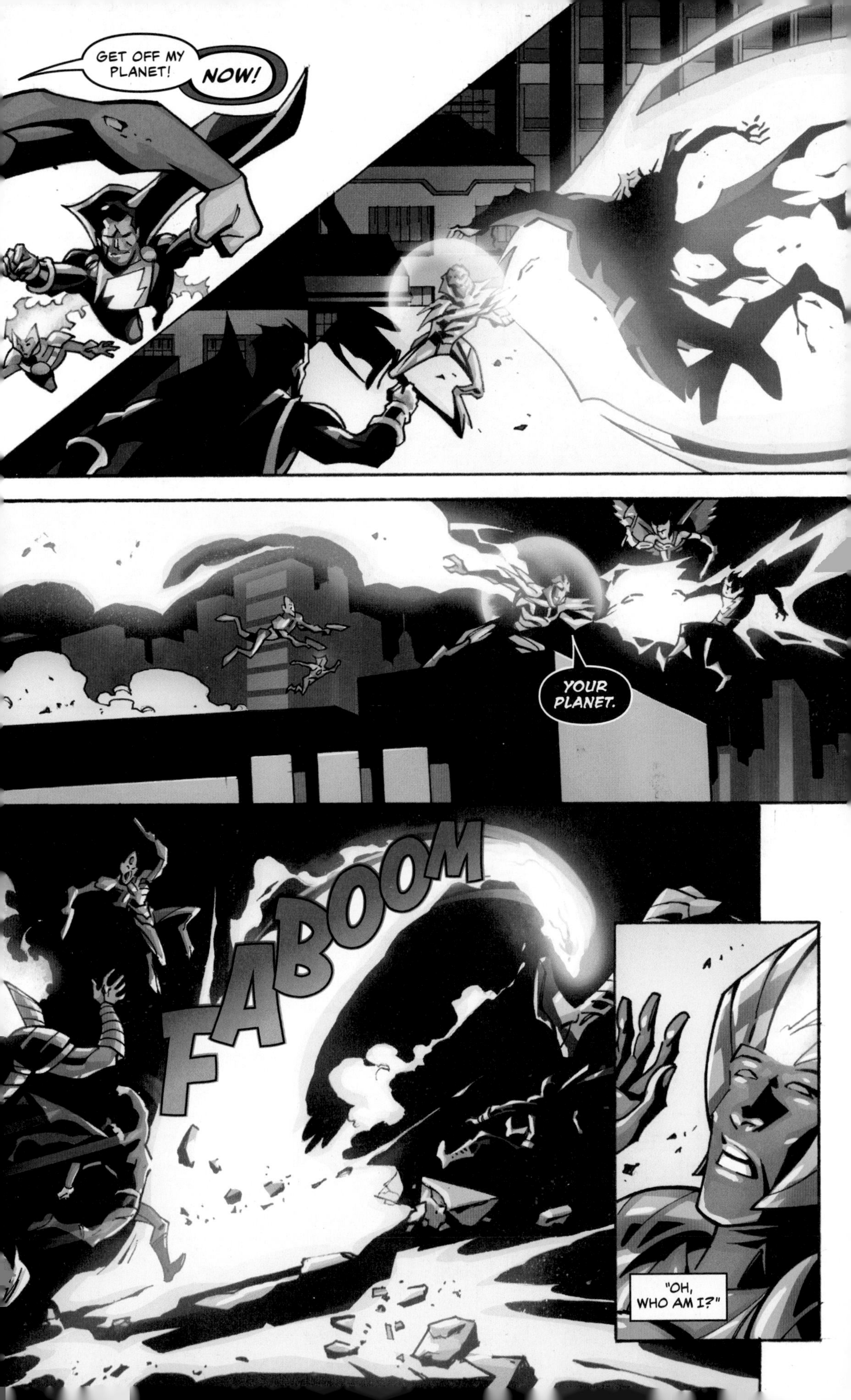
GET OFF MY PLANET!
NOW!
YOUR PLANET.
FABOOM
"OH, WHO AM I?"

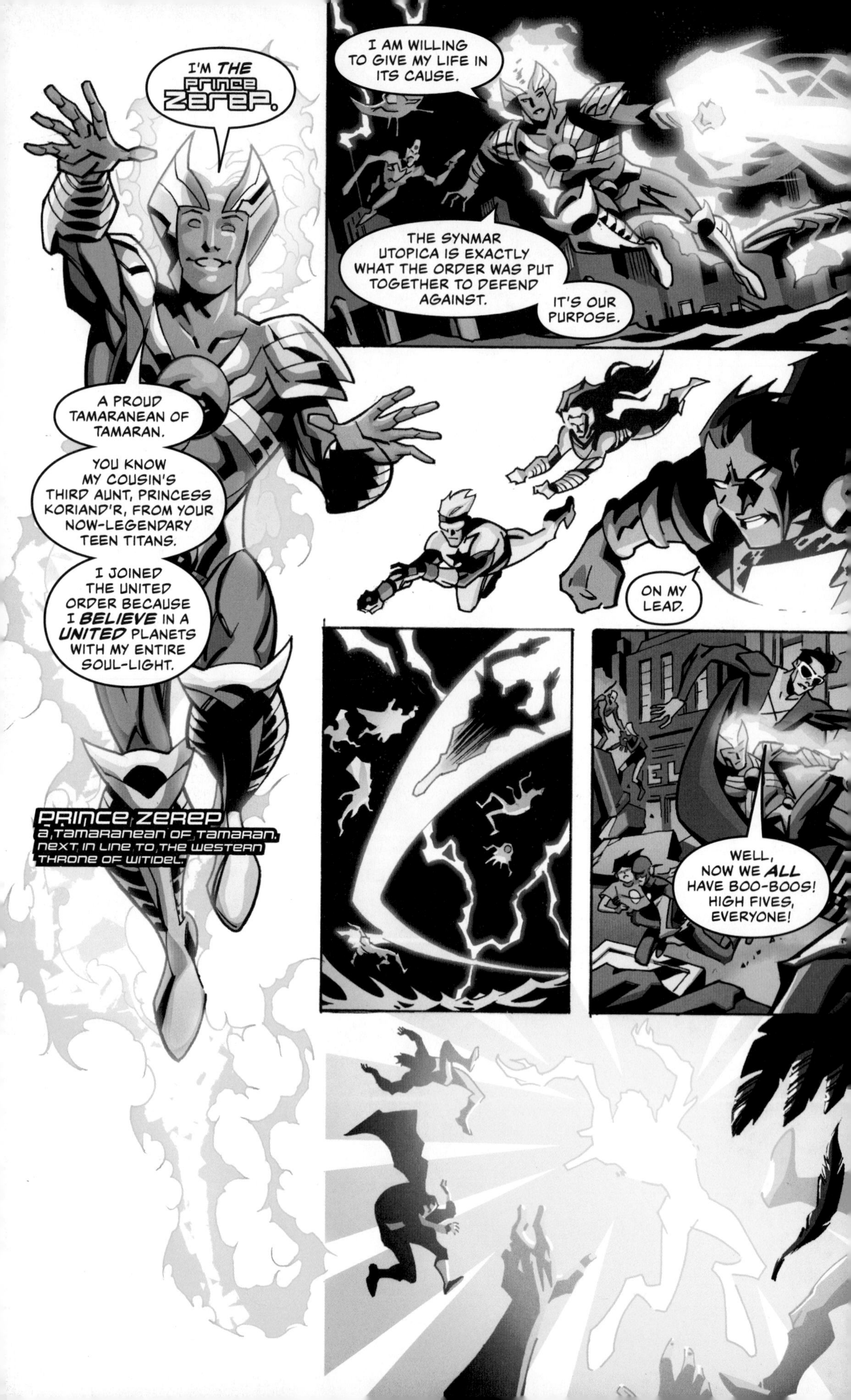
I'M THE PRINCE ZEREP.
A PROUD TAMARANEAN OF TAMARAN.
YOU KNOW MY COUSIN'S THIRD AUNT, PRINCESS KORIAND'R, FROM YOUR NOW-LEGENDARY TEEN TITANS.
I JOINED THE UNITED ORDER BECAUSE I BELIEVE IN A UNITED PLANETS WITH MY ENTIRE SOUL-LIGHT.
PRINCE ZEREP
A TAMARANEAN OF TAMARAN. NEXT IN LINE TO THE WESTERN THRONE OF WITIDEL.
I AM WILLING TO GIVE MY LIFE IN ITS CAUSE.
THE SYNMAR UTOPICA IS EXACTLY WHAT THE ORDER WAS PUT TOGETHER TO DEFEND AGAINST.
IT'S OUR PURPOSE.
ON MY LEAD.
WELL, NOW WE ALL HAVE BOO-BOOS! HIGH FIVES, EVERYONE!

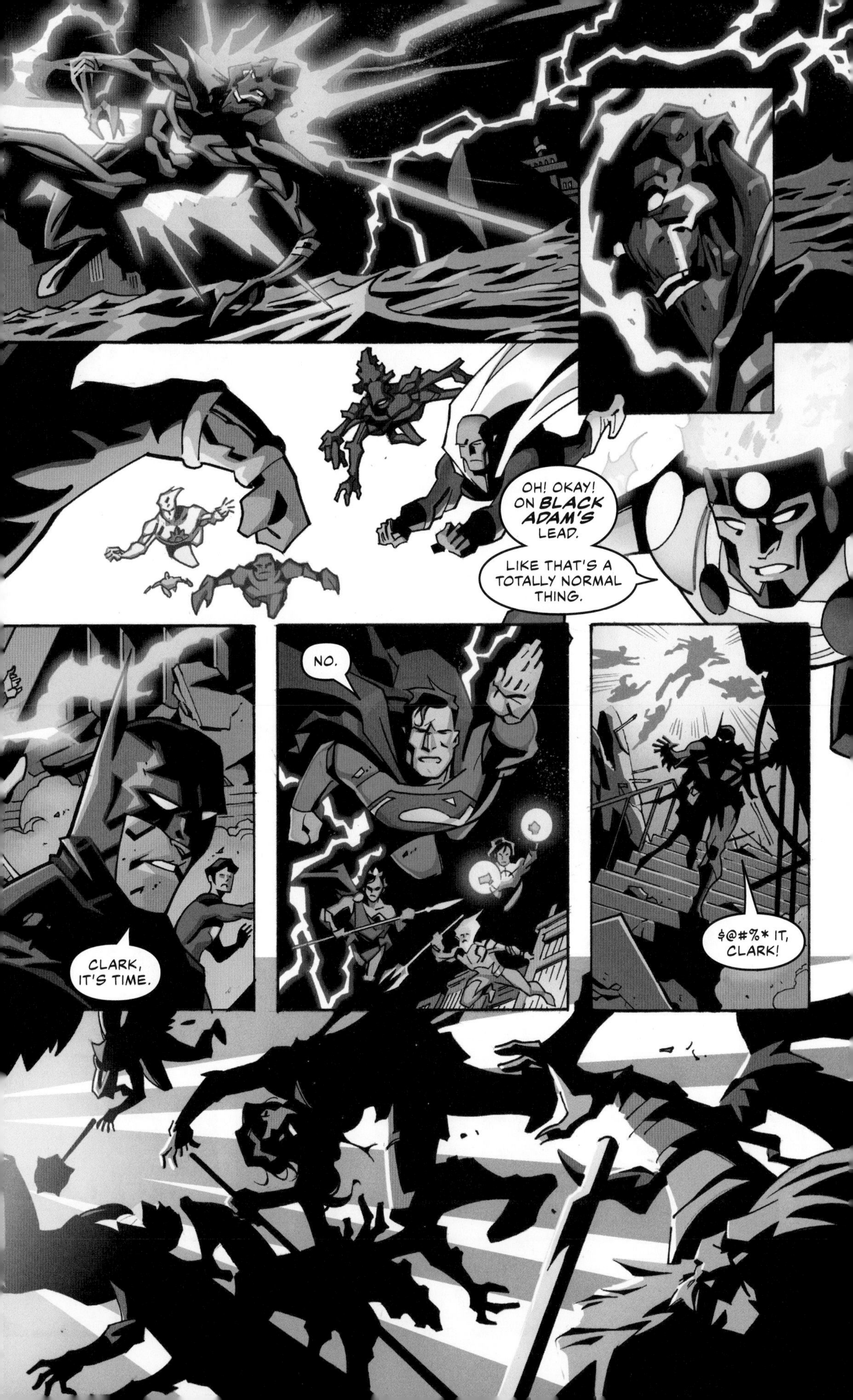
OH! OKAY! ON BLACK ADAM'S LEAD.
LIKE THAT'S A TOTALLY NORMAL THING.
CLARK, IT'S TIME.
NO.
$@#%* IT, CLARK!

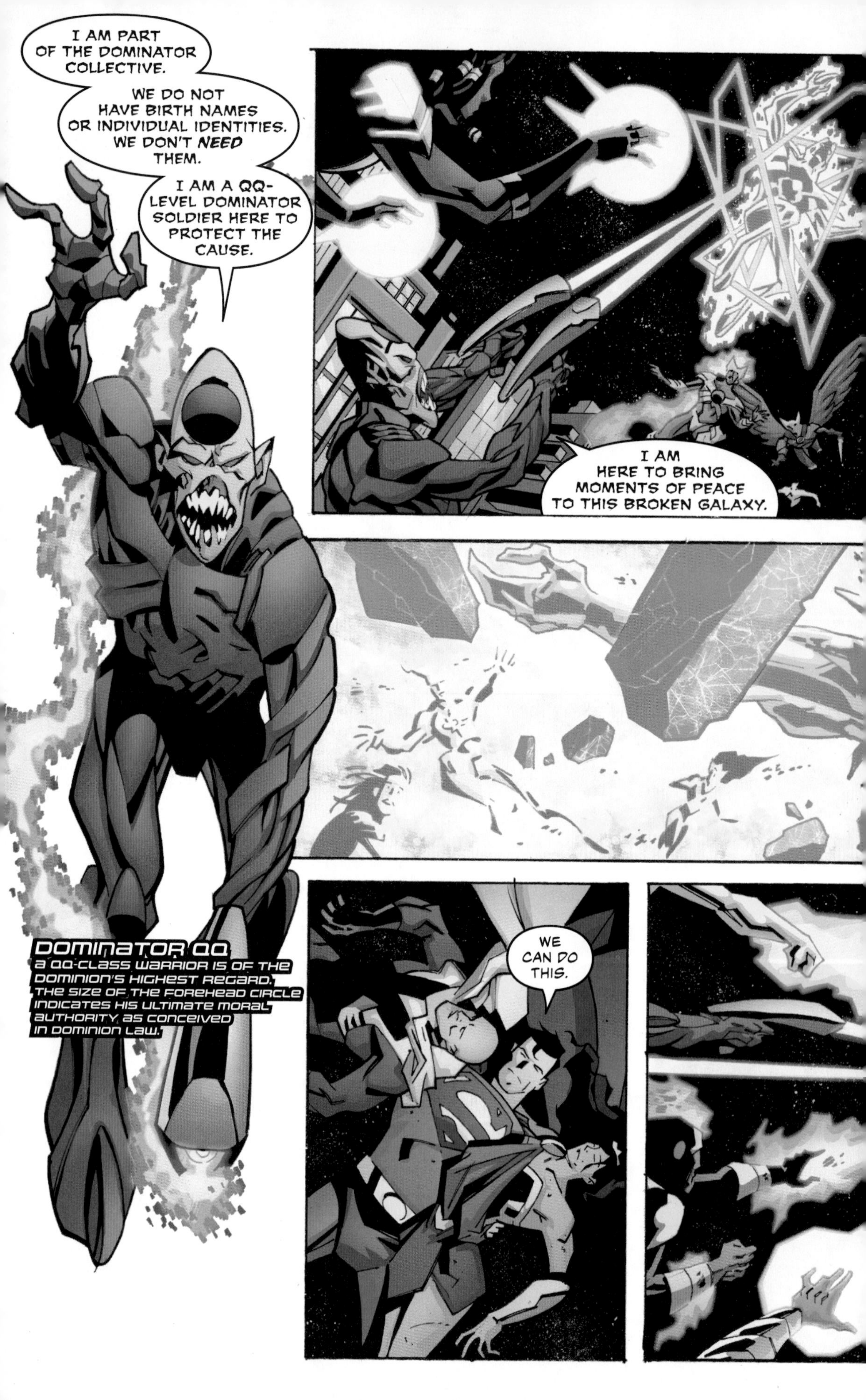
I AM PART OF THE DOMINATOR COLLECTIVE.
WE DO NOT HAVE BIRTH NAMES OR INDIVIDUAL IDENTITIES. WE DON'T *NEED* THEM.
I AM A QQ-LEVEL DOMINATOR SOLDIER HERE TO PROTECT THE CAUSE.
I AM HERE TO BRING MOMENTS OF PEACE TO THIS BROKEN GALAXY.
DOMINATOR QQ
A QQ-CLASS WARRIOR IS OF THE DOMINION'S HIGHEST REGARD. THE SIZE OF THE FOREHEAD CIRCLE INDICATES HIS ULTIMATE MORAL AUTHORITY AS CONCEIVED IN DOMINION LAW.
WE CAN DO THIS.

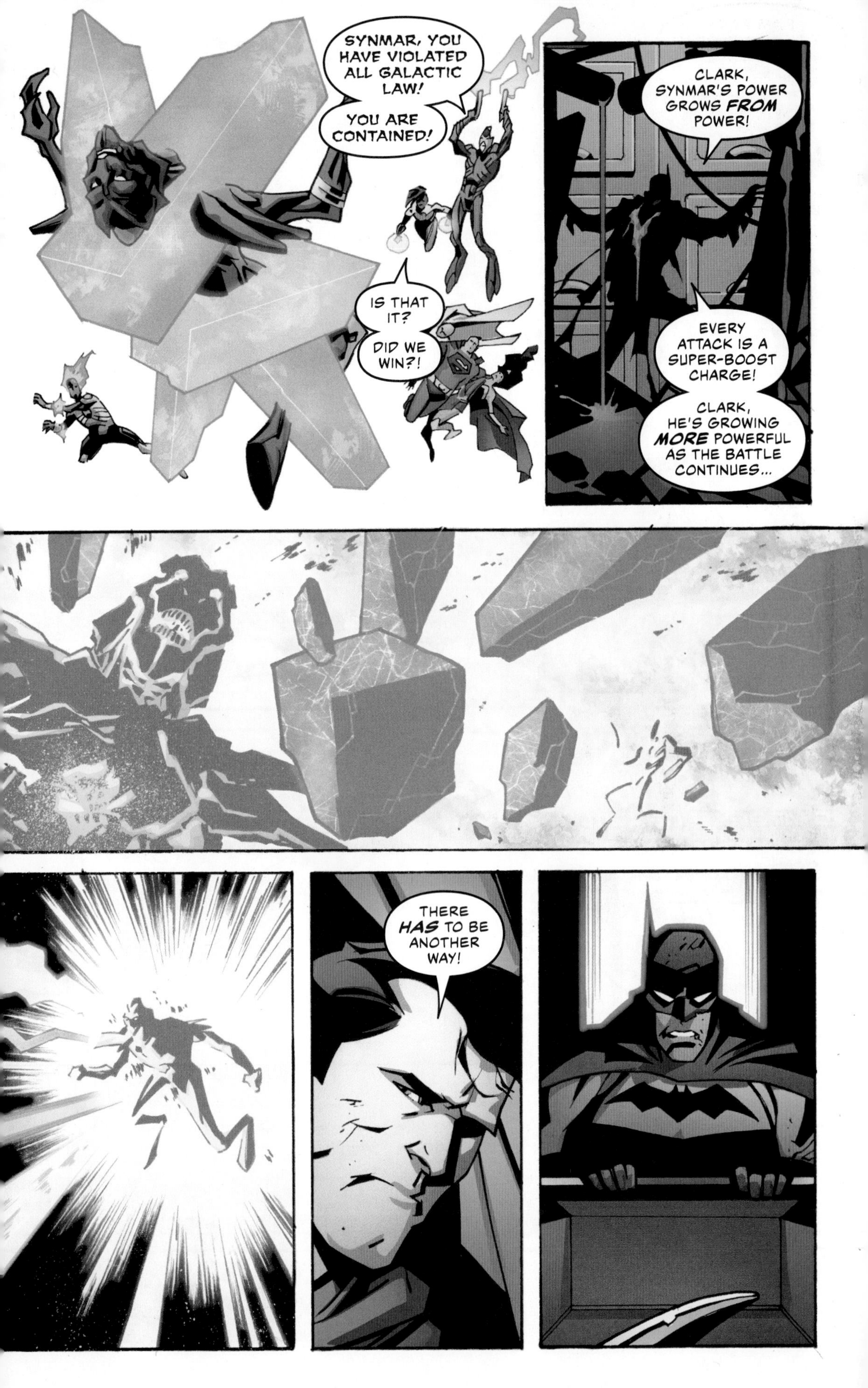
SYNMAR, YOU HAVE VIOLATED ALL GALACTIC LAW!
YOU ARE CONTAINED!
IS THAT IT?
DID WE WIN?!
CLARK, SYNMAR'S POWER GROWS FROM POWER!
EVERY ATTACK IS A SUPER-BOOST CHARGE!
CLARK, HE'S GROWING MORE POWERFUL AS THE BATTLE CONTINUES...
THERE HAS TO BE ANOTHER WAY!

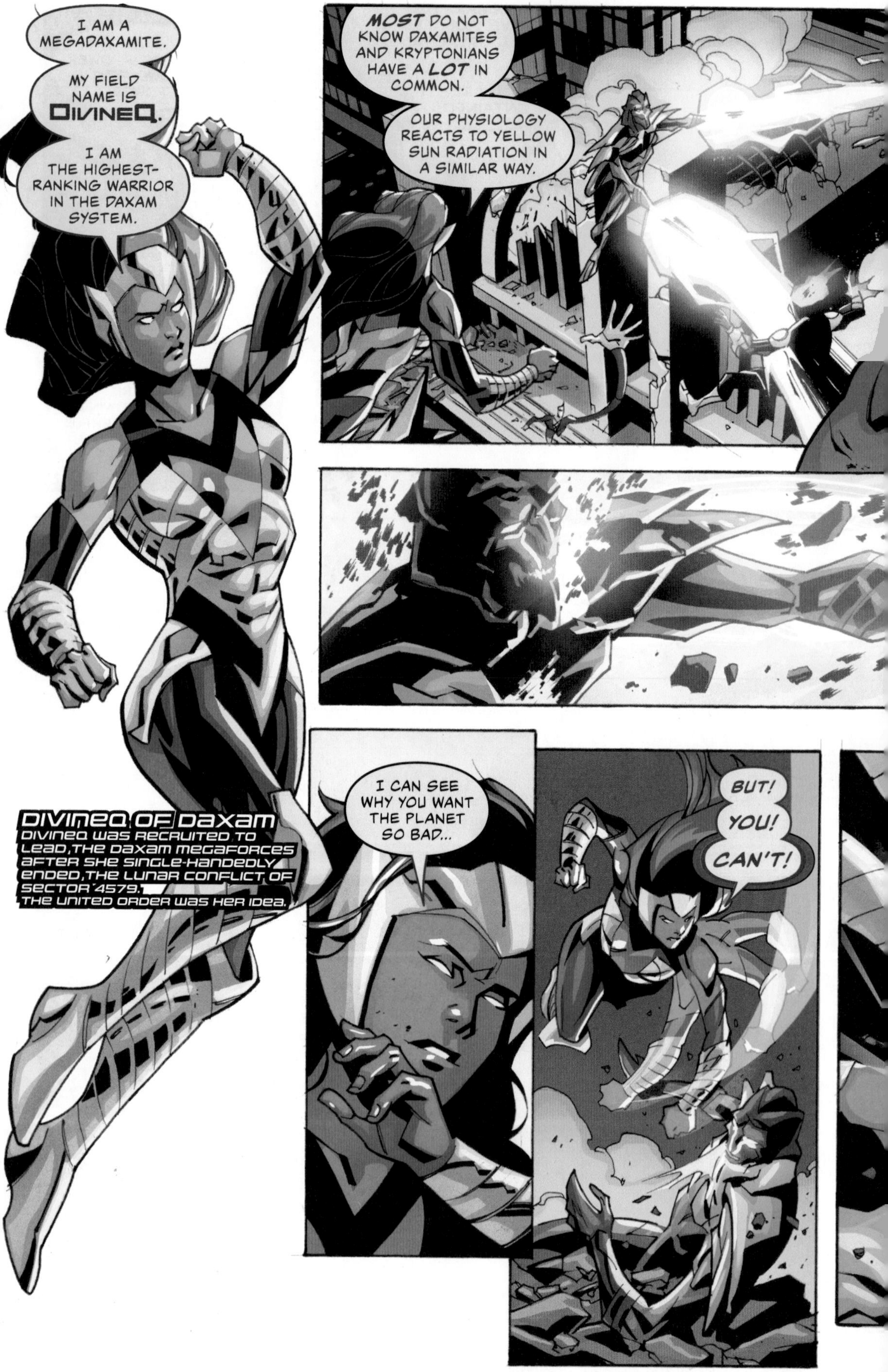
I AM A MEGADAXAMITE.
MY FIELD NAME IS DIVINEQ.
I AM THE HIGHEST-RANKING WARRIOR IN THE DAXAM SYSTEM.
MOST DO NOT KNOW DAXAMITES AND KRYPTONIANS HAVE A LOT IN COMMON.
OUR PHYSIOLOGY REACTS TO YELLOW SUN RADIATION IN A SIMILAR WAY.
DIVINEQ OF DAXAM
DIVINEQ WAS RECRUITED TO LEAD THE DAXAM MEGAFORCES AFTER SHE SINGLE-HANDEDLY ENDED THE LUNAR CONFLICT OF SECTOR 4579. THE UNITED ORDER WAS HER IDEA.
I CAN SEE WHY YOU WANT THE PLANET SO BAD...
BUT!
YOU!
CAN'T!

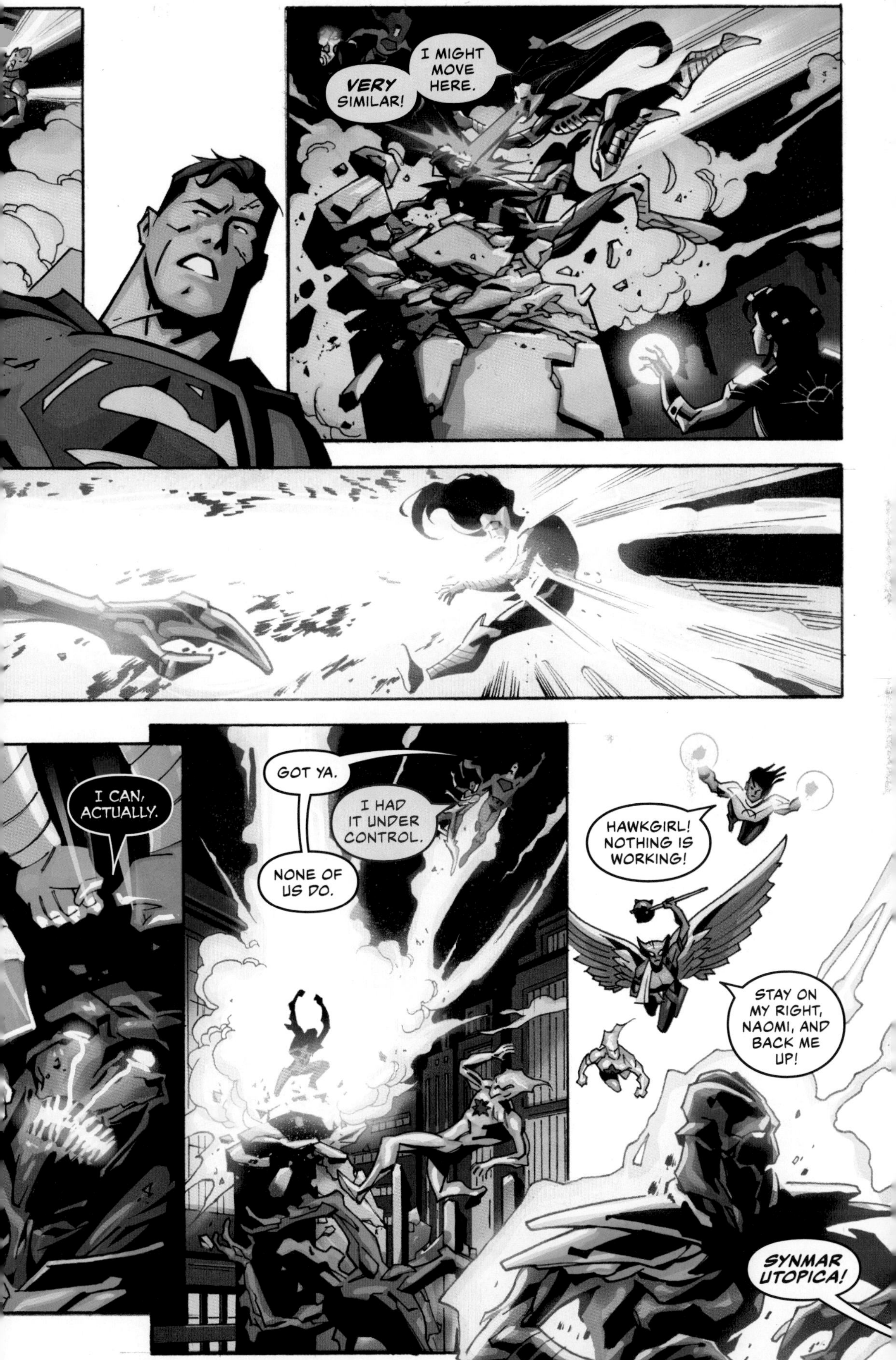
VERY SIMILAR!
I MIGHT MOVE HERE.
I CAN, ACTUALLY.
GOT YA.
I HAD IT UNDER CONTROL.
NONE OF US DO.
HAWKGIRL! NOTHING IS WORKING!
STAY ON MY RIGHT, NAOMI, AND BACK ME UP!
SYNMAR UTOPICA!

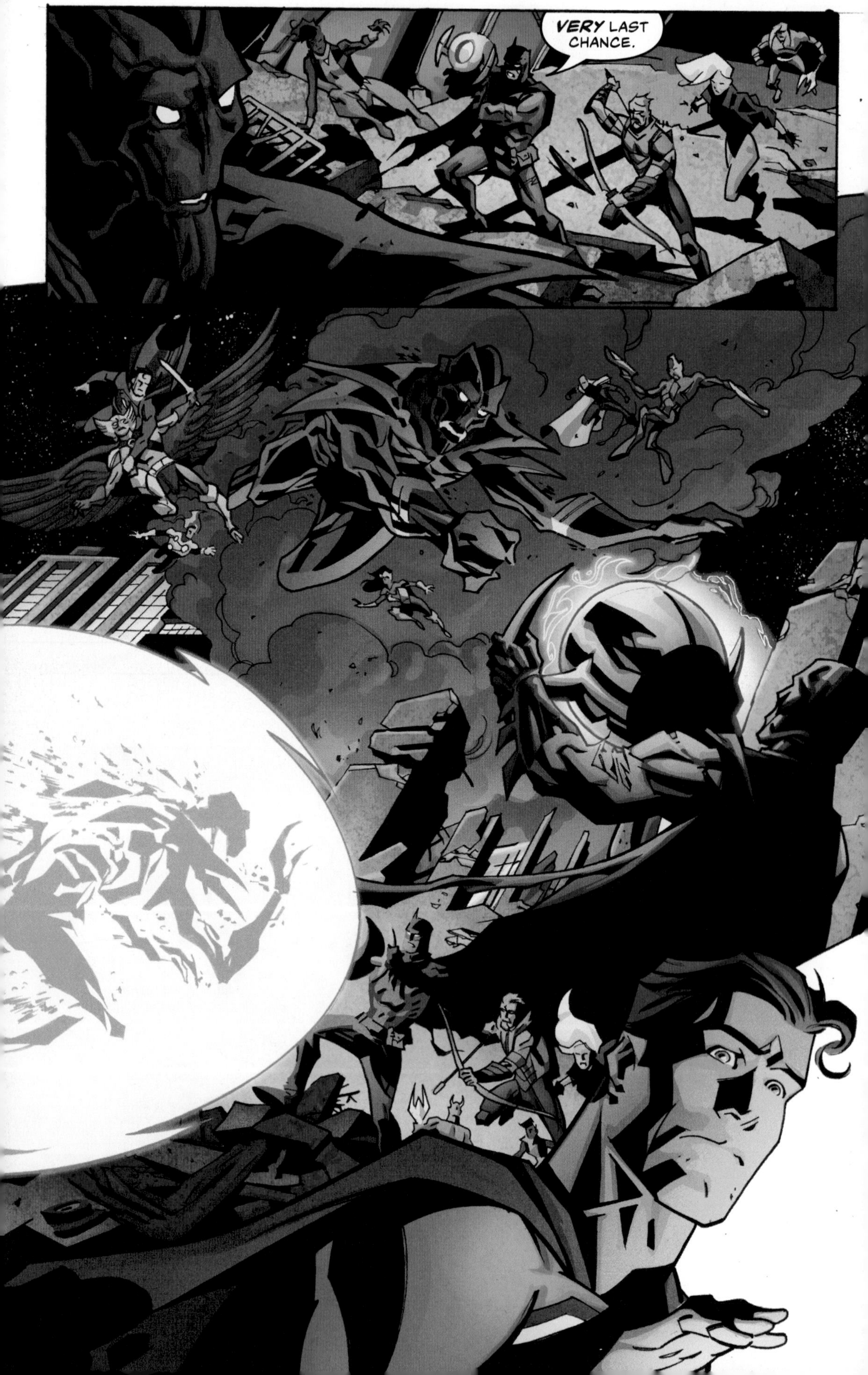
VERY LAST CHANCE.

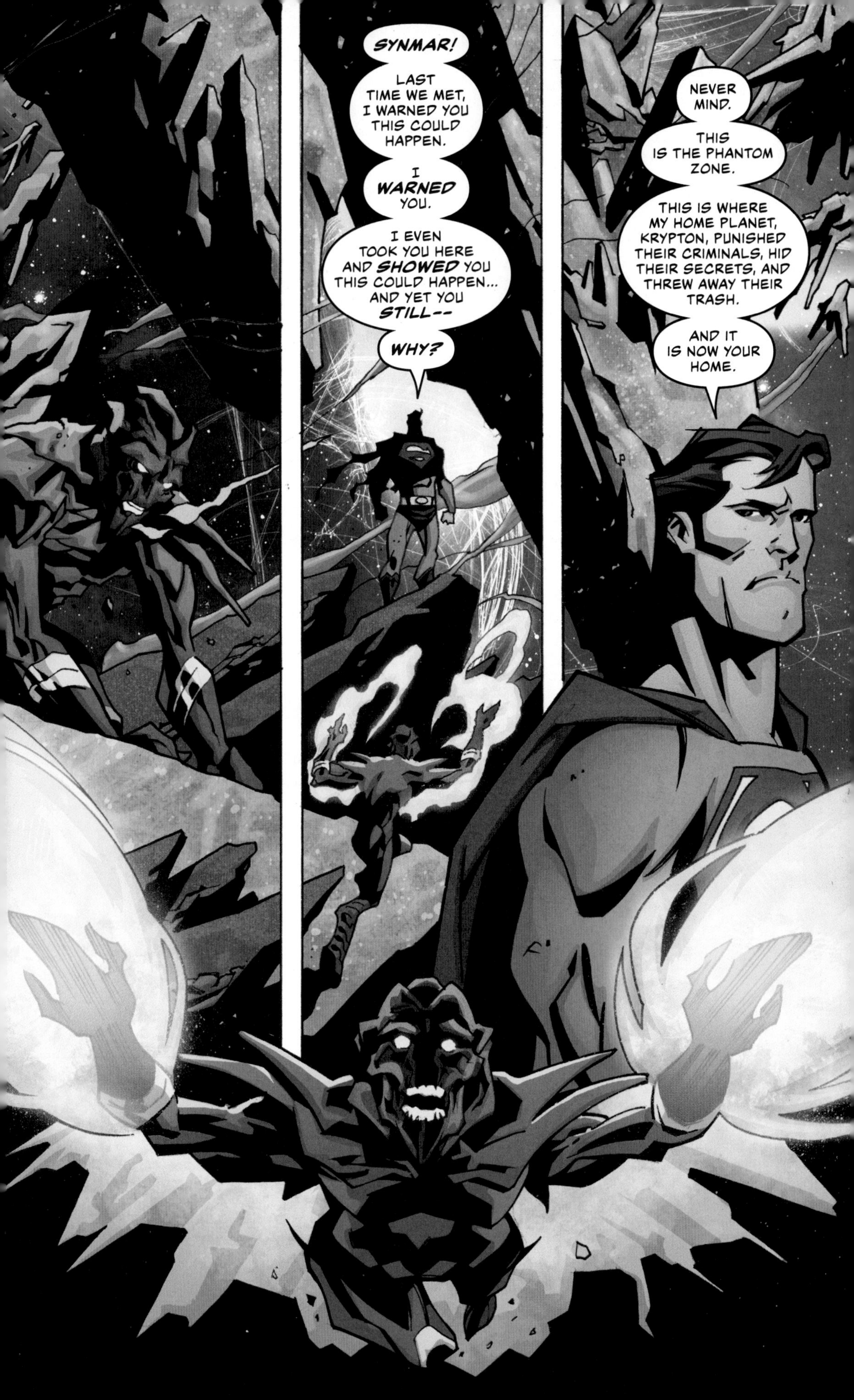
SYNMAR!
LAST TIME WE MET, I WARNED YOU THIS COULD HAPPEN.
I WARNED YOU.
I EVEN TOOK YOU HERE AND SHOWED YOU THIS COULD HAPPEN... AND YET YOU STILL--
WHY?
NEVER MIND.
THIS IS THE PHANTOM ZONE.
THIS IS WHERE MY HOME PLANET, KRYPTON, PUNISHED THEIR CRIMINALS, HID THEIR SECRETS, AND THREW AWAY THEIR TRASH.
AND IT IS NOW YOUR HOME.

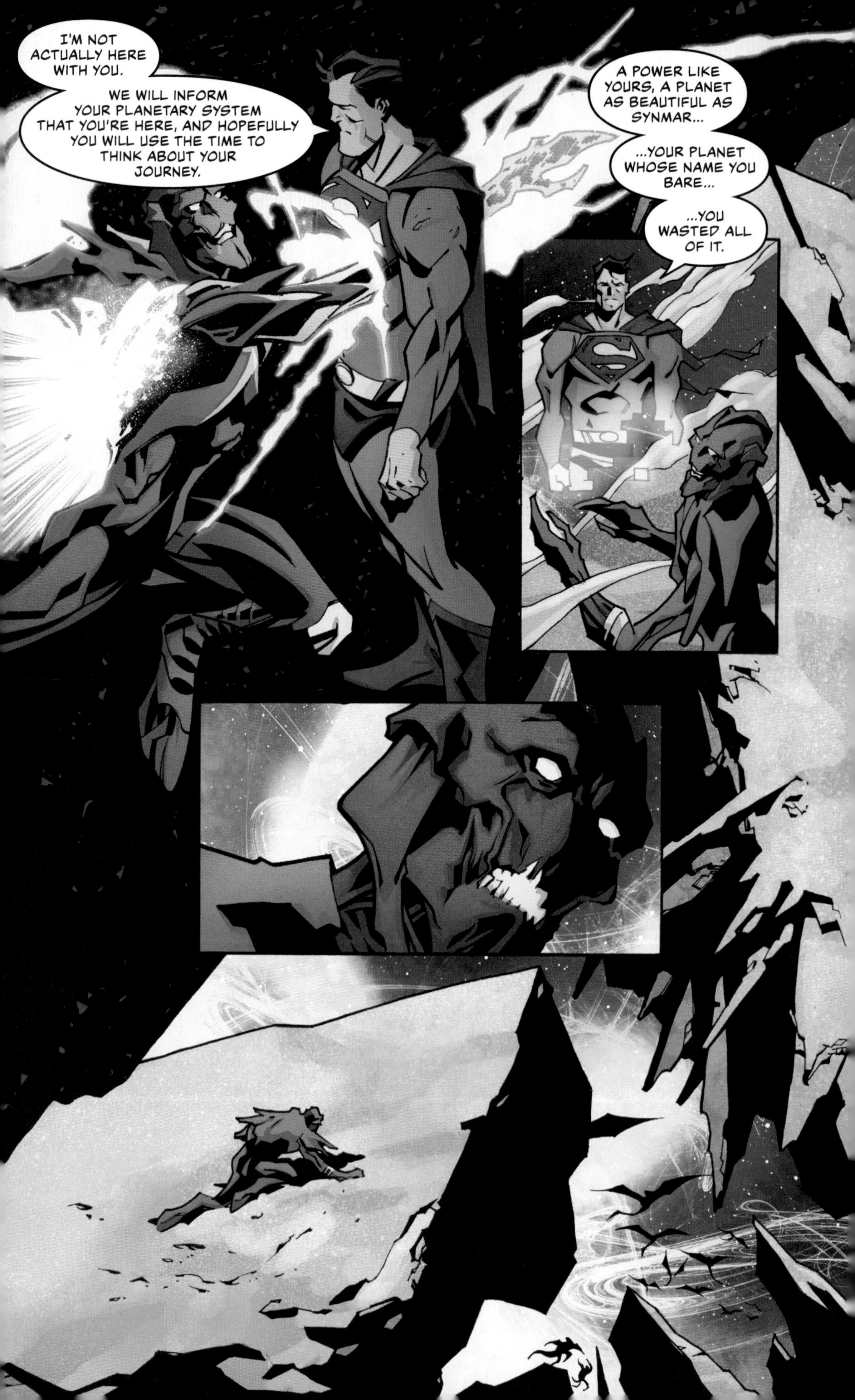
I'M NOT ACTUALLY HERE WITH YOU.
WE WILL INFORM YOUR PLANETARY SYSTEM THAT YOU'RE HERE, AND HOPEFULLY YOU WILL USE THE TIME TO THINK ABOUT YOUR JOURNEY.
A POWER LIKE YOURS, A PLANET AS BEAUTIFUL AS SYNMAR...
...YOUR PLANET WHOSE NAME YOU BARE...
...YOU WASTED ALL OF IT.

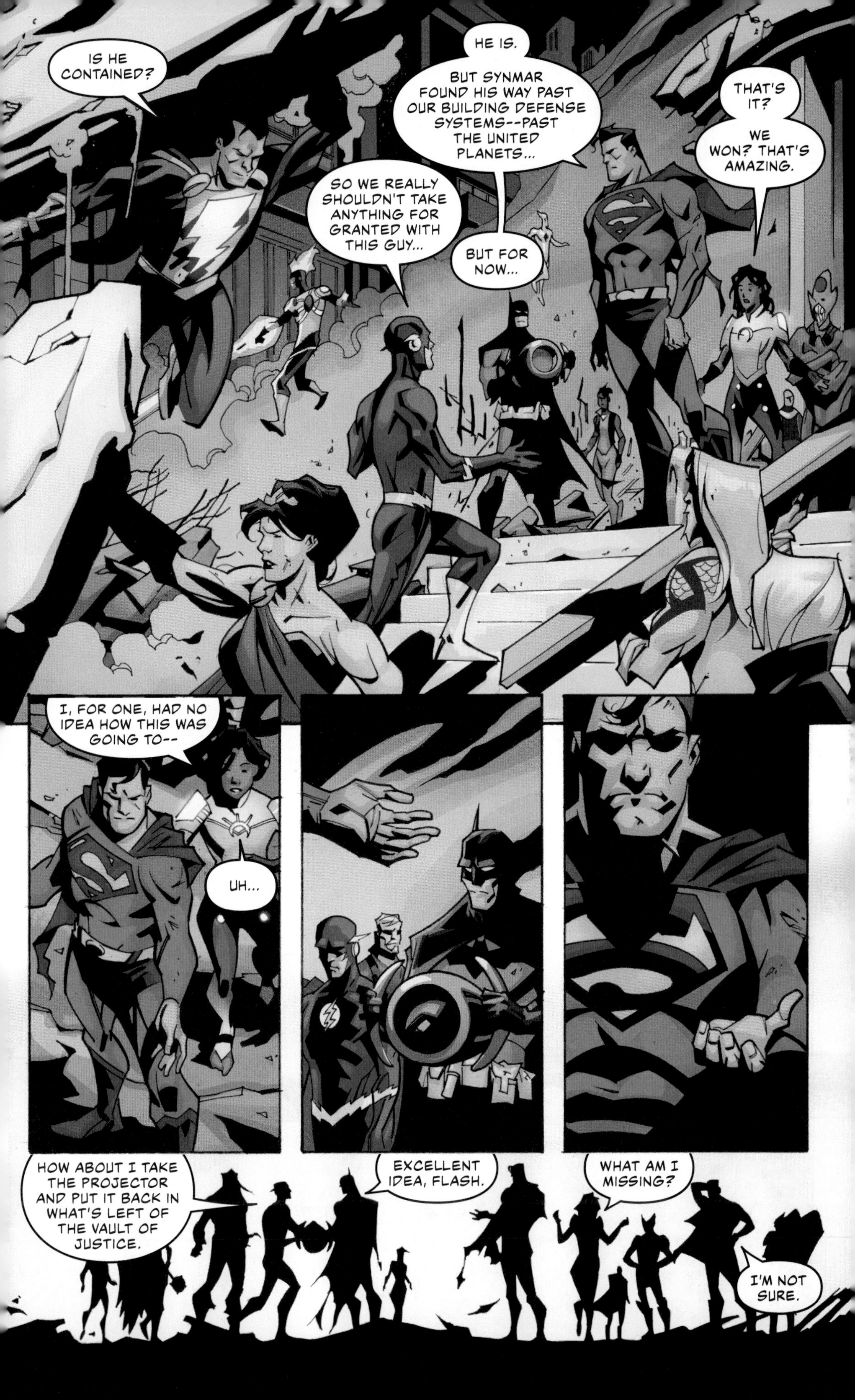
IS HE CONTAINED?
HE IS.
BUT SYNMAR FOUND HIS WAY PAST OUR BUILDING DEFENSE SYSTEMS--PAST THE UNITED PLANETS...
BUT FOR NOW...
SO WE REALLY SHOULDN'T TAKE ANYTHING FOR GRANTED WITH THIS GUY...
THAT'S IT?
WE WON? THAT'S AMAZING.
I, FOR ONE, HAD NO IDEA HOW THIS WAS GOING TO--
UH...
HOW ABOUT I TAKE THE PROJECTOR AND PUT IT BACK IN WHAT'S LEFT OF THE VAULT OF JUSTICE.
EXCELLENT IDEA, FLASH.
WHAT AM I MISSING?
I'M NOT SURE.

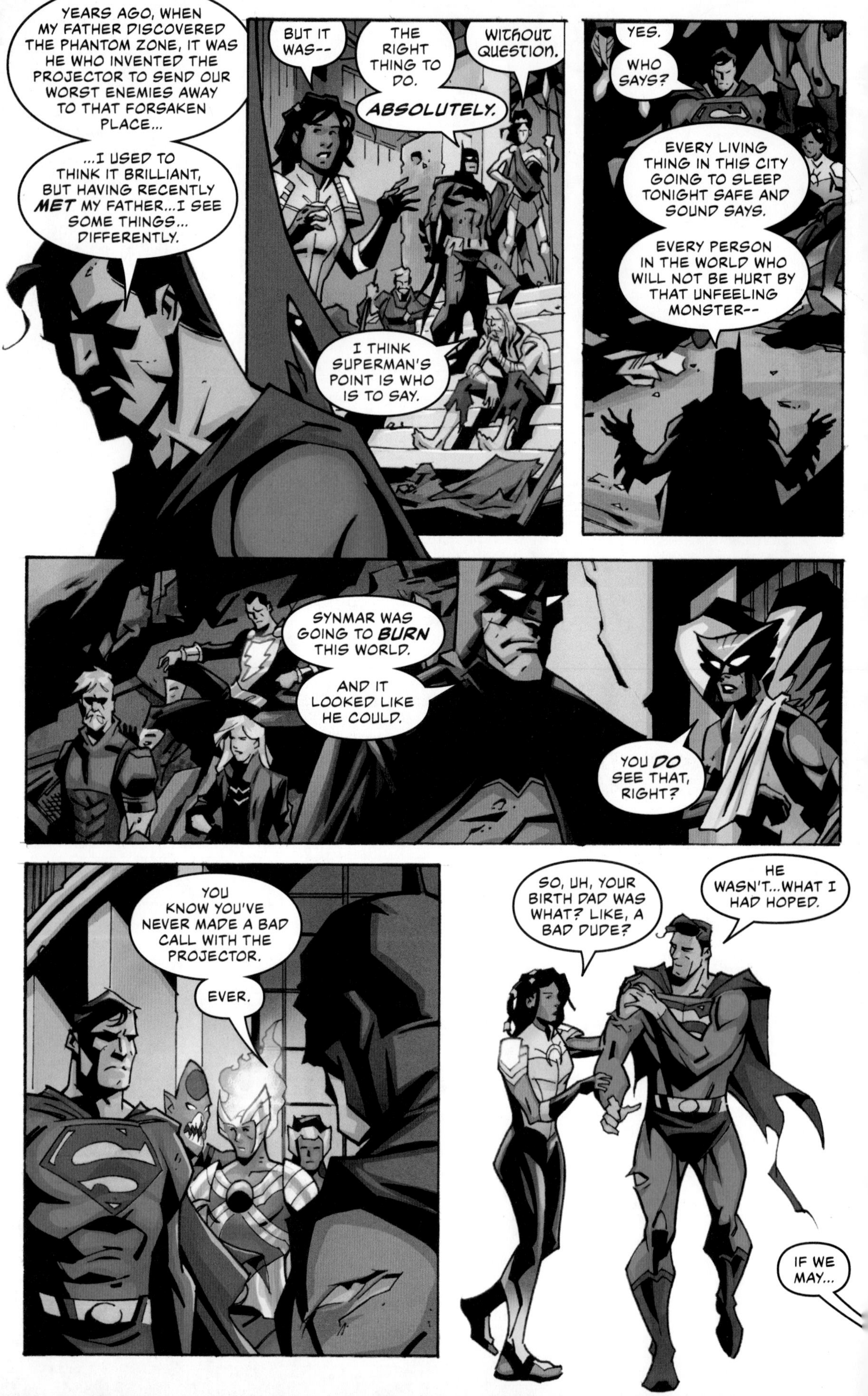
YEARS AGO, WHEN MY FATHER DISCOVERED THE PHANTOM ZONE, IT WAS HE WHO INVENTED THE PROJECTOR TO SEND OUR WORST ENEMIES AWAY TO THAT FORSAKEN PLACE...
...I USED TO THINK IT BRILLIANT, BUT HAVING RECENTLY MET MY FATHER...I SEE SOME THINGS... DIFFERENTLY.
BUT IT WAS--
THE RIGHT THING TO DO.
ABSOLUTELY.
WITHOUT QUESTION.
I THINK SUPERMAN'S POINT IS WHO IS TO SAY.
YES.
WHO SAYS?
EVERY LIVING THING IN THIS CITY GOING TO SLEEP TONIGHT SAFE AND SOUND SAYS.
EVERY PERSON IN THE WORLD WHO WILL NOT BE HURT BY THAT UNFEELING MONSTER--
SYNMAR WAS GOING TO BURN THIS WORLD.
AND IT LOOKED LIKE HE COULD.
YOU DO SEE THAT, RIGHT?
YOU KNOW YOU'VE NEVER MADE A BAD CALL WITH THE PROJECTOR.
EVER.
SO, UH, YOUR BIRTH DAD WAS WHAT? LIKE, A BAD DUDE?
HE WASN'T...WHAT I HAD HOPED.
IF WE MAY...

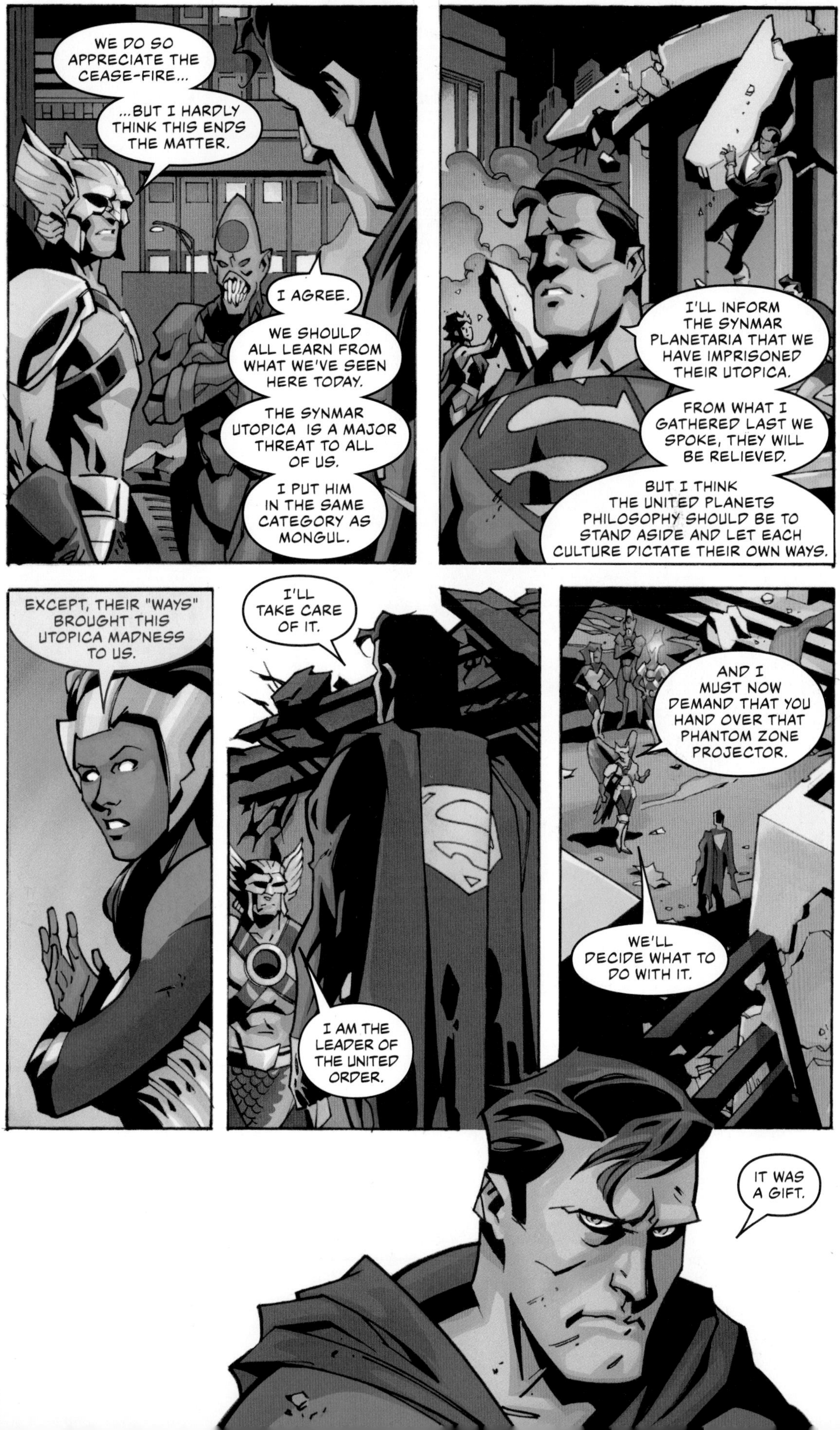
WE DO SO APPRECIATE THE CEASE-FIRE...
...BUT I HARDLY THINK THIS ENDS THE MATTER.
I AGREE.
WE SHOULD ALL LEARN FROM WHAT WE'VE SEEN HERE TODAY.
THE SYNMAR UTOPICA IS A MAJOR THREAT TO ALL OF US.
I PUT HIM IN THE SAME CATEGORY AS MONGUL.
I'LL INFORM THE SYNMAR PLANETARIA THAT WE HAVE IMPRISONED THEIR UTOPICA.
FROM WHAT I GATHERED LAST WE SPOKE, THEY WILL BE RELIEVED.
BUT I THINK THE UNITED PLANETS PHILOSOPHY SHOULD BE TO STAND ASIDE AND LET EACH CULTURE DICTATE THEIR OWN WAYS.
EXCEPT, THEIR "WAYS" BROUGHT THIS UTOPICA MADNESS TO US.
I'LL TAKE CARE OF IT.
I AM THE LEADER OF THE UNITED ORDER.
AND I MUST NOW DEMAND THAT YOU HAND OVER THAT PHANTOM ZONE PROJECTOR.
WE'LL DECIDE WHAT TO DO WITH IT.
IT WAS A GIFT.

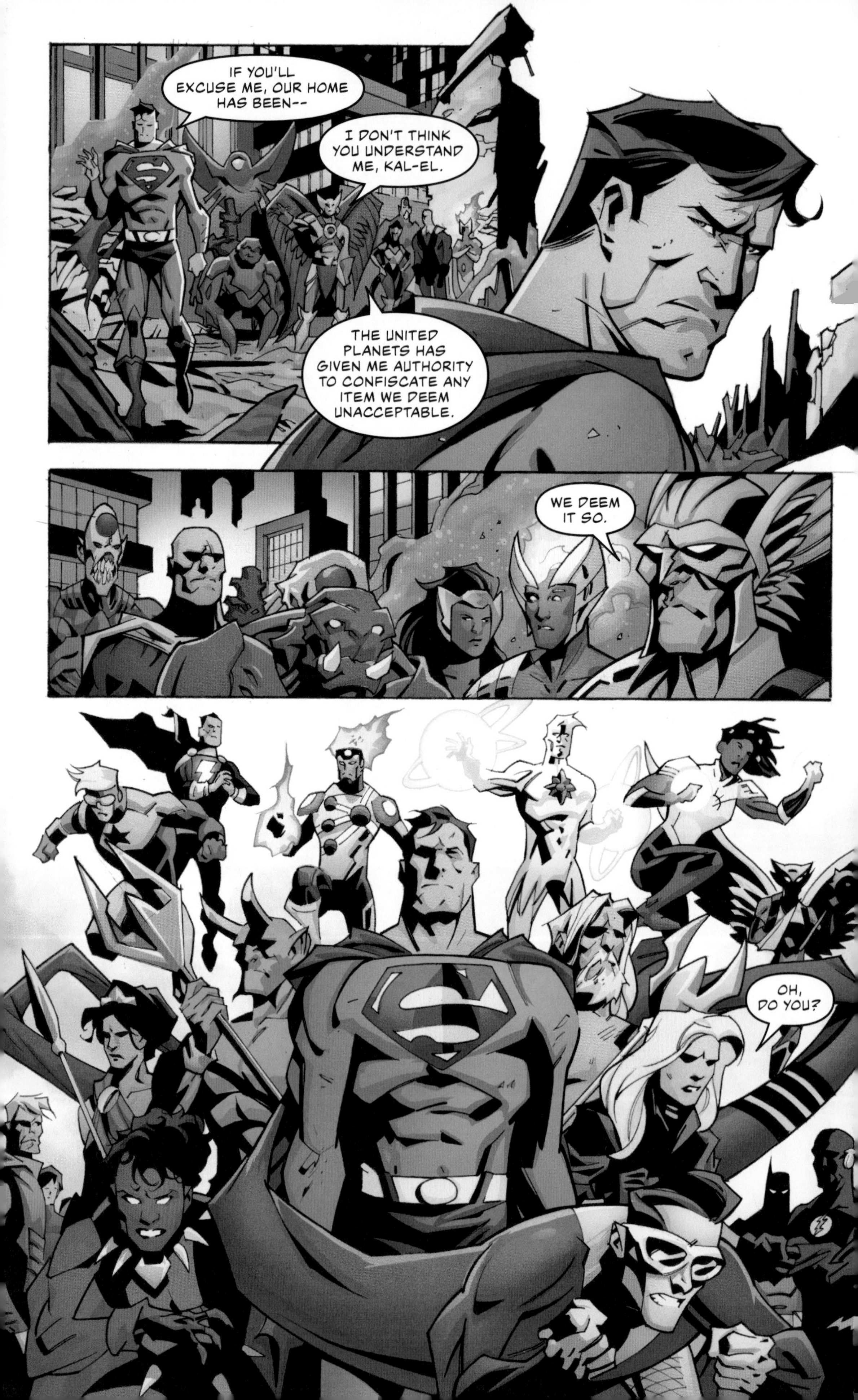
IF YOU'LL EXCUSE ME, OUR HOME HAS BEEN--
I DON'T THINK YOU UNDERSTAND ME, KAL-EL.
THE UNITED PLANETS HAS GIVEN ME AUTHORITY TO CONFISCATE ANY ITEM WE DEEM UNACCEPTABLE.
WE DEEM IT SO.
OH, DO YOU?

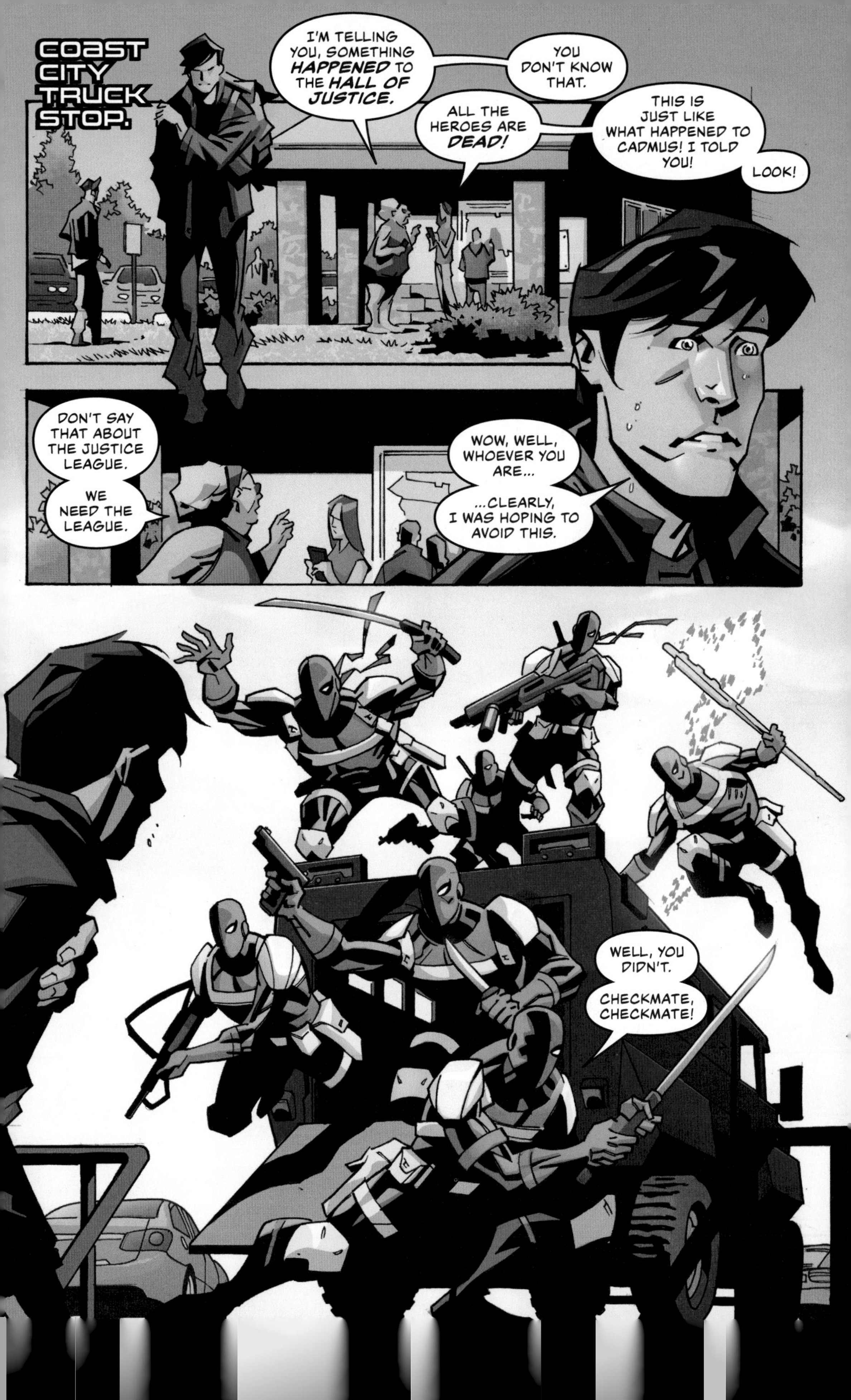
COAST CITY TRUCK STOP.
I'M TELLING YOU, SOMETHING HAPPENED TO THE HALL OF JUSTICE.
YOU DON'T KNOW THAT.
ALL THE HEROES ARE DEAD!
THIS IS JUST LIKE WHAT HAPPENED TO CADMUS! I TOLD YOU!
LOOK!
DON'T SAY THAT ABOUT THE JUSTICE LEAGUE.
WE NEED THE LEAGUE.
WOW, WELL, WHOEVER YOU ARE...
...CLEARLY, I WAS HOPING TO AVOID THIS.
WELL, YOU DIDN'T.
CHECKMATE, CHECKMATE!

Justice League #68 cover art by
David Marquez & Ivan Plascencia

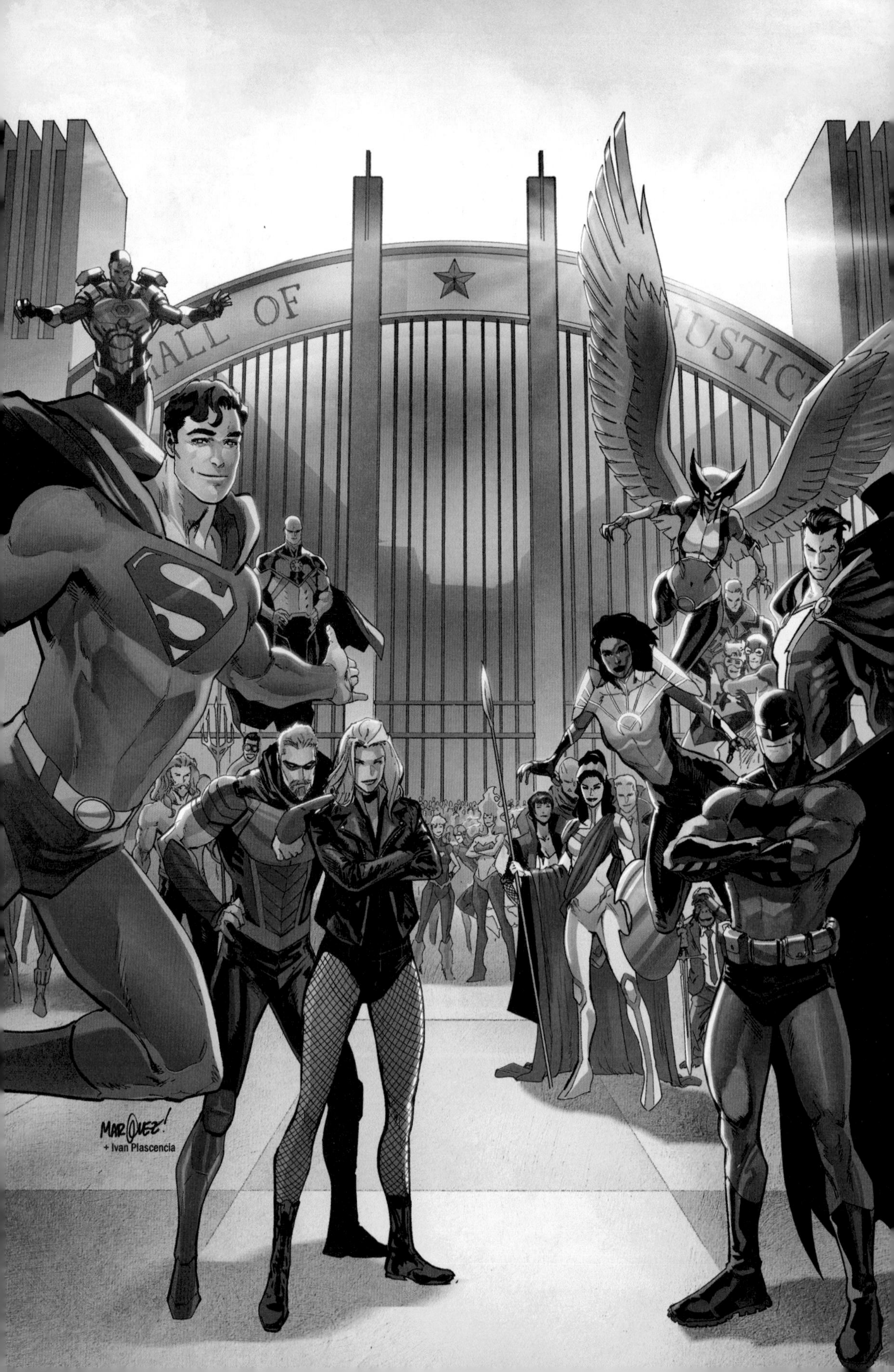
HALL OF JUSTICE
MARQUEZ!
+ Ivan Plascencia

Justice League #68 variant cover art by
Alexander Lozano

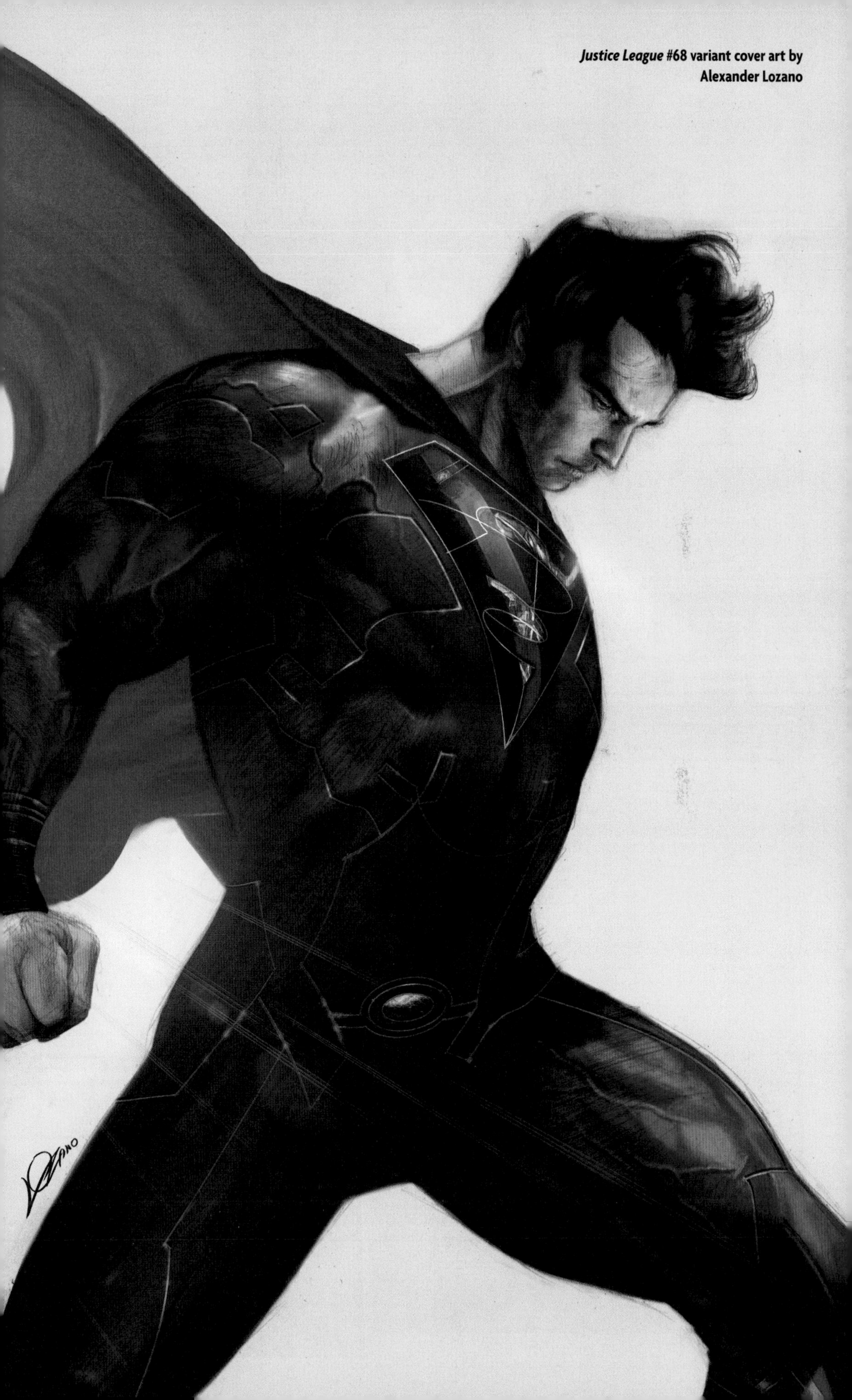

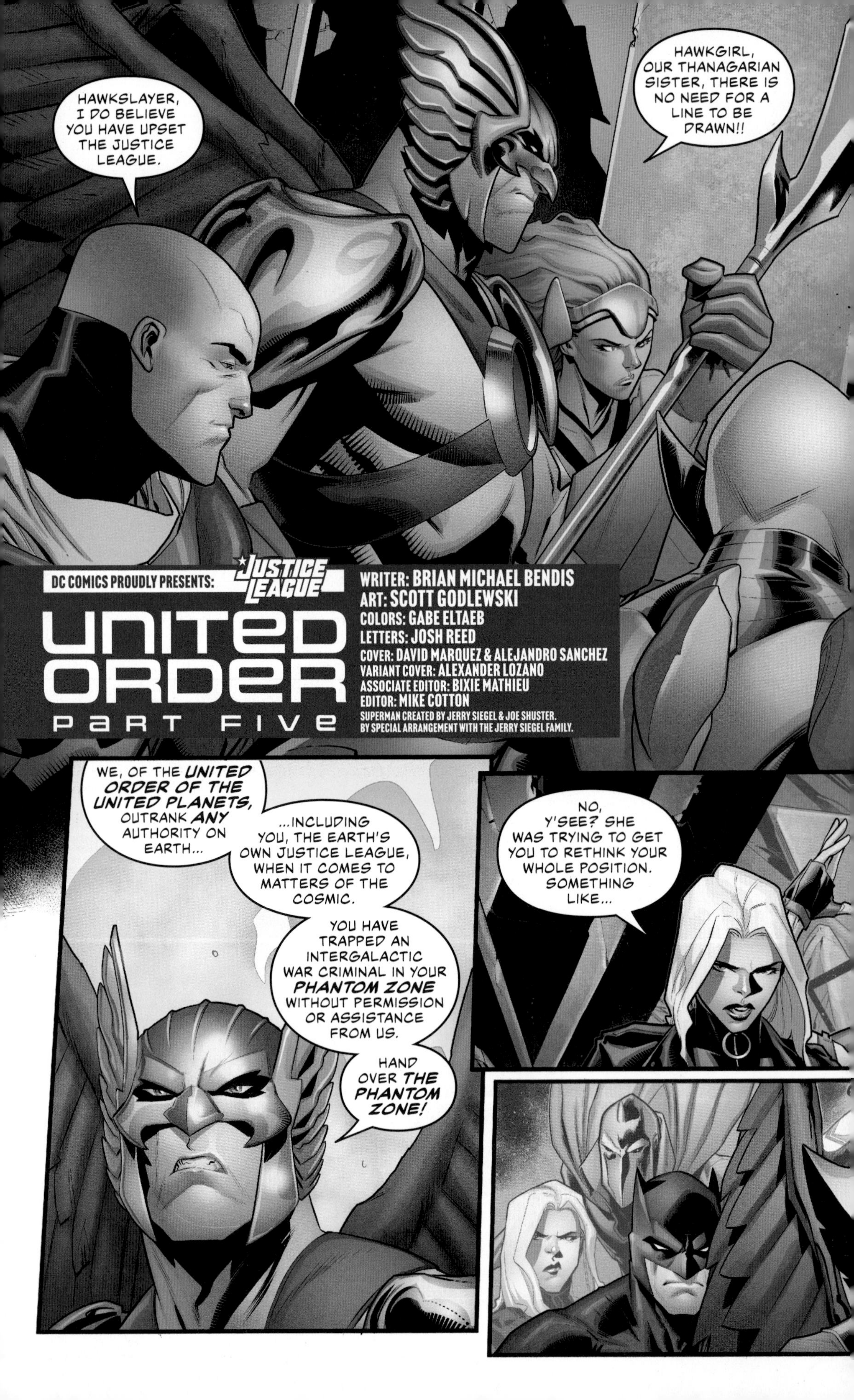
HAWKSLAYER, I DO BELIEVE YOU HAVE UPSET THE JUSTICE LEAGUE.
HAWKGIRL, OUR THANAGARIAN SISTER, THERE IS NO NEED FOR A LINE TO BE DRAWN!!
DC COMICS PROUDLY PRESENTS: JUSTICE LEAGUE
UNITED ORDER
PART FIVE
WRITER: BRIAN MICHAEL BENDIS
ART: SCOTT GODLEWSKI
COLORS: GABE ELTAEB
LETTERS: JOSH REED
COVER: DAVID MARQUEZ & ALEJANDRO SANCHEZ
VARIANT COVER: ALEXANDER LOZANO
ASSOCIATE EDITOR: BIXIE MATHIEU
EDITOR: MIKE COTTON
SUPERMAN CREATED BY JERRY SIEGEL & JOE SHUSTER. BY SPECIAL ARRANGEMENT WITH THE JERRY SIEGEL FAMILY.
WE, OF THE *UNITED ORDER OF THE UNITED PLANETS,* OUTRANK *ANY* AUTHORITY ON EARTH...
...INCLUDING YOU, THE EARTH'S OWN JUSTICE LEAGUE, WHEN IT COMES TO MATTERS OF THE COSMIC.
YOU HAVE TRAPPED AN INTERGALACTIC WAR CRIMINAL IN YOUR *PHANTOM ZONE* WITHOUT PERMISSION OR ASSISTANCE FROM US.
HAND OVER *THE PHANTOM ZONE!*
NO, Y'SEE? SHE WAS TRYING TO GET YOU TO RETHINK YOUR WHOLE POSITION. SOMETHING LIKE...

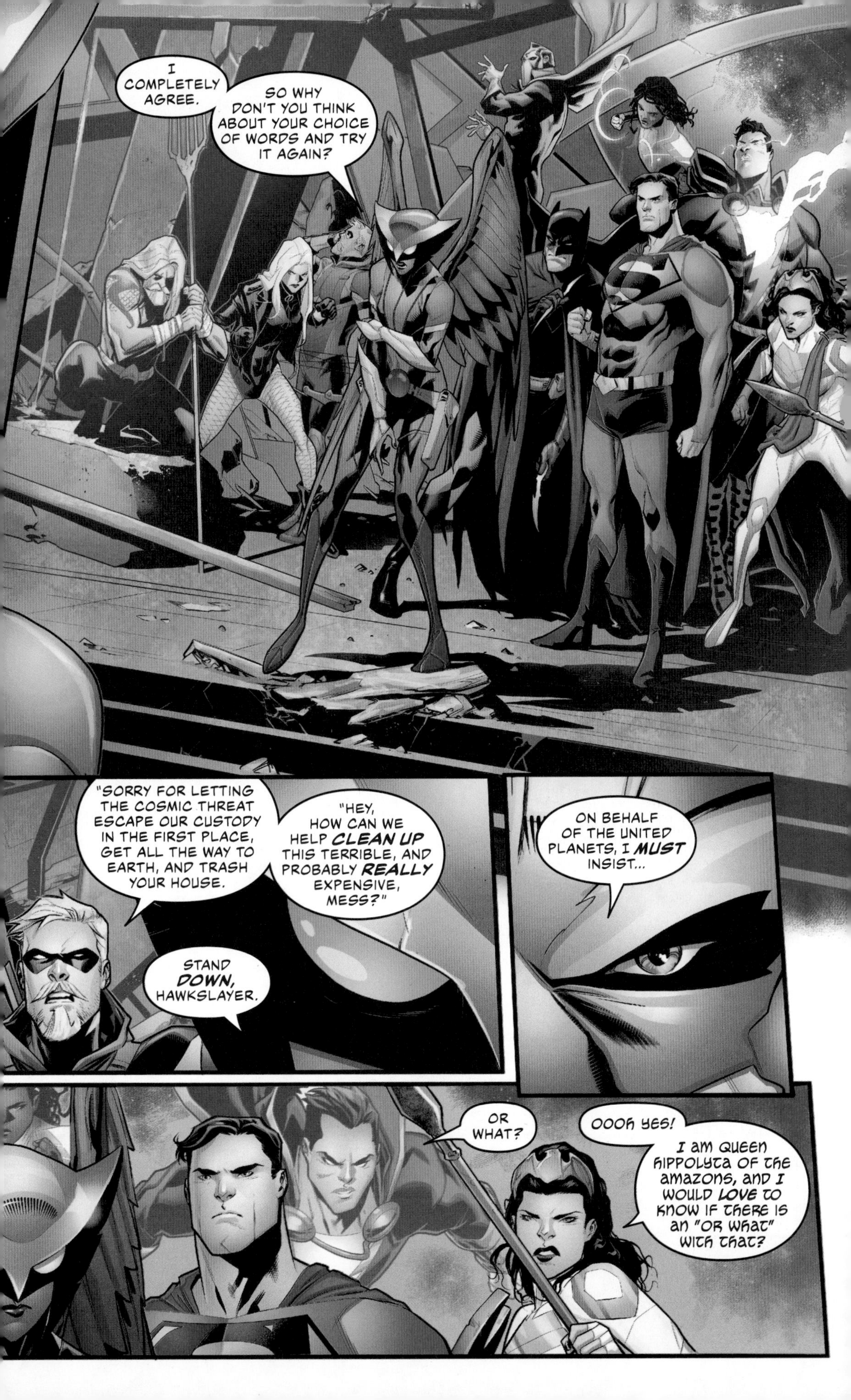
I COMPLETELY AGREE.
SO WHY DON'T YOU THINK ABOUT YOUR CHOICE OF WORDS AND TRY IT AGAIN?
"SORRY FOR LETTING THE COSMIC THREAT ESCAPE OUR CUSTODY IN THE FIRST PLACE, GET ALL THE WAY TO EARTH, AND TRASH YOUR HOUSE.
"HEY, HOW CAN WE HELP CLEAN UP THIS TERRIBLE, AND PROBABLY REALLY EXPENSIVE, MESS?"
STAND DOWN, HAWKSLAYER.
ON BEHALF OF THE UNITED PLANETS, I MUST INSIST...
OR WHAT?
OOOH YES!
I AM QUEEN HIPPOLYTA OF THE AMAZONS, AND I WOULD LOVE TO KNOW IF THERE IS AN "OR WHAT" WITH THAT?

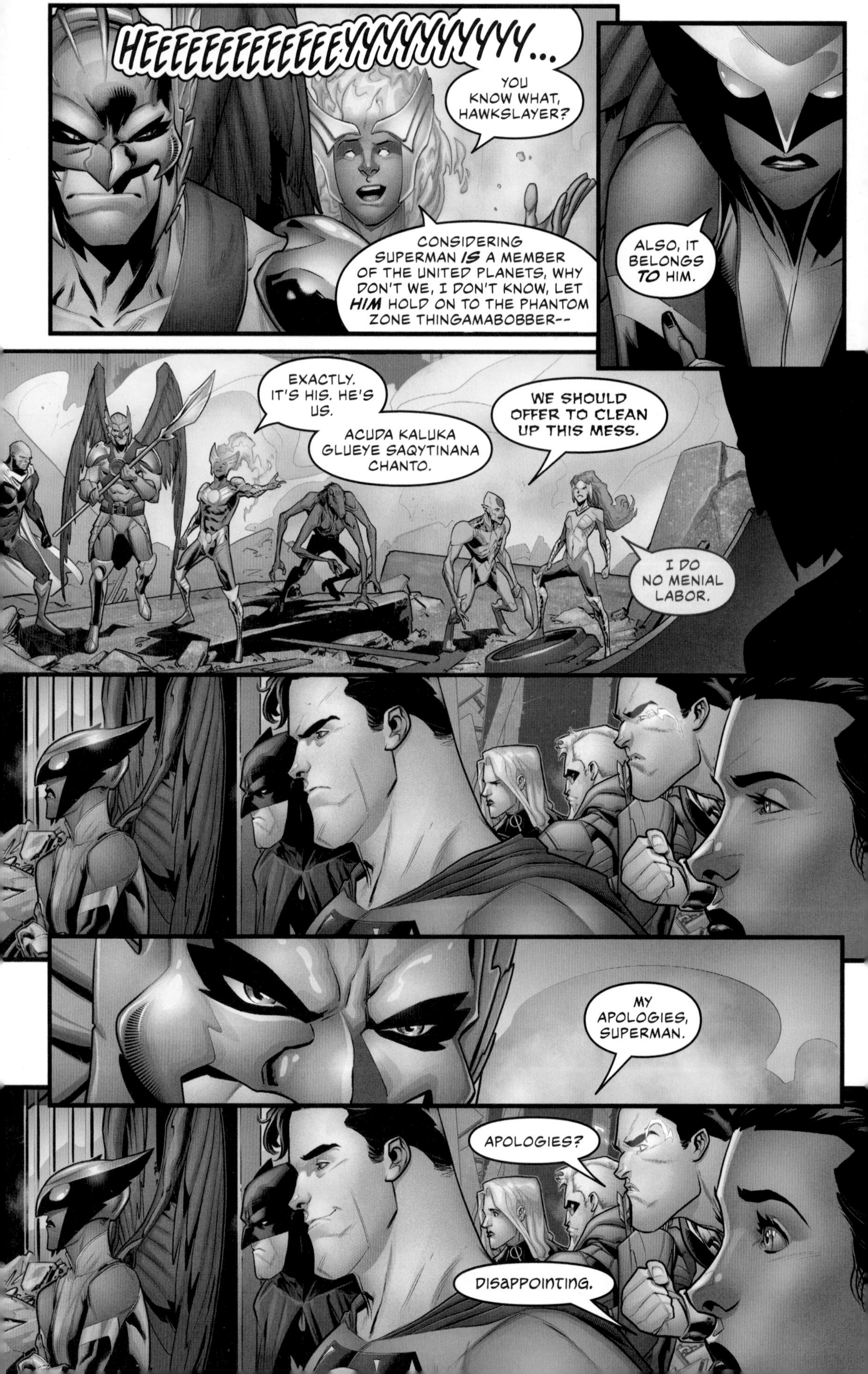
HEEEEEEEEEEEEEEYYYYYYYYYY...
YOU KNOW WHAT, HAWKSLAYER?
CONSIDERING SUPERMAN IS A MEMBER OF THE UNITED PLANETS, WHY DON'T WE, I DON'T KNOW, LET HIM HOLD ON TO THE PHANTOM ZONE THINGAMABOBBER--
ALSO, IT BELONGS TO HIM.
EXACTLY. IT'S HIS. HE'S US.
ACUDA KALUKA GLUEYE SAQYTINANA CHANTO.
WE SHOULD OFFER TO CLEAN UP THIS MESS.
I DO NO MENIAL LABOR.
MY APOLOGIES, SUPERMAN.
APOLOGIES?
DISAPPOINTING.

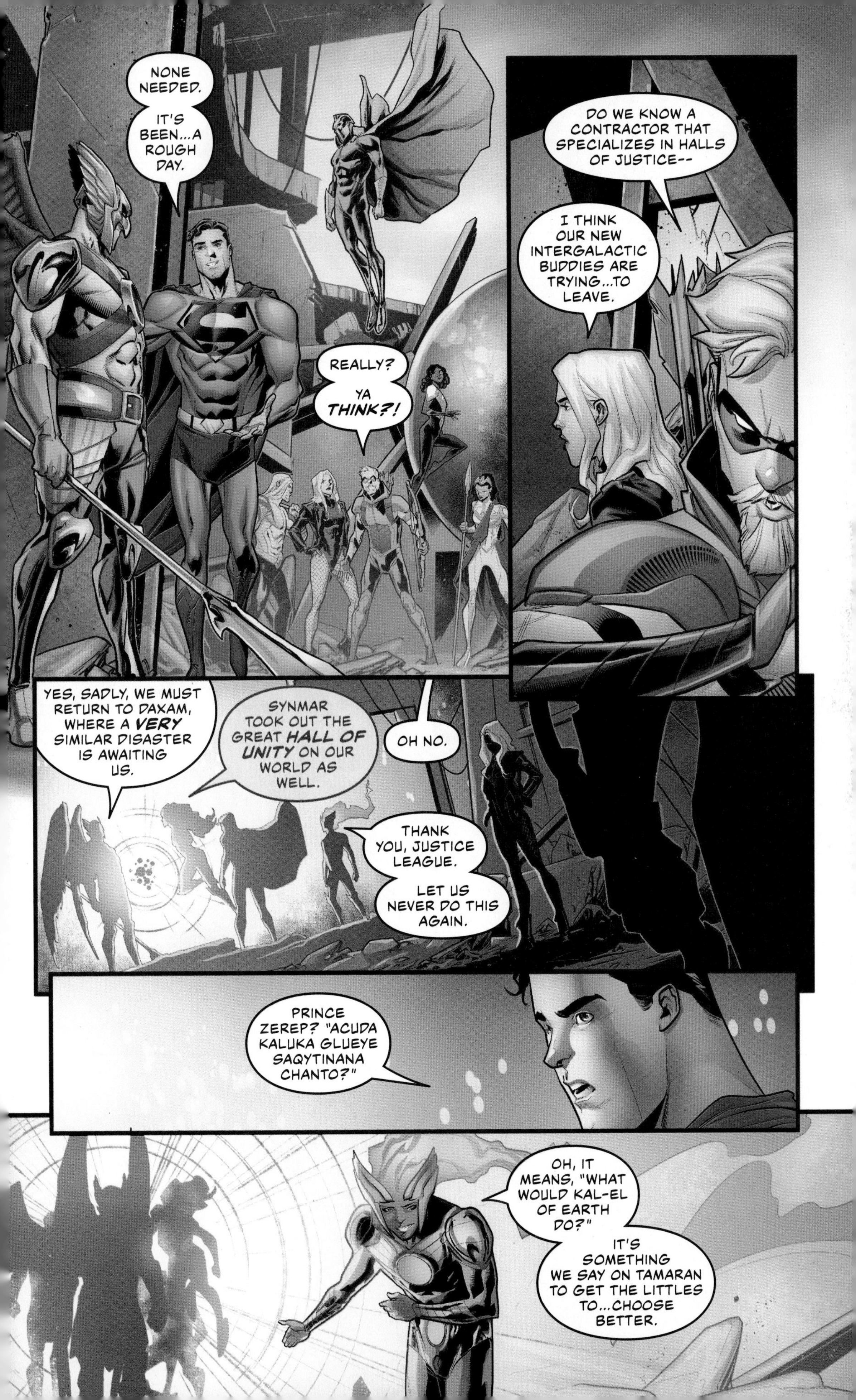

NONE NEEDED.
IT'S BEEN...A ROUGH DAY.
REALLY?
YA THINK?!
DO WE KNOW A CONTRACTOR THAT SPECIALIZES IN HALLS OF JUSTICE--
I THINK OUR NEW INTERGALACTIC BUDDIES ARE TRYING...TO LEAVE.
YES, SADLY, WE MUST RETURN TO DAXAM, WHERE A VERY SIMILAR DISASTER IS AWAITING US.
SYNMAR TOOK OUT THE GREAT HALL OF UNITY ON OUR WORLD AS WELL.
OH NO.
THANK YOU, JUSTICE LEAGUE.
LET US NEVER DO THIS AGAIN.
PRINCE ZEREP? "ACUDA KALUKA GLUEYE SAQYTINANA CHANTO?"
OH, IT MEANS, "WHAT WOULD KAL-EL OF EARTH DO?"
IT'S SOMETHING WE SAY ON TAMARAN TO GET THE LITTLES TO...CHOOSE BETTER.

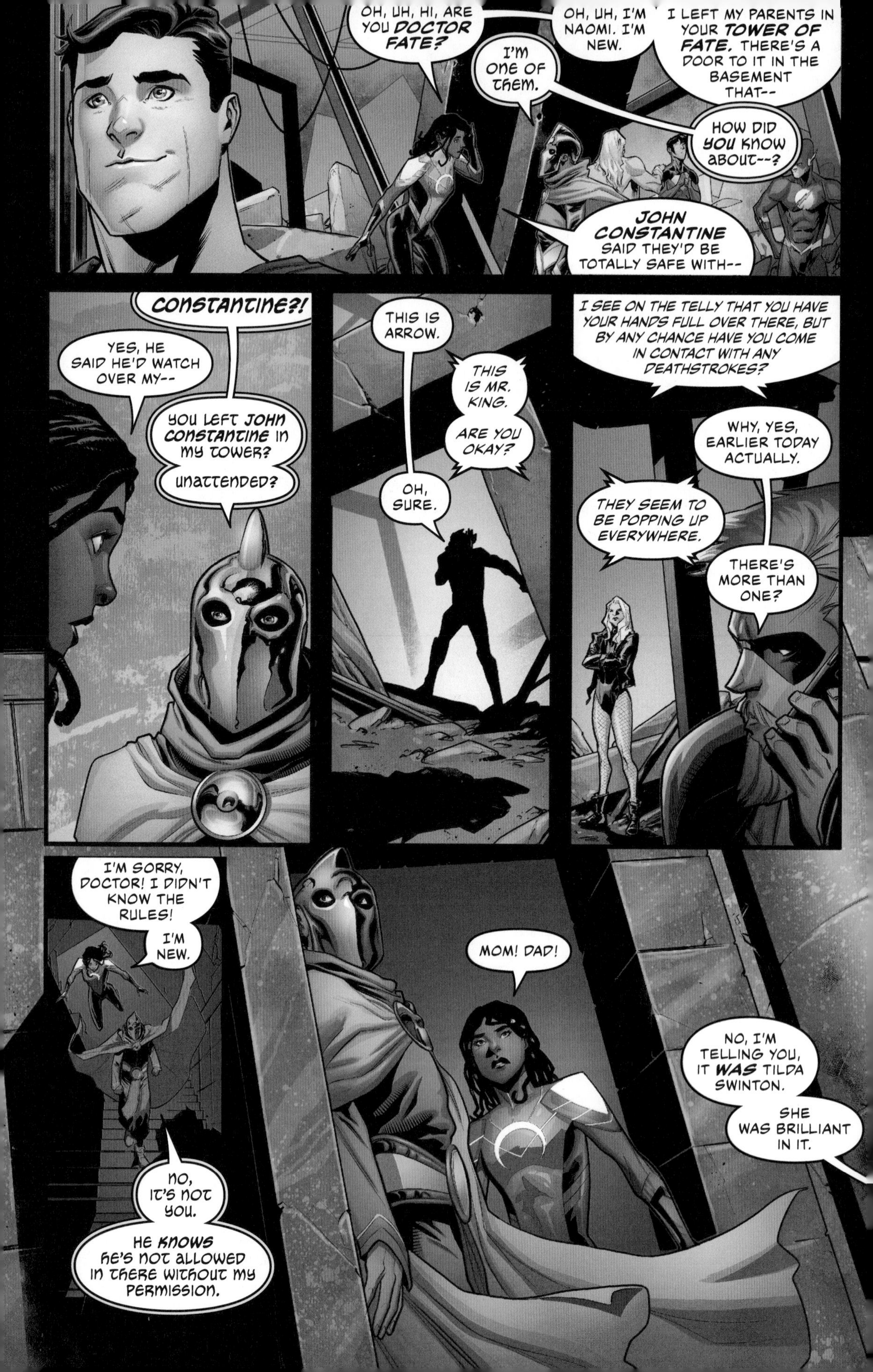
OH, UH, HI, ARE YOU DOCTOR FATE?
I'M ONE OF THEM.
OH, UH, I'M NAOMI. I'M NEW.
I LEFT MY PARENTS IN YOUR TOWER OF FATE. THERE'S A DOOR TO IT IN THE BASEMENT THAT--
HOW DID YOU KNOW ABOUT--?
JOHN CONSTANTINE SAID THEY'D BE TOTALLY SAFE WITH--
CONSTANTINE?!
YES, HE SAID HE'D WATCH OVER MY--
YOU LEFT JOHN CONSTANTINE IN MY TOWER?
UNATTENDED?
THIS IS ARROW.
THIS IS MR. KING.
ARE YOU OKAY?
OH, SURE.
I SEE ON THE TELLY THAT YOU HAVE YOUR HANDS FULL OVER THERE, BUT BY ANY CHANCE HAVE YOU COME IN CONTACT WITH ANY DEATHSTROKES?
WHY, YES, EARLIER TODAY ACTUALLY.
THEY SEEM TO BE POPPING UP EVERYWHERE.
THERE'S MORE THAN ONE?
I'M SORRY, DOCTOR! I DIDN'T KNOW THE RULES!
I'M NEW.
NO, IT'S NOT YOU.
HE KNOWS HE'S NOT ALLOWED IN THERE WITHOUT MY PERMISSION.
MOM! DAD!
NO, I'M TELLING YOU, IT WAS TILDA SWINTON.
SHE WAS BRILLIANT IN IT.

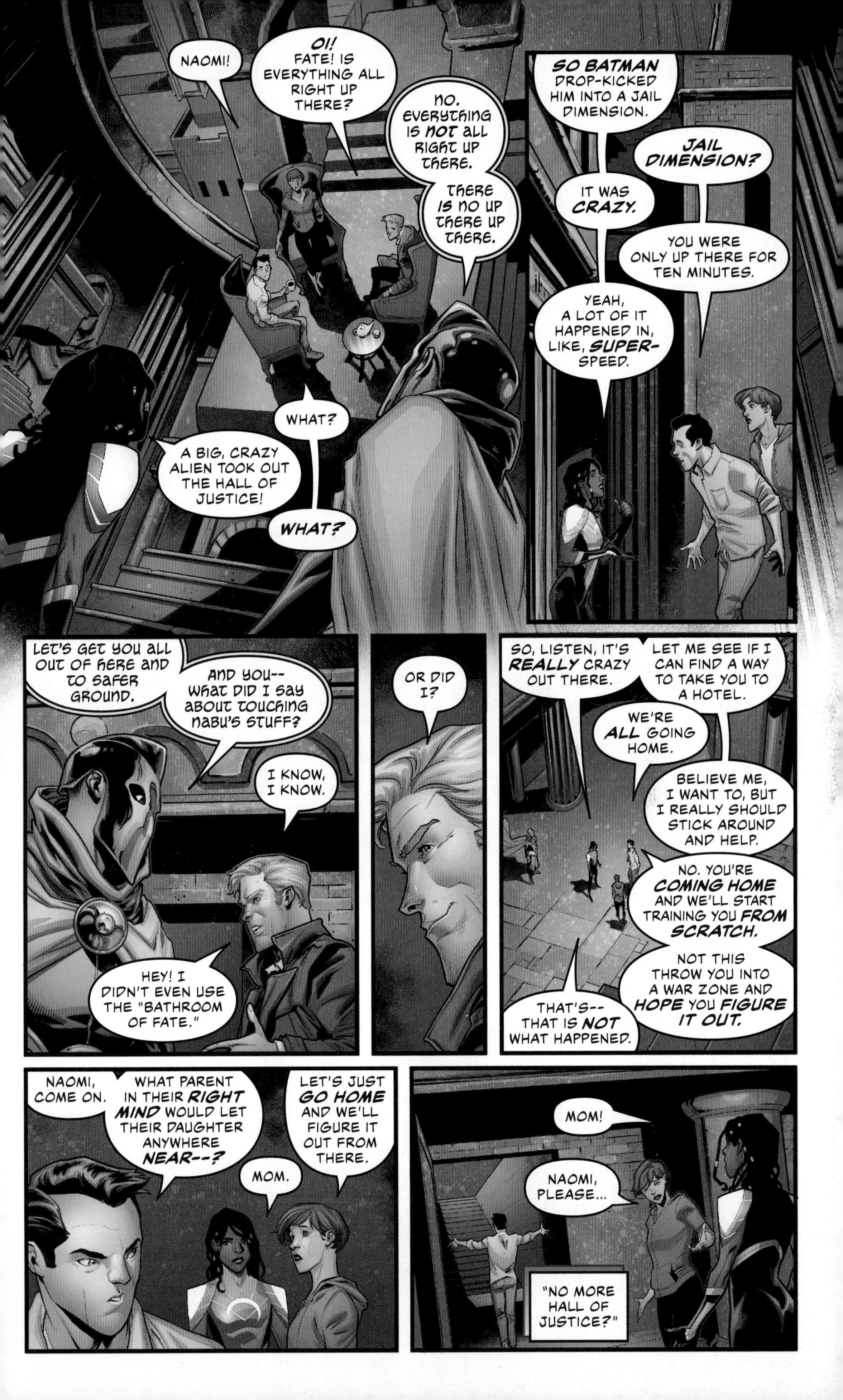
NAOMI!
OI! FATE! IS EVERYTHING ALL RIGHT UP THERE?
NO. EVERYTHING IS NOT ALL RIGHT UP THERE.
THERE IS NO UP THERE UP THERE.
WHAT?
A BIG, CRAZY ALIEN TOOK OUT THE HALL OF JUSTICE!
WHAT?
SO BATMAN DROP-KICKED HIM INTO A JAIL DIMENSION.
JAIL DIMENSION?
IT WAS CRAZY.
YOU WERE ONLY UP THERE FOR TEN MINUTES.
YEAH, A LOT OF IT HAPPENED IN, LIKE, SUPER-SPEED.
LET'S GET YOU ALL OUT OF HERE AND TO SAFER GROUND.
AND YOU-- WHAT DID I SAY ABOUT TOUCHING NABU'S STUFF?
I KNOW, I KNOW.
HEY! I DIDN'T EVEN USE THE "BATHROOM OF FATE."
OR DID I?
SO, LISTEN, IT'S REALLY CRAZY OUT THERE.
LET ME SEE IF I CAN FIND A WAY TO TAKE YOU TO A HOTEL.
WE'RE ALL GOING HOME.
BELIEVE ME, I WANT TO, BUT I REALLY SHOULD STICK AROUND AND HELP.
NO. YOU'RE COMING HOME AND WE'LL START TRAINING YOU FROM SCRATCH.
NOT THIS THROW YOU INTO A WAR ZONE AND HOPE YOU FIGURE IT OUT.
THAT'S-- THAT IS NOT WHAT HAPPENED.
NAOMI, COME ON.
WHAT PARENT IN THEIR RIGHT MIND WOULD LET THEIR DAUGHTER ANYWHERE NEAR--?
MOM.
LET'S JUST GO HOME AND WE'LL FIGURE IT OUT FROM THERE.
MOM!
NAOMI, PLEASE...
"NO MORE HALL OF JUSTICE?"

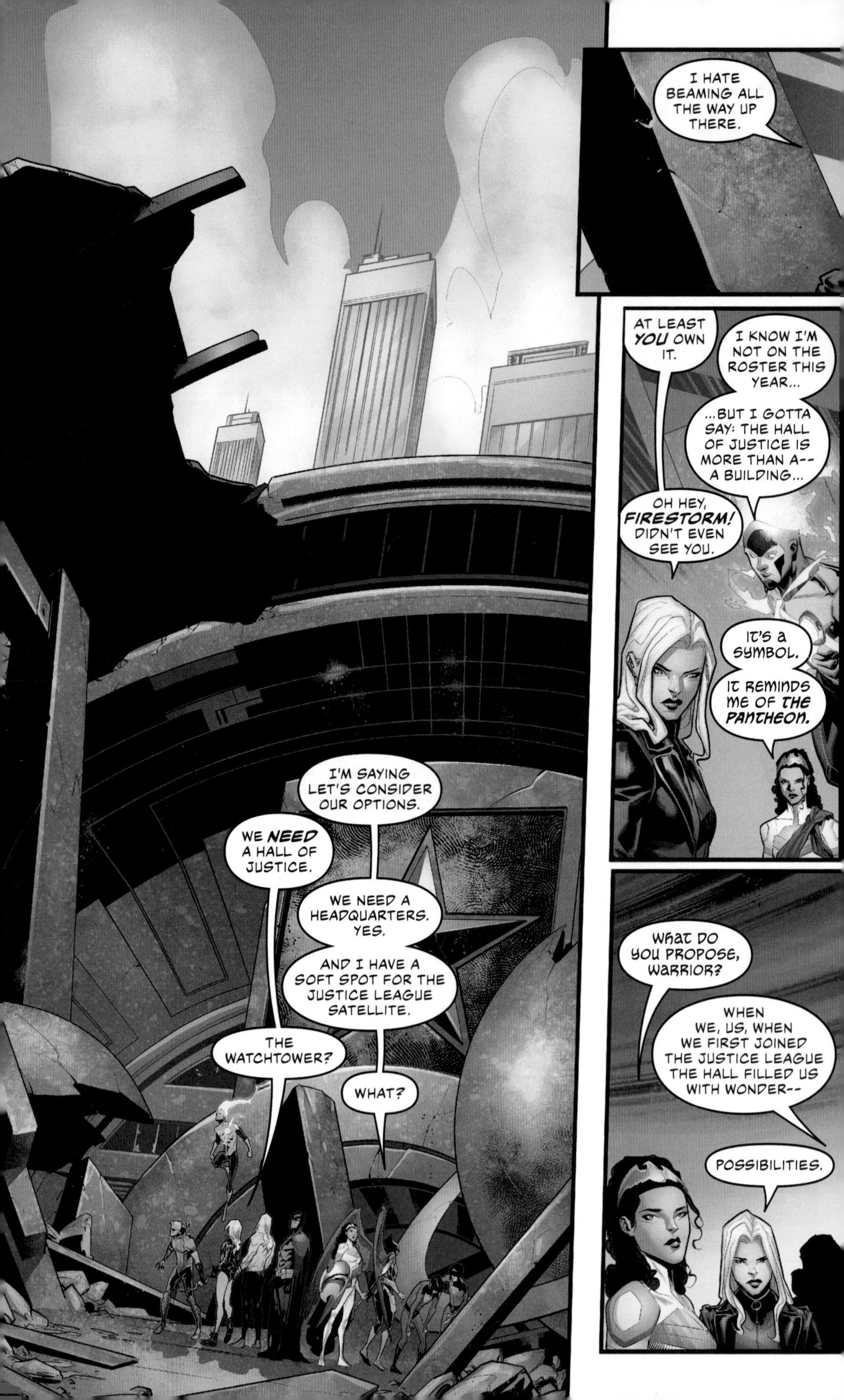

I HATE BEAMING ALL THE WAY UP THERE.
AT LEAST YOU OWN IT.
I KNOW I'M NOT ON THE ROSTER THIS YEAR...
...BUT I GOTTA SAY: THE HALL OF JUSTICE IS MORE THAN A-- A BUILDING...
OH HEY, FIRESTORM! DIDN'T EVEN SEE YOU.
IT'S A SYMBOL.
IT REMINDS ME OF THE PANTHEON.
WHAT DO YOU PROPOSE, WARRIOR?
WHEN WE, US, WHEN WE FIRST JOINED THE JUSTICE LEAGUE THE HALL FILLED US WITH WONDER--
POSSIBILITIES.
I'M SAYING LET'S CONSIDER OUR OPTIONS.
WE NEED A HALL OF JUSTICE.
WE NEED A HEADQUARTERS. YES.
AND I HAVE A SOFT SPOT FOR THE JUSTICE LEAGUE SATELLITE.
THE WATCHTOWER?
WHAT?

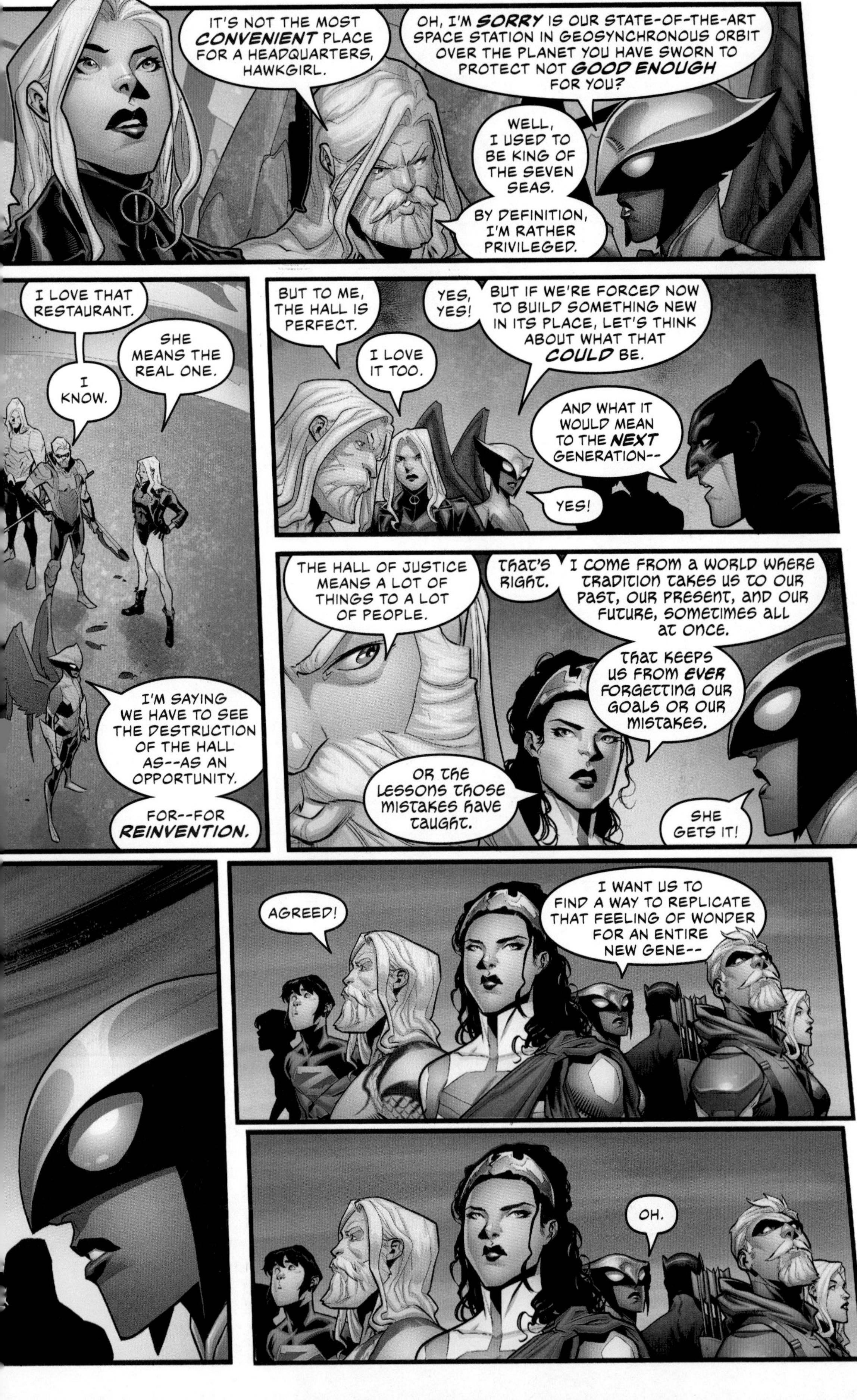
IT'S NOT THE MOST CONVENIENT PLACE FOR A HEADQUARTERS, HAWKGIRL.
OH, I'M SORRY IS OUR STATE-OF-THE-ART SPACE STATION IN GEOSYNCHRONOUS ORBIT OVER THE PLANET YOU HAVE SWORN TO PROTECT NOT GOOD ENOUGH FOR YOU?
WELL, I USED TO BE KING OF THE SEVEN SEAS.
BY DEFINITION, I'M RATHER PRIVILEGED.
I LOVE THAT RESTAURANT.
SHE MEANS THE REAL ONE.
I KNOW.
I'M SAYING WE HAVE TO SEE THE DESTRUCTION OF THE HALL AS--AS AN OPPORTUNITY.
FOR--FOR REINVENTION.
BUT TO ME, THE HALL IS PERFECT.
YES, YES!
BUT IF WE'RE FORCED NOW TO BUILD SOMETHING NEW IN ITS PLACE, LET'S THINK ABOUT WHAT THAT COULD BE.
I LOVE IT TOO.
AND WHAT IT WOULD MEAN TO THE NEXT GENERATION--
YES!
THE HALL OF JUSTICE MEANS A LOT OF THINGS TO A LOT OF PEOPLE.
THAT'S RIGHT.
I COME FROM A WORLD WHERE TRADITION TAKES US TO OUR PAST, OUR PRESENT, AND OUR FUTURE, SOMETIMES ALL AT ONCE.
THAT KEEPS US FROM EVER FORGETTING OUR GOALS OR OUR MISTAKES.
OR THE LESSONS THOSE MISTAKES HAVE TAUGHT.
SHE GETS IT!
AGREED!
I WANT US TO FIND A WAY TO REPLICATE THAT FEELING OF WONDER FOR AN ENTIRE NEW GENE--
OH.

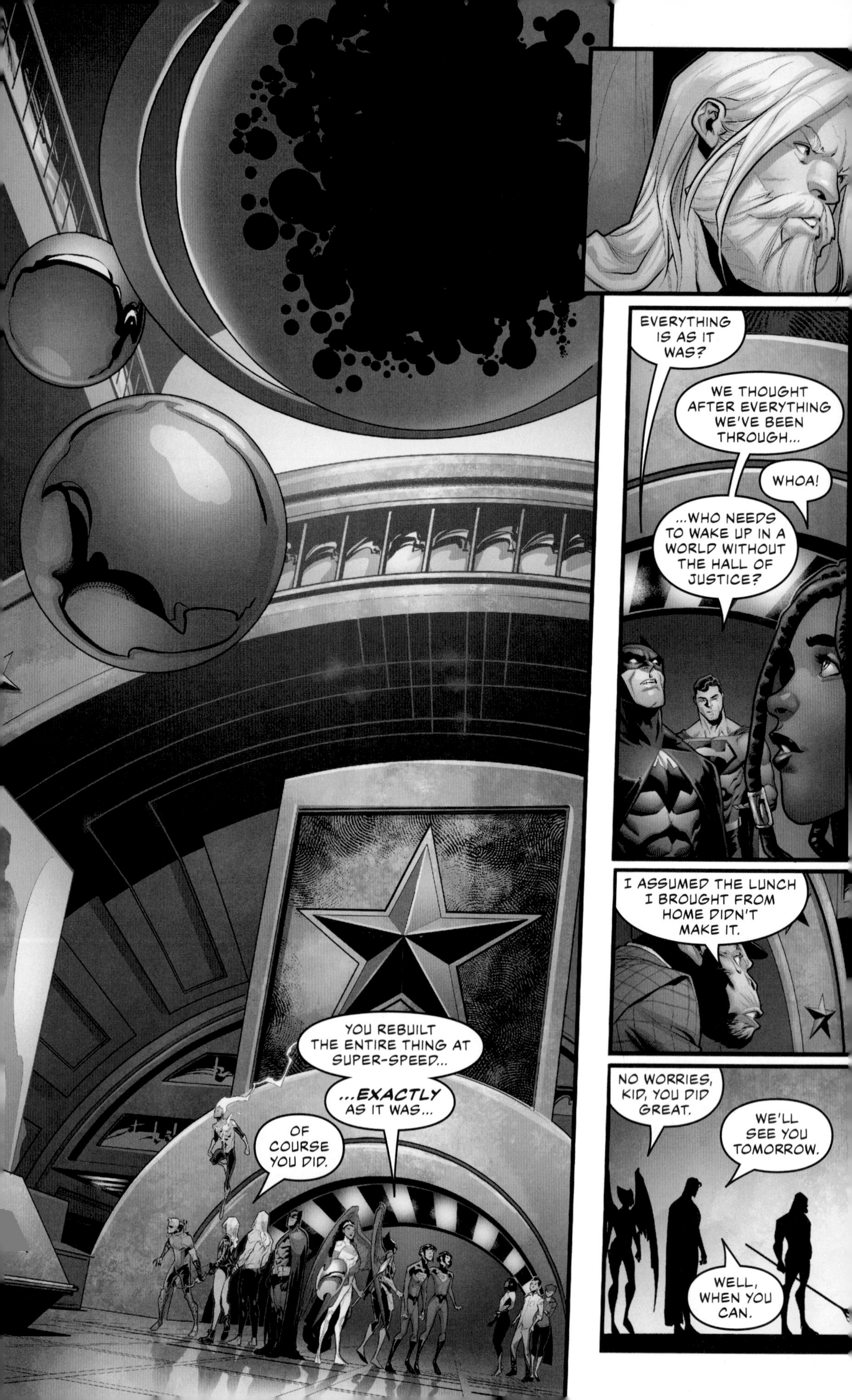
EVERYTHING IS AS IT WAS?
WE THOUGHT AFTER EVERYTHING WE'VE BEEN THROUGH...
WHOA!
...WHO NEEDS TO WAKE UP IN A WORLD WITHOUT THE HALL OF JUSTICE?
YOU REBUILT THE ENTIRE THING AT SUPER-SPEED...
...*EXACTLY* AS IT WAS...
OF COURSE YOU DID.
I ASSUMED THE LUNCH I BROUGHT FROM HOME DIDN'T MAKE IT.
NO WORRIES, KID, YOU DID GREAT.
WE'LL SEE YOU TOMORROW.
WELL, WHEN YOU CAN.

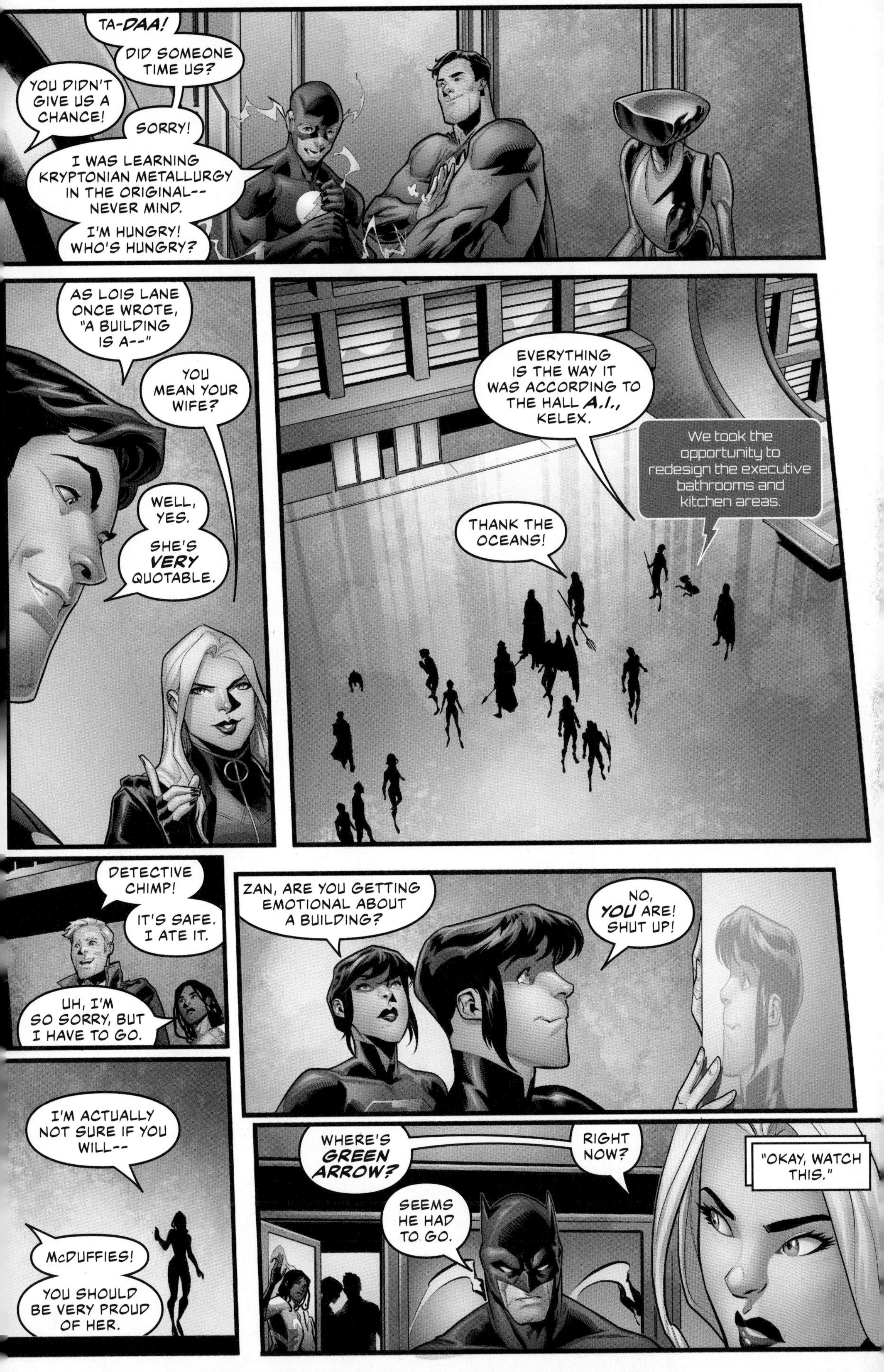
TA-DAA!
DID SOMEONE TIME US?
YOU DIDN'T GIVE US A CHANCE!
SORRY!
I WAS LEARNING KRYPTONIAN METALLURGY IN THE ORIGINAL-- NEVER MIND.
I'M HUNGRY! WHO'S HUNGRY?
AS LOIS LANE ONCE WROTE, "A BUILDING IS A--"
YOU MEAN YOUR WIFE?
WELL, YES.
SHE'S VERY QUOTABLE.
EVERYTHING IS THE WAY IT WAS ACCORDING TO THE HALL A.I., KELEX.
We took the opportunity to redesign the executive bathrooms and kitchen areas.
THANK THE OCEANS!
DETECTIVE CHIMP!
IT'S SAFE. I ATE IT.
UH, I'M SO SORRY, BUT I HAVE TO GO.
ZAN, ARE YOU GETTING EMOTIONAL ABOUT A BUILDING?
NO, YOU ARE! SHUT UP!
I'M ACTUALLY NOT SURE IF YOU WILL--
McDUFFIES!
YOU SHOULD BE VERY PROUD OF HER.
WHERE'S GREEN ARROW?
RIGHT NOW?
SEEMS HE HAD TO GO.
"OKAY, WATCH THIS."

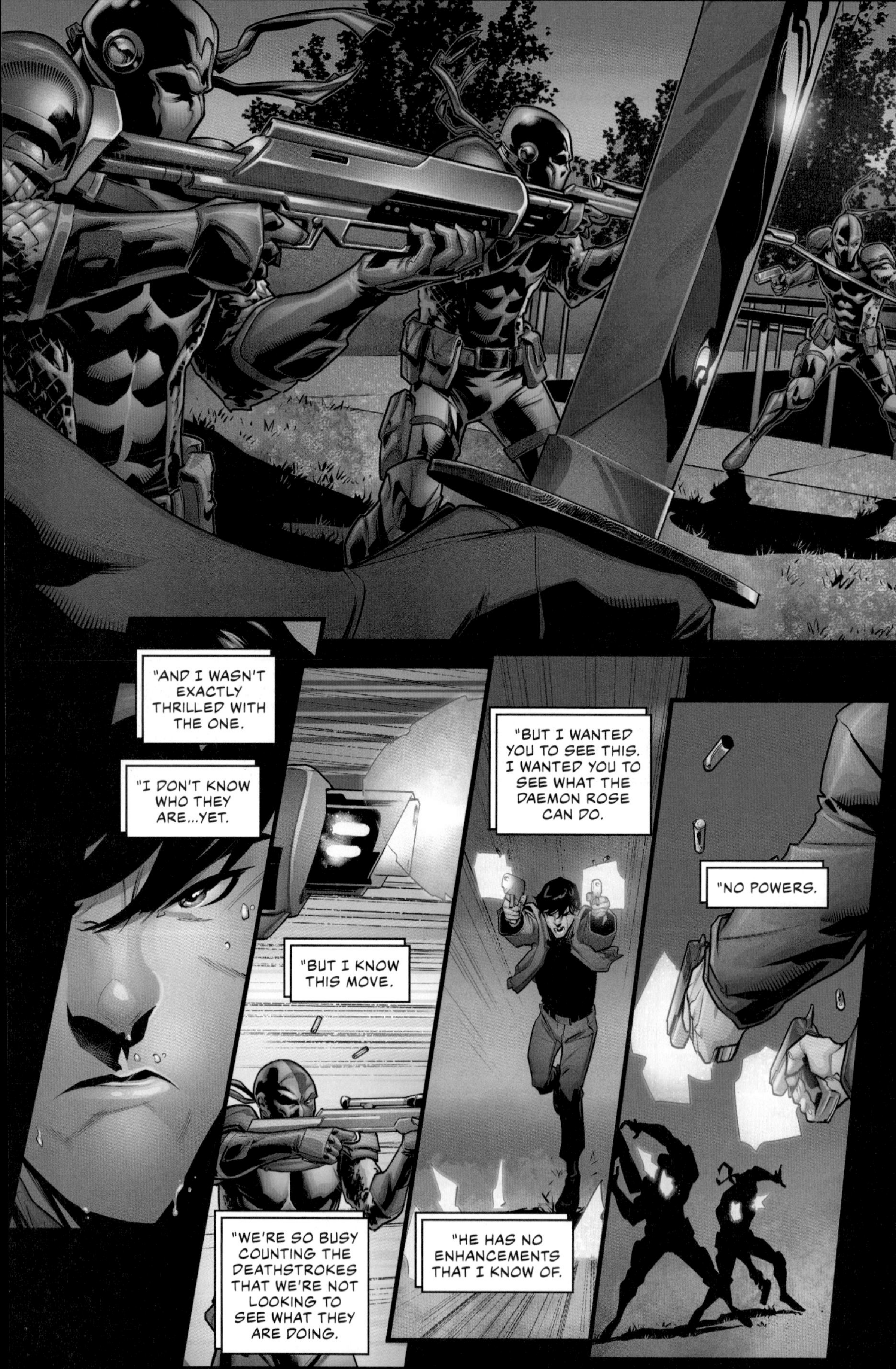
"AND I WASN'T EXACTLY THRILLED WITH THE ONE.
"I DON'T KNOW WHO THEY ARE...YET.
"BUT I KNOW THIS MOVE.
"WE'RE SO BUSY COUNTING THE DEATHSTROKES THAT WE'RE NOT LOOKING TO SEE WHAT THEY ARE DOING.
"BUT I WANTED YOU TO SEE THIS. I WANTED YOU TO SEE WHAT THE DAEMON ROSE CAN DO.
"HE HAS NO ENHANCEMENTS THAT I KNOW OF.
"NO POWERS.

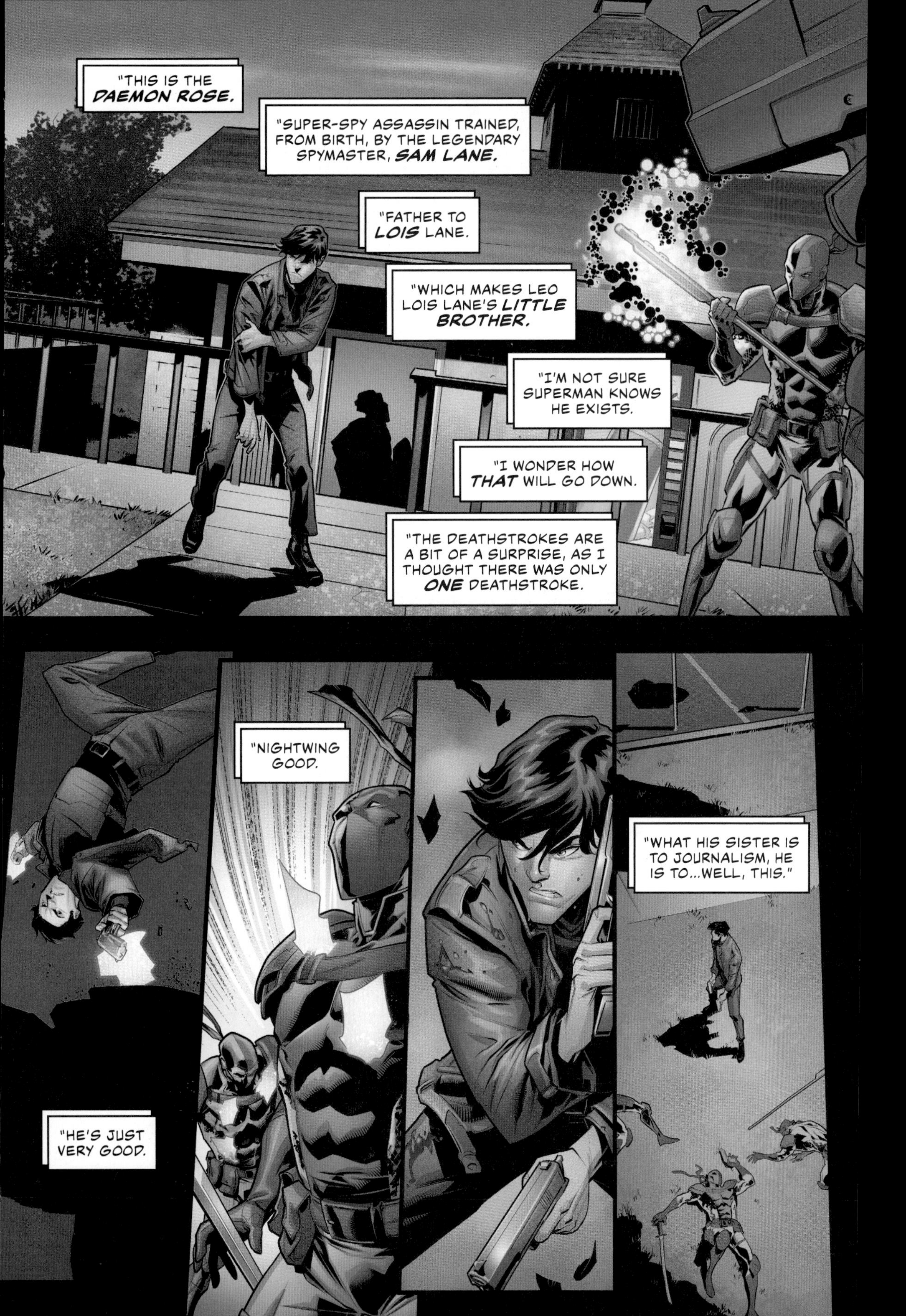
"THIS IS THE DAEMON ROSE.
"SUPER-SPY ASSASSIN TRAINED, FROM BIRTH, BY THE LEGENDARY SPYMASTER, SAM LANE.
"FATHER TO LOIS LANE.
"WHICH MAKES LEO LOIS LANE'S LITTLE BROTHER.
"I'M NOT SURE SUPERMAN KNOWS HE EXISTS.
"I WONDER HOW THAT WILL GO DOWN.
"THE DEATHSTROKES ARE A BIT OF A SURPRISE, AS I THOUGHT THERE WAS ONLY ONE DEATHSTROKE.
"NIGHTWING GOOD.
"HE'S JUST VERY GOOD.
"WHAT HIS SISTER IS TO JOURNALISM, HE IS TO...WELL, THIS."

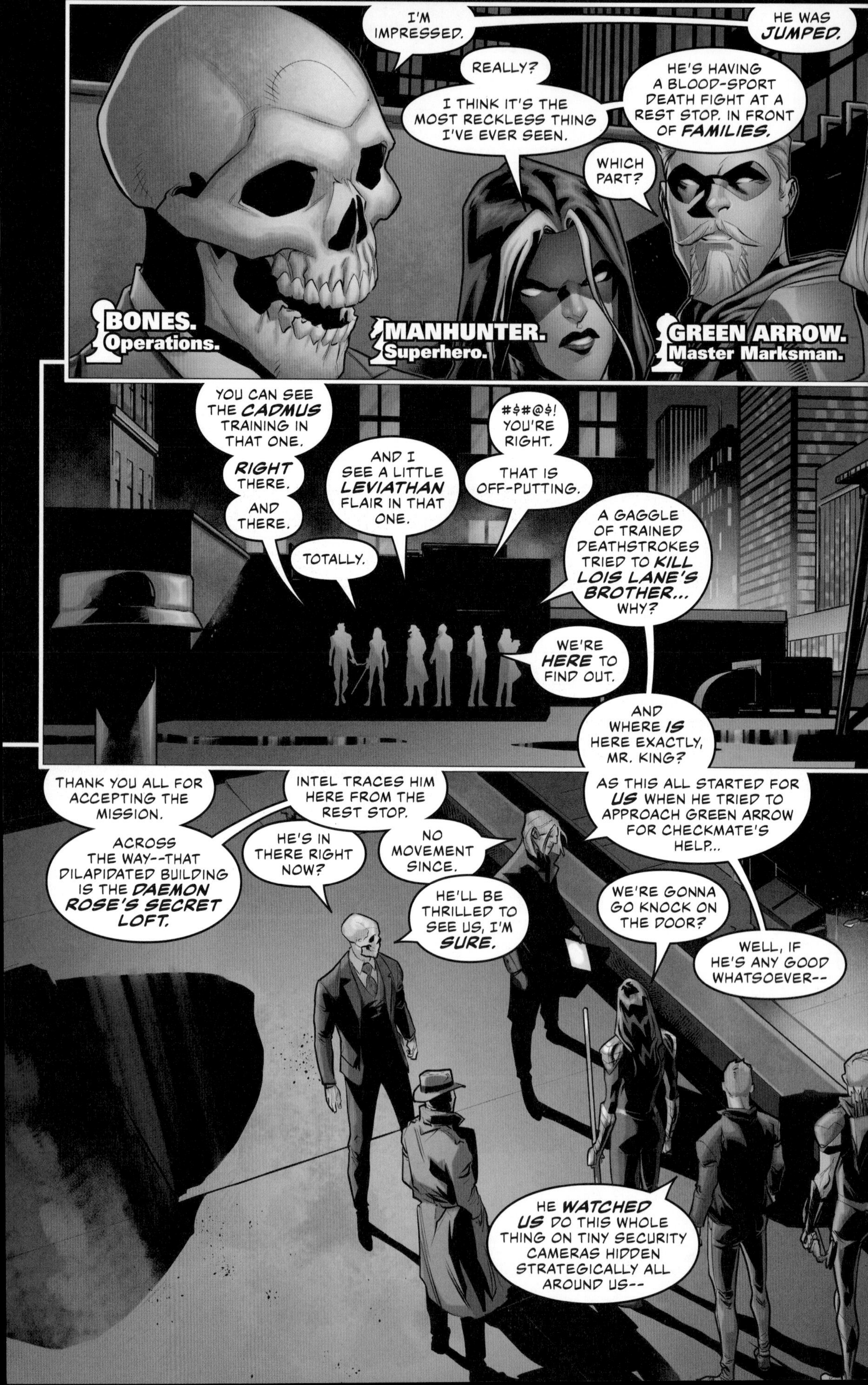
I'M IMPRESSED.
HE WAS JUMPED.
REALLY?
I THINK IT'S THE MOST RECKLESS THING I'VE EVER SEEN.
HE'S HAVING A BLOOD-SPORT DEATH FIGHT AT A REST STOP. IN FRONT OF FAMILIES.
WHICH PART?
BONES. Operations.
MANHUNTER. Superhero.
GREEN ARROW. Master Marksman.
YOU CAN SEE THE CADMUS TRAINING IN THAT ONE.
RIGHT THERE.
AND THERE.
TOTALLY.
AND I SEE A LITTLE LEVIATHAN FLAIR IN THAT ONE.
#$#@$! YOU'RE RIGHT.
THAT IS OFF-PUTTING.
A GAGGLE OF TRAINED DEATHSTROKES TRIED TO KILL LOIS LANE'S BROTHER... WHY?
WE'RE HERE TO FIND OUT.
AND WHERE IS HERE EXACTLY, MR. KING?
THANK YOU ALL FOR ACCEPTING THE MISSION.
ACROSS THE WAY--THAT DILAPIDATED BUILDING IS THE DAEMON ROSE'S SECRET LOFT.
INTEL TRACES HIM HERE FROM THE REST STOP.
HE'S IN THERE RIGHT NOW?
NO MOVEMENT SINCE.
HE'LL BE THRILLED TO SEE US, I'M SURE.
AS THIS ALL STARTED FOR US WHEN HE TRIED TO APPROACH GREEN ARROW FOR CHECKMATE'S HELP...
WE'RE GONNA GO KNOCK ON THE DOOR?
WELL, IF HE'S ANY GOOD WHATSOEVER--
HE WATCHED US DO THIS WHOLE THING ON TINY SECURITY CAMERAS HIDDEN STRATEGICALLY ALL AROUND US--

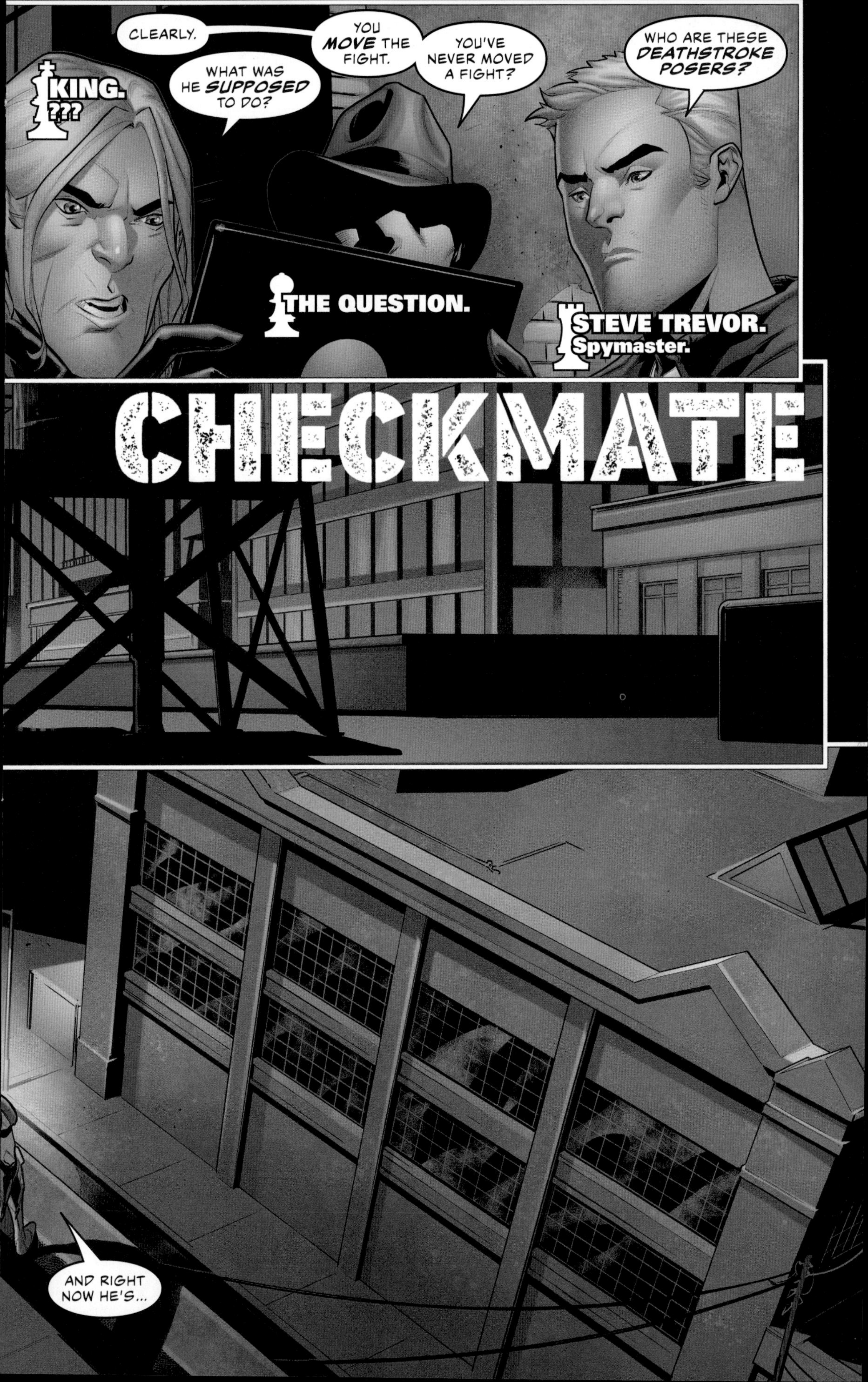
CLEARLY.
WHAT WAS HE SUPPOSED TO DO?
YOU MOVE THE FIGHT.
YOU'VE NEVER MOVED A FIGHT?
WHO ARE THESE DEATHSTROKE POSERS?
KING. ???
THE QUESTION.
STEVE TREVOR. Spymaster.
CHECKMATE
AND RIGHT NOW HE'S...

...RIGHT BEHIND US.

OH HEY, KID.

HEY... "POPS."

HOW'D YOU FIND ME HERE?

I THOUGHT I CLOAKED MYSELF FROM SATELLITE TRACE.

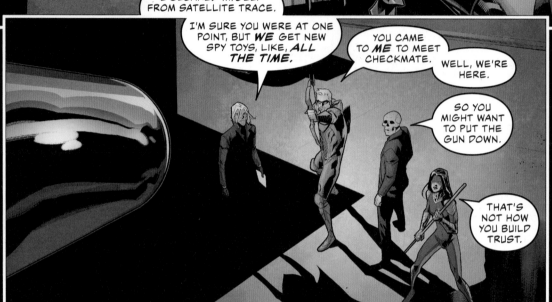

I'M SURE YOU WERE AT ONE POINT, BUT WE GET NEW SPY TOYS, LIKE, ALL THE TIME.

YOU CAME TO ME TO MEET CHECKMATE.

WELL, WE'RE HERE.

SO YOU MIGHT WANT TO PUT THE GUN DOWN.

THAT'S NOT HOW YOU BUILD TRUST.

I'M NOT TRYING TO "BUILD TRUST."

I'M TRYING TO STAY ALIVE LONG ENOUGH TO GET CHECKMATE TO HELP ME SHUT DOWN THIS NEW @#$@#$.

A NETWORK OF DEATHSTROKES IS THE NEW $@#$$?

YEAH, THAT'S PRETTY MUCH A NORMAL THURSDAY IN GOTHAM CITY.

WHY ARE THEY TRYING TO KILL YOU?

WHO ARE THEY?

THEY'RE TRYING TO KILL ME BECAUSE, WELL, THEY CAN'T HAVE ME.

I WON'T KILL THE JUSTICE LEAGUE.

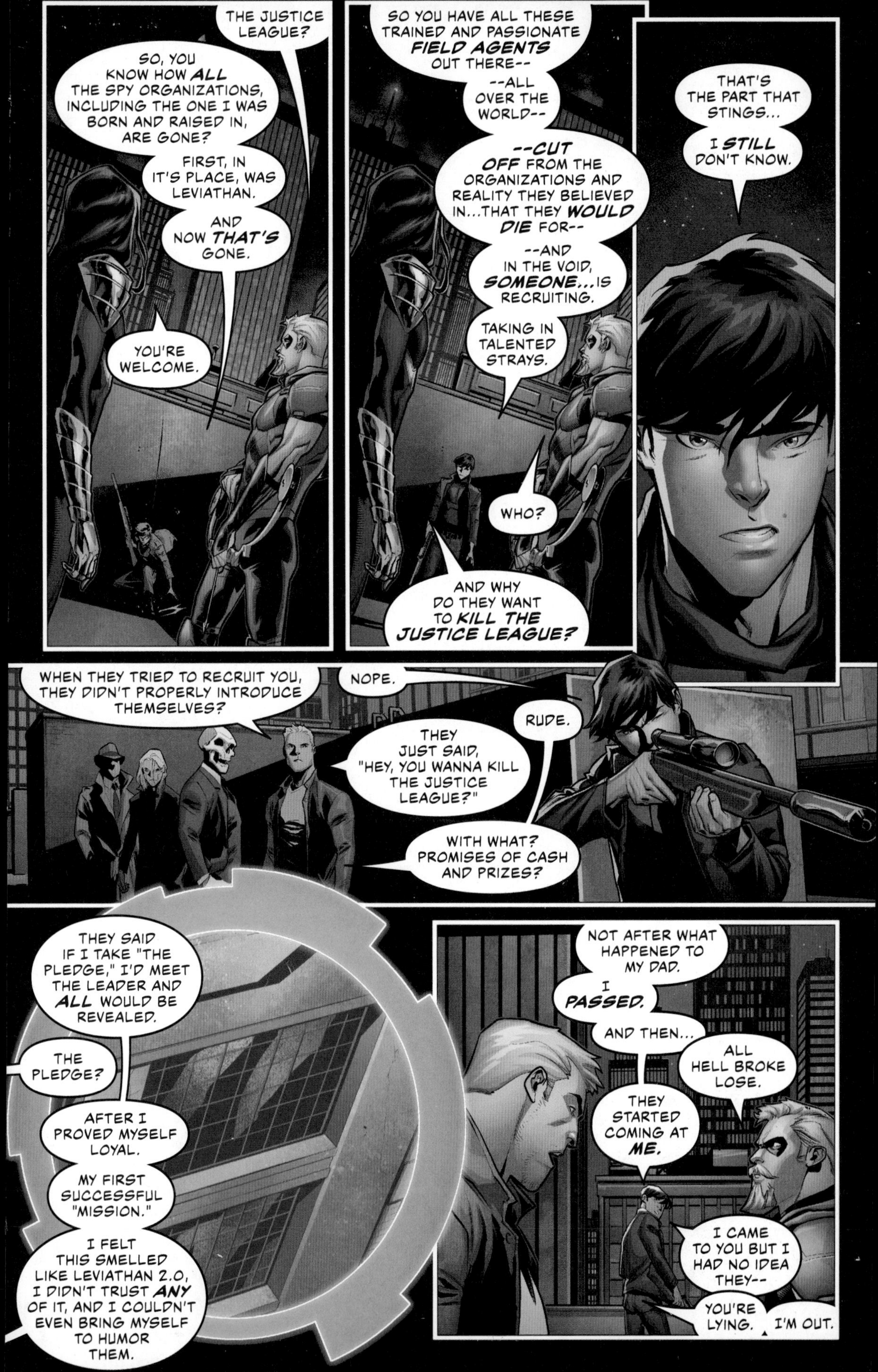
THE JUSTICE LEAGUE?
SO, YOU KNOW HOW ALL THE SPY ORGANIZATIONS, INCLUDING THE ONE I WAS BORN AND RAISED IN, ARE GONE?
FIRST, IN IT'S PLACE, WAS LEVIATHAN.
AND NOW THAT'S GONE.
YOU'RE WELCOME.
SO YOU HAVE ALL THESE TRAINED AND PASSIONATE FIELD AGENTS OUT THERE--
--ALL OVER THE WORLD--
--CUT OFF FROM THE ORGANIZATIONS AND REALITY THEY BELIEVED IN...THAT THEY WOULD DIE FOR--
--AND IN THE VOID, SOMEONE...IS RECRUITING.
TAKING IN TALENTED STRAYS.
WHO?
AND WHY DO THEY WANT TO KILL THE JUSTICE LEAGUE?
THAT'S THE PART THAT STINGS...
I STILL DON'T KNOW.
WHEN THEY TRIED TO RECRUIT YOU, THEY DIDN'T PROPERLY INTRODUCE THEMSELVES?
NOPE.
RUDE.
THEY JUST SAID, "HEY, YOU WANNA KILL THE JUSTICE LEAGUE?"
WITH WHAT? PROMISES OF CASH AND PRIZES?
THEY SAID IF I TAKE "THE PLEDGE," I'D MEET THE LEADER AND ALL WOULD BE REVEALED.
THE PLEDGE?
AFTER I PROVED MYSELF LOYAL.
MY FIRST SUCCESSFUL "MISSION."
I FELT THIS SMELLED LIKE LEVIATHAN 2.0, I DIDN'T TRUST ANY OF IT, AND I COULDN'T EVEN BRING MYSELF TO HUMOR THEM.
NOT AFTER WHAT HAPPENED TO MY DAD.
I PASSED.
AND THEN...
ALL HELL BROKE LOSE.
THEY STARTED COMING AT ME.
I CAME TO YOU BUT I HAD NO IDEA THEY--
YOU'RE LYING.
I'M OUT.

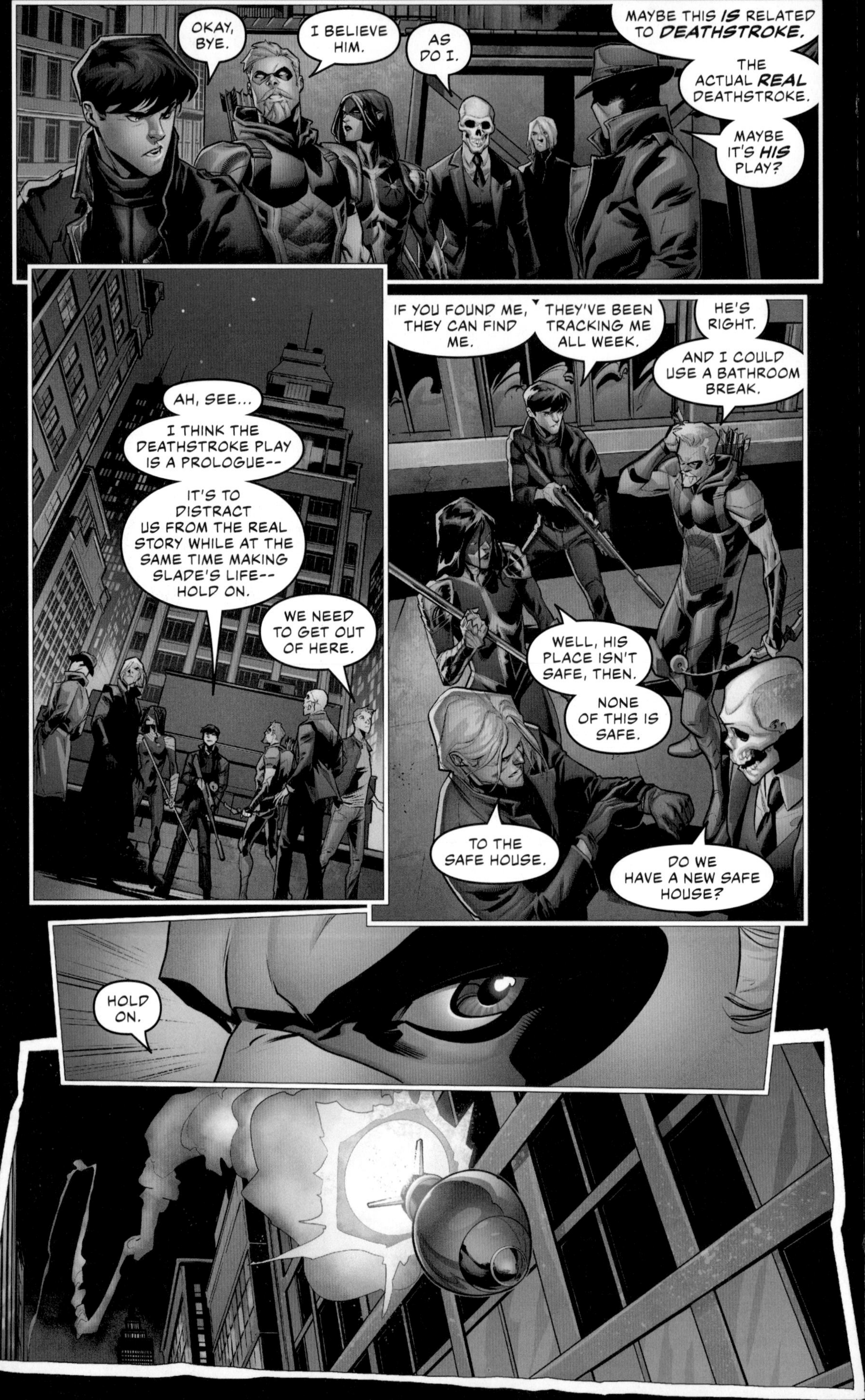
OKAY, BYE.
I BELIEVE HIM.
AS DO I.
MAYBE THIS IS RELATED TO DEATHSTROKE.
THE ACTUAL REAL DEATHSTROKE.
MAYBE IT'S HIS PLAY?
AH, SEE...
I THINK THE DEATHSTROKE PLAY IS A PROLOGUE--
IT'S TO DISTRACT US FROM THE REAL STORY WHILE AT THE SAME TIME MAKING SLADE'S LIFE-- HOLD ON.
WE NEED TO GET OUT OF HERE.
IF YOU FOUND ME, THEY CAN FIND ME.
THEY'VE BEEN TRACKING ME ALL WEEK.
HE'S RIGHT.
AND I COULD USE A BATHROOM BREAK.
WELL, HIS PLACE ISN'T SAFE, THEN.
NONE OF THIS IS SAFE.
TO THE SAFE HOUSE.
DO WE HAVE A NEW SAFE HOUSE?
HOLD ON.

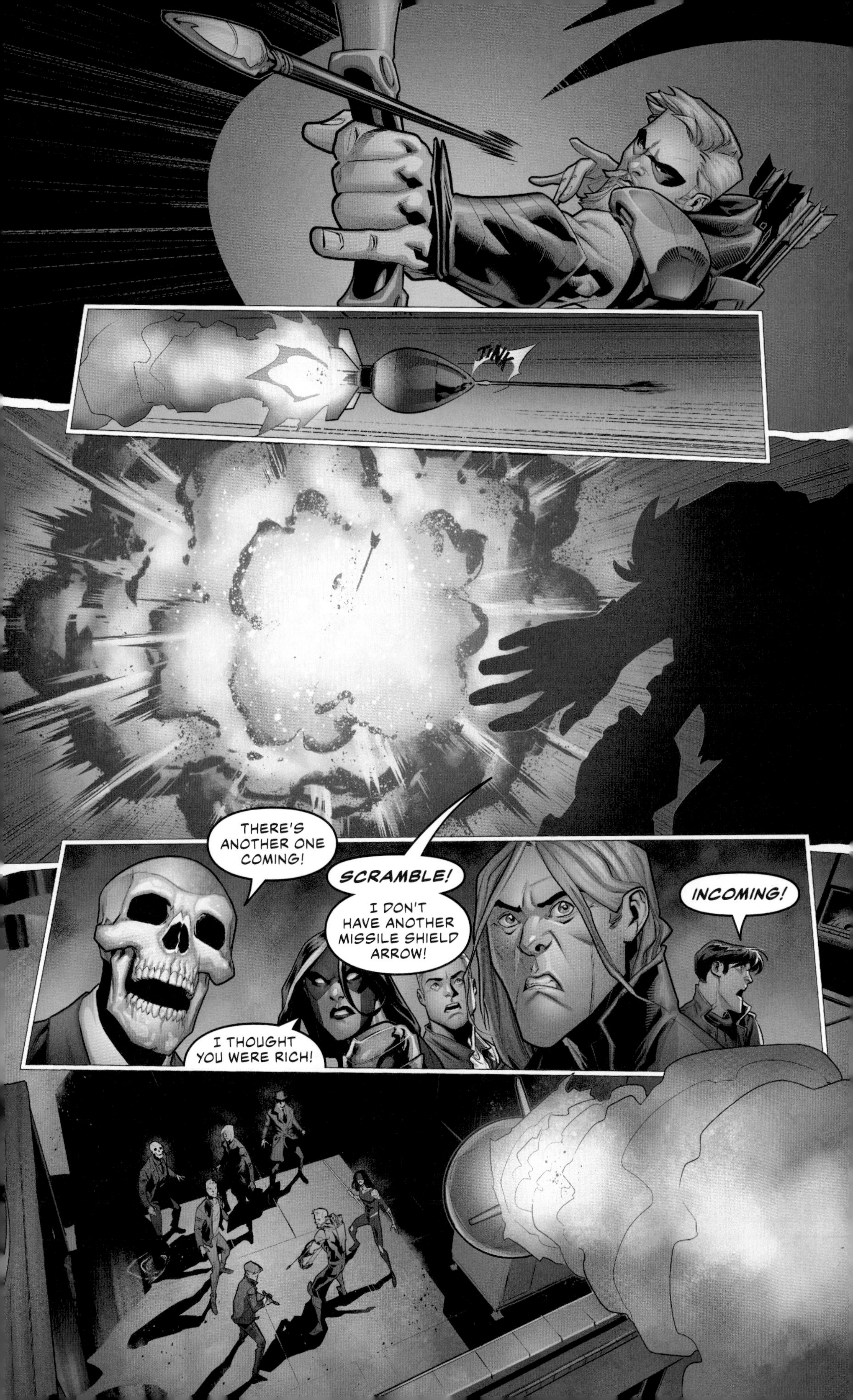
TINK
THERE'S ANOTHER ONE COMING!
SCRAMBLE!
I DON'T HAVE ANOTHER MISSILE SHIELD ARROW!
INCOMING!
I THOUGHT YOU WERE RICH!

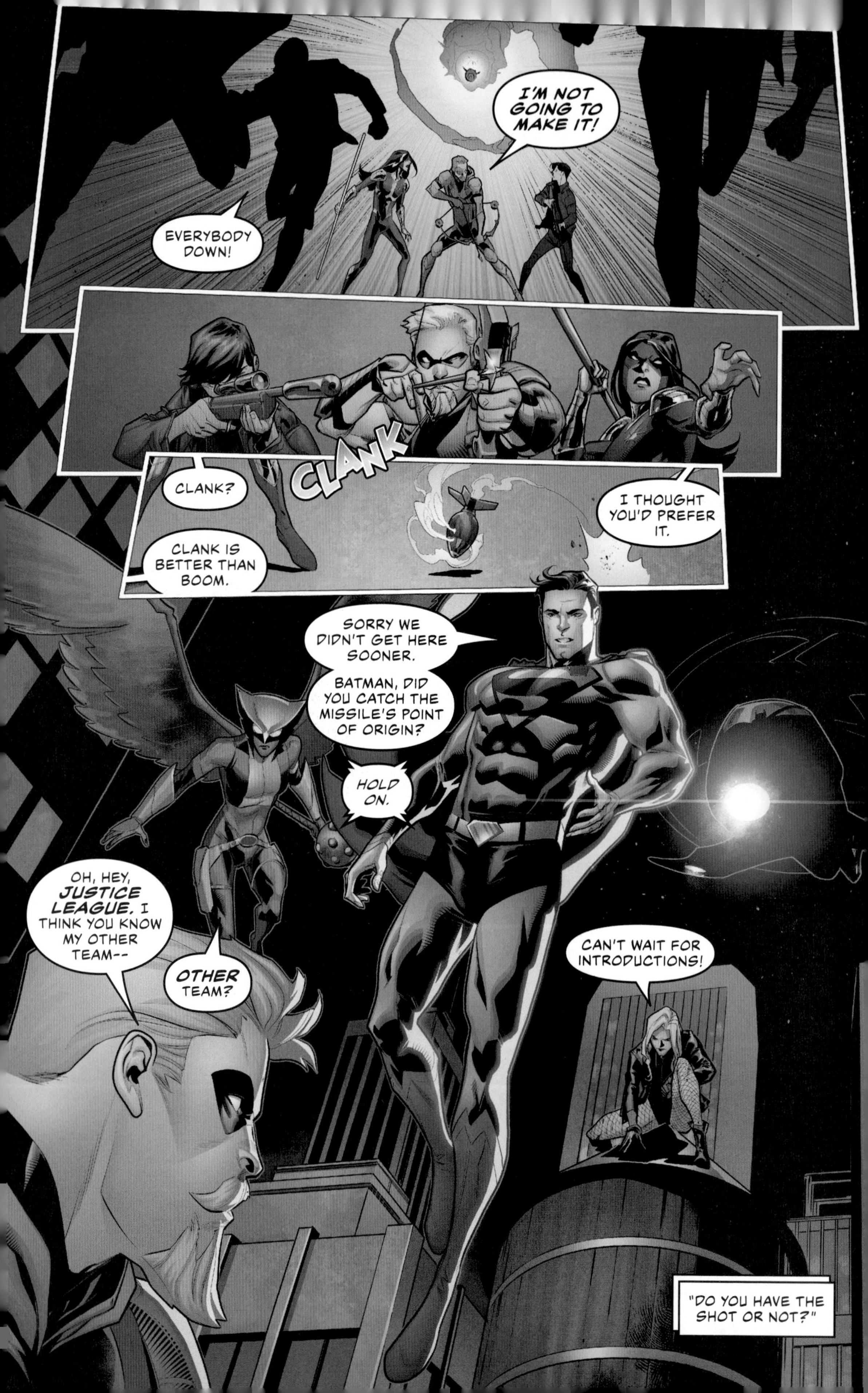
I'M NOT GOING TO MAKE IT!
EVERYBODY DOWN!
CLANK
CLANK?
CLANK IS BETTER THAN BOOM.
I THOUGHT YOU'D PREFER IT.
SORRY WE DIDN'T GET HERE SOONER.
BATMAN, DID YOU CATCH THE MISSILE'S POINT OF ORIGIN?
HOLD ON.
OH, HEY, JUSTICE LEAGUE. I THINK YOU KNOW MY OTHER TEAM--
OTHER TEAM?
CAN'T WAIT FOR INTRODUCTIONS!
"DO YOU HAVE THE SHOT OR NOT?"

I GOT IT.
ARE THE TARGETS DOWN?
SOMETHING WRONG.
HOLD ON.
WHO ELSE IS OUT THERE?
WHAT?
THERE'S A GUY WITH A SKULL HEAD, A GUY WITH A RATHER NICE HAT AND NO FACE.
THERE'S A ROBIN HOOD--HEY!
WHAT ARE YOU EVEN TALKING ABOUT?
ON THE ROOF.
LET ME SEE.
STOP IT.
THEY CAN'T SEE US.
LET ME SEE!
I DON'T SEE *ANYTHING.*
HERE!
YOU DON'T SEE A GAGGLE OF SUPER-WEIRDOS ON THE ROOF FIVE BLOCKS THAT--
NO.
YOU DON'T SEE--
ALL I *SEE* IS A BLURRY *SUPERMAN* LOGO THAT-- OH.
UH-OH.

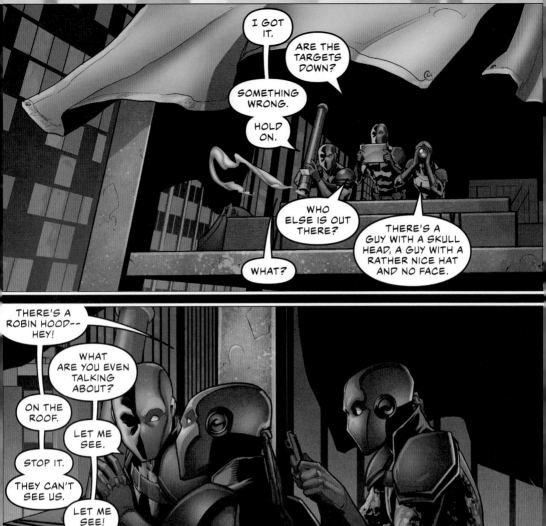

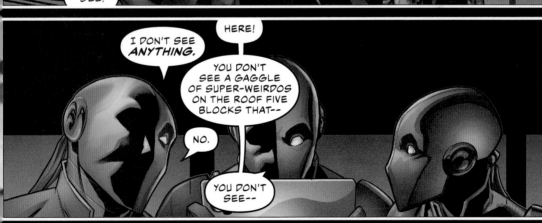

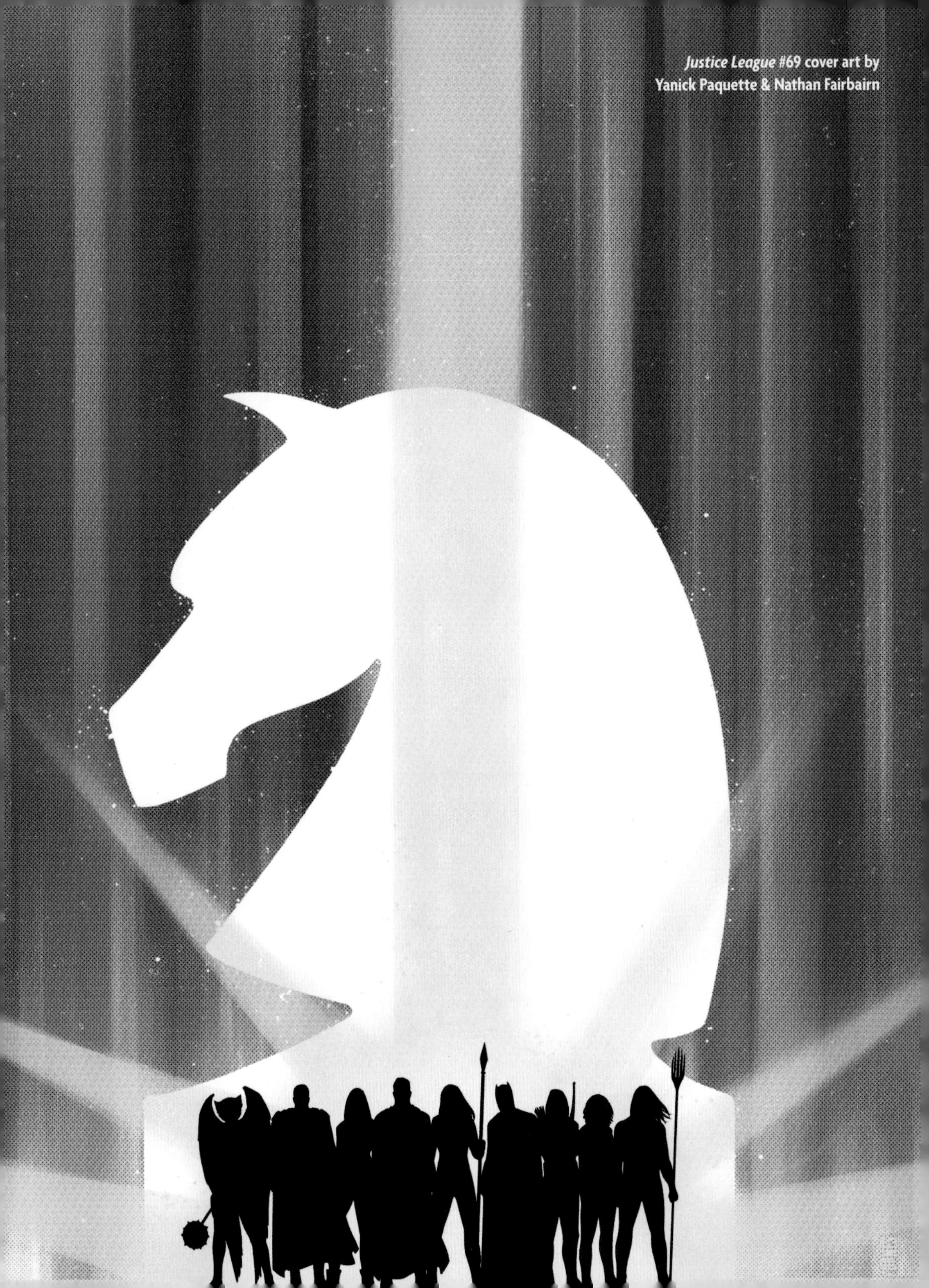

Justice League #69 cover art by
Yanick Paquette & Nathan Fairbairn

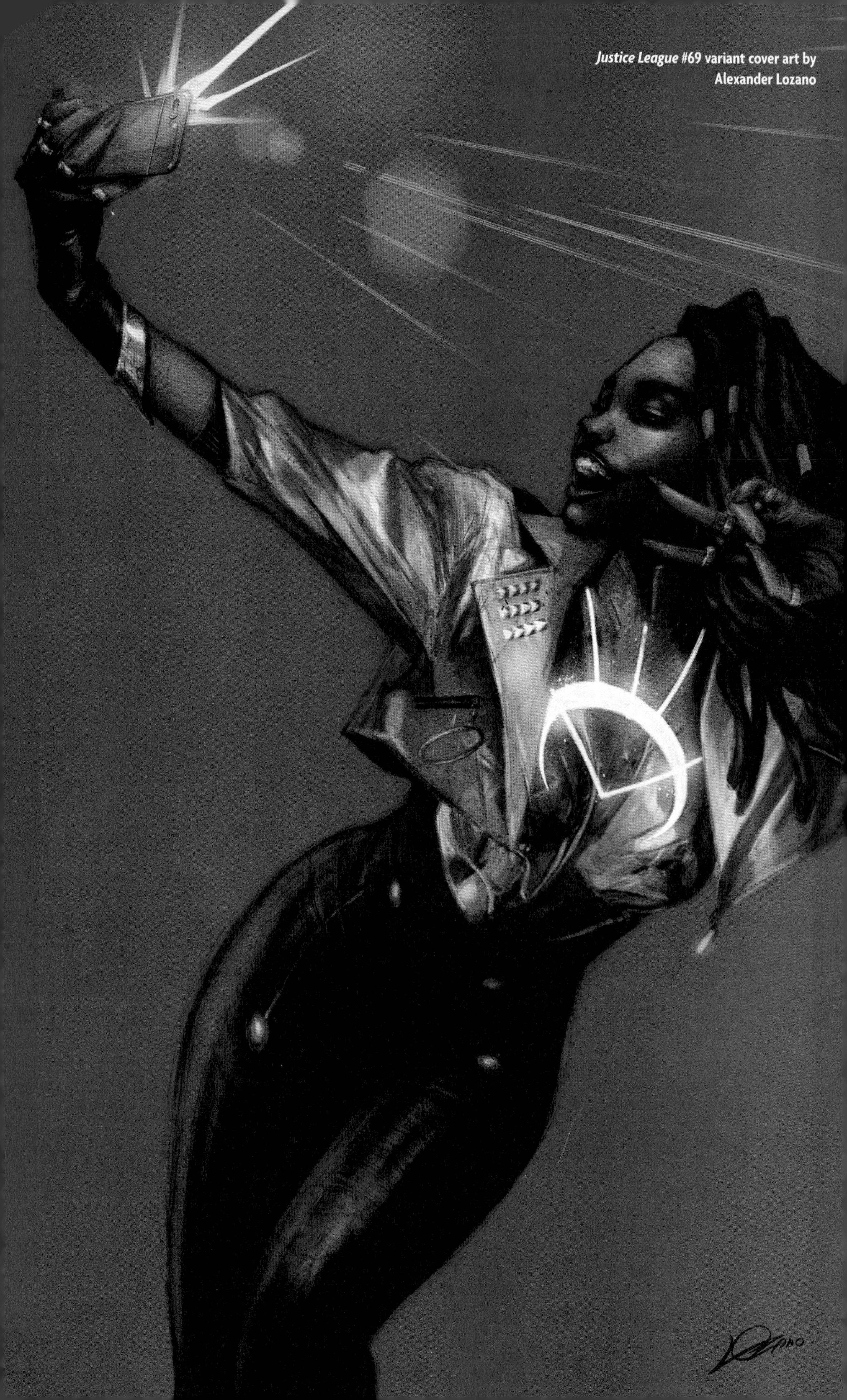

Justice League #69 variant cover art by Alexander Lozano

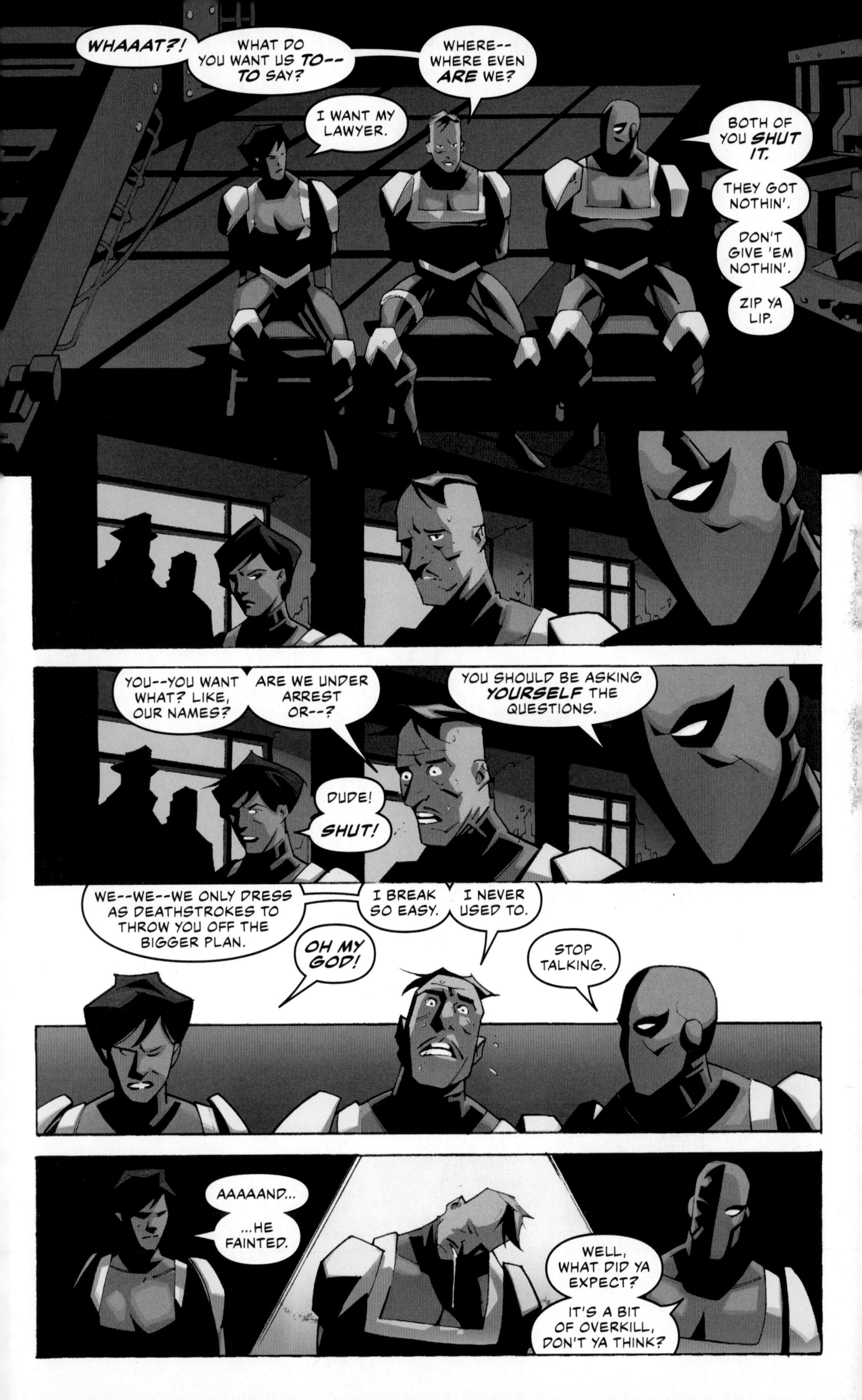
WHAAAT?!
WHAT DO YOU WANT US TO-- TO SAY?
WHERE-- WHERE EVEN ARE WE?
I WANT MY LAWYER.
BOTH OF YOU SHUT IT.
THEY GOT NOTHIN'.
DON'T GIVE 'EM NOTHIN'.
ZIP YA LIP.
YOU--YOU WANT WHAT? LIKE, OUR NAMES?
ARE WE UNDER ARREST OR--?
YOU SHOULD BE ASKING YOURSELF THE QUESTIONS.
DUDE!
SHUT!
WE--WE--WE ONLY DRESS AS DEATHSTROKES TO THROW YOU OFF THE BIGGER PLAN.
I BREAK SO EASY.
I NEVER USED TO.
OH MY GOD!
STOP TALKING.
AAAAAND...
...HE FAINTED.
WELL, WHAT DID YA EXPECT?
IT'S A BIT OF OVERKILL, DON'T YA THINK?

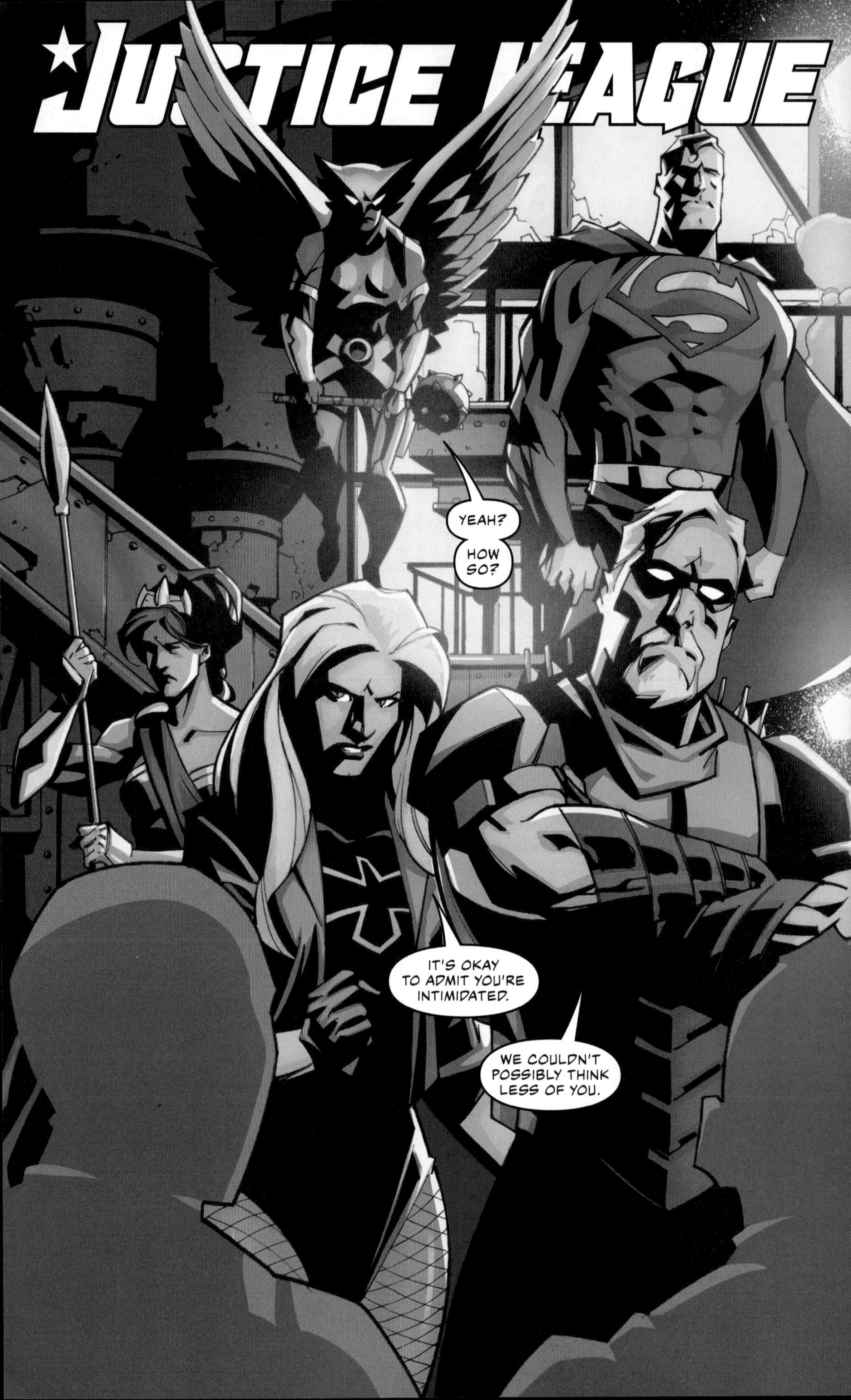
JUSTICE LEAGUE
YEAH?
HOW SO?
IT'S OKAY TO ADMIT YOU'RE INTIMIDATED.
WE COULDN'T POSSIBLY THINK LESS OF YOU.

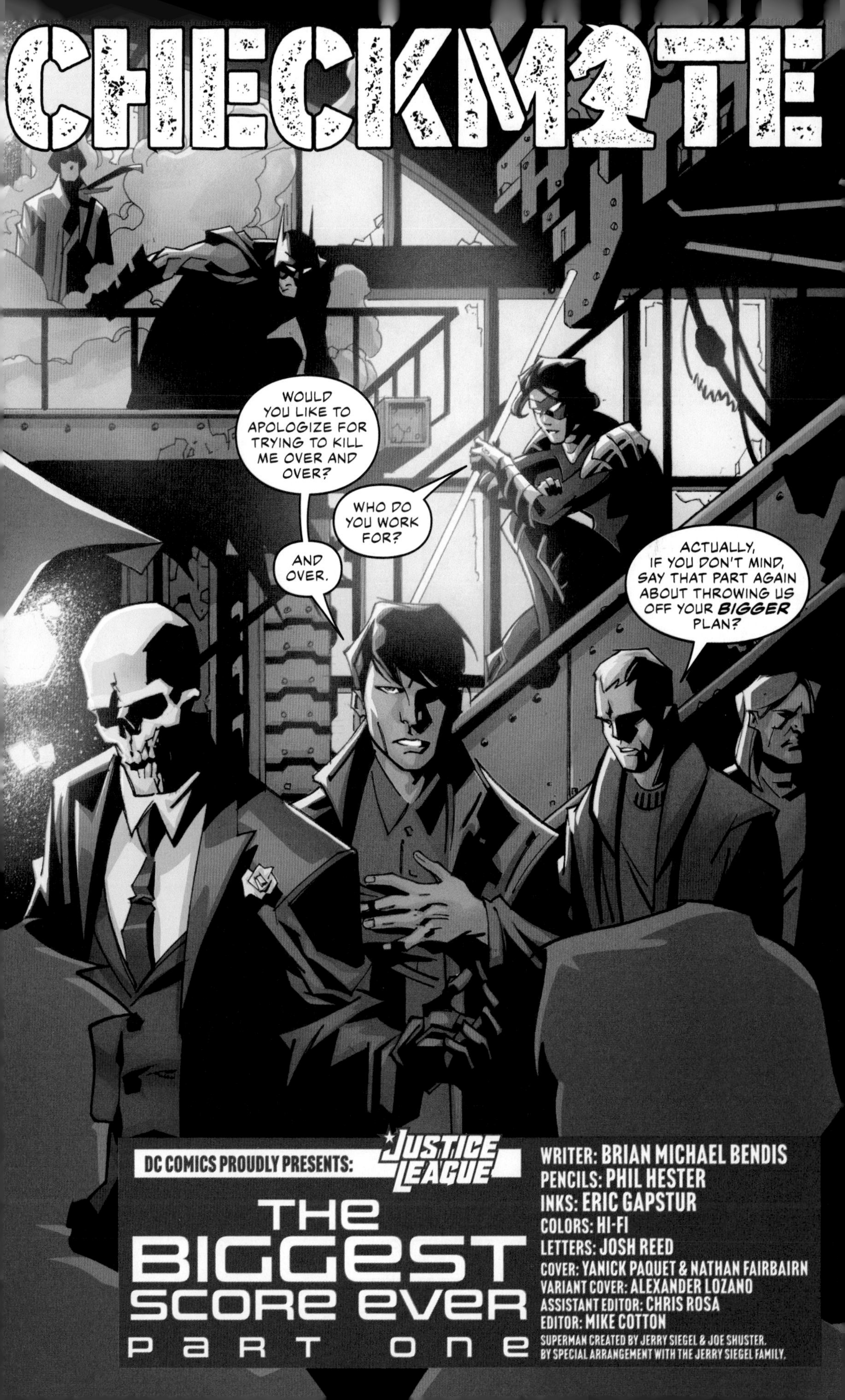
CHECKMATE
WOULD YOU LIKE TO APOLOGIZE FOR TRYING TO KILL ME OVER AND OVER?
AND OVER.
WHO DO YOU WORK FOR?
ACTUALLY, IF YOU DON'T MIND, SAY THAT PART AGAIN ABOUT THROWING US OFF YOUR BIGGER PLAN?
DC COMICS PROUDLY PRESENTS: JUSTICE LEAGUE
THE BIGGEST SCORE EVER PART ONE
WRITER: BRIAN MICHAEL BENDIS
PENCILS: PHIL HESTER
INKS: ERIC GAPSTUR
COLORS: HI-FI
LETTERS: JOSH REED
COVER: YANICK PAQUET & NATHAN FAIRBAIRN
VARIANT COVER: ALEXANDER LOZANO
ASSISTANT EDITOR: CHRIS ROSA
EDITOR: MIKE COTTON
SUPERMAN CREATED BY JERRY SIEGEL & JOE SHUSTER. BY SPECIAL ARRANGEMENT WITH THE JERRY SIEGEL FAMILY.

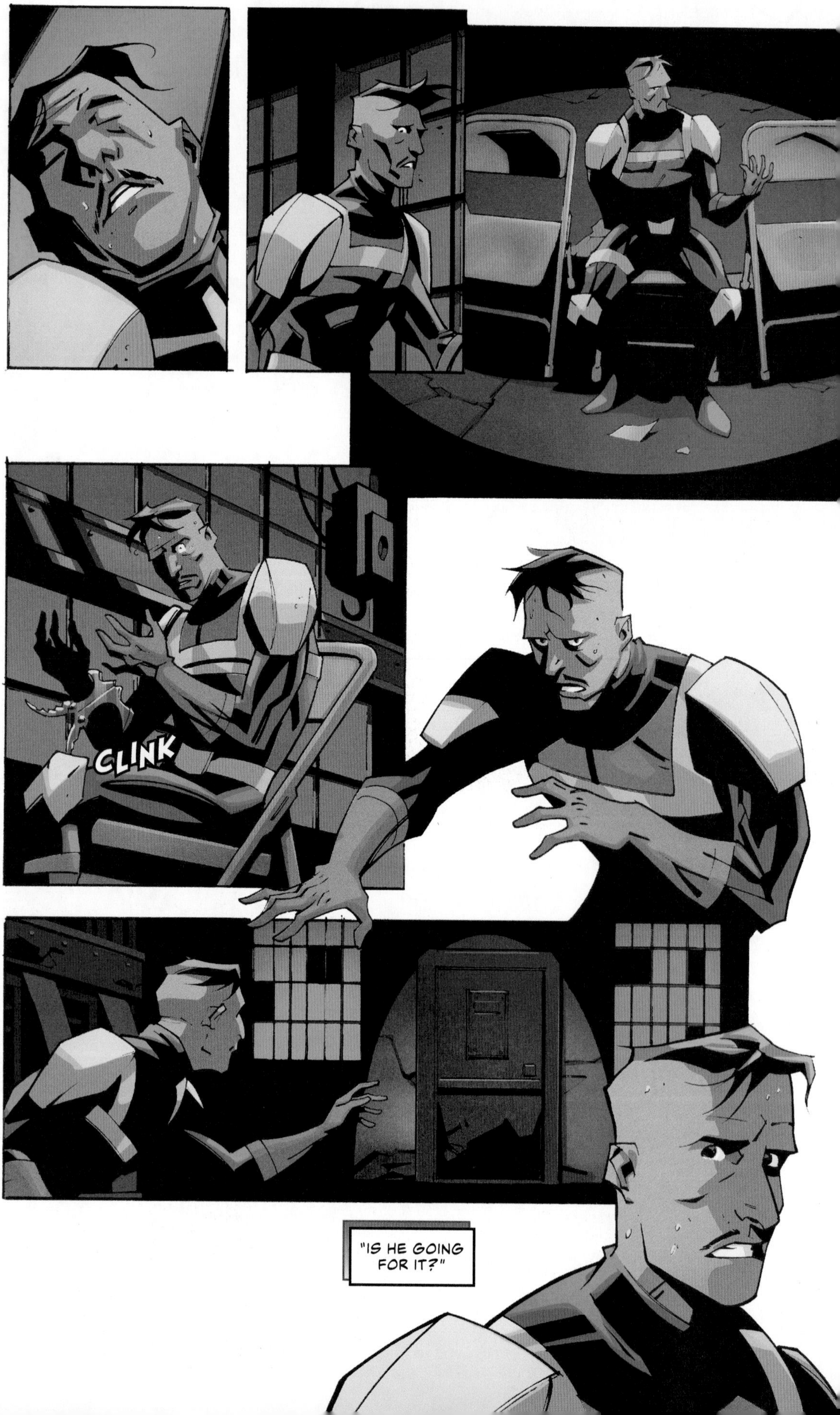
CLINK
"IS HE GOING FOR IT?"

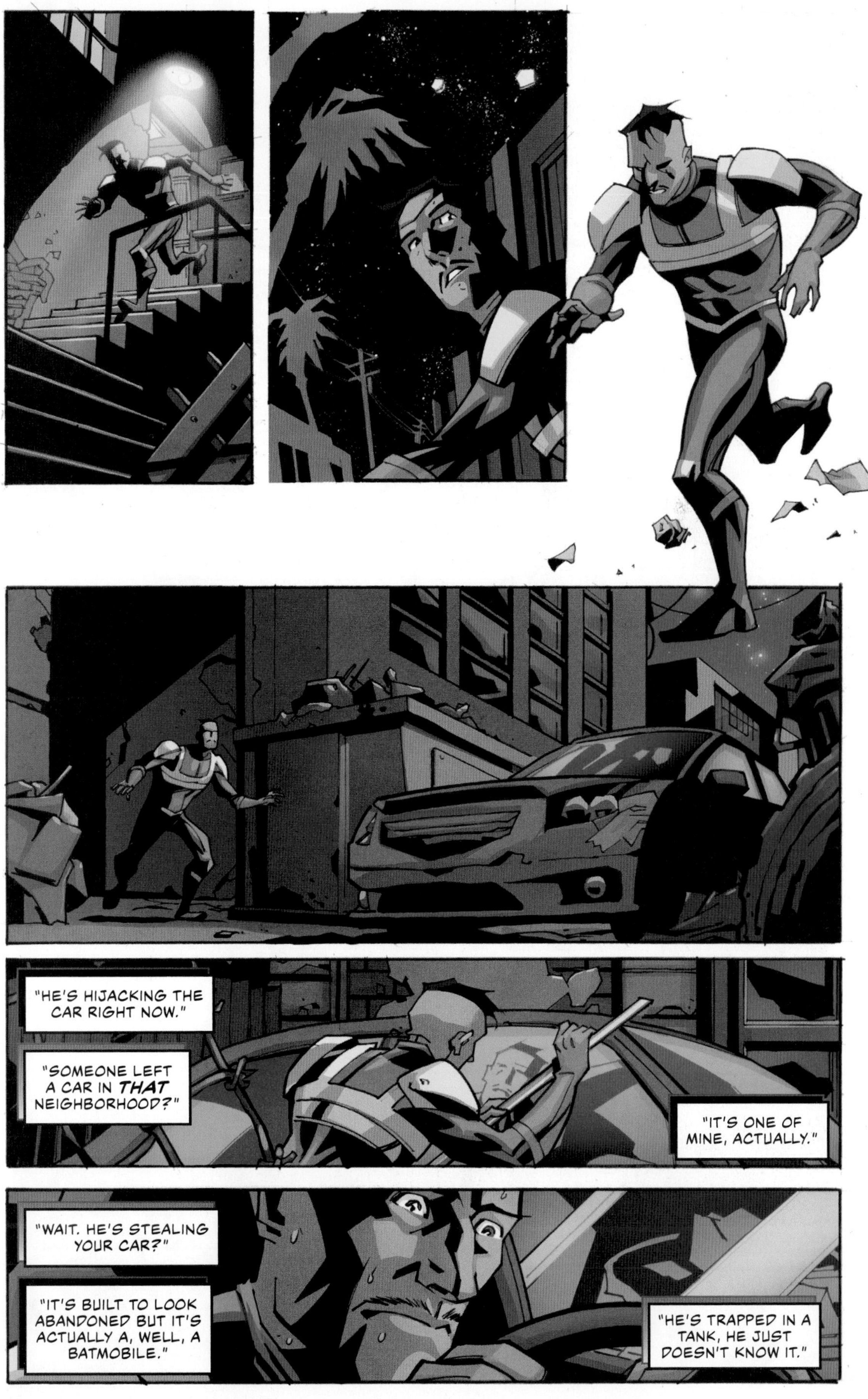
"HE'S HIJACKING THE CAR RIGHT NOW."
"SOMEONE LEFT A CAR IN *THAT* NEIGHBORHOOD?"
"IT'S ONE OF MINE, ACTUALLY."
"WAIT. HE'S STEALING YOUR CAR?"
"IT'S BUILT TO LOOK ABANDONED BUT IT'S ACTUALLY A, WELL, A BATMOBILE."
"HE'S TRAPPED IN A TANK, HE JUST DOESN'T KNOW IT."

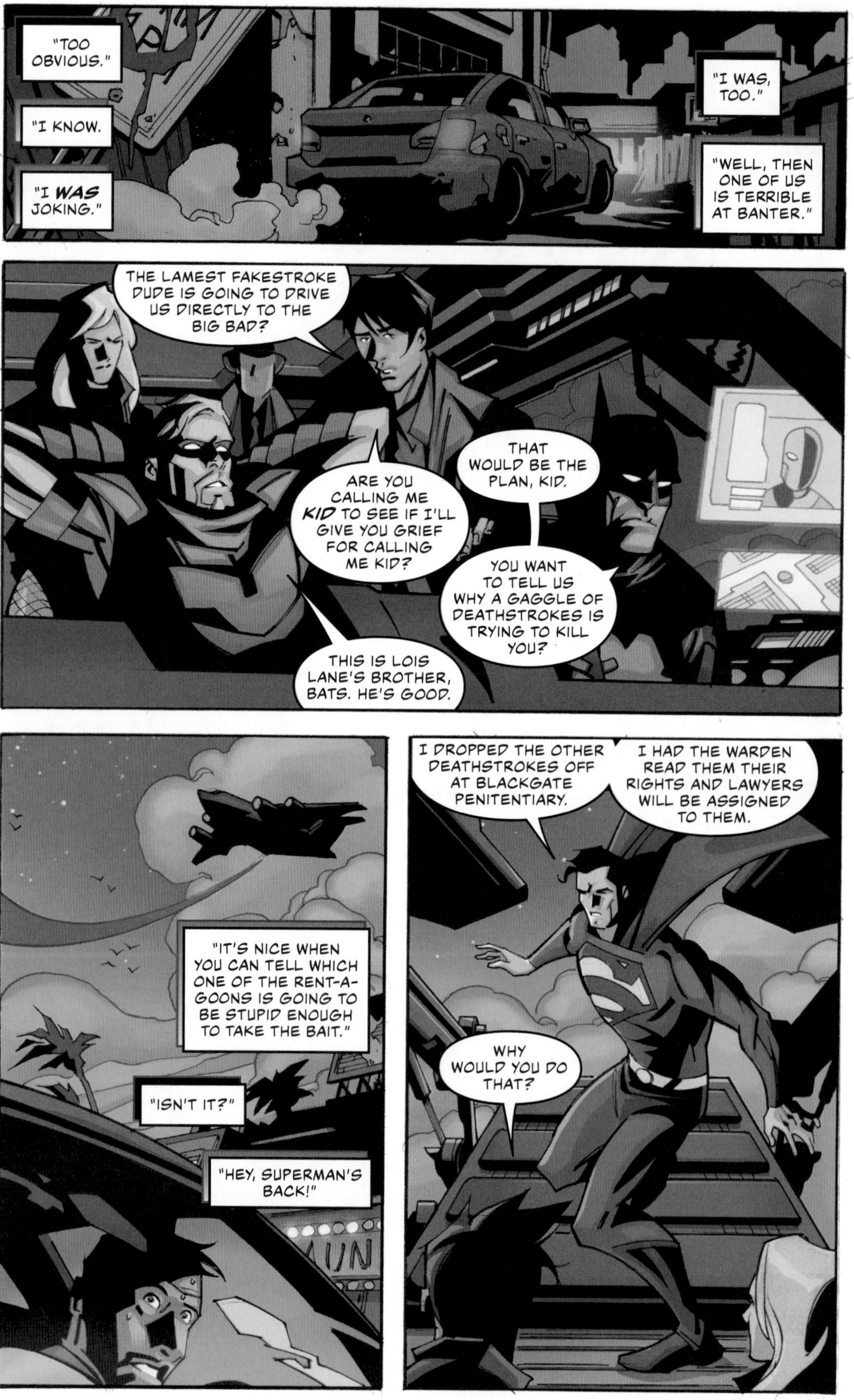
"TOO OBVIOUS."
"I KNOW.
"I *WAS* JOKING."
"I WAS, TOO."
"WELL, THEN ONE OF US IS TERRIBLE AT BANTER."
THE LAMEST FAKESTROKE DUDE IS GOING TO DRIVE US DIRECTLY TO THE BIG BAD?
THAT WOULD BE THE PLAN, KID.
ARE YOU CALLING ME *KID* TO SEE IF I'LL GIVE YOU GRIEF FOR CALLING ME KID?
THIS IS LOIS LANE'S BROTHER, BATS. HE'S GOOD.
YOU WANT TO TELL US WHY A GAGGLE OF DEATHSTROKES IS TRYING TO KILL YOU?
"IT'S NICE WHEN YOU CAN TELL WHICH ONE OF THE RENT-A-GOONS IS GOING TO BE STUPID ENOUGH TO TAKE THE BAIT."
"ISN'T IT?"
"HEY, SUPERMAN'S BACK!"
I DROPPED THE OTHER DEATHSTROKES OFF AT BLACKGATE PENITENTIARY.
I HAD THE WARDEN READ THEM THEIR RIGHTS AND LAWYERS WILL BE ASSIGNED TO THEM.
WHY WOULD YOU DO THAT?

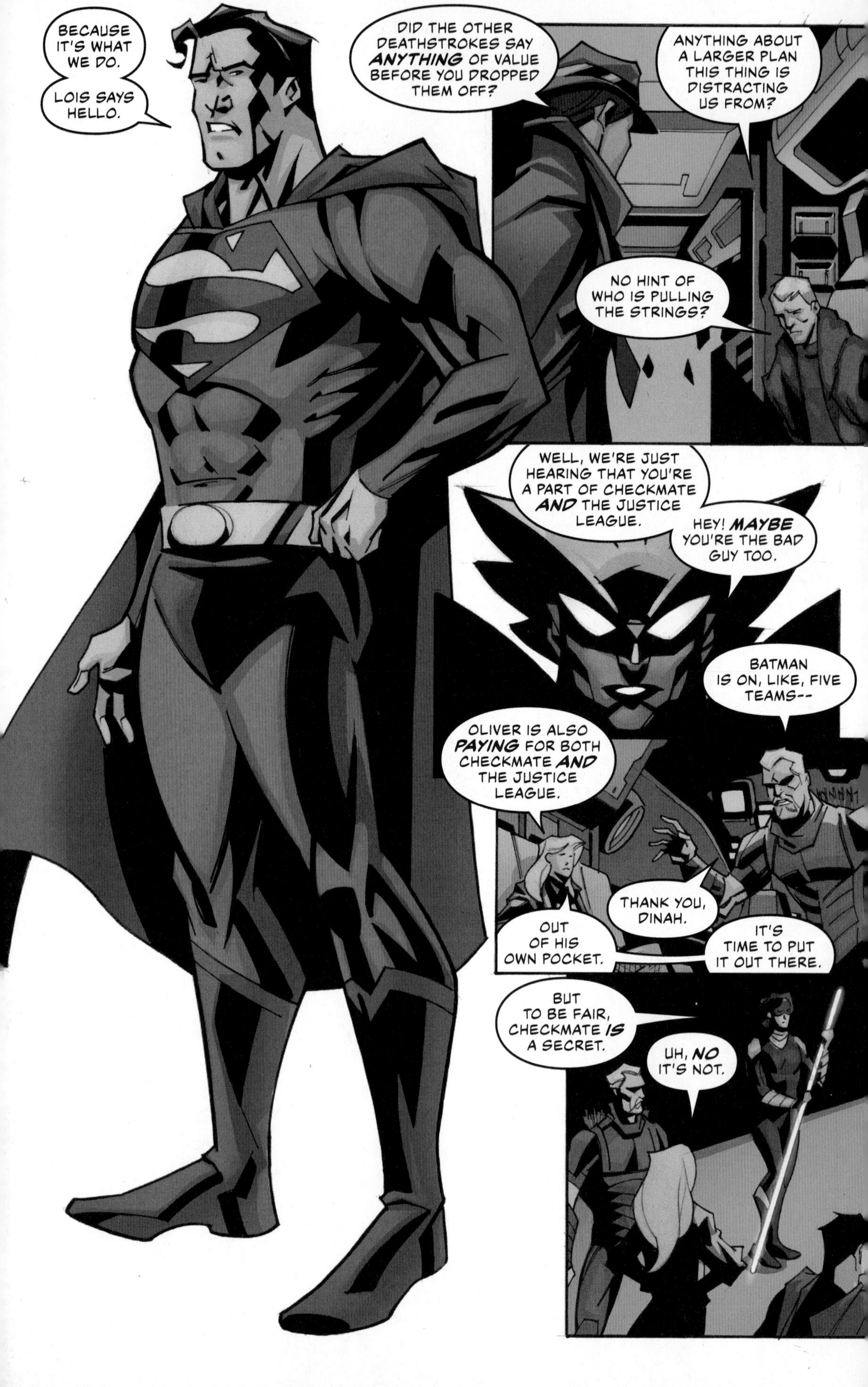
BECAUSE IT'S WHAT WE DO.
LOIS SAYS HELLO.
DID THE OTHER DEATHSTROKES SAY ANYTHING OF VALUE BEFORE YOU DROPPED THEM OFF?
ANYTHING ABOUT A LARGER PLAN THIS THING IS DISTRACTING US FROM?
NO HINT OF WHO IS PULLING THE STRINGS?
WELL, WE'RE JUST HEARING THAT YOU'RE A PART OF CHECKMATE AND THE JUSTICE LEAGUE.
HEY! MAYBE YOU'RE THE BAD GUY TOO.
BATMAN IS ON, LIKE, FIVE TEAMS--
OLIVER IS ALSO PAYING FOR BOTH CHECKMATE AND THE JUSTICE LEAGUE.
THANK YOU, DINAH.
OUT OF HIS OWN POCKET.
IT'S TIME TO PUT IT OUT THERE.
BUT TO BE FAIR, CHECKMATE IS A SECRET.
UH, NO IT'S NOT.

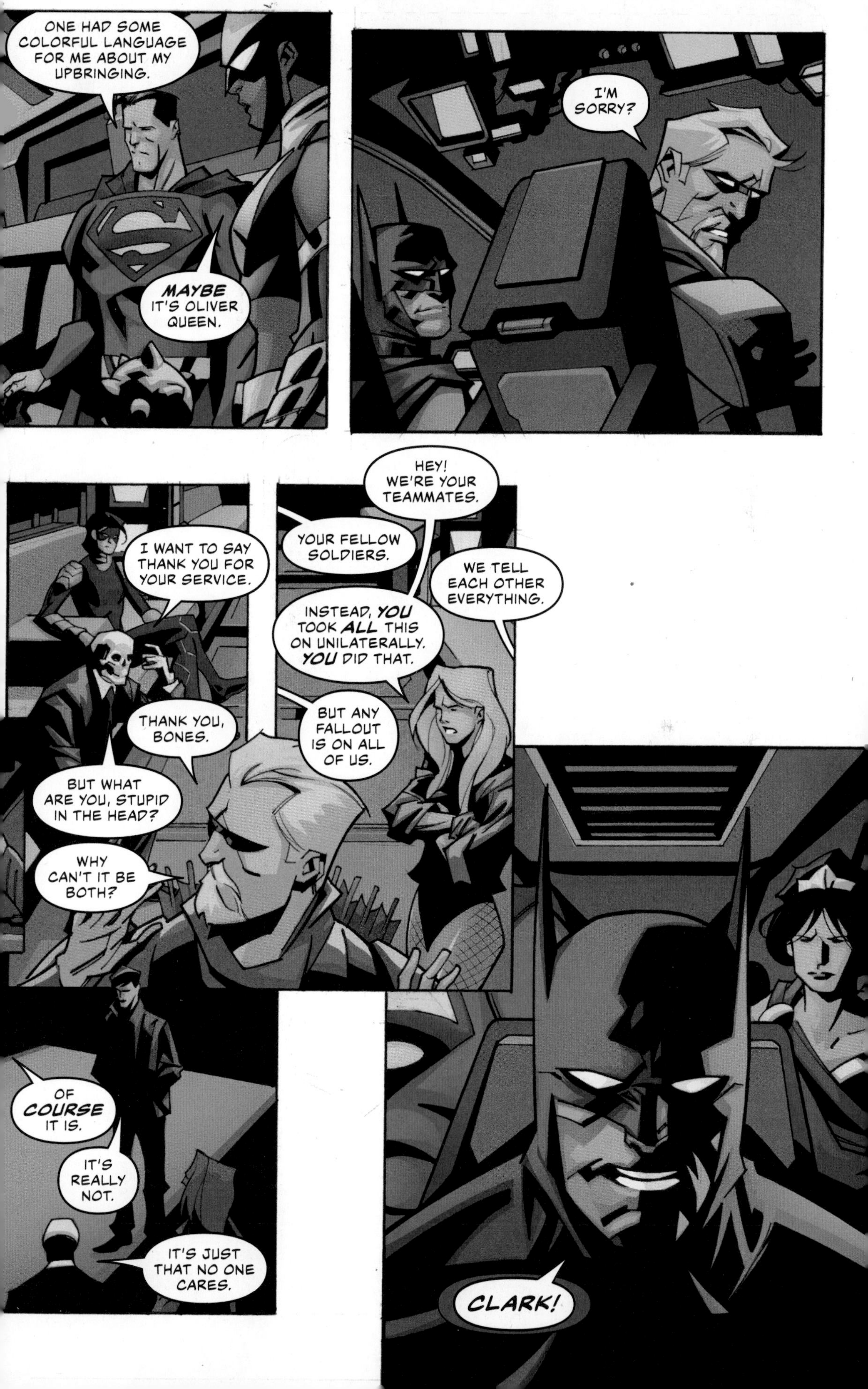
ONE HAD SOME COLORFUL LANGUAGE FOR ME ABOUT MY UPBRINGING.
MAYBE IT'S OLIVER QUEEN.
I'M SORRY?
I WANT TO SAY THANK YOU FOR YOUR SERVICE.
THANK YOU, BONES.
BUT WHAT ARE YOU, STUPID IN THE HEAD?
WHY CAN'T IT BE BOTH?
HEY! WE'RE YOUR TEAMMATES.
YOUR FELLOW SOLDIERS.
WE TELL EACH OTHER EVERYTHING.
INSTEAD, YOU TOOK ALL THIS ON UNILATERALLY. YOU DID THAT.
BUT ANY FALLOUT IS ON ALL OF US.
OF COURSE IT IS.
IT'S REALLY NOT.
IT'S JUST THAT NO ONE CARES.
CLARK!

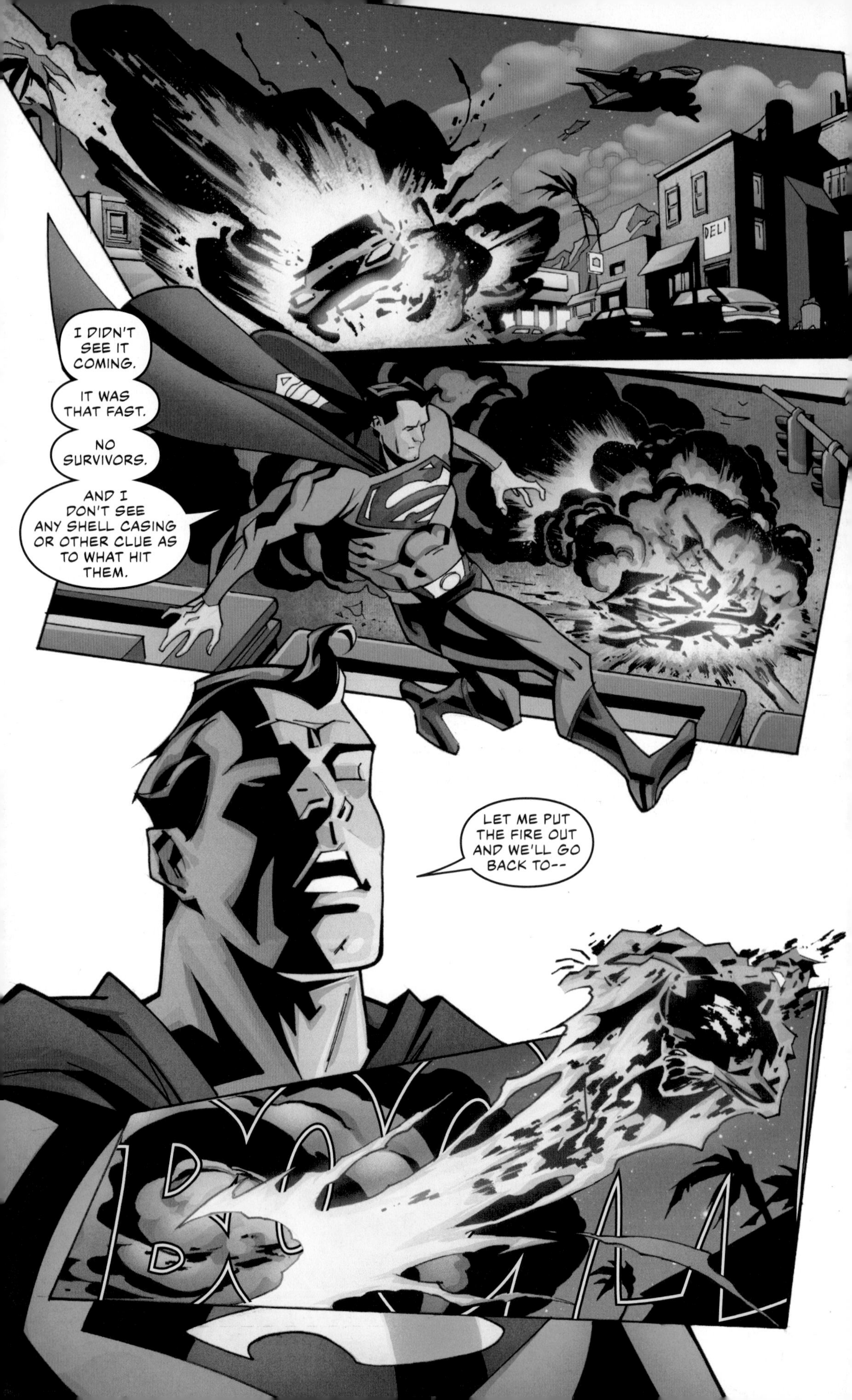
I DIDN'T SEE IT COMING.
IT WAS THAT FAST.
NO SURVIVORS.
AND I DON'T SEE ANY SHELL CASING OR OTHER CLUE AS TO WHAT HIT THEM.
DELI
LET ME PUT THE FIRE OUT AND WE'LL GO BACK TO--
BOOM

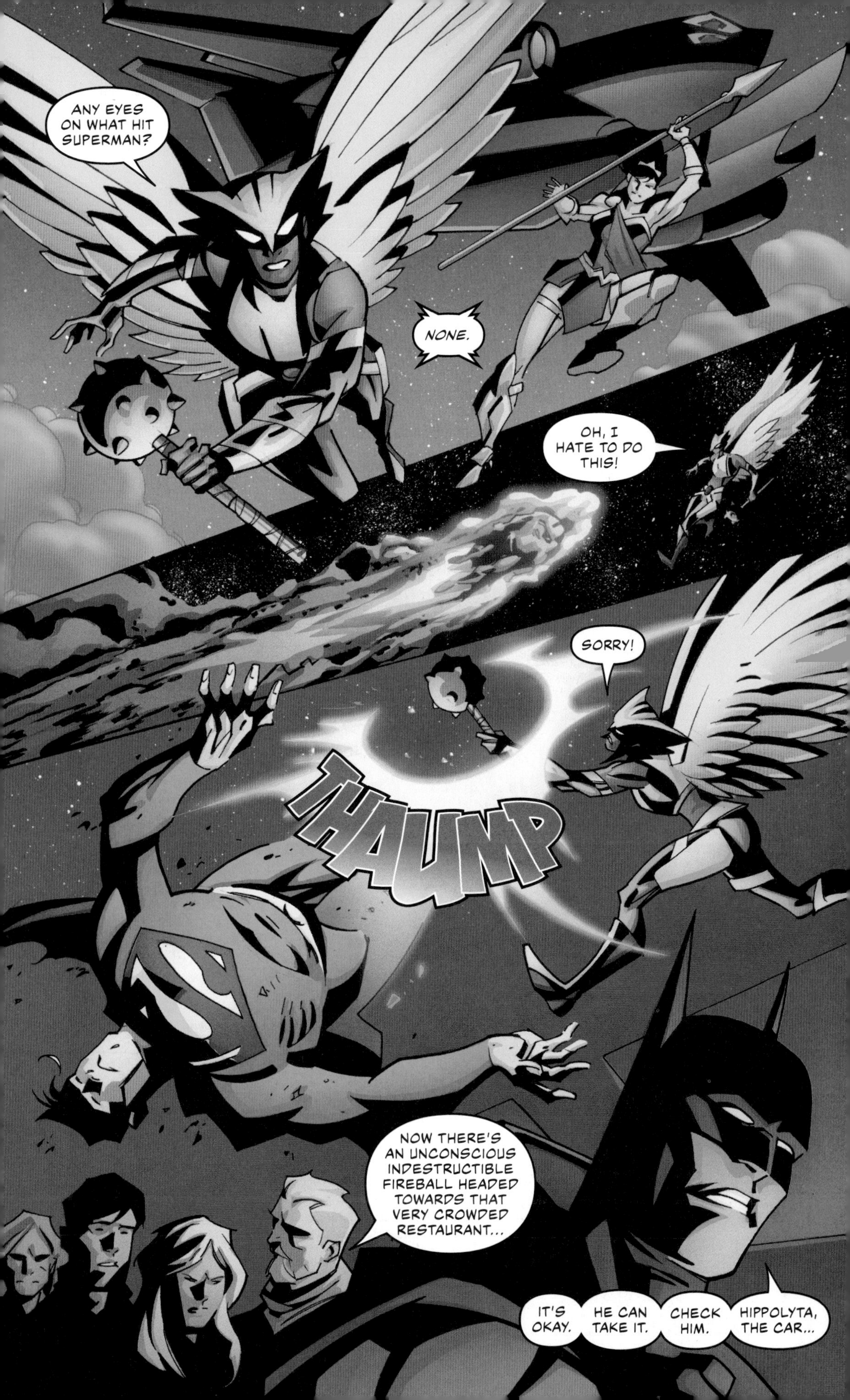
ANY EYES ON WHAT HIT SUPERMAN?
NONE.
OH, I HATE TO DO THIS!
SORRY!
THAUMP
NOW THERE'S AN UNCONSCIOUS INDESTRUCTIBLE FIREBALL HEADED TOWARDS THAT VERY CROWDED RESTAURANT...
HIPPOLYTA, THE CAR...
CHECK HIM.
HE CAN TAKE IT.
IT'S OKAY.

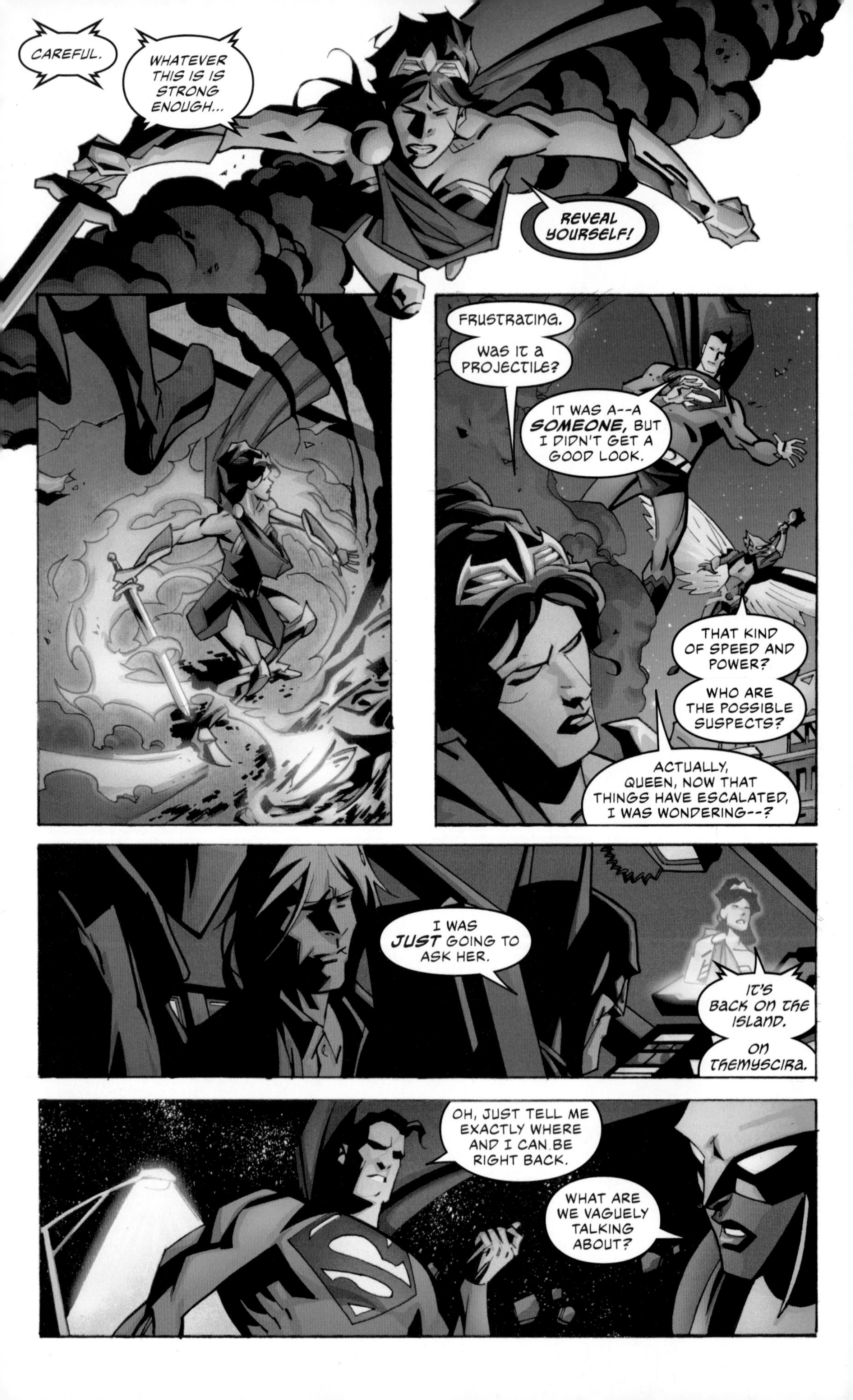
CAREFUL.
WHATEVER THIS IS IS STRONG ENOUGH...
REVEAL YOURSELF!
FRUSTRATING.
WAS IT A PROJECTILE?
IT WAS A--A SOMEONE, BUT I DIDN'T GET A GOOD LOOK.
THAT KIND OF SPEED AND POWER?
WHO ARE THE POSSIBLE SUSPECTS?
ACTUALLY, QUEEN, NOW THAT THINGS HAVE ESCALATED, I WAS WONDERING--?
I WAS JUST GOING TO ASK HER.
IT'S BACK ON THE ISLAND.
ON THEMYSCIRA.
OH, JUST TELL ME EXACTLY WHERE AND I CAN BE RIGHT BACK.
WHAT ARE WE VAGUELY TALKING ABOUT?

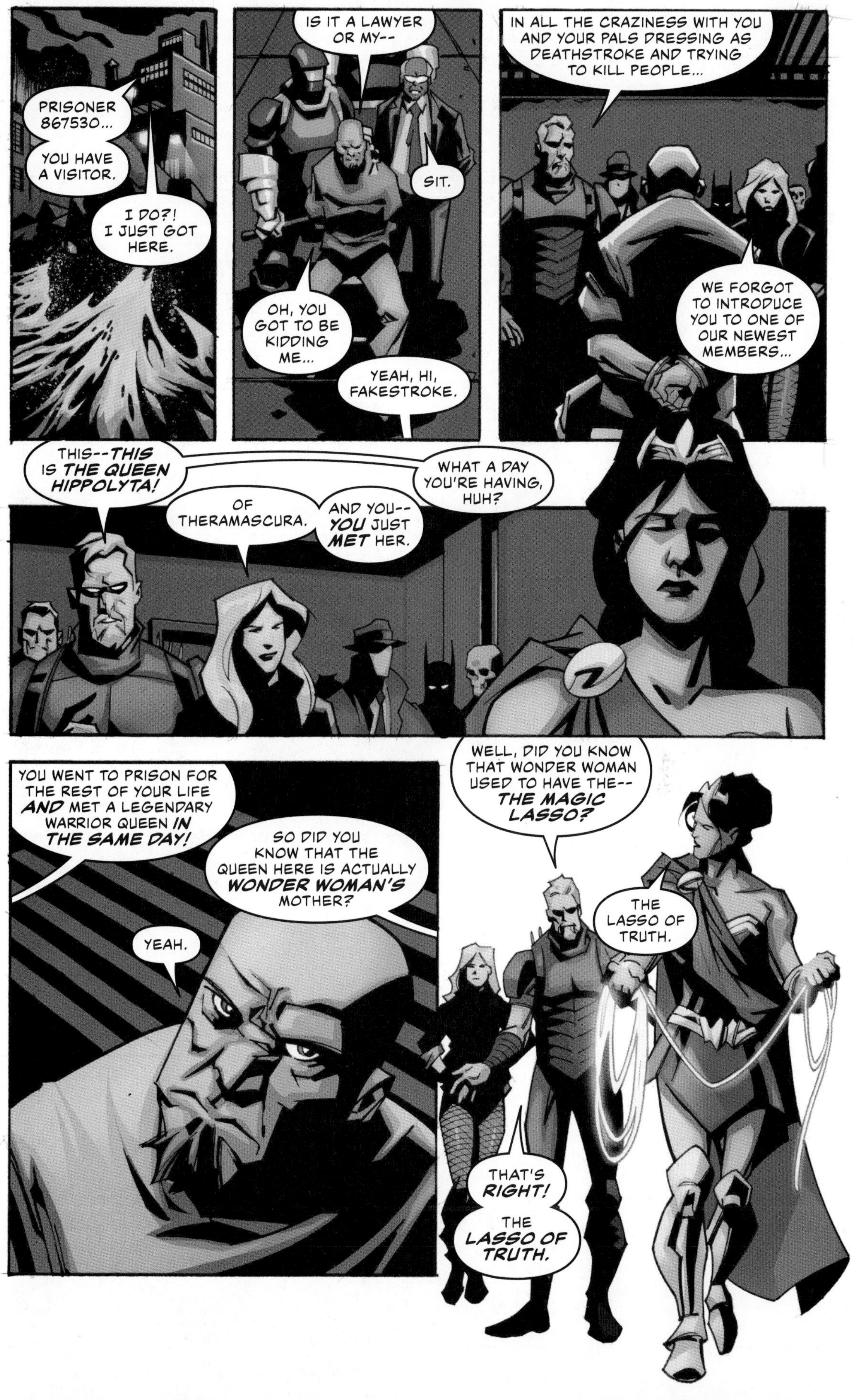
PRISONER 867530...
YOU HAVE A VISITOR.
I DO?! I JUST GOT HERE.
IS IT A LAWYER OR MY--
SIT.
OH, YOU GOT TO BE KIDDING ME...
YEAH, HI, FAKESTROKE.
IN ALL THE CRAZINESS WITH YOU AND YOUR PALS DRESSING AS DEATHSTROKE AND TRYING TO KILL PEOPLE...
WE FORGOT TO INTRODUCE YOU TO ONE OF OUR NEWEST MEMBERS...
THIS--THIS IS THE QUEEN HIPPOLYTA!
OF THERAMASCURA.
AND YOU--YOU JUST MET HER.
WHAT A DAY YOU'RE HAVING, HUH?
YOU WENT TO PRISON FOR THE REST OF YOUR LIFE AND MET A LEGENDARY WARRIOR QUEEN IN THE SAME DAY!
SO DID YOU KNOW THAT THE QUEEN HERE IS ACTUALLY WONDER WOMAN'S MOTHER?
YEAH.
WELL, DID YOU KNOW THAT WONDER WOMAN USED TO HAVE THE--THE MAGIC LASSO?
THE LASSO OF TRUTH.
THAT'S RIGHT!
THE LASSO OF TRUTH.

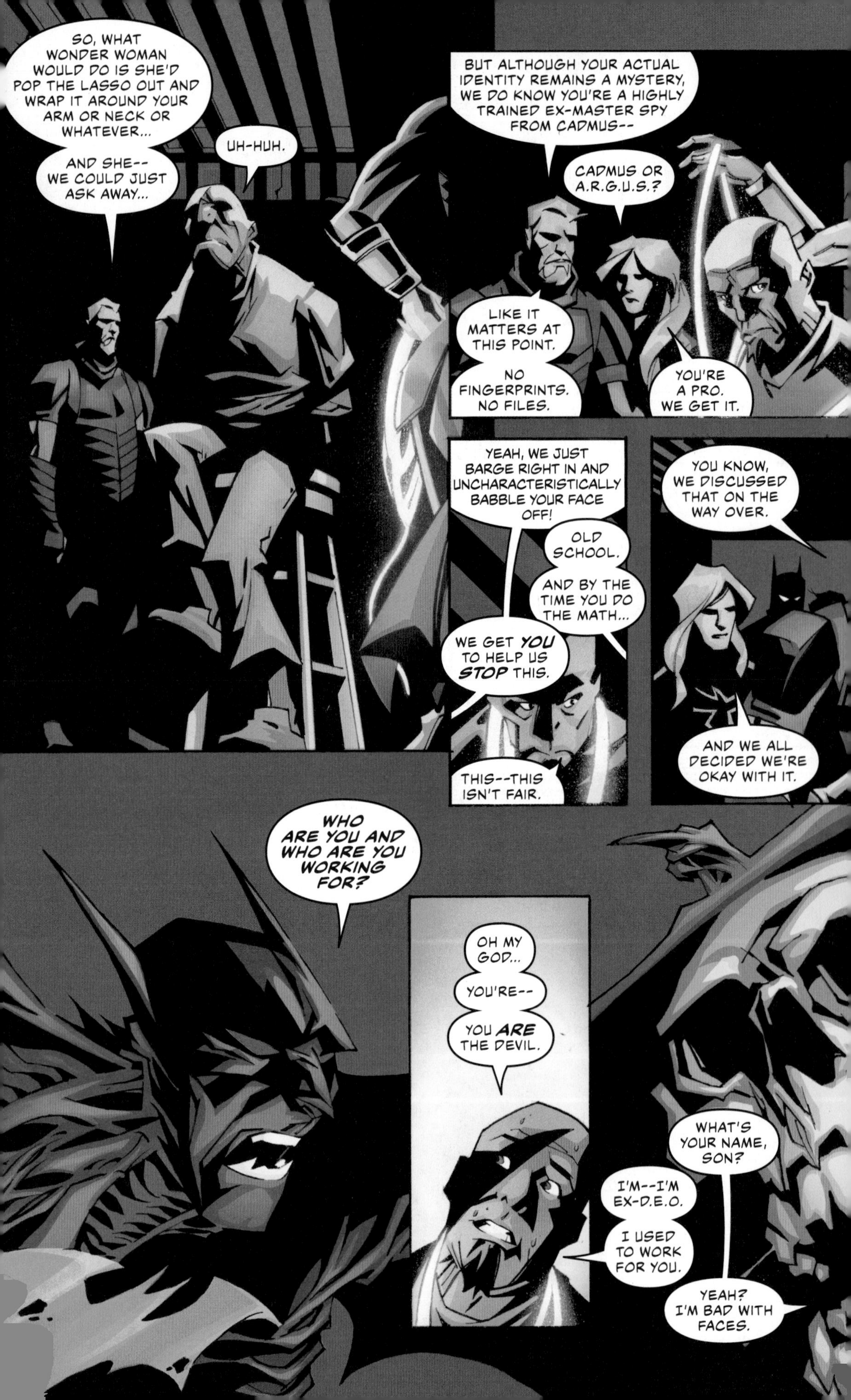
SO, WHAT WONDER WOMAN WOULD DO IS SHE'D POP THE LASSO OUT AND WRAP IT AROUND YOUR ARM OR NECK OR WHATEVER...
AND SHE-- WE COULD JUST ASK AWAY...
UH-HUH.
BUT ALTHOUGH YOUR ACTUAL IDENTITY REMAINS A MYSTERY, WE DO KNOW YOU'RE A HIGHLY TRAINED EX-MASTER SPY FROM CADMUS--
CADMUS OR A.R.G.U.S.?
LIKE IT MATTERS AT THIS POINT.
NO FINGERPRINTS. NO FILES.
YOU'RE A PRO. WE GET IT.
YEAH, WE JUST BARGE RIGHT IN AND UNCHARACTERISTICALLY BABBLE YOUR FACE OFF!
OLD SCHOOL.
AND BY THE TIME YOU DO THE MATH...
WE GET YOU TO HELP US STOP THIS.
THIS--THIS ISN'T FAIR.
YOU KNOW, WE DISCUSSED THAT ON THE WAY OVER.
AND WE ALL DECIDED WE'RE OKAY WITH IT.
WHO ARE YOU AND WHO ARE YOU WORKING FOR?
OH MY GOD...
YOU'RE--
YOU ARE THE DEVIL.
WHAT'S YOUR NAME, SON?
I'M--I'M EX-D.E.O.
I USED TO WORK FOR YOU.
YEAH? I'M BAD WITH FACES.

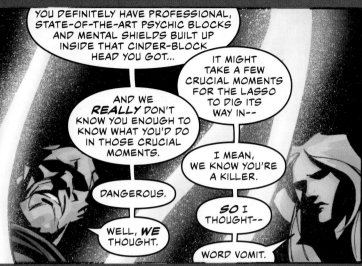

YOU DEFINITELY HAVE PROFESSIONAL, STATE-OF-THE-ART PSYCHIC BLOCKS AND MENTAL SHIELDS BUILT UP INSIDE THAT CINDER-BLOCK HEAD YOU GOT...

IT MIGHT TAKE A FEW CRUCIAL MOMENTS FOR THE LASSO TO DIG ITS WAY IN--

AND WE *REALLY* DON'T KNOW YOU ENOUGH TO KNOW WHAT YOU'D DO IN THOSE CRUCIAL MOMENTS.

I MEAN, WE KNOW YOU'RE A KILLER.

DANGEROUS.

SO I THOUGHT--

WELL, *WE* THOUGHT.

WORD VOMIT.

WASN'T EVEN MUCH OF A VOTE.

HOW ARE YOU FEELING?

I-- I ONCE ATE BIRD-SEED.

I THINK THAT MEANS IT'S WORKING.

THANK YOU, MY QUEEN.

'KAY.

WHO WANTS TO *A.M.A.* WITH FAKESTROKE FIRST?

I D-DON'T WORK FOR--FOR *ANYBODY* NOW THOUGH.

I'M *PART* OF SOMETHING.

WE'RE *ALL* PART OF SOMETHING!

BUT I--I DON'T HAVE TOP ACCESS YET.

I HAVEN'T EARNED MY WAY UP YET.

WHO DO YOU ANSWER TO?!

AAGGHH!

I'LL TELL YOU EXACTLY WHERE THEY ARE!

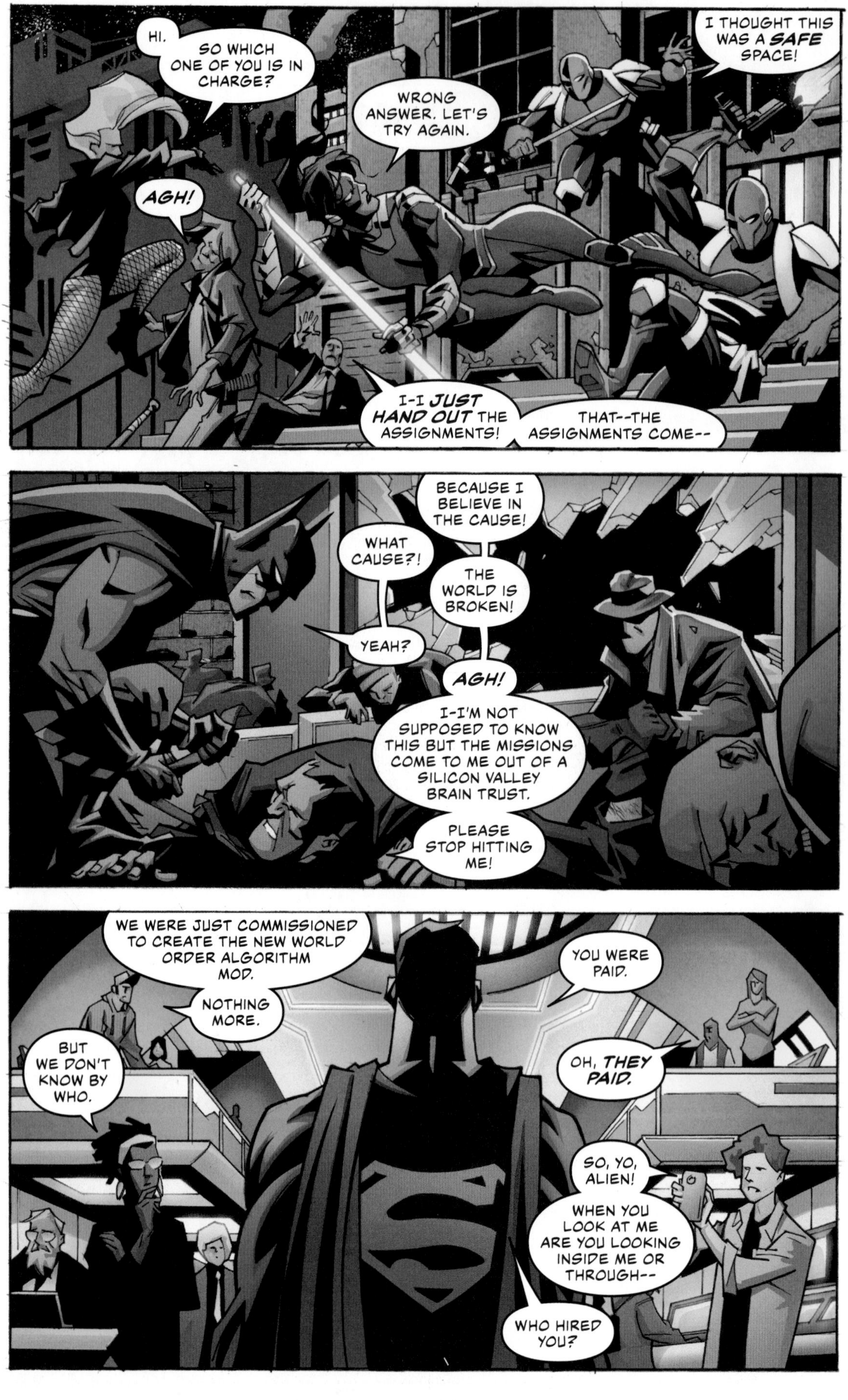
HI.
SO WHICH ONE OF YOU IS IN CHARGE?
AGH!
WRONG ANSWER. LET'S TRY AGAIN.
I THOUGHT THIS WAS A ***SAFE*** SPACE!
I-I ***JUST HAND OUT*** THE ASSIGNMENTS!
THAT--THE ASSIGNMENTS COME--
BECAUSE I BELIEVE IN THE CAUSE!
WHAT CAUSE?!
THE WORLD IS BROKEN!
YEAH?
AGH!
I-I'M NOT SUPPOSED TO KNOW THIS BUT THE MISSIONS COME TO ME OUT OF A SILICON VALLEY BRAIN TRUST.
PLEASE STOP HITTING ME!
WE WERE JUST COMMISSIONED TO CREATE THE NEW WORLD ORDER ALGORITHM MOD.
NOTHING MORE.
BUT WE DON'T KNOW BY WHO.
YOU WERE PAID.
OH, ***THEY PAID.***
SO, YO, ALIEN!
WHEN YOU LOOK AT ME ARE YOU LOOKING INSIDE ME OR THROUGH--
WHO HIRED YOU?

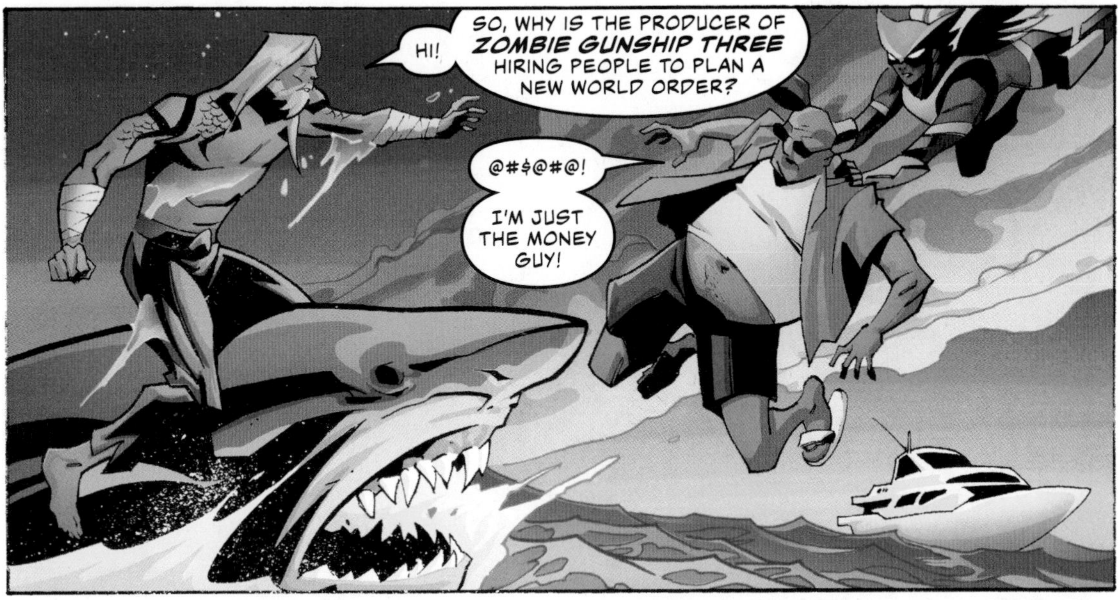
HI!
SO, WHY IS THE PRODUCER OF ZOMBIE GUNSHIP THREE HIRING PEOPLE TO PLAN A NEW WORLD ORDER?
@#$@#@!
I'M JUST THE MONEY GUY!

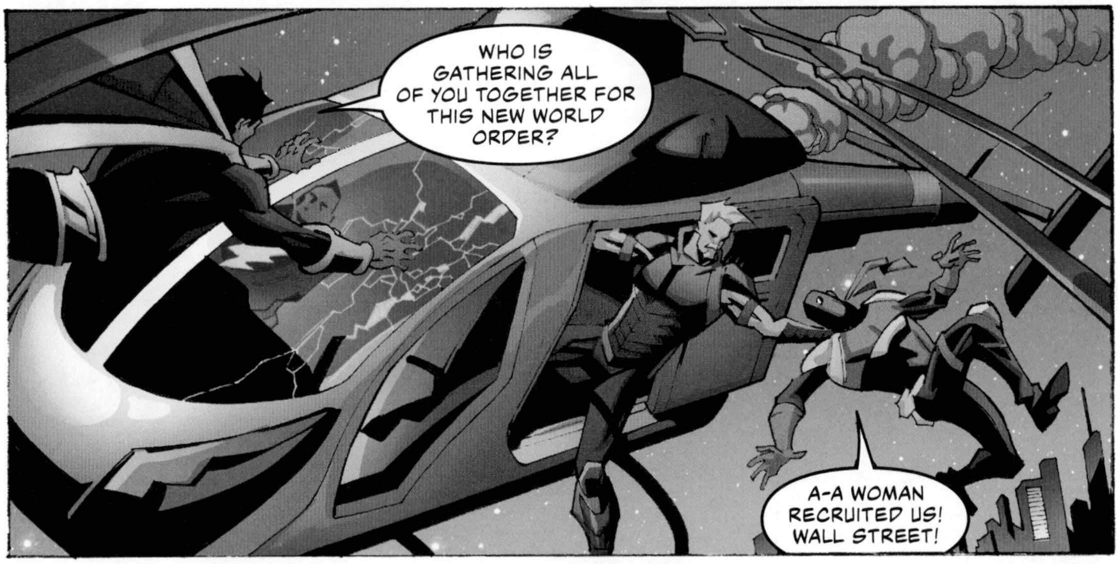
WHO IS GATHERING ALL OF YOU TOGETHER FOR THIS NEW WORLD ORDER?
A-A WOMAN RECRUITED US! WALL STREET!

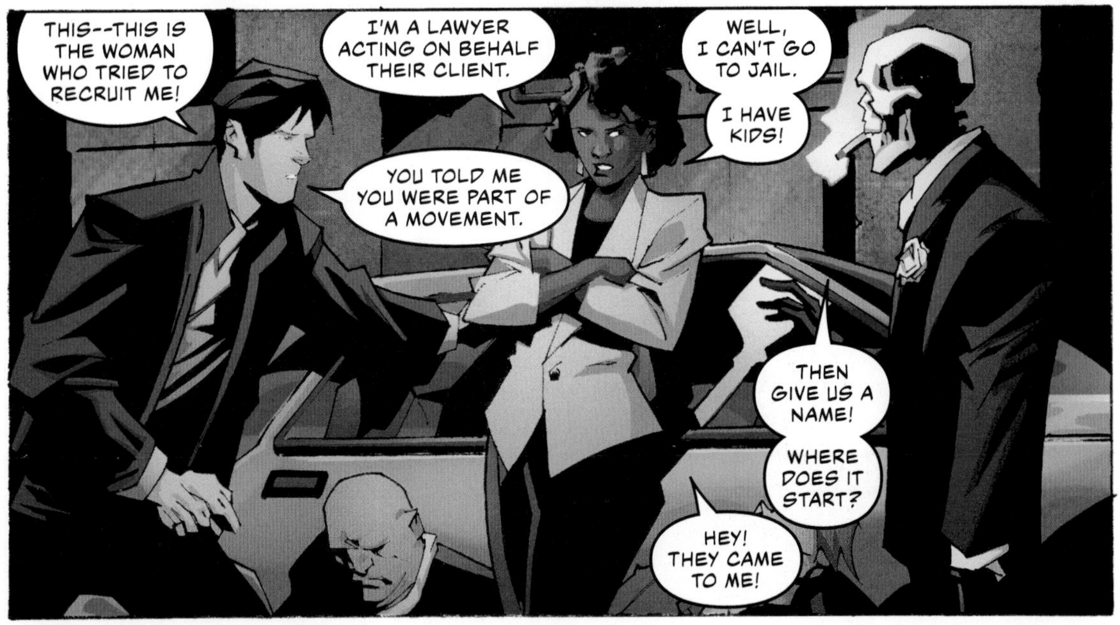
THIS--THIS IS THE WOMAN WHO TRIED TO RECRUIT ME!
I'M A LAWYER ACTING ON BEHALF THEIR CLIENT.
WELL, I CAN'T GO TO JAIL.
I HAVE KIDS!
YOU TOLD ME YOU WERE PART OF A MOVEMENT.
THEN GIVE US A NAME!
WHERE DOES IT START?
HEY! THEY CAME TO ME!

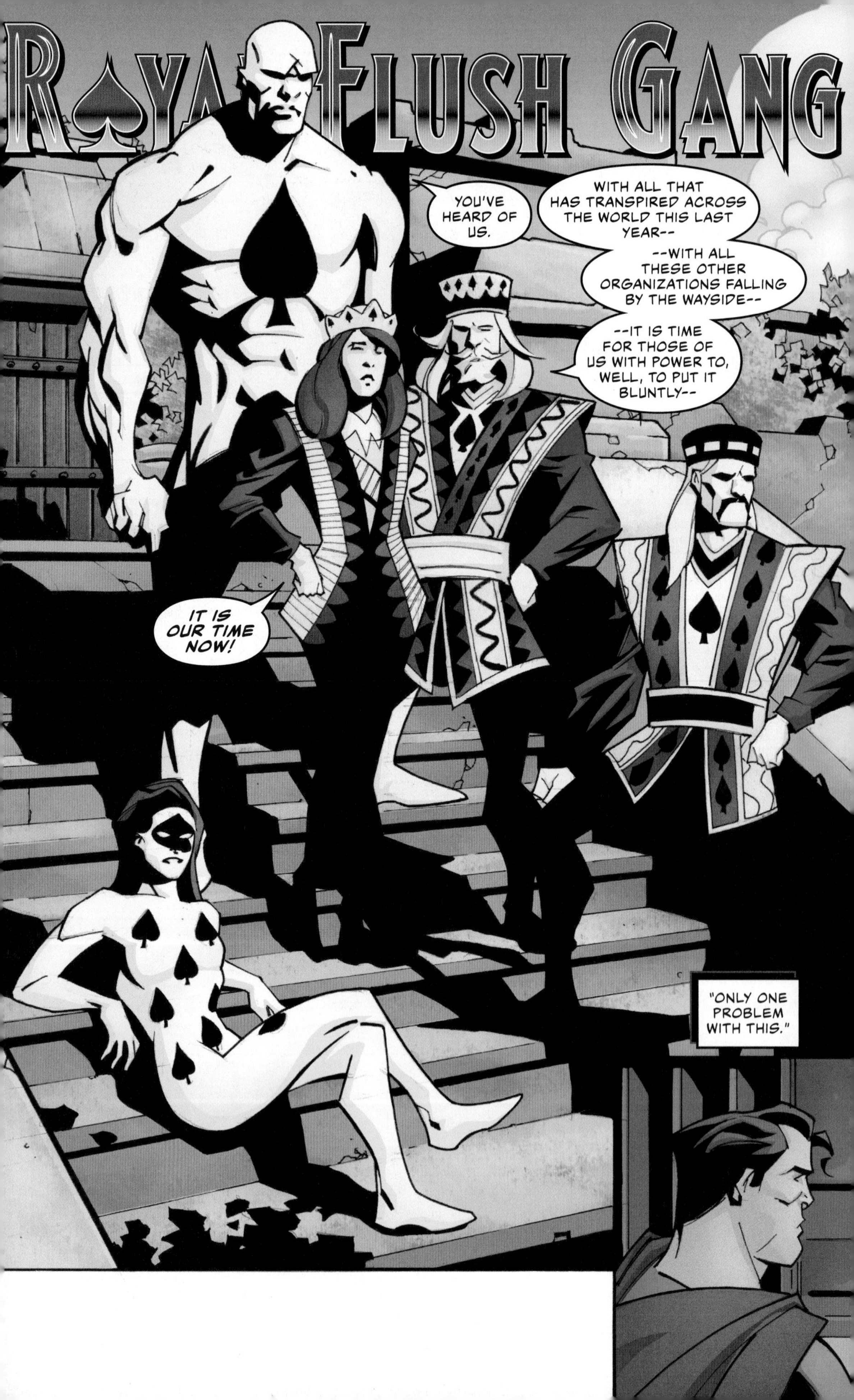
ROYAL FLUSH GANG
YOU'VE HEARD OF US.
WITH ALL THAT HAS TRANSPIRED ACROSS THE WORLD THIS LAST YEAR--
--WITH ALL THESE OTHER ORGANIZATIONS FALLING BY THE WAYSIDE--
--IT IS TIME FOR THOSE OF US WITH POWER TO, WELL, TO PUT IT BLUNTLY--
IT IS OUR TIME NOW!
"ONLY ONE PROBLEM WITH THIS."

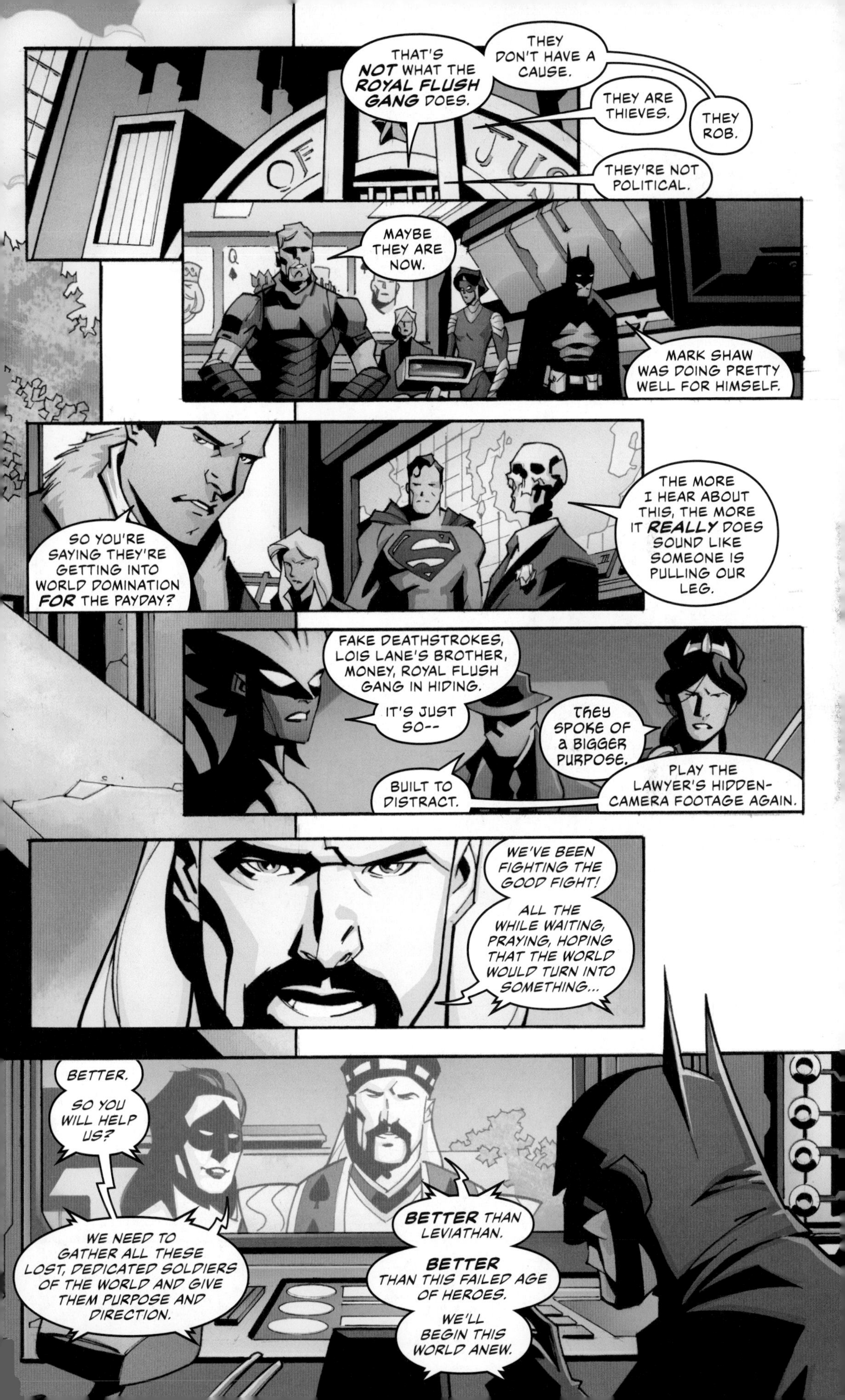
THAT'S NOT WHAT THE ROYAL FLUSH GANG DOES.
THEY DON'T HAVE A CAUSE.
THEY ARE THIEVES.
THEY ROB.
THEY'RE NOT POLITICAL.
MAYBE THEY ARE NOW.
MARK SHAW WAS DOING PRETTY WELL FOR HIMSELF.
SO YOU'RE SAYING THEY'RE GETTING INTO WORLD DOMINATION FOR THE PAYDAY?
THE MORE I HEAR ABOUT THIS, THE MORE IT REALLY DOES SOUND LIKE SOMEONE IS PULLING OUR LEG.
FAKE DEATHSTROKES, LOIS LANE'S BROTHER, MONEY, ROYAL FLUSH GANG IN HIDING.
IT'S JUST SO--
THEY SPOKE OF A BIGGER PURPOSE.
BUILT TO DISTRACT.
PLAY THE LAWYER'S HIDDEN-CAMERA FOOTAGE AGAIN.
WE'VE BEEN FIGHTING THE GOOD FIGHT!
ALL THE WHILE WAITING, PRAYING, HOPING THAT THE WORLD WOULD TURN INTO SOMETHING...
BETTER.
SO YOU WILL HELP US?
WE NEED TO GATHER ALL THESE LOST, DEDICATED SOLDIERS OF THE WORLD AND GIVE THEM PURPOSE AND DIRECTION.
BETTER THAN LEVIATHAN.
BETTER THAN THIS FAILED AGE OF HEROES.
WE'LL BEGIN THIS WORLD ANEW.

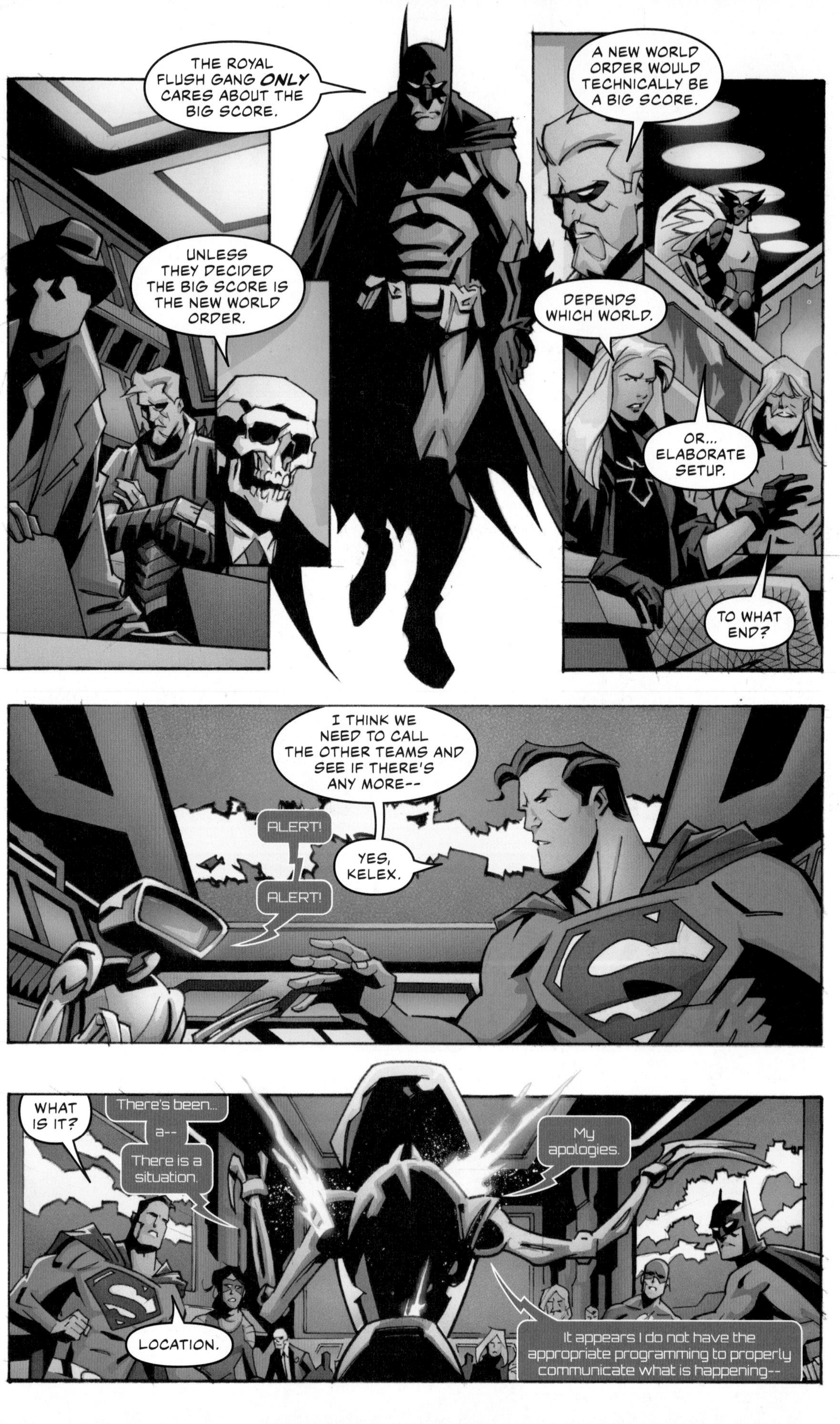
THE ROYAL FLUSH GANG ONLY CARES ABOUT THE BIG SCORE.
A NEW WORLD ORDER WOULD TECHNICALLY BE A BIG SCORE.
UNLESS THEY DECIDED THE BIG SCORE IS THE NEW WORLD ORDER.
DEPENDS WHICH WORLD.
OR... ELABORATE SETUP.
TO WHAT END?
I THINK WE NEED TO CALL THE OTHER TEAMS AND SEE IF THERE'S ANY MORE--
ALERT!
YES, KELEX.
ALERT!
WHAT IS IT?
There's been...
a--
There is a situation.
My apologies.
LOCATION.
It appears I do not have the appropriate programming to properly communicate what is happening--

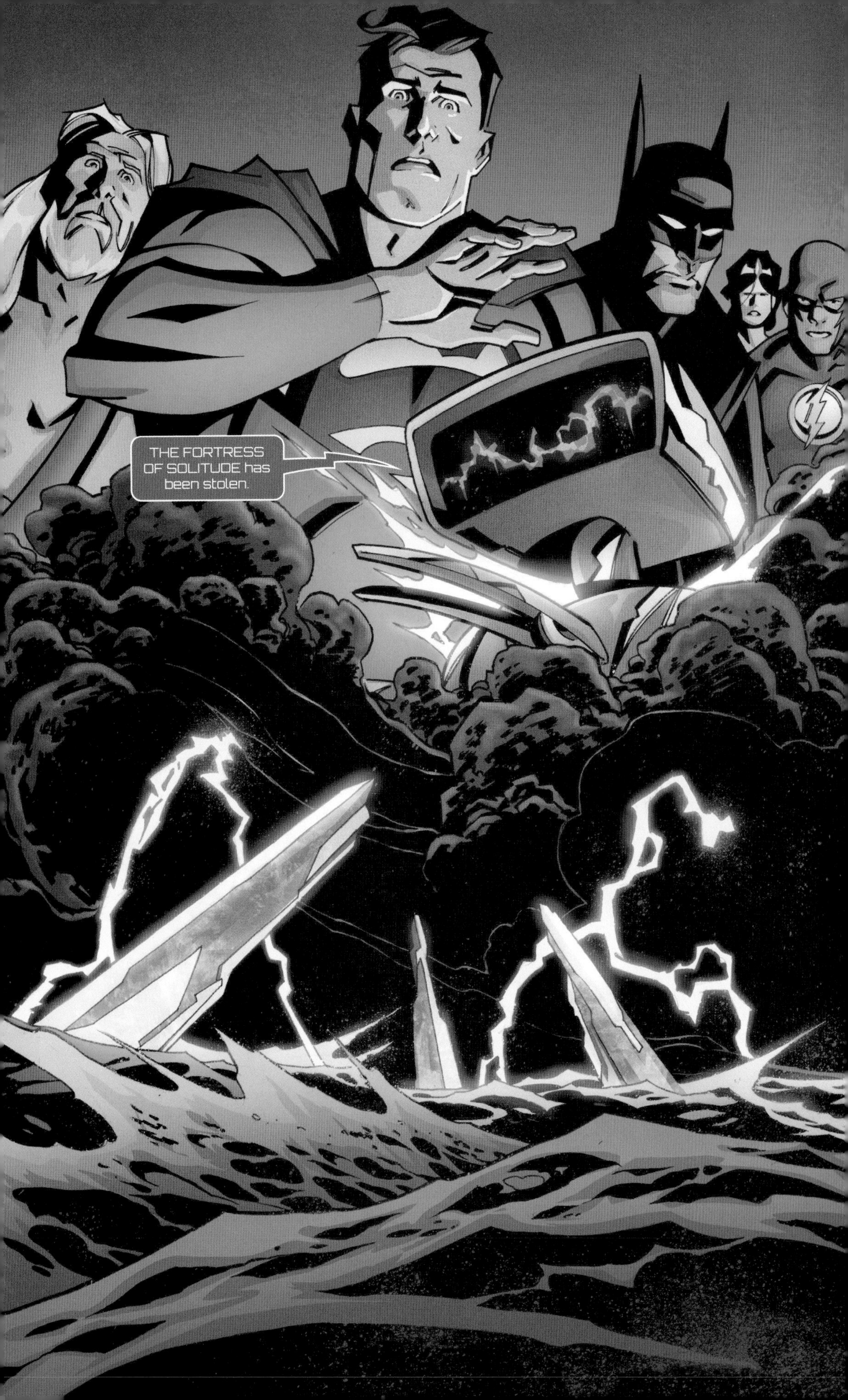
THE FORTRESS OF SOLITUDE has been stolen.

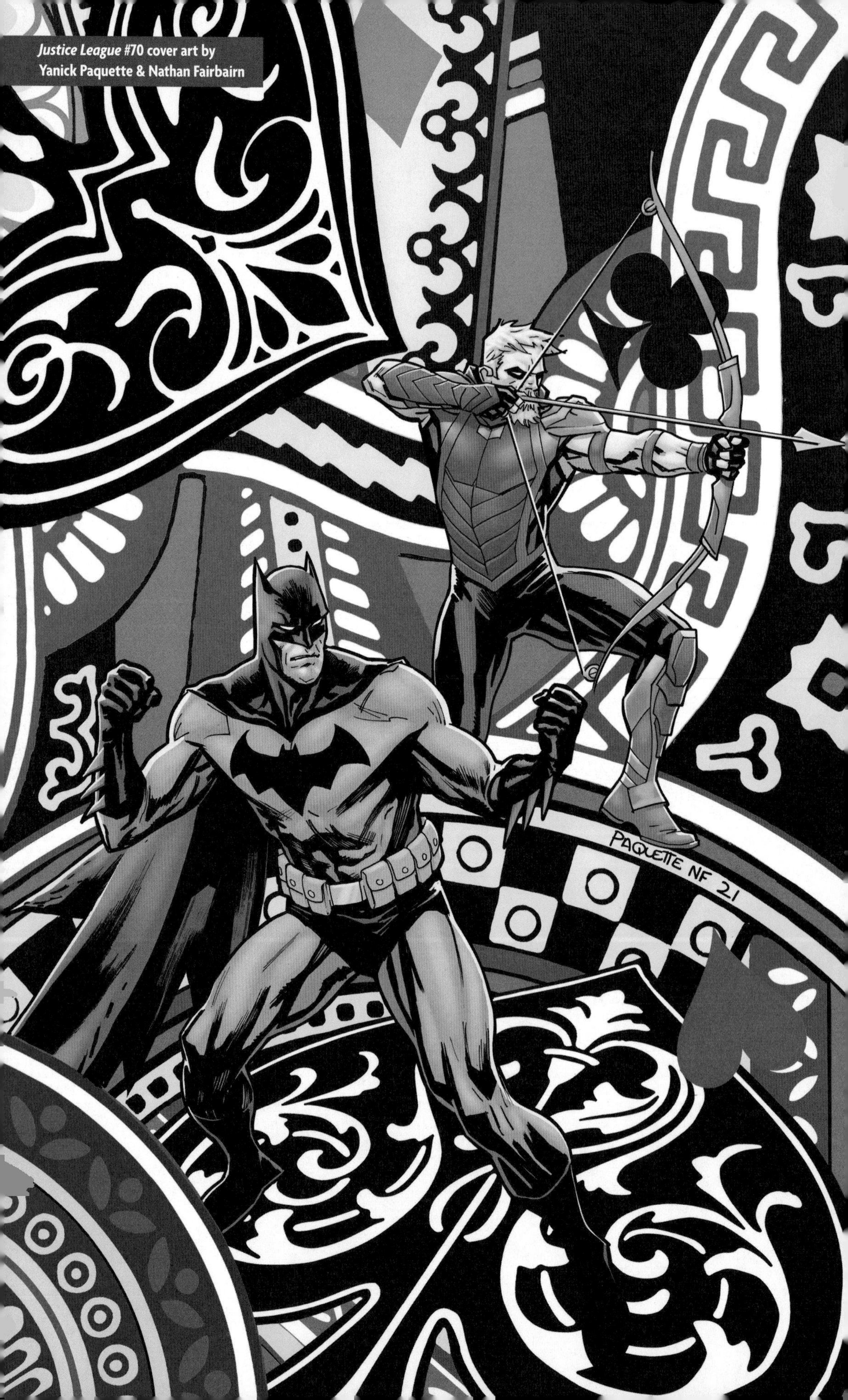
PAQUETTE NF 21

Justice League #70 cover art by
Yanick Paquette & Nathan Fairbairn

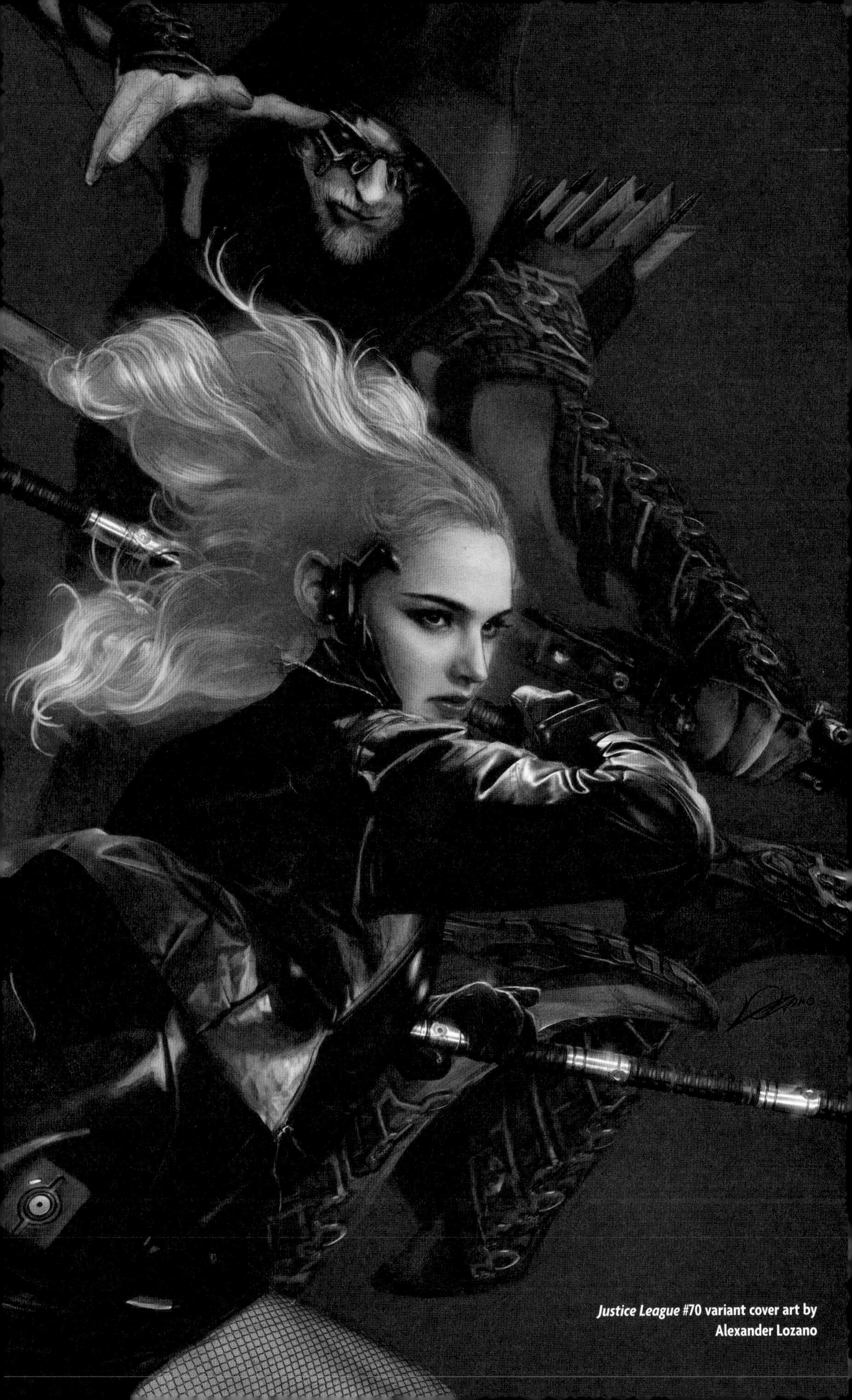

Justice League #70 variant cover art by
Alexander Lozano

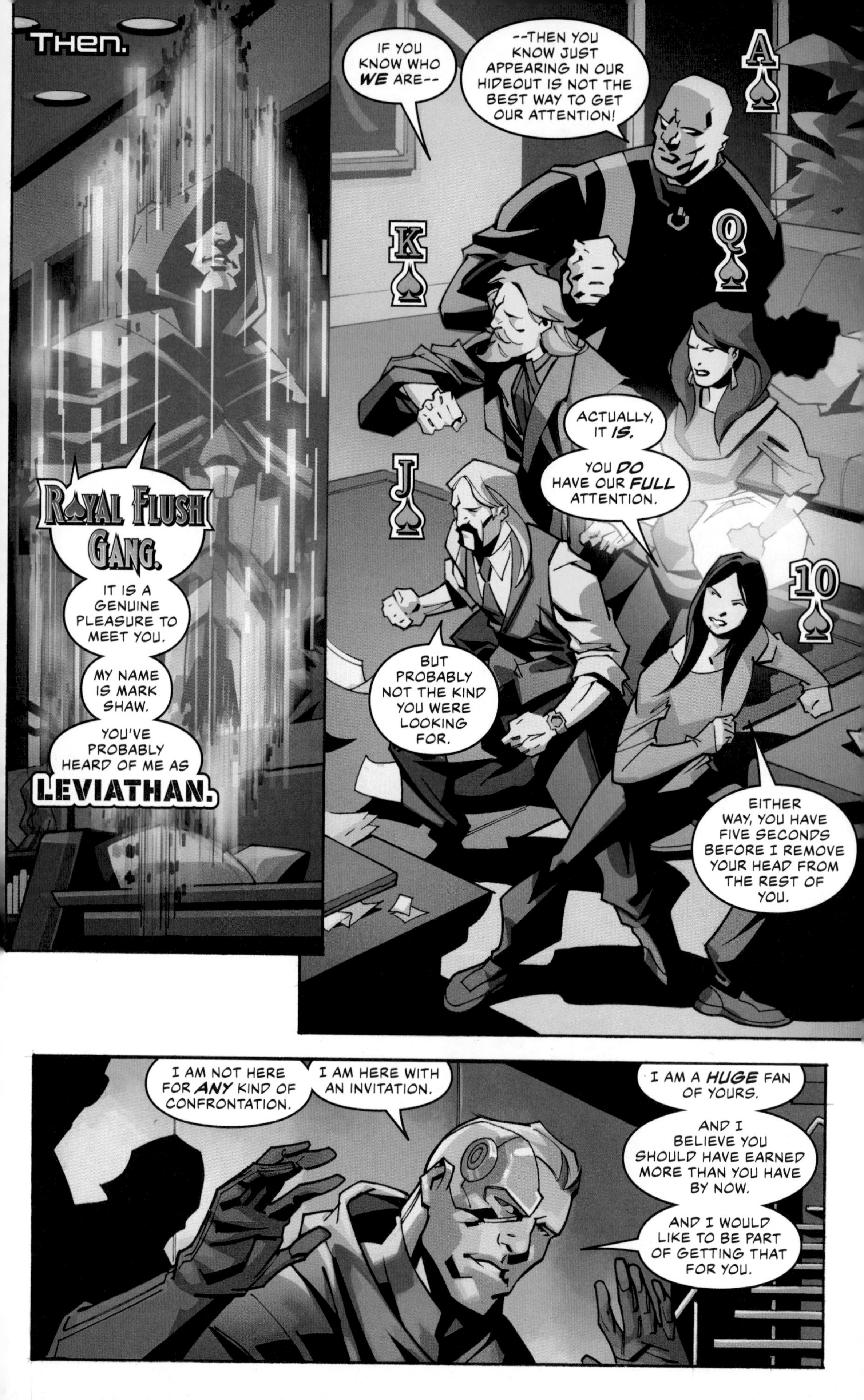
THEN.
ROYAL FLUSH GANG.
IT IS A GENUINE PLEASURE TO MEET YOU.
MY NAME IS MARK SHAW.
YOU'VE PROBABLY HEARD OF ME AS LEVIATHAN.
IF YOU KNOW WHO WE ARE--
--THEN YOU KNOW JUST APPEARING IN OUR HIDEOUT IS NOT THE BEST WAY TO GET OUR ATTENTION!
A
K
Q
J
10
ACTUALLY, IT IS.
YOU DO HAVE OUR FULL ATTENTION.
BUT PROBABLY NOT THE KIND YOU WERE LOOKING FOR.
EITHER WAY, YOU HAVE FIVE SECONDS BEFORE I REMOVE YOUR HEAD FROM THE REST OF YOU.
I AM NOT HERE FOR ANY KIND OF CONFRONTATION.
I AM HERE WITH AN INVITATION.
I AM A HUGE FAN OF YOURS.
AND I BELIEVE YOU SHOULD HAVE EARNED MORE THAN YOU HAVE BY NOW.
AND I WOULD LIKE TO BE PART OF GETTING THAT FOR YOU.

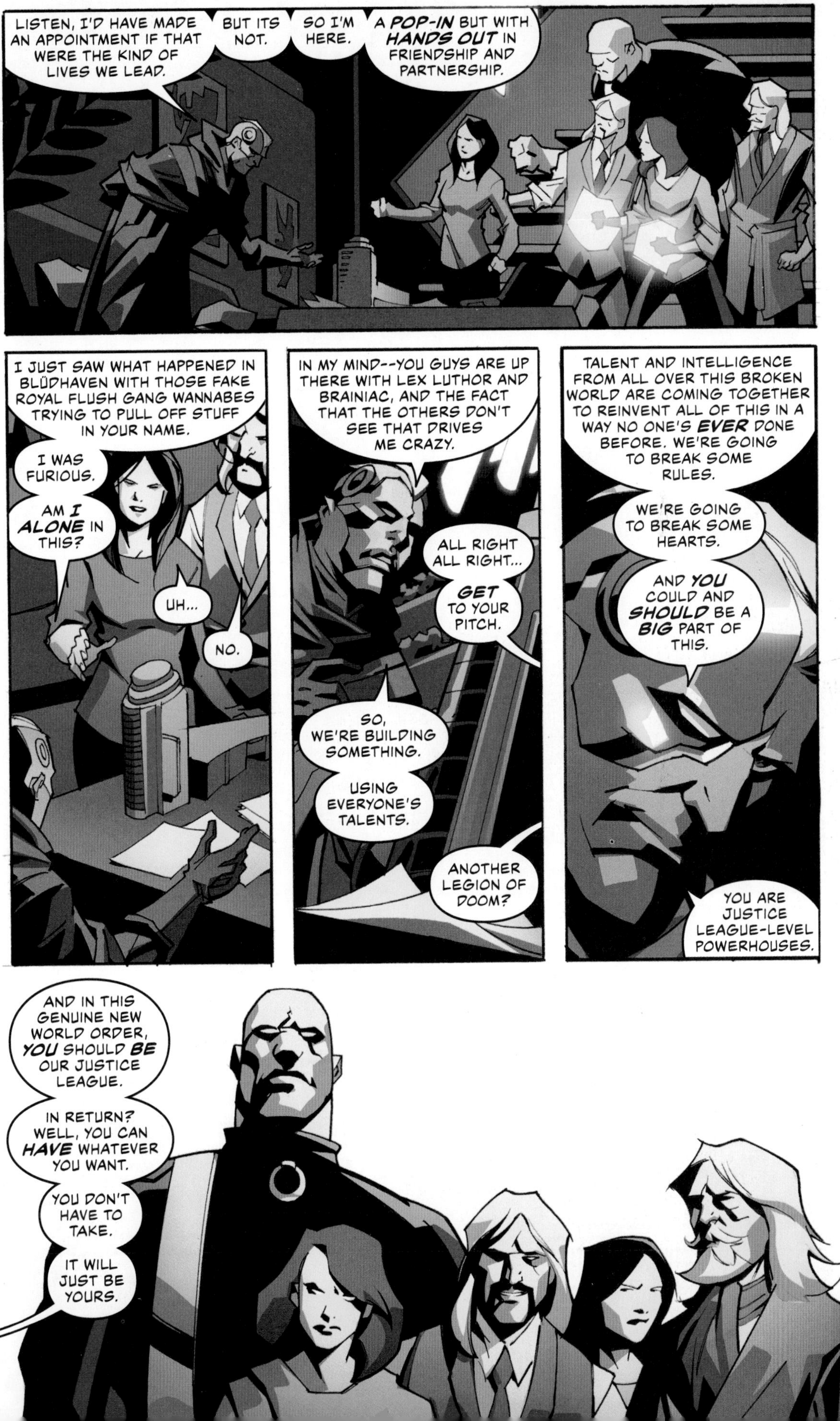
LISTEN, I'D HAVE MADE AN APPOINTMENT IF THAT WERE THE KIND OF LIVES WE LEAD.
BUT ITS NOT.
SO I'M HERE.
A POP-IN BUT WITH HANDS OUT IN FRIENDSHIP AND PARTNERSHIP.
I JUST SAW WHAT HAPPENED IN BLÜDHAVEN WITH THOSE FAKE ROYAL FLUSH GANG WANNABES TRYING TO PULL OFF STUFF IN YOUR NAME.
I WAS FURIOUS.
AM I ALONE IN THIS?
UH...
NO.
IN MY MIND--YOU GUYS ARE UP THERE WITH LEX LUTHOR AND BRAINIAC, AND THE FACT THAT THE OTHERS DON'T SEE THAT DRIVES ME CRAZY.
ALL RIGHT ALL RIGHT...
GET TO YOUR PITCH.
SO, WE'RE BUILDING SOMETHING.
USING EVERYONE'S TALENTS.
ANOTHER LEGION OF DOOM?
TALENT AND INTELLIGENCE FROM ALL OVER THIS BROKEN WORLD ARE COMING TOGETHER TO REINVENT ALL OF THIS IN A WAY NO ONE'S EVER DONE BEFORE. WE'RE GOING TO BREAK SOME RULES.
WE'RE GOING TO BREAK SOME HEARTS.
AND YOU COULD AND SHOULD BE A BIG PART OF THIS.
YOU ARE JUSTICE LEAGUE-LEVEL POWERHOUSES.
AND IN THIS GENUINE NEW WORLD ORDER, YOU SHOULD BE OUR JUSTICE LEAGUE.
IN RETURN? WELL, YOU CAN HAVE WHATEVER YOU WANT.
YOU DON'T HAVE TO TAKE.
IT WILL JUST BE YOURS.

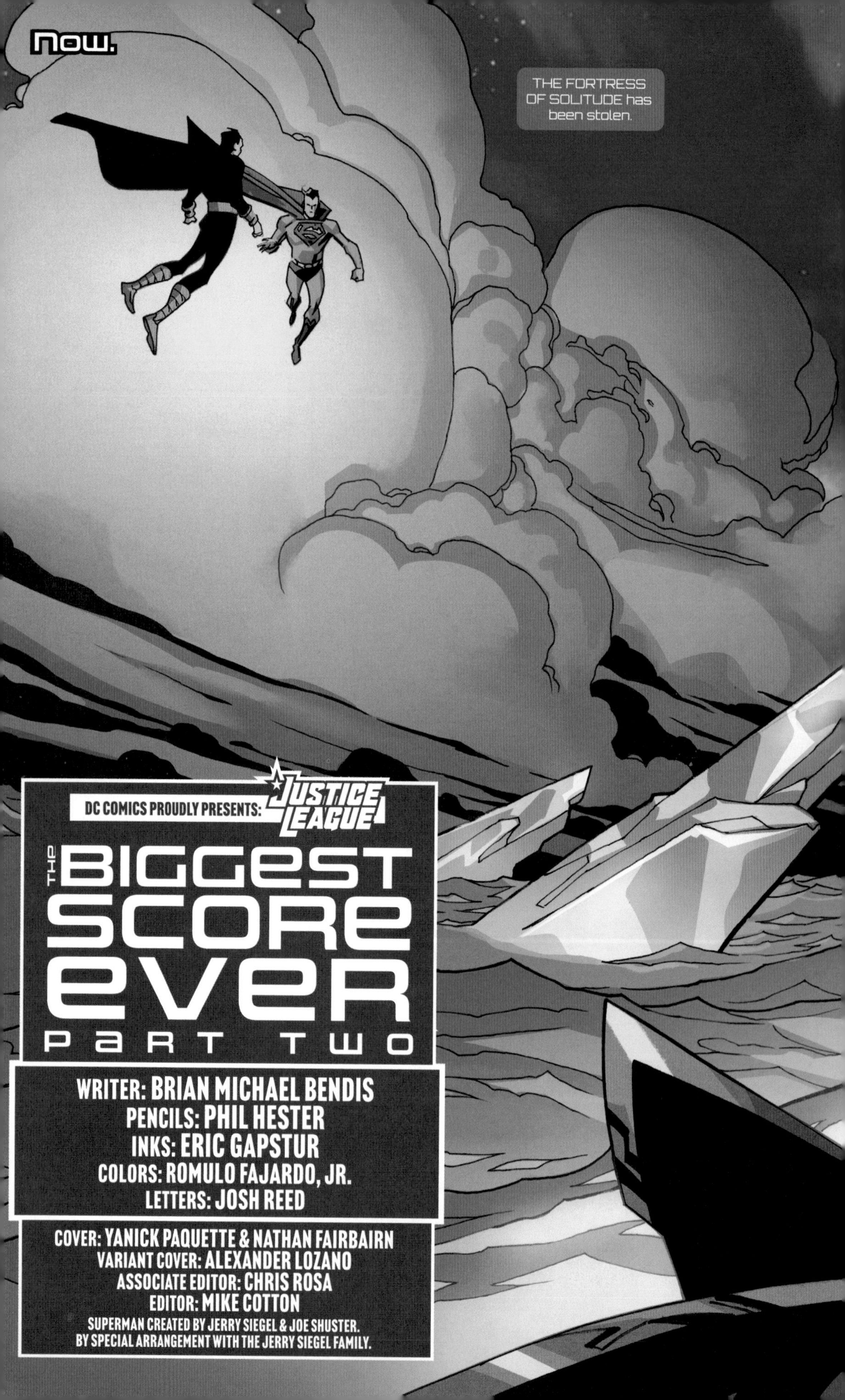
NOW.
THE FORTRESS OF SOLITUDE has been stolen.
DC COMICS PROUDLY PRESENTS: JUSTICE LEAGUE
THE BIGGEST SCORE EVER
PART TWO
WRITER: BRIAN MICHAEL BENDIS
PENCILS: PHIL HESTER
INKS: ERIC GAPSTUR
COLORS: ROMULO FAJARDO, JR.
LETTERS: JOSH REED
COVER: YANICK PAQUETTE & NATHAN FAIRBAIRN
VARIANT COVER: ALEXANDER LOZANO
ASSOCIATE EDITOR: CHRIS ROSA
EDITOR: MIKE COTTON
SUPERMAN CREATED BY JERRY SIEGEL & JOE SHUSTER.
BY SPECIAL ARRANGEMENT WITH THE JERRY SIEGEL FAMILY.

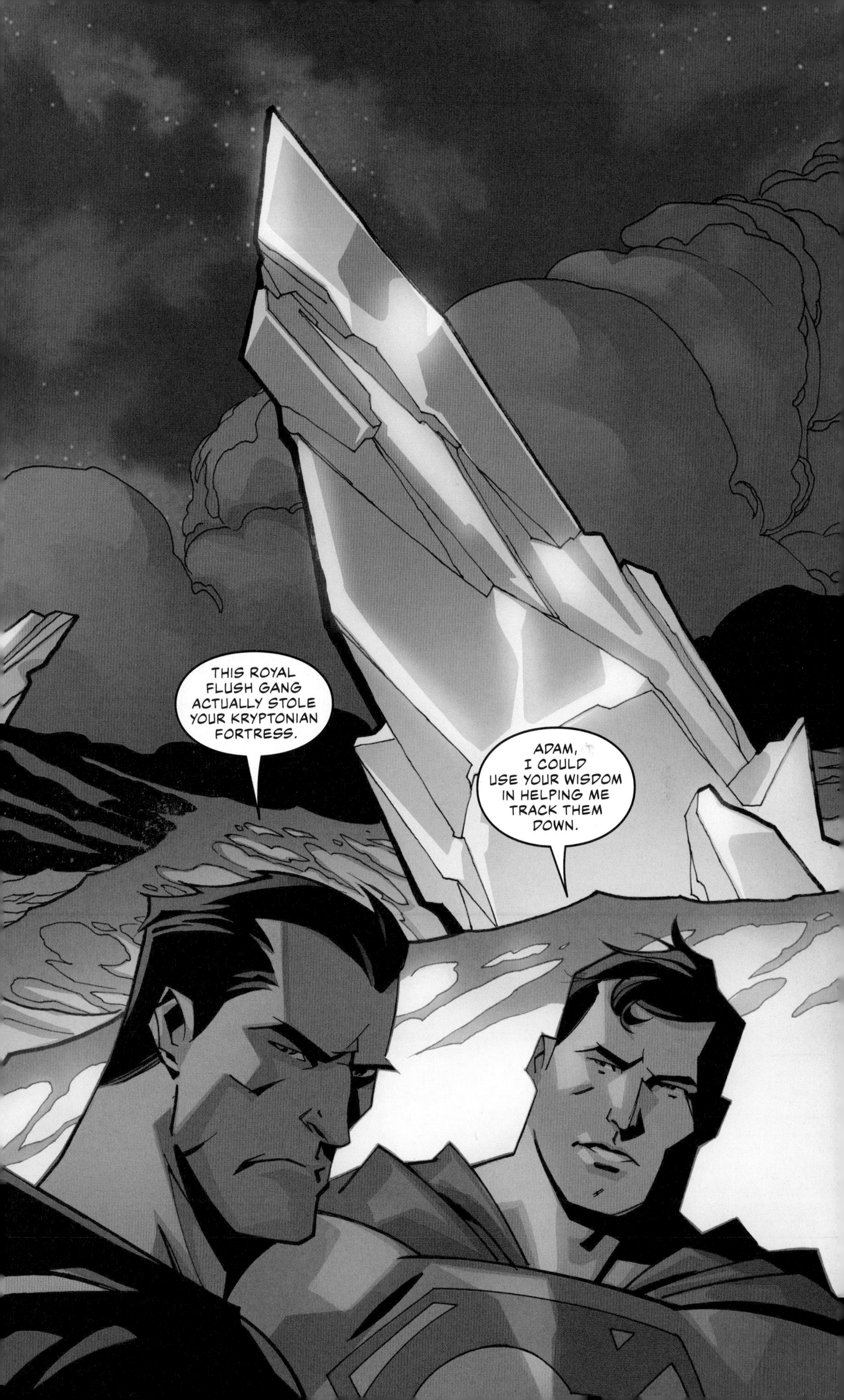
THIS ROYAL FLUSH GANG ACTUALLY STOLE YOUR KRYPTONIAN FORTRESS.
ADAM, I COULD USE YOUR WISDOM IN HELPING ME TRACK THEM DOWN.

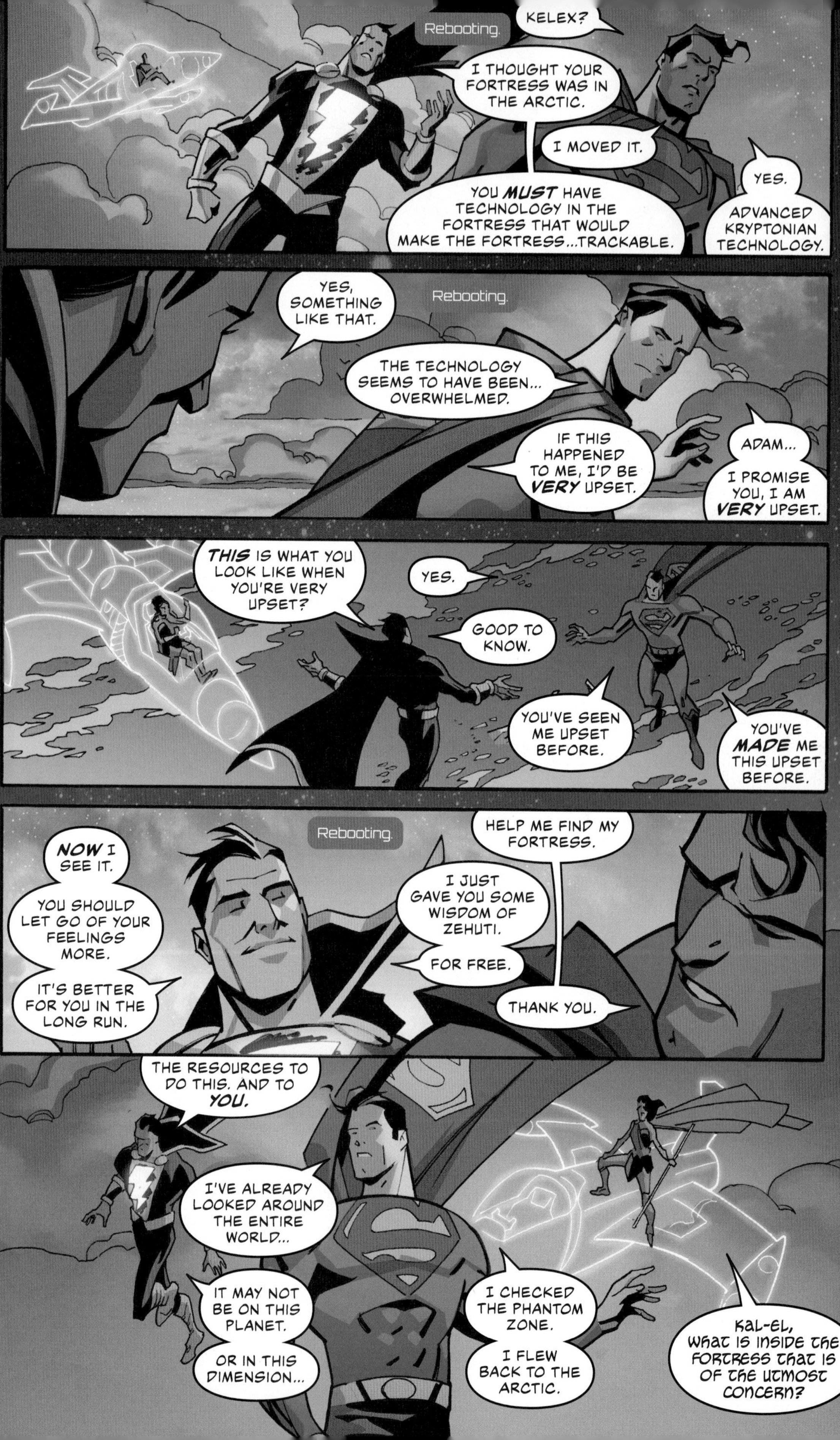

Rebooting.
KELEX?
I THOUGHT YOUR FORTRESS WAS IN THE ARCTIC.
I MOVED IT.
YOU MUST HAVE TECHNOLOGY IN THE FORTRESS THAT WOULD MAKE THE FORTRESS...TRACKABLE.
YES.
ADVANCED KRYPTONIAN TECHNOLOGY.
YES, SOMETHING LIKE THAT.
Rebooting.
THE TECHNOLOGY SEEMS TO HAVE BEEN... OVERWHELMED.
IF THIS HAPPENED TO ME, I'D BE VERY UPSET.
ADAM...
I PROMISE YOU, I AM VERY UPSET.
THIS IS WHAT YOU LOOK LIKE WHEN YOU'RE VERY UPSET?
YES.
GOOD TO KNOW.
YOU'VE SEEN ME UPSET BEFORE.
YOU'VE MADE ME THIS UPSET BEFORE.
Rebooting.
NOW I SEE IT.
YOU SHOULD LET GO OF YOUR FEELINGS MORE.
IT'S BETTER FOR YOU IN THE LONG RUN.
HELP ME FIND MY FORTRESS.
I JUST GAVE YOU SOME WISDOM OF ZEHUTI.
FOR FREE.
THANK YOU.
THE RESOURCES TO DO THIS. AND TO YOU.
I'VE ALREADY LOOKED AROUND THE ENTIRE WORLD...
IT MAY NOT BE ON THIS PLANET.
OR IN THIS DIMENSION...
I CHECKED THE PHANTOM ZONE.
I FLEW BACK TO THE ARCTIC.
KAL-EL, WHAT IS INSIDE THE FORTRESS THAT IS OF THE UTMOST CONCERN?

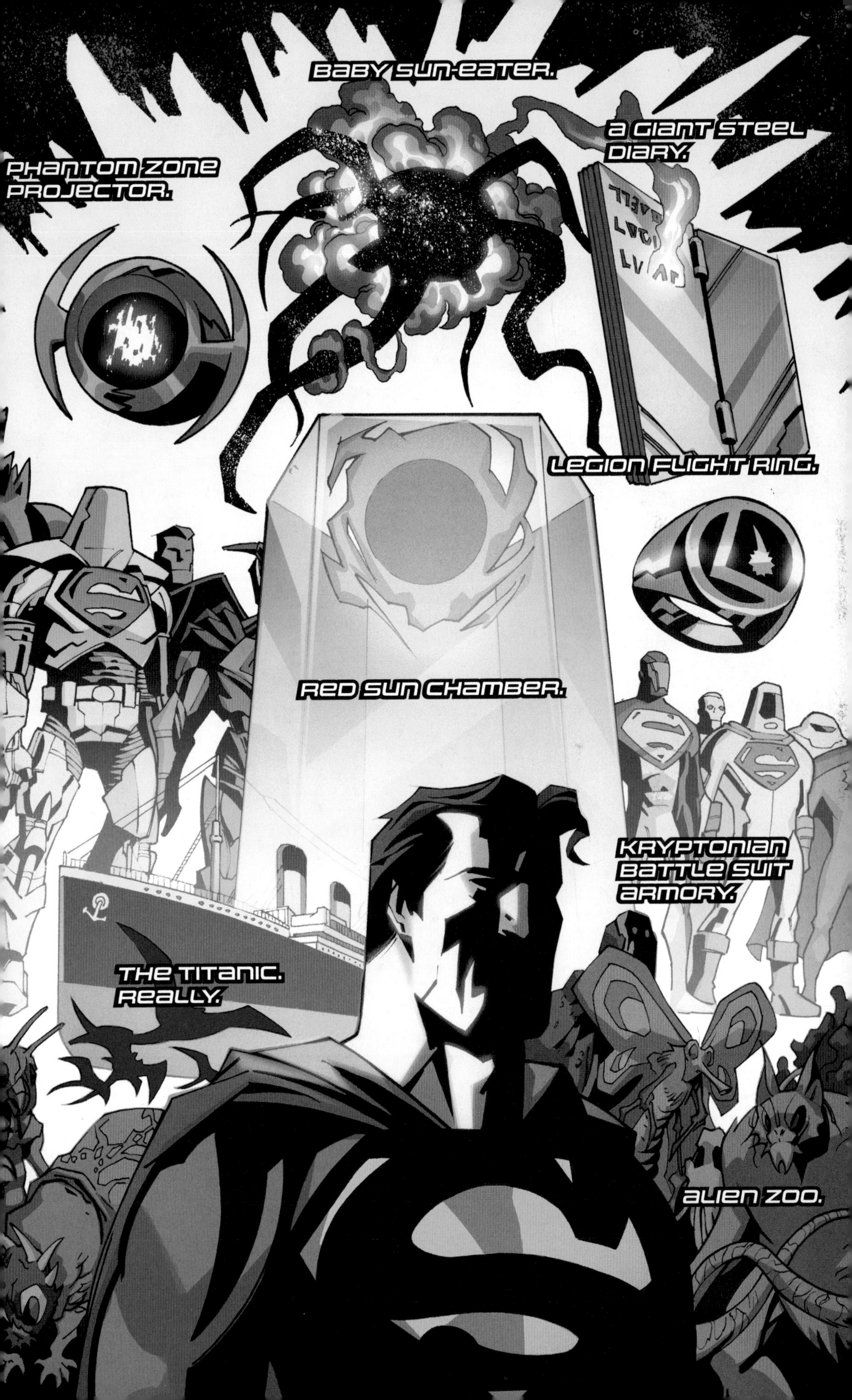

BABY SUN-EATER.
A GIANT STEEL DIARY.
PHANTOM ZONE PROJECTOR.
LEGION FLIGHT RING.
RED SUN CHAMBER.
KRYPTONIAN BATTLE SUIT ARMORY.
THE TITANIC. REALLY.
ALIEN ZOO.

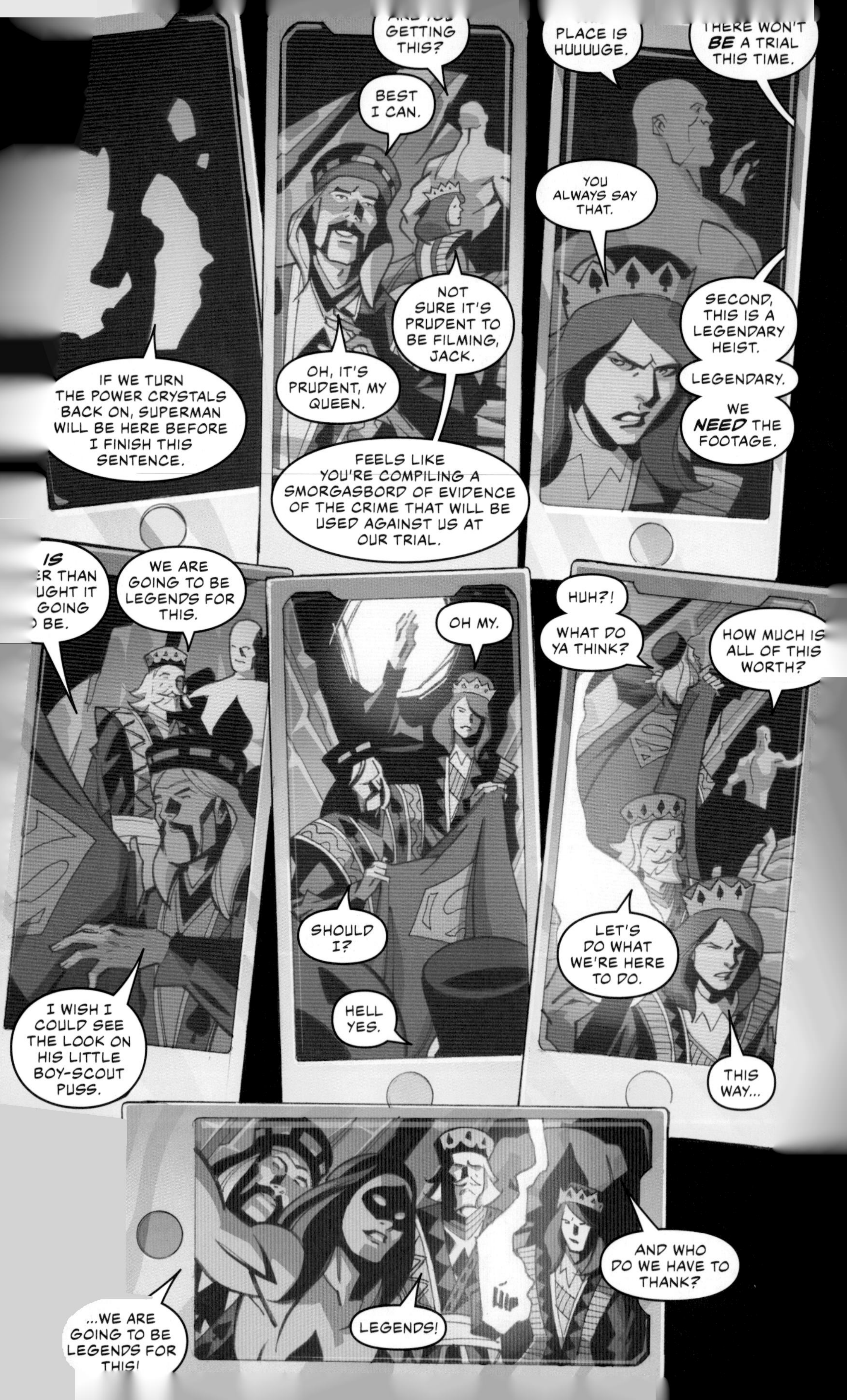
IF WE TURN THE POWER CRYSTALS BACK ON, SUPERMAN WILL BE HERE BEFORE I FINISH THIS SENTENCE.
GETTING THIS?
BEST I CAN.
NOT SURE IT'S PRUDENT TO BE FILMING, JACK.
OH, IT'S PRUDENT, MY QUEEN.
FEELS LIKE YOU'RE COMPILING A SMORGASBORD OF EVIDENCE OF THE CRIME THAT WILL BE USED AGAINST US AT OUR TRIAL.
PLACE IS HUUUUGE.
THERE WON'T BE A TRIAL THIS TIME.
YOU ALWAYS SAY THAT.
SECOND, THIS IS A LEGENDARY HEIST.
LEGENDARY.
WE NEED THE FOOTAGE.
WE ARE GOING TO BE LEGENDS FOR THIS.
I WISH I COULD SEE THE LOOK ON HIS LITTLE BOY-SCOUT PUSS.
OH MY.
SHOULD I?
HELL YES.
HUH?!
WHAT DO YA THINK?
HOW MUCH IS ALL OF THIS WORTH?
LET'S DO WHAT WE'RE HERE TO DO.
THIS WAY...
...WE ARE GOING TO BE LEGENDS FOR THIS!
LEGENDS!
AND WHO DO WE HAVE TO THANK?

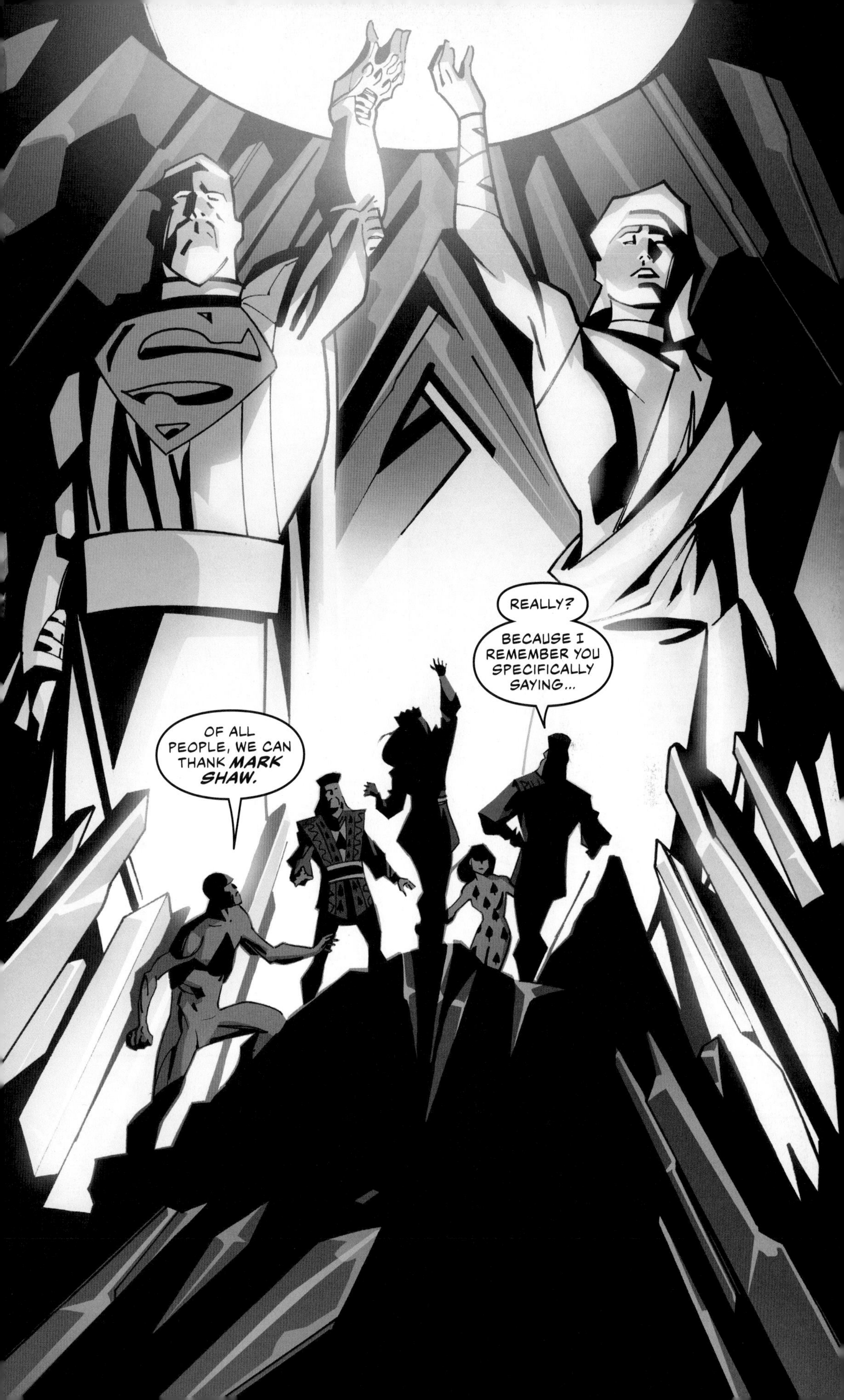
REALLY?
BECAUSE I REMEMBER YOU SPECIFICALLY SAYING...
OF ALL PEOPLE, WE CAN THANK MARK SHAW.

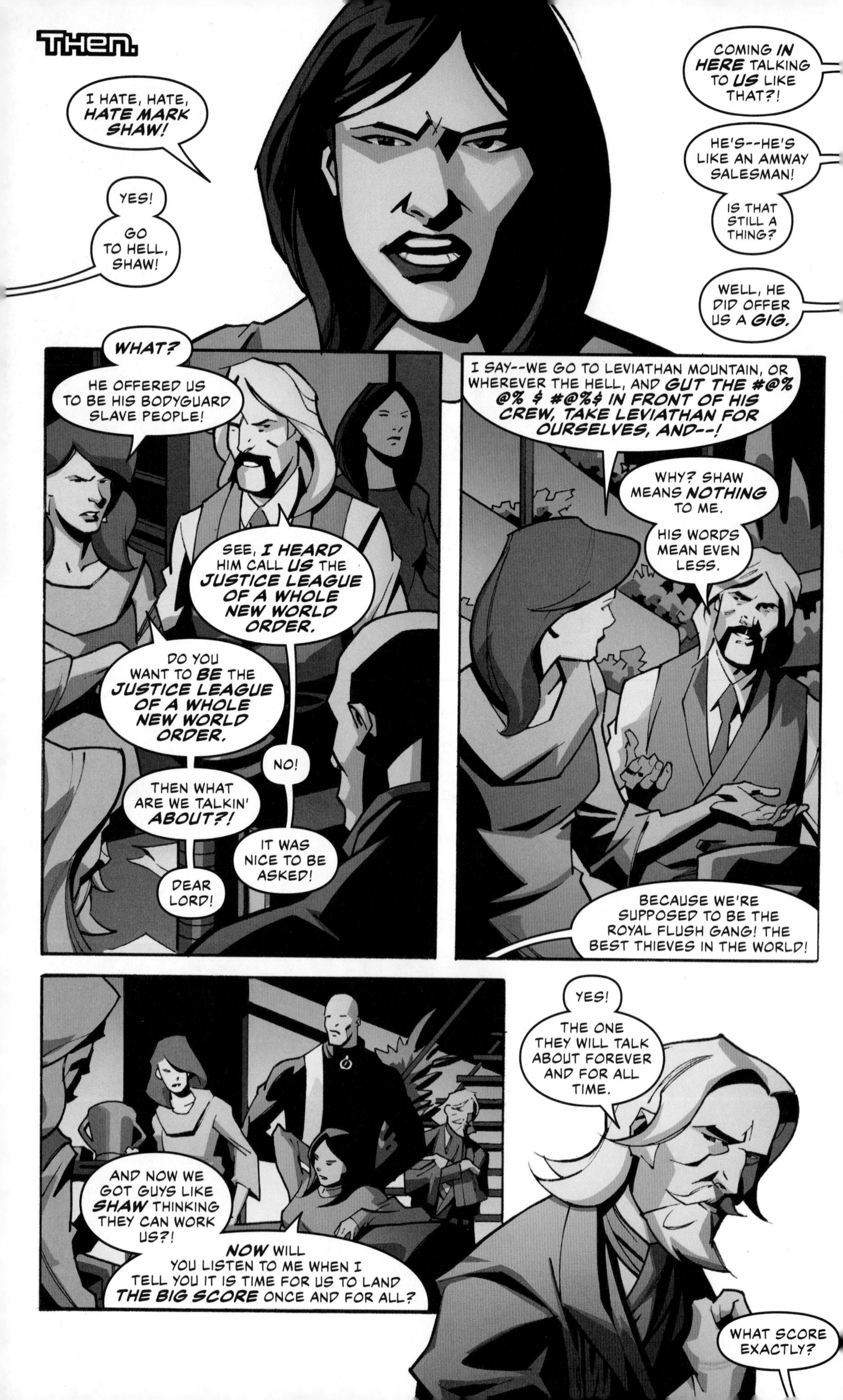
THEN.
I HATE, HATE, HATE MARK SHAW!
YES!
GO TO HELL, SHAW!
COMING IN HERE TALKING TO US LIKE THAT?!
HE'S--HE'S LIKE AN AMWAY SALESMAN!
IS THAT STILL A THING?
WELL, HE DID OFFER US A GIG.
WHAT?
HE OFFERED US TO BE HIS BODYGUARD SLAVE PEOPLE!
SEE, I HEARD HIM CALL US THE JUSTICE LEAGUE OF A WHOLE NEW WORLD ORDER.
DO YOU WANT TO BE THE JUSTICE LEAGUE OF A WHOLE NEW WORLD ORDER.
NO!
THEN WHAT ARE WE TALKIN' ABOUT?!
IT WAS NICE TO BE ASKED!
DEAR LORD!
I SAY--WE GO TO LEVIATHAN MOUNTAIN, OR WHEREVER THE HELL, AND GUT THE #@% @% $ #@%$ IN FRONT OF HIS CREW, TAKE LEVIATHAN FOR OURSELVES, AND--!
WHY? SHAW MEANS NOTHING TO ME.
HIS WORDS MEAN EVEN LESS.
BECAUSE WE'RE SUPPOSED TO BE THE ROYAL FLUSH GANG! THE BEST THIEVES IN THE WORLD!
YES!
THE ONE THEY WILL TALK ABOUT FOREVER AND FOR ALL TIME.
AND NOW WE GOT GUYS LIKE SHAW THINKING THEY CAN WORK US?!
NOW WILL YOU LISTEN TO ME WHEN I TELL YOU IT IS TIME FOR US TO LAND THE BIG SCORE ONCE AND FOR ALL?
WHAT SCORE EXACTLY?

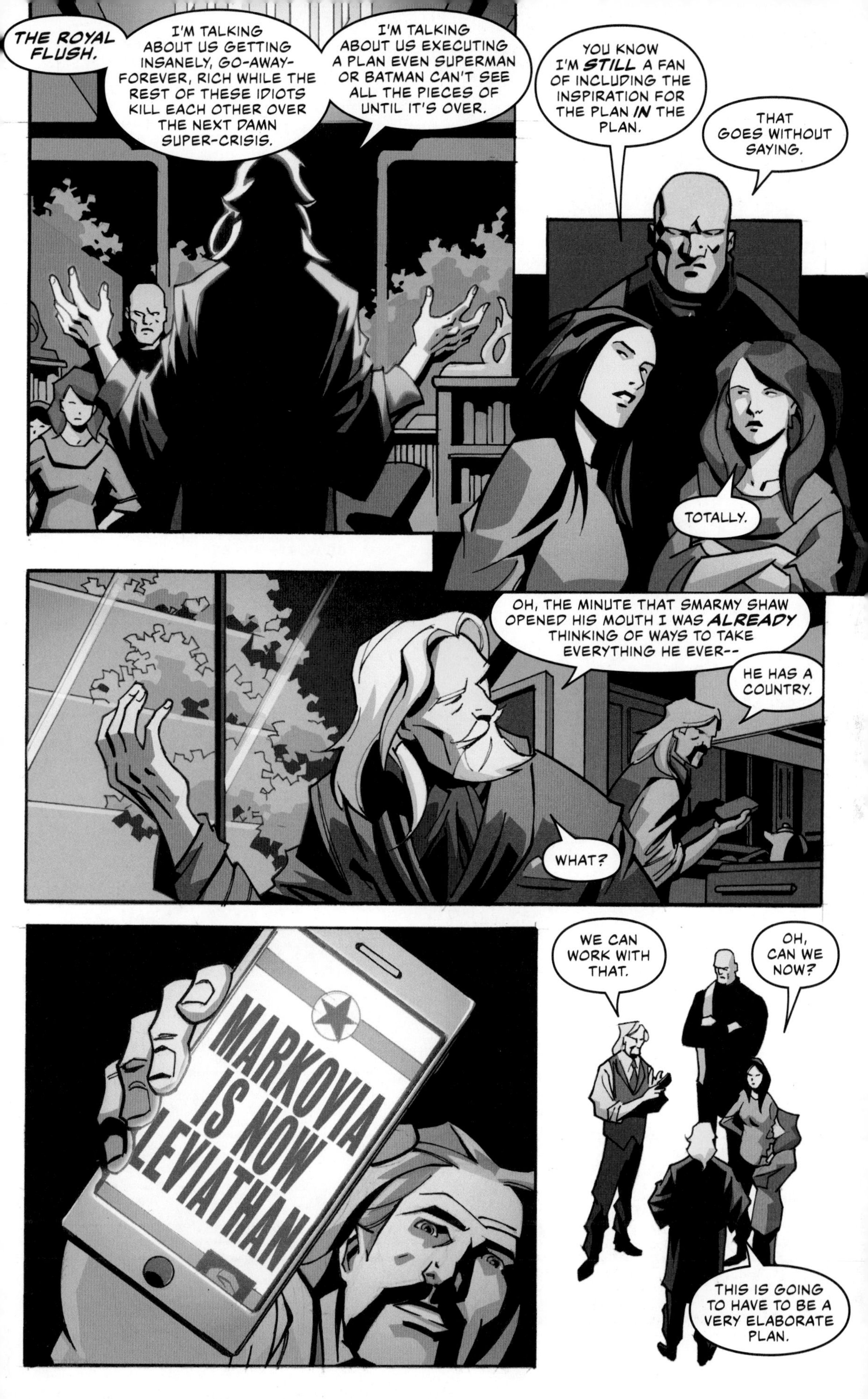
THE ROYAL FLUSH.
I'M TALKING ABOUT US GETTING INSANELY, GO-AWAY-FOREVER, RICH WHILE THE REST OF THESE IDIOTS KILL EACH OTHER OVER THE NEXT DAMN SUPER-CRISIS.
I'M TALKING ABOUT US EXECUTING A PLAN EVEN SUPERMAN OR BATMAN CAN'T SEE ALL THE PIECES OF UNTIL IT'S OVER.
YOU KNOW I'M STILL A FAN OF INCLUDING THE INSPIRATION FOR THE PLAN IN THE PLAN.
THAT GOES WITHOUT SAYING.
TOTALLY.
OH, THE MINUTE THAT SMARMY SHAW OPENED HIS MOUTH I WAS ALREADY THINKING OF WAYS TO TAKE EVERYTHING HE EVER--
HE HAS A COUNTRY.
WHAT?
MARKOVIA IS NOW LEVIATHAN
WE CAN WORK WITH THAT.
OH, CAN WE NOW?
THIS IS GOING TO HAVE TO BE A VERY ELABORATE PLAN.

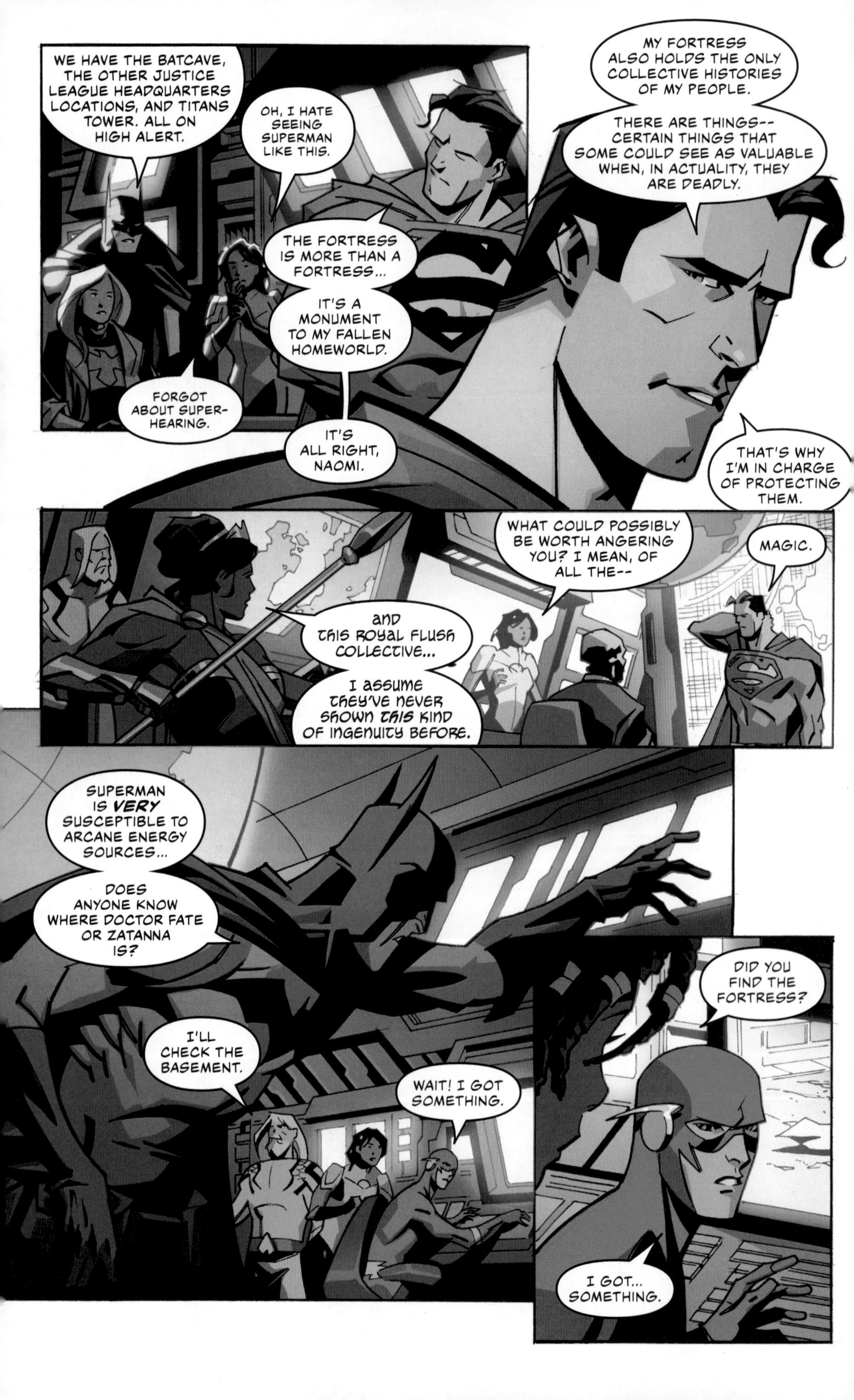
WE HAVE THE BATCAVE, THE OTHER JUSTICE LEAGUE HEADQUARTERS LOCATIONS, AND TITANS TOWER. ALL ON HIGH ALERT.
OH, I HATE SEEING SUPERMAN LIKE THIS.
THE FORTRESS IS MORE THAN A FORTRESS...
IT'S A MONUMENT TO MY FALLEN HOMEWORLD.
FORGOT ABOUT SUPER-HEARING.
IT'S ALL RIGHT, NAOMI.
MY FORTRESS ALSO HOLDS THE ONLY COLLECTIVE HISTORIES OF MY PEOPLE.
THERE ARE THINGS--CERTAIN THINGS THAT SOME COULD SEE AS VALUABLE WHEN, IN ACTUALITY, THEY ARE DEADLY.
THAT'S WHY I'M IN CHARGE OF PROTECTING THEM.
WHAT COULD POSSIBLY BE WORTH ANGERING YOU? I MEAN, OF ALL THE--
MAGIC.
AND THIS ROYAL FLUSH COLLECTIVE...
I ASSUME THEY'VE NEVER SHOWN THIS KIND OF INGENUITY BEFORE.
SUPERMAN IS VERY SUSCEPTIBLE TO ARCANE ENERGY SOURCES...
DOES ANYONE KNOW WHERE DOCTOR FATE OR ZATANNA IS?
I'LL CHECK THE BASEMENT.
WAIT! I GOT SOMETHING.
DID YOU FIND THE FORTRESS?
I GOT... SOMETHING.

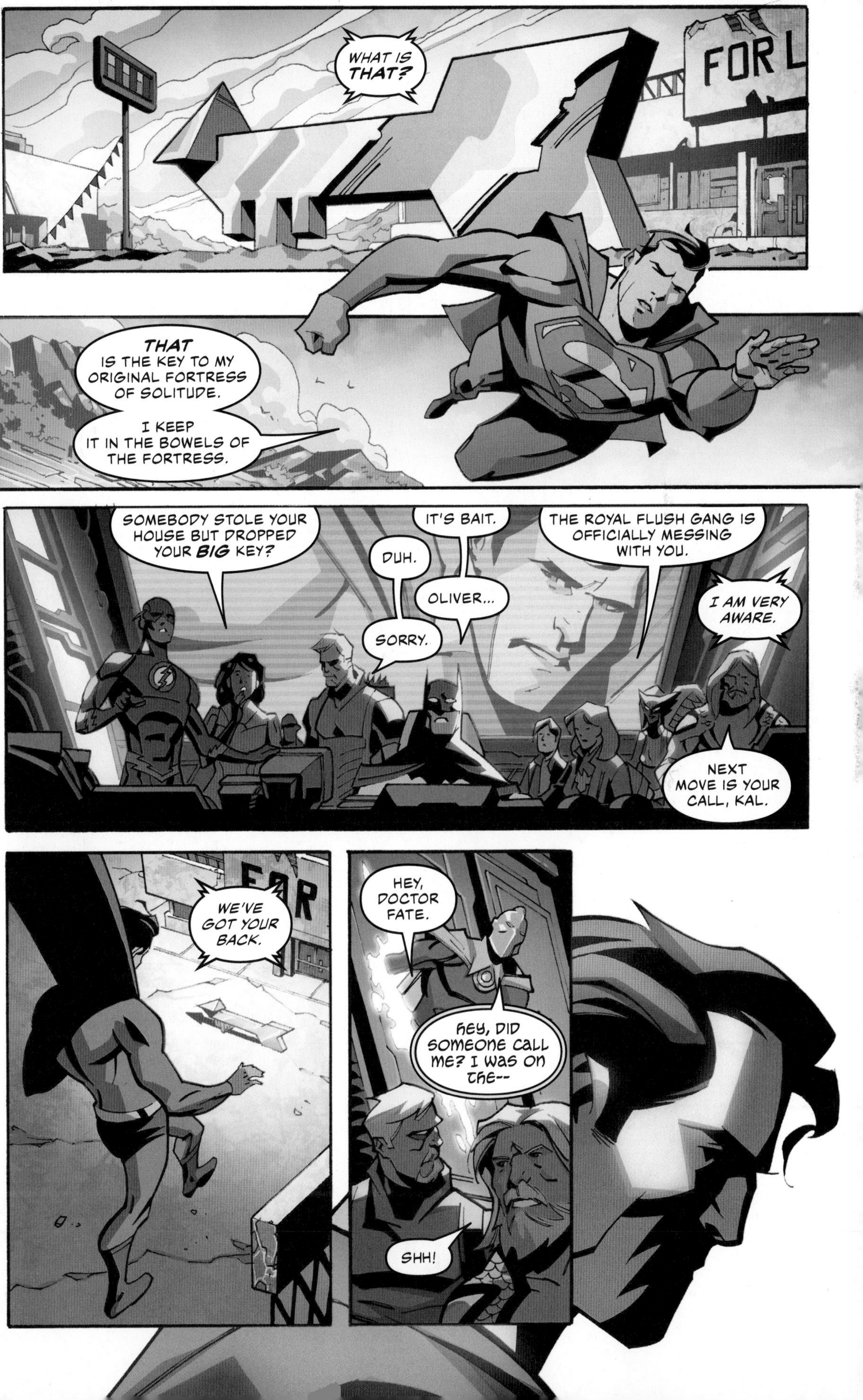

FOR L
WHAT IS THAT?
THAT IS THE KEY TO MY ORIGINAL FORTRESS OF SOLITUDE.
I KEEP IT IN THE BOWELS OF THE FORTRESS.
SOMEBODY STOLE YOUR HOUSE BUT DROPPED YOUR BIG KEY?
DUH.
IT'S BAIT.
OLIVER...
SORRY.
THE ROYAL FLUSH GANG IS OFFICIALLY MESSING WITH YOU.
I AM VERY AWARE.
NEXT MOVE IS YOUR CALL, KAL.
WE'VE GOT YOUR BACK.
HEY, DOCTOR FATE.
HEY, DID SOMEONE CALL ME? I WAS ON THE--
SHH!

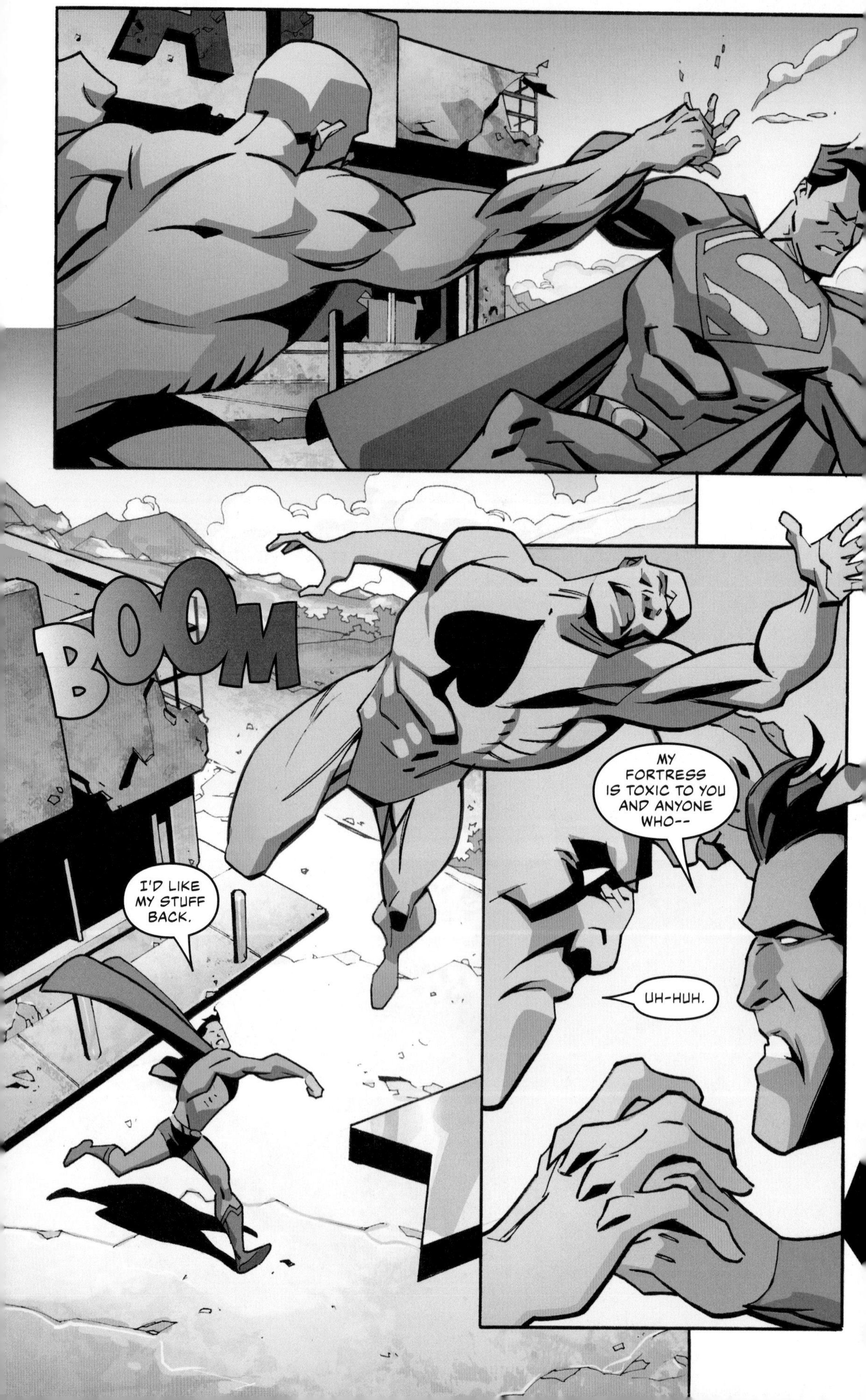
BOOM
I'D LIKE MY STUFF BACK.
MY FORTRESS IS TOXIC TO YOU AND ANYONE WHO--
UH-HUH.

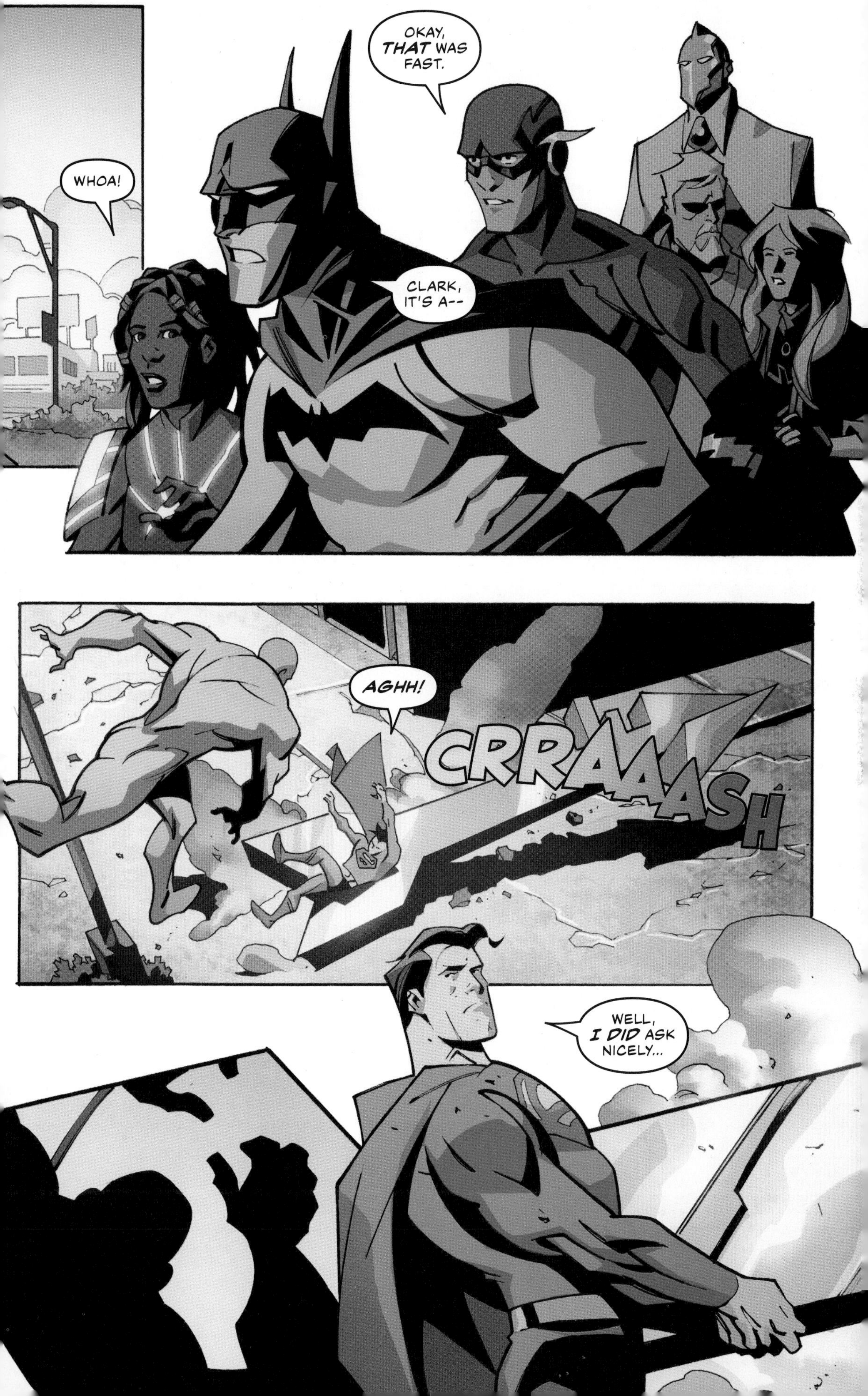
WHOA!
OKAY, THAT WAS FAST.
CLARK, IT'S A--
AGHH!
CRRAAAASH
WELL, I DID ASK NICELY...

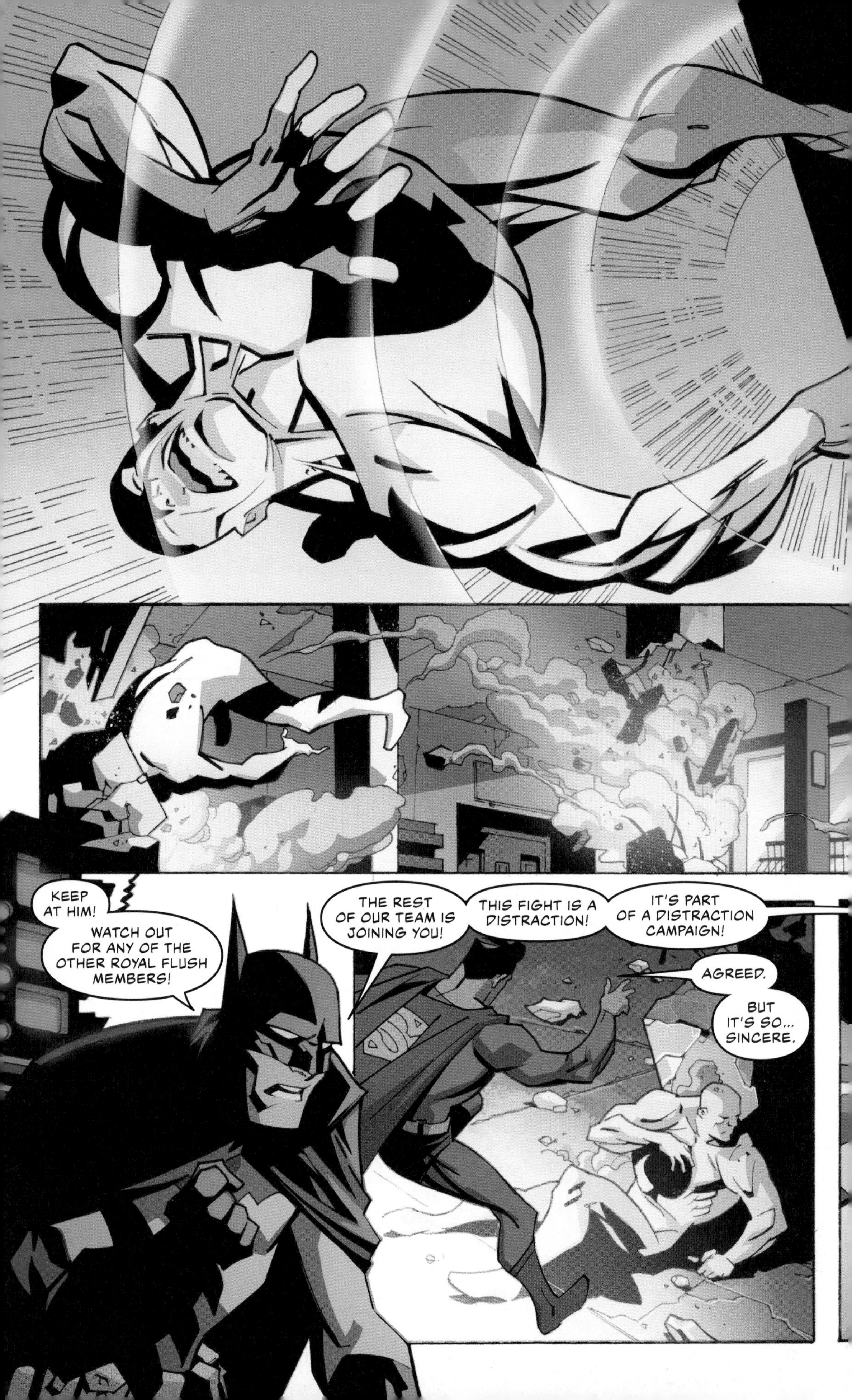
KEEP AT HIM!
WATCH OUT FOR ANY OF THE OTHER ROYAL FLUSH MEMBERS!
THE REST OF OUR TEAM IS JOINING YOU!
THIS FIGHT IS A DISTRACTION!
IT'S PART OF A DISTRACTION CAMPAIGN!
AGREED.
BUT IT'S SO... SINCERE.

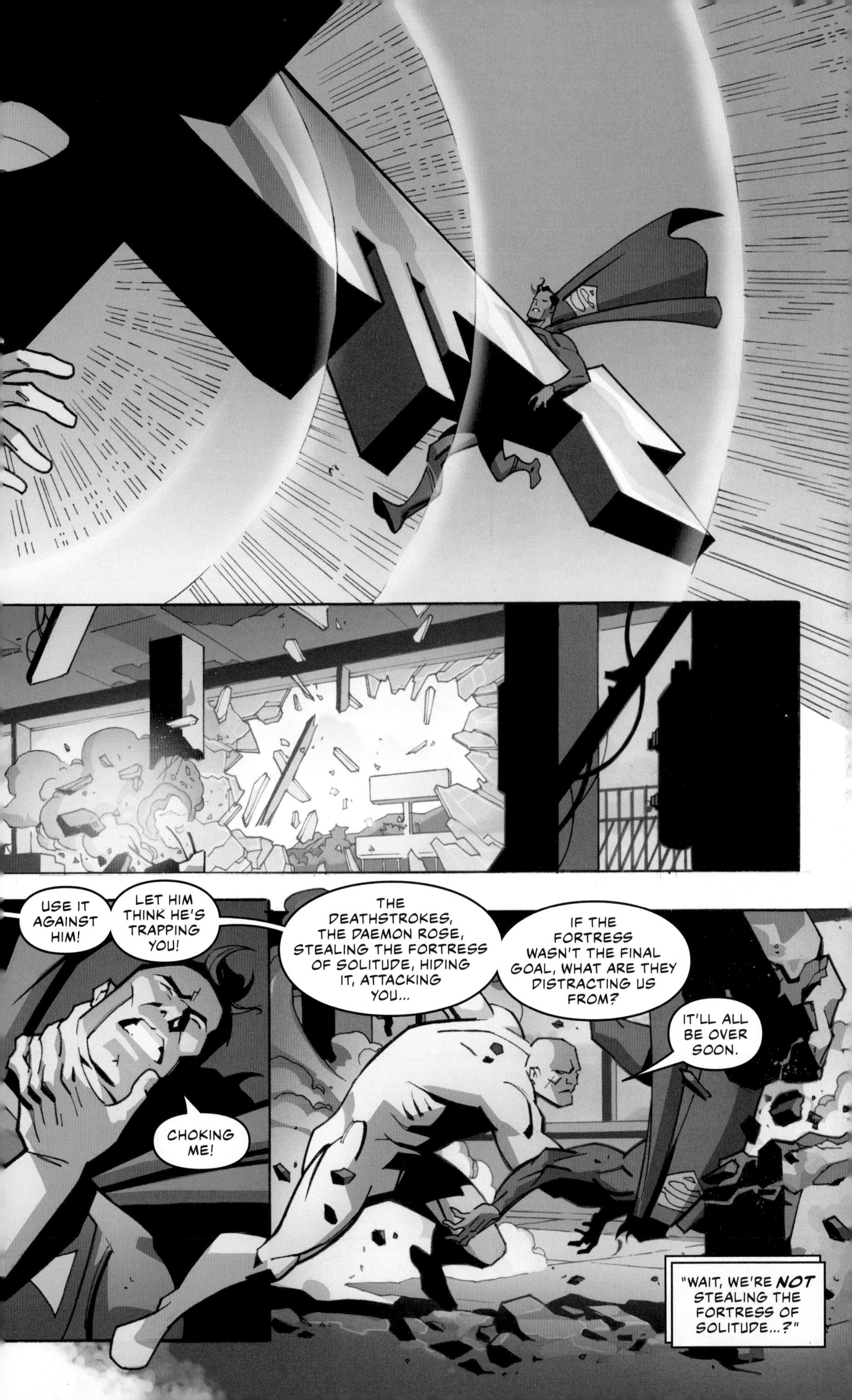
USE IT AGAINST HIM!
LET HIM THINK HE'S TRAPPING YOU!
THE DEATHSTROKES, THE DAEMON ROSE, STEALING THE FORTRESS OF SOLITUDE, HIDING IT, ATTACKING YOU...
IF THE FORTRESS WASN'T THE FINAL GOAL, WHAT ARE THEY DISTRACTING US FROM?
CHOKING ME!
IT'LL ALL BE OVER SOON.
"WAIT, WE'RE NOT STEALING THE FORTRESS OF SOLITUDE...?"

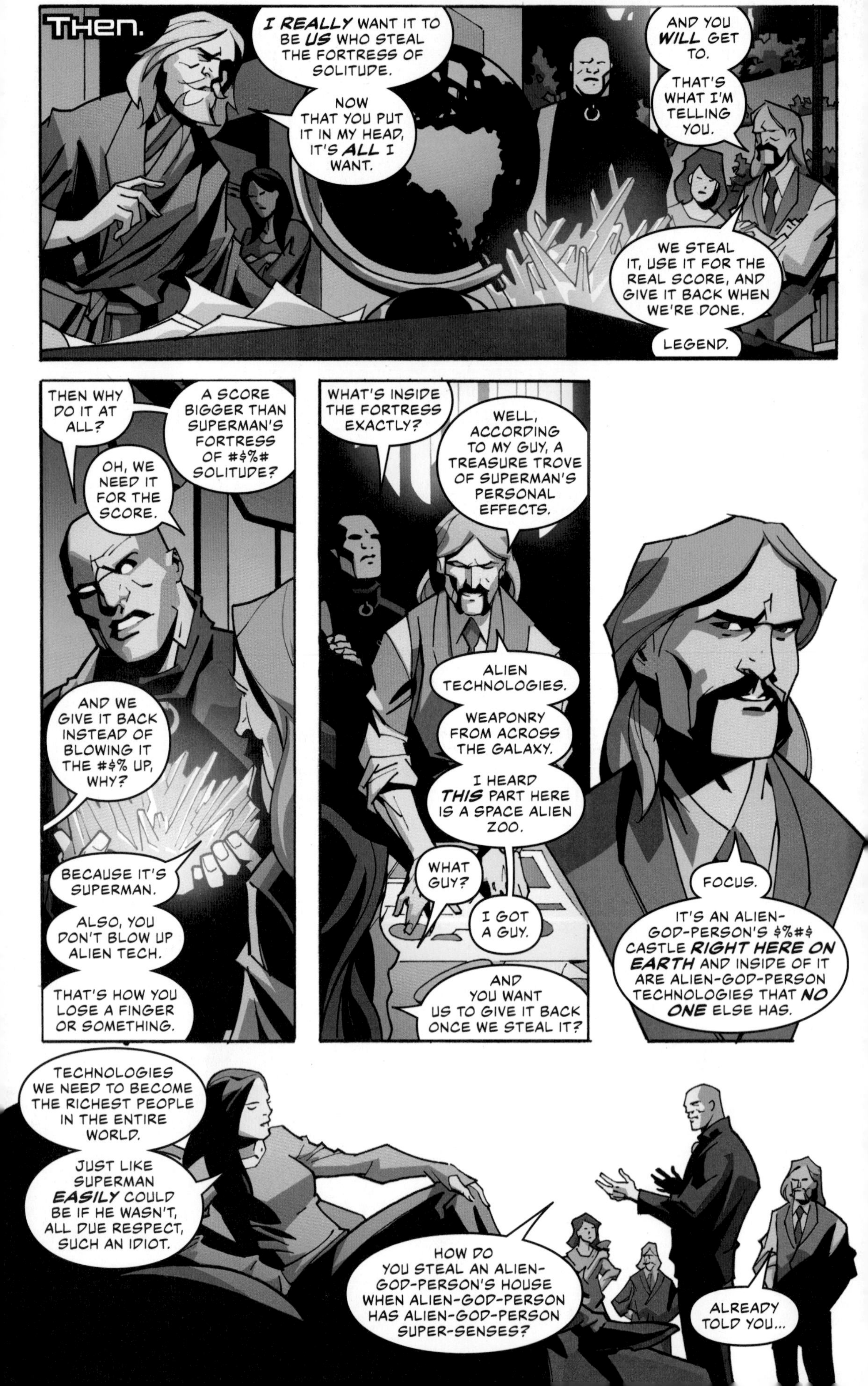
THEN.
I REALLY WANT IT TO BE US WHO STEAL THE FORTRESS OF SOLITUDE.
NOW THAT YOU PUT IT IN MY HEAD, IT'S ALL I WANT.
AND YOU WILL GET TO.
THAT'S WHAT I'M TELLING YOU.
WE STEAL IT, USE IT FOR THE REAL SCORE, AND GIVE IT BACK WHEN WE'RE DONE.
LEGEND.
THEN WHY DO IT AT ALL?
A SCORE BIGGER THAN SUPERMAN'S FORTRESS OF #$%# SOLITUDE?
OH, WE NEED IT FOR THE SCORE.
AND WE GIVE IT BACK INSTEAD OF BLOWING IT THE #$% UP, WHY?
BECAUSE IT'S SUPERMAN.
ALSO, YOU DON'T BLOW UP ALIEN TECH.
THAT'S HOW YOU LOSE A FINGER OR SOMETHING.
WHAT'S INSIDE THE FORTRESS EXACTLY?
WELL, ACCORDING TO MY GUY, A TREASURE TROVE OF SUPERMAN'S PERSONAL EFFECTS.
ALIEN TECHNOLOGIES.
WEAPONRY FROM ACROSS THE GALAXY.
I HEARD THIS PART HERE IS A SPACE ALIEN ZOO.
WHAT GUY?
I GOT A GUY.
AND YOU WANT US TO GIVE IT BACK ONCE WE STEAL IT?
FOCUS.
IT'S AN ALIEN-GOD-PERSON'S $%#$ CASTLE RIGHT HERE ON EARTH AND INSIDE OF IT ARE ALIEN-GOD-PERSON TECHNOLOGIES THAT NO ONE ELSE HAS.
TECHNOLOGIES WE NEED TO BECOME THE RICHEST PEOPLE IN THE ENTIRE WORLD.
JUST LIKE SUPERMAN EASILY COULD BE IF HE WASN'T, ALL DUE RESPECT, SUCH AN IDIOT.
HOW DO YOU STEAL AN ALIEN-GOD-PERSON'S HOUSE WHEN ALIEN-GOD-PERSON HAS ALIEN-GOD-PERSON SUPER-SENSES?
ALREADY TOLD YOU...

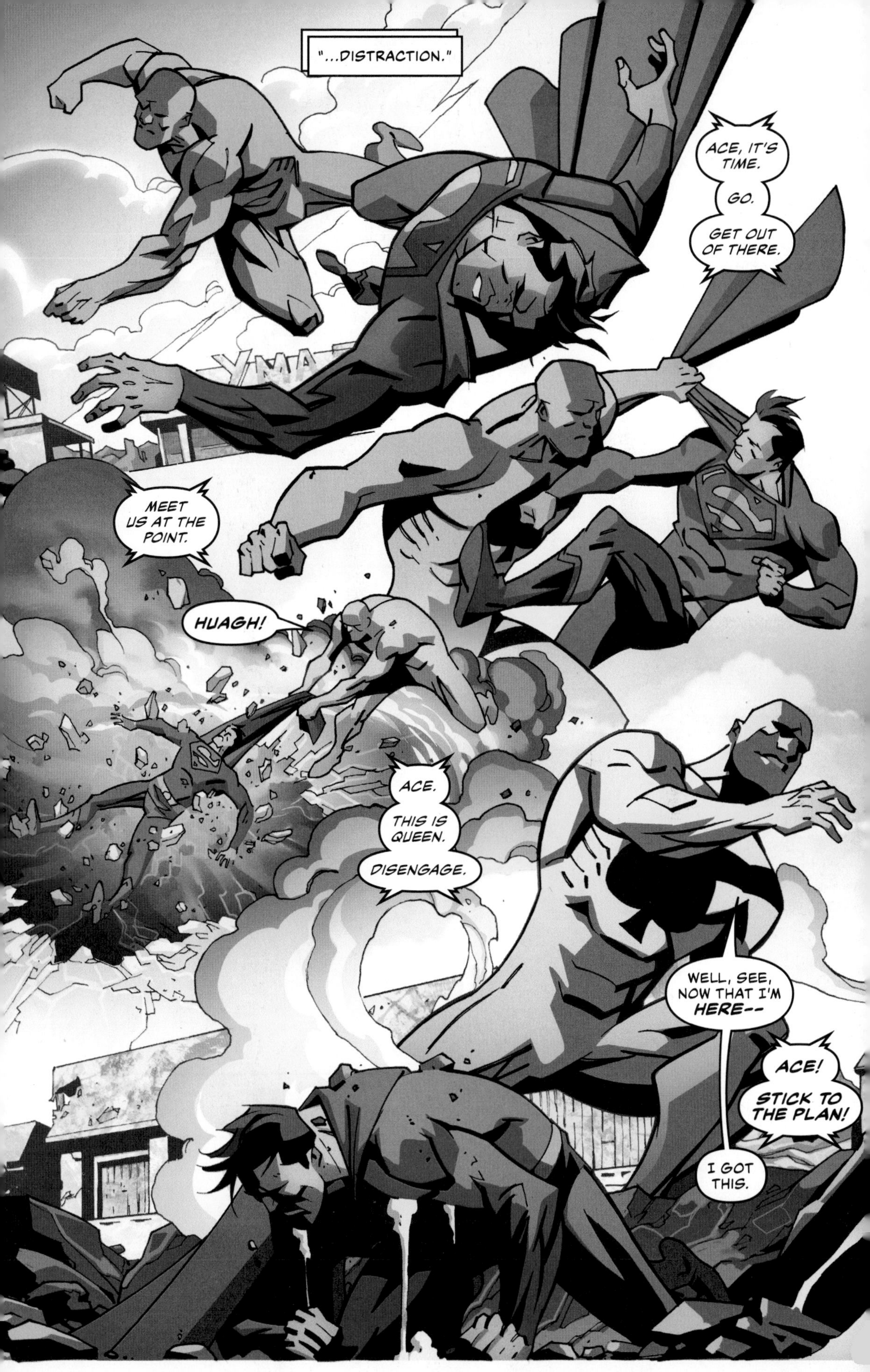
"...DISTRACTION."
ACE, IT'S TIME.
GO.
GET OUT OF THERE.
MEET US AT THE POINT.
HUAGH!
ACE.
THIS IS QUEEN.
DISENGAGE.
WELL, SEE, NOW THAT I'M HERE--
ACE!
STICK TO THE PLAN!
I GOT THIS.

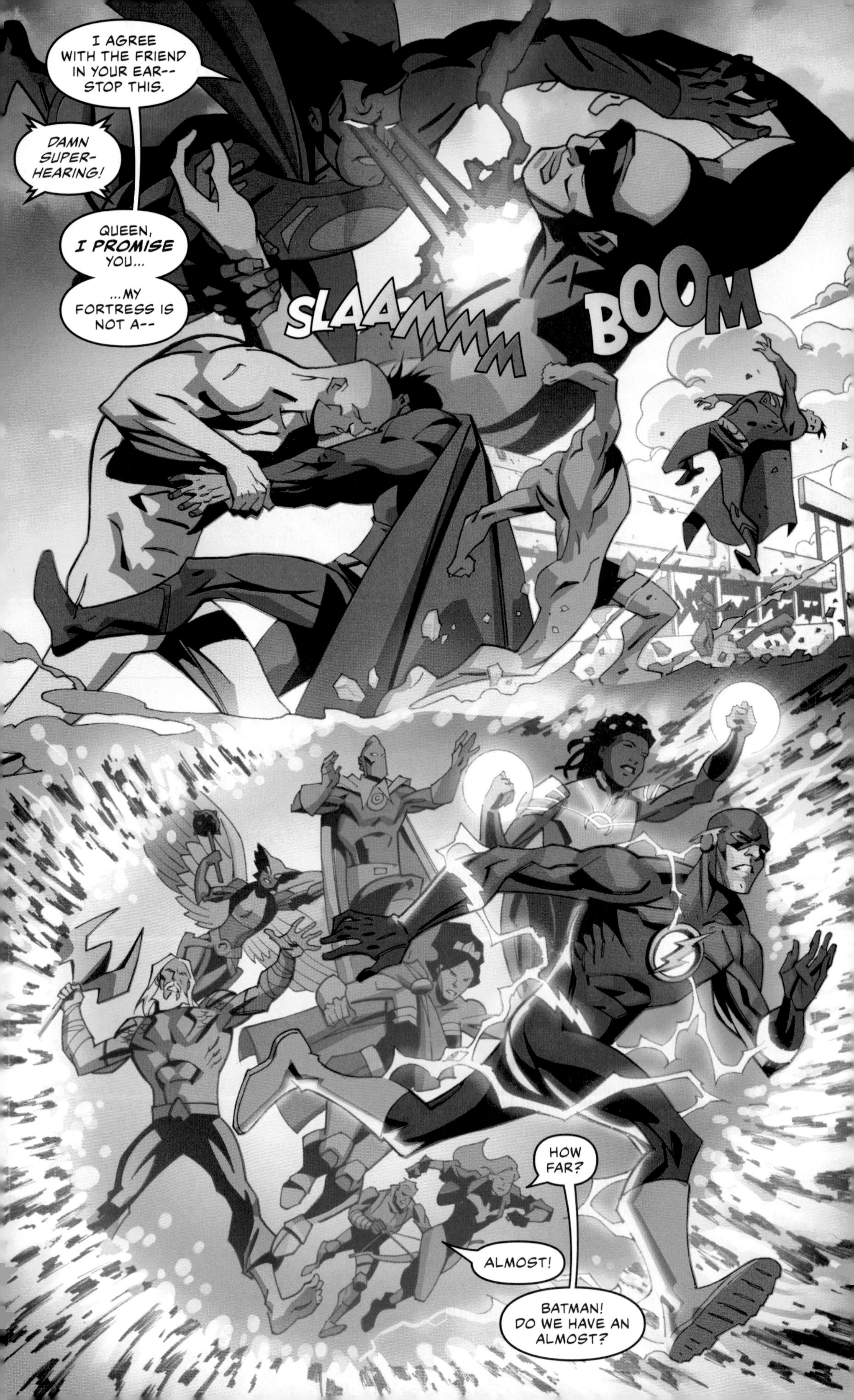
I AGREE WITH THE FRIEND IN YOUR EAR-- STOP THIS.
DAMN SUPER-HEARING!
QUEEN, I PROMISE YOU...
...MY FORTRESS IS NOT A--
SLAAMMMM
BOOM
HOW FAR?
ALMOST!
BATMAN! DO WE HAVE AN ALMOST?

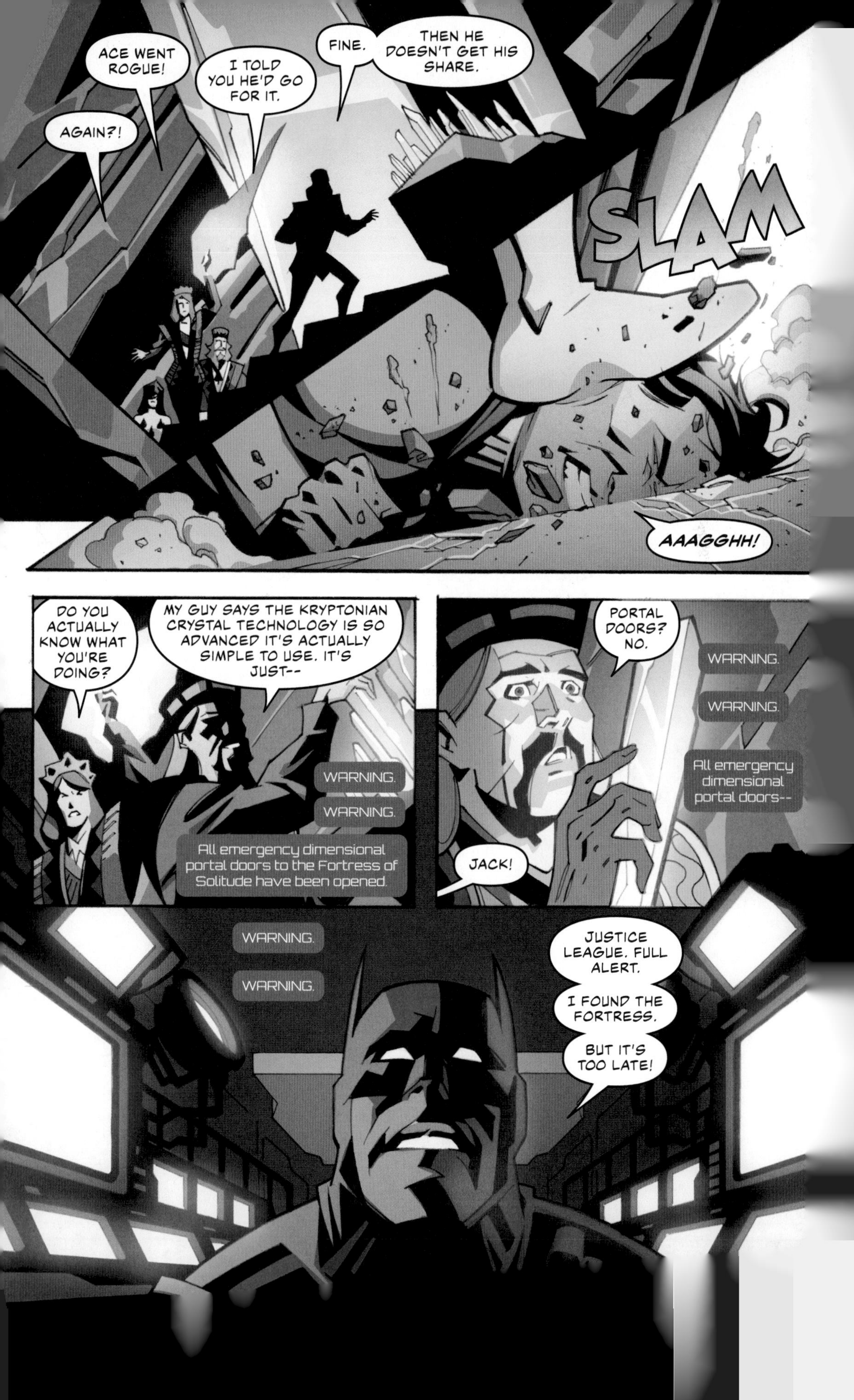
ACE WENT ROGUE!
AGAIN?!
I TOLD YOU HE'D GO FOR IT.
FINE.
THEN HE DOESN'T GET HIS SHARE.
SLAM
AAAGGHH!
DO YOU ACTUALLY KNOW WHAT YOU'RE DOING?
MY GUY SAYS THE KRYPTONIAN CRYSTAL TECHNOLOGY IS SO ADVANCED IT'S ACTUALLY SIMPLE TO USE. IT'S JUST--
WARNING.
WARNING.
All emergency dimensional portal doors to the Fortress of Solitude have been opened.
PORTAL DOORS? NO.
WARNING.
WARNING.
All emergency dimensional portal doors--
JACK!
WARNING.
WARNING.
JUSTICE LEAGUE. FULL ALERT.
I FOUND THE FORTRESS.
BUT IT'S TOO LATE!

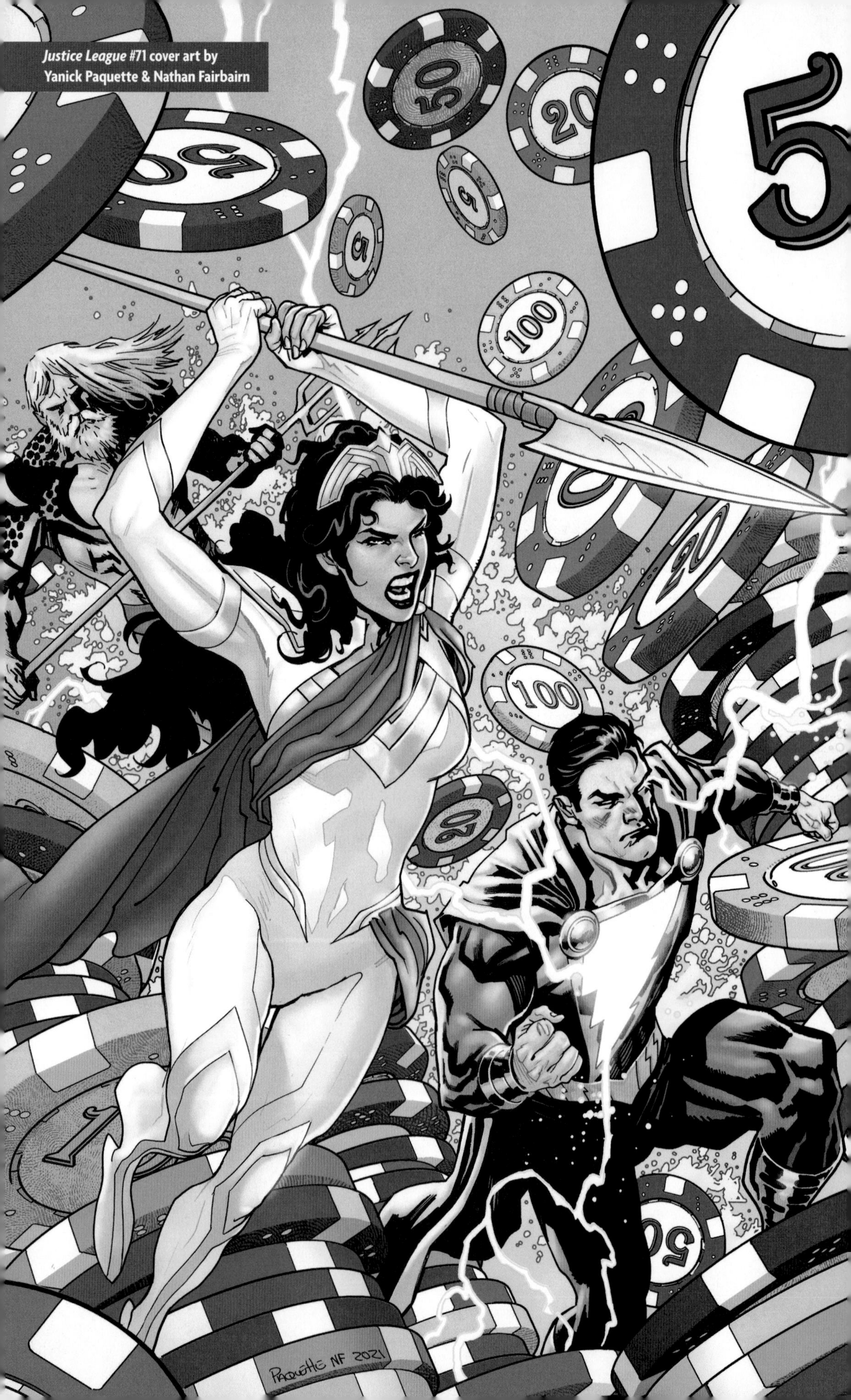
PAQUETTE NF 2021

Justice League #71 cover art by
Yanick Paquette & Nathan Fairbairn

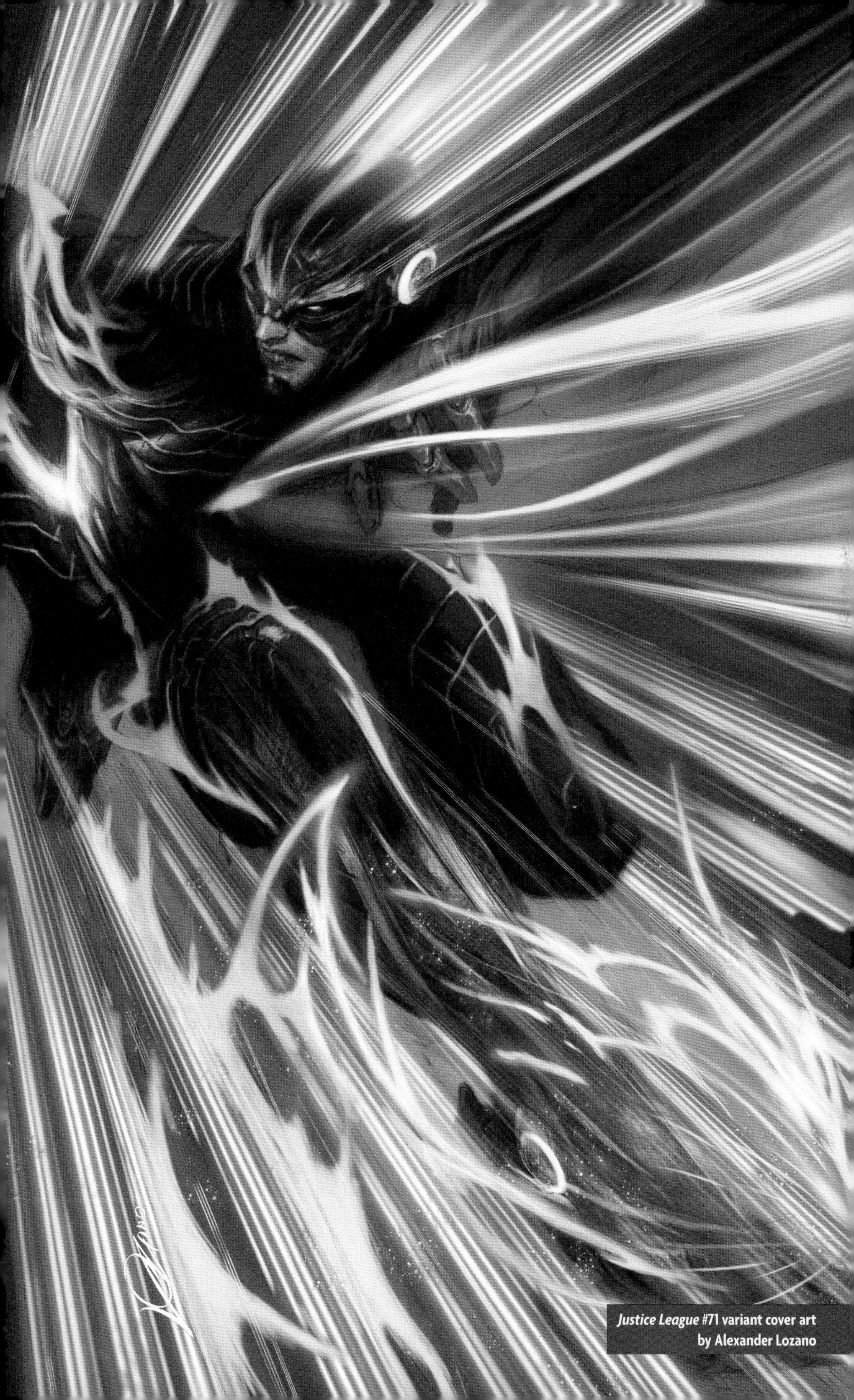

Justice League #71 variant cover art
by Alexander Lozano

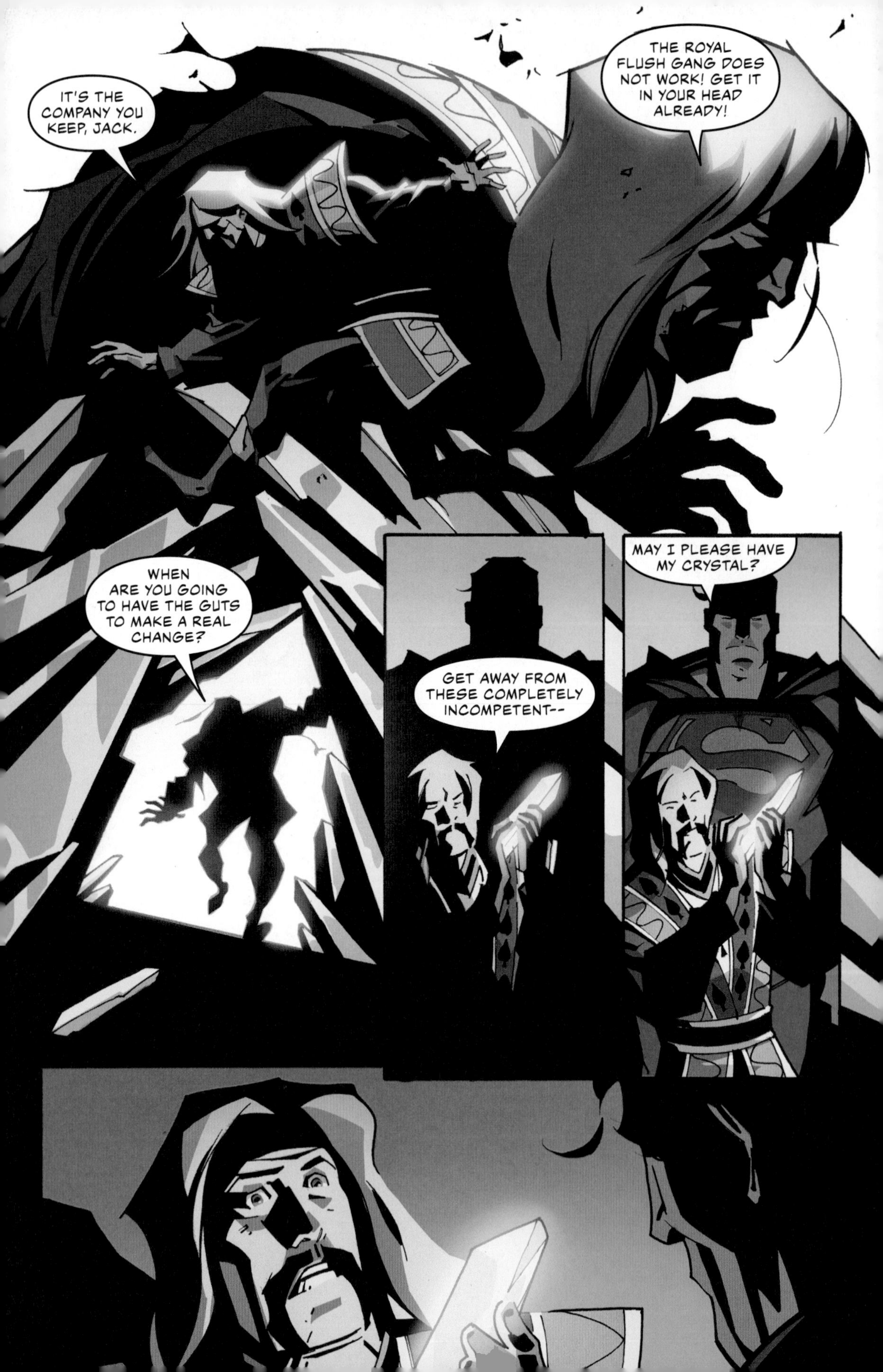
IT'S THE COMPANY YOU KEEP, JACK.
THE ROYAL FLUSH GANG DOES NOT WORK! GET IT IN YOUR HEAD ALREADY!
WHEN ARE YOU GOING TO HAVE THE GUTS TO MAKE A REAL CHANGE?
GET AWAY FROM THESE COMPLETELY INCOMPETENT--
MAY I PLEASE HAVE MY CRYSTAL?

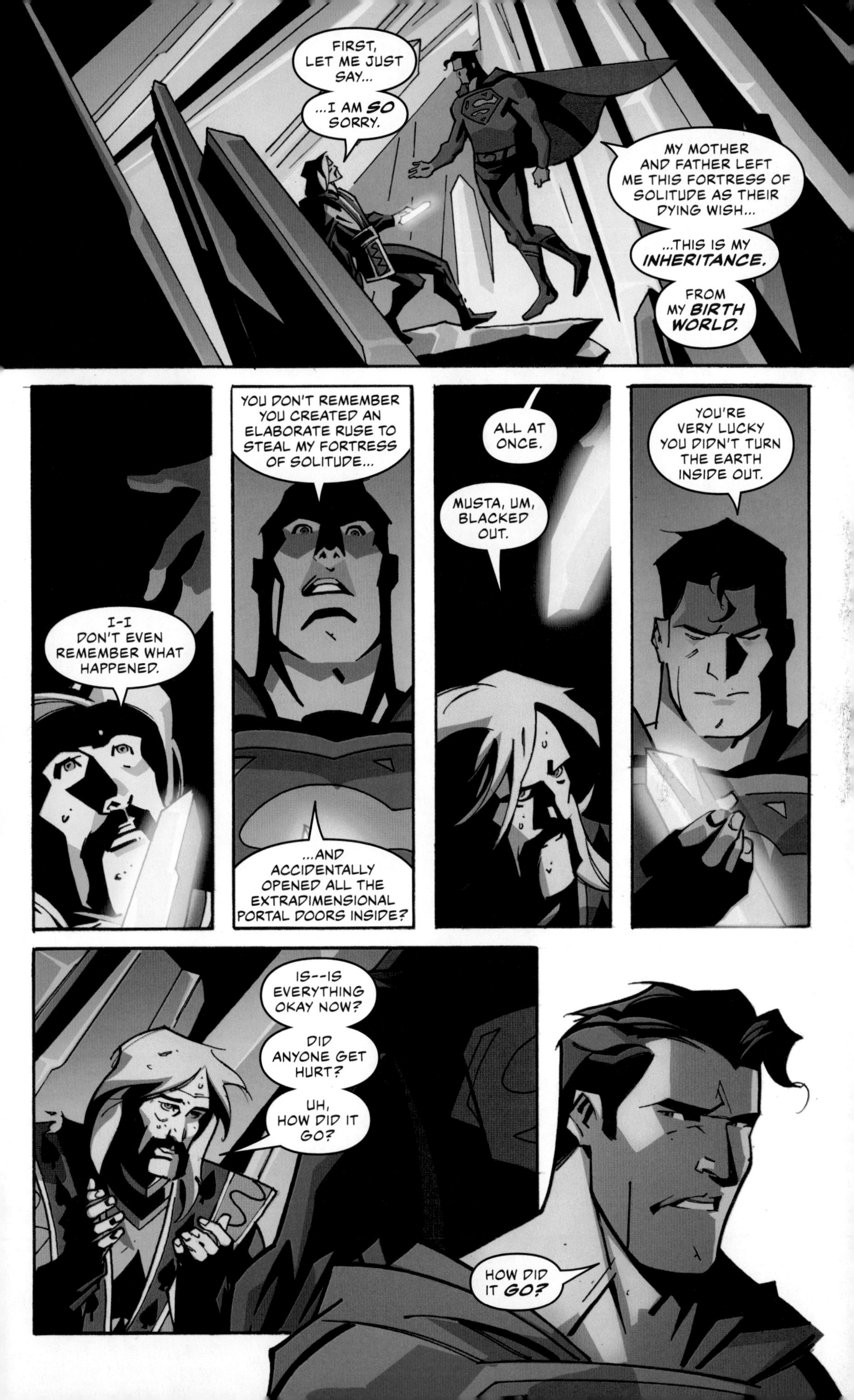
FIRST, LET ME JUST SAY...
...I AM SO SORRY.
MY MOTHER AND FATHER LEFT ME THIS FORTRESS OF SOLITUDE AS THEIR DYING WISH...
...THIS IS MY INHERITANCE.
FROM MY BIRTH WORLD.
I-I DON'T EVEN REMEMBER WHAT HAPPENED.
YOU DON'T REMEMBER YOU CREATED AN ELABORATE RUSE TO STEAL MY FORTRESS OF SOLITUDE...
...AND ACCIDENTALLY OPENED ALL THE EXTRADIMENSIONAL PORTAL DOORS INSIDE?
ALL AT ONCE.
MUSTA, UM, BLACKED OUT.
YOU'RE VERY LUCKY YOU DIDN'T TURN THE EARTH INSIDE OUT.
IS--IS EVERYTHING OKAY NOW?
DID ANYONE GET HURT?
UH, HOW DID IT GO?
HOW DID IT GO?

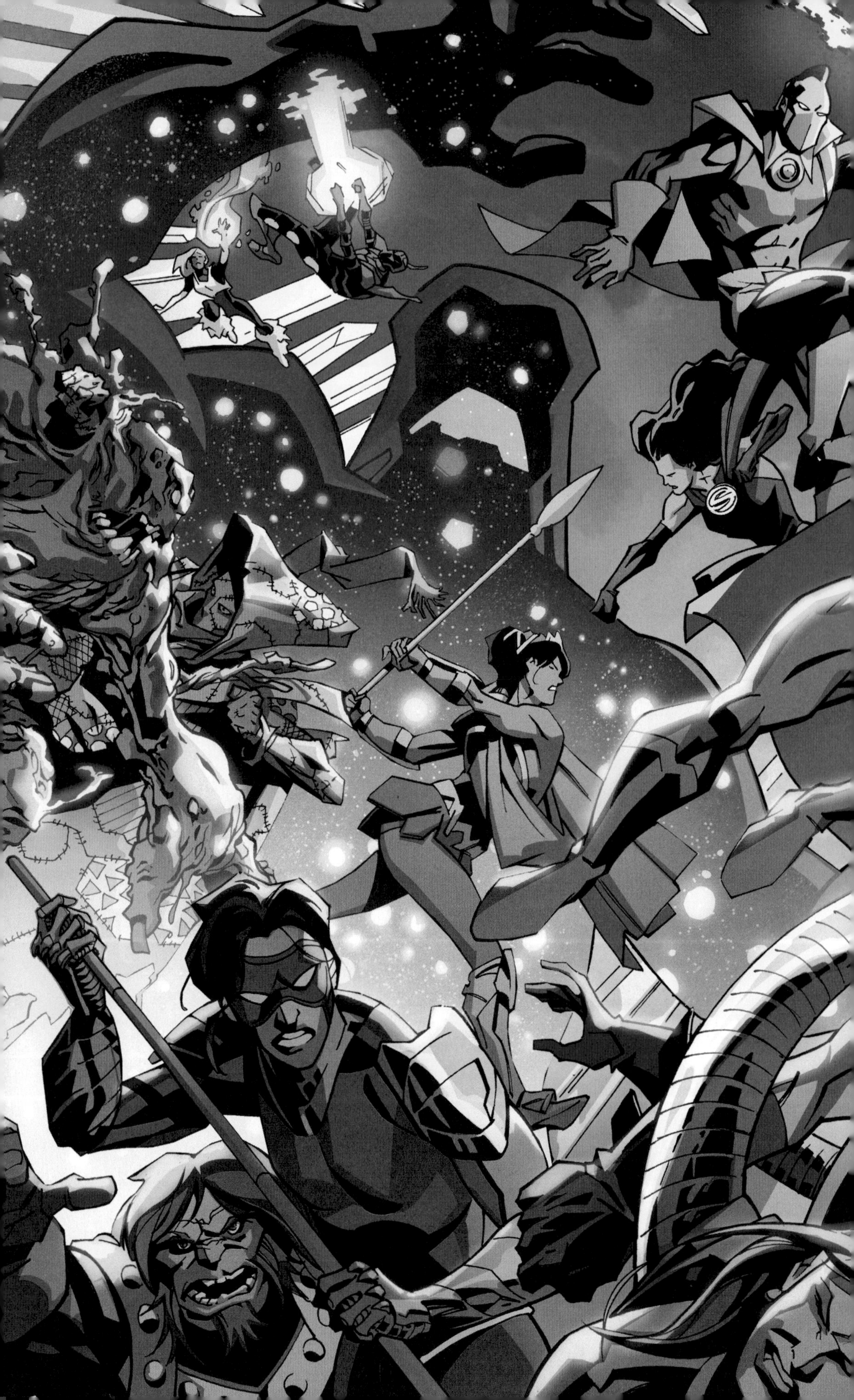

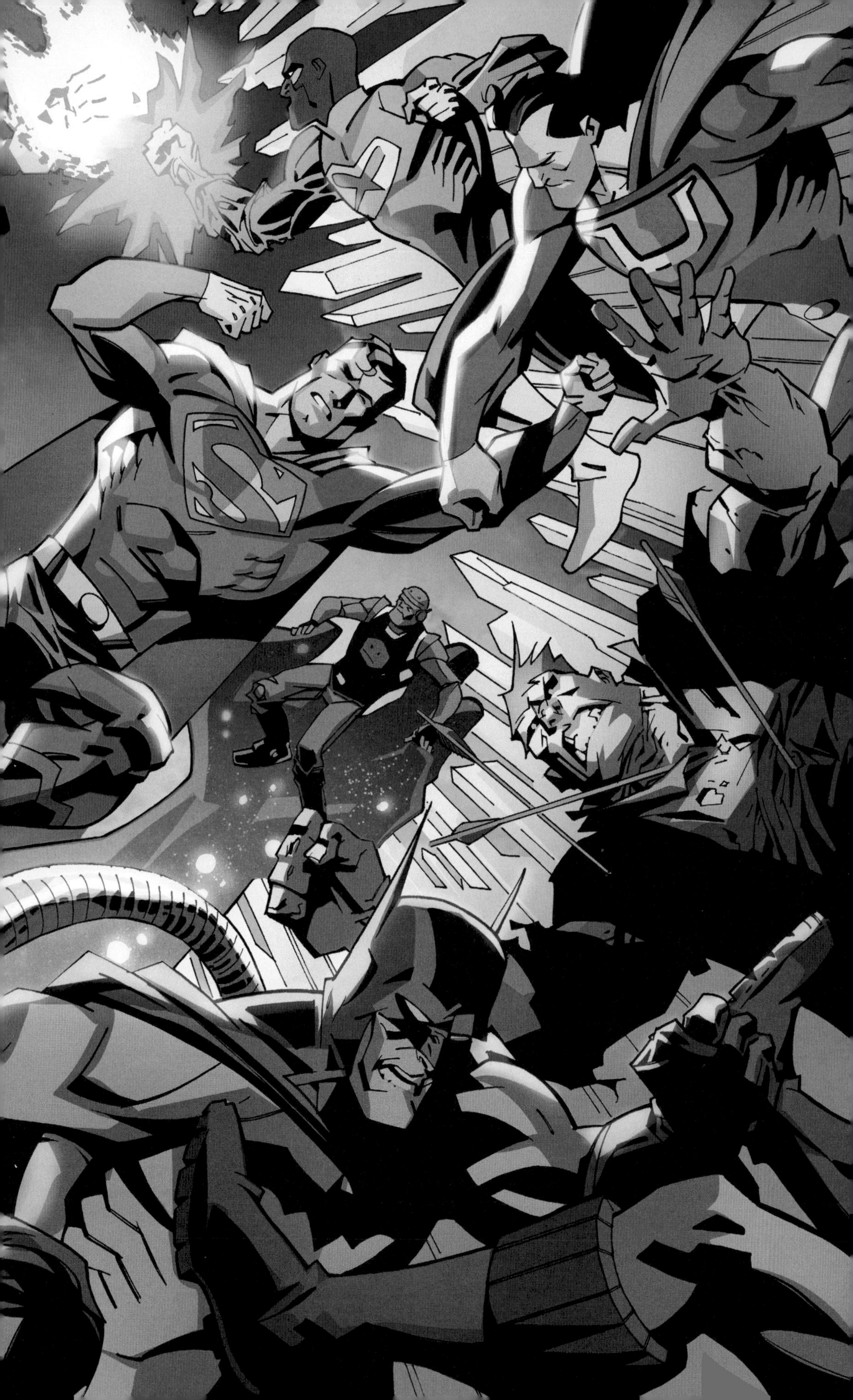

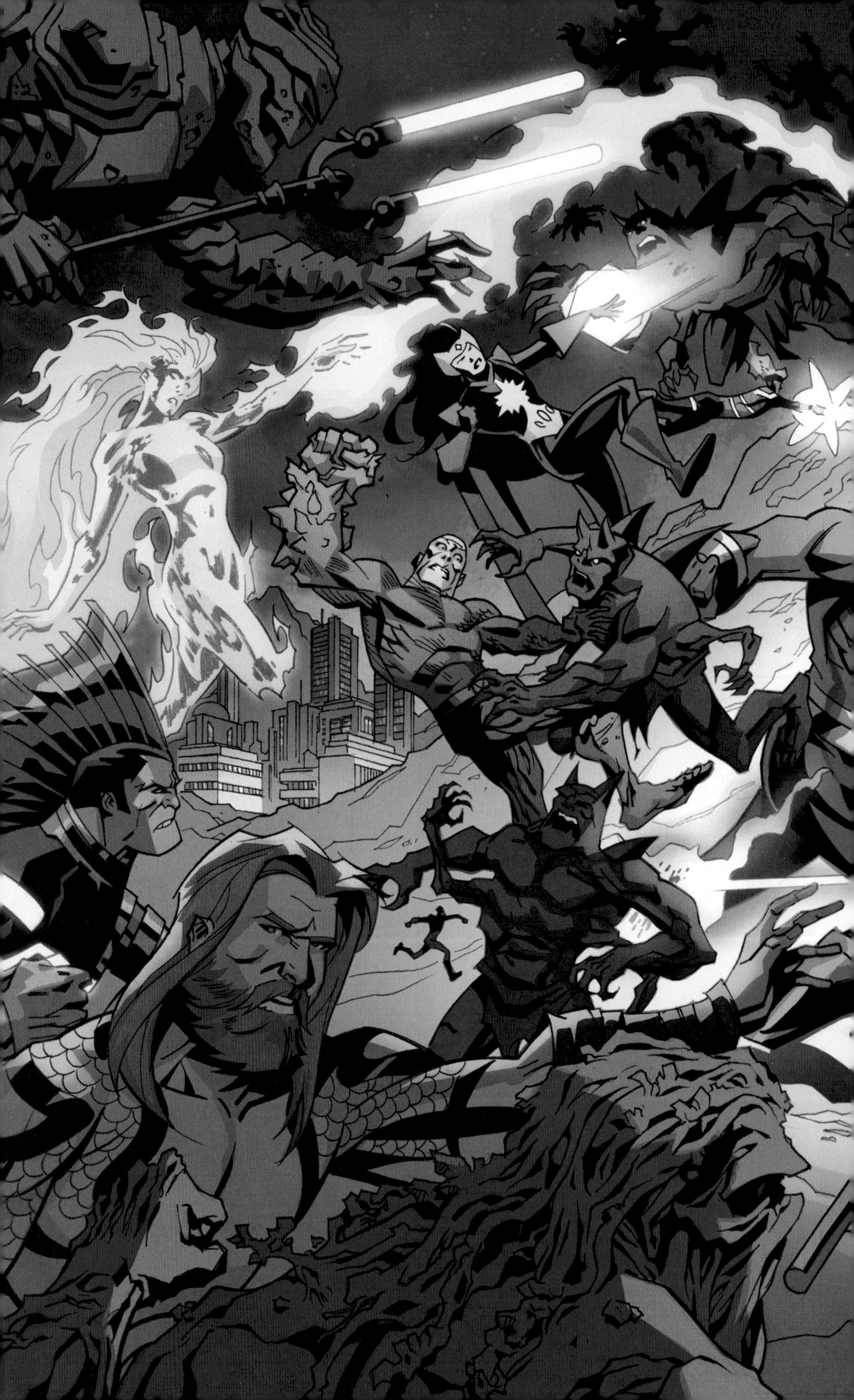

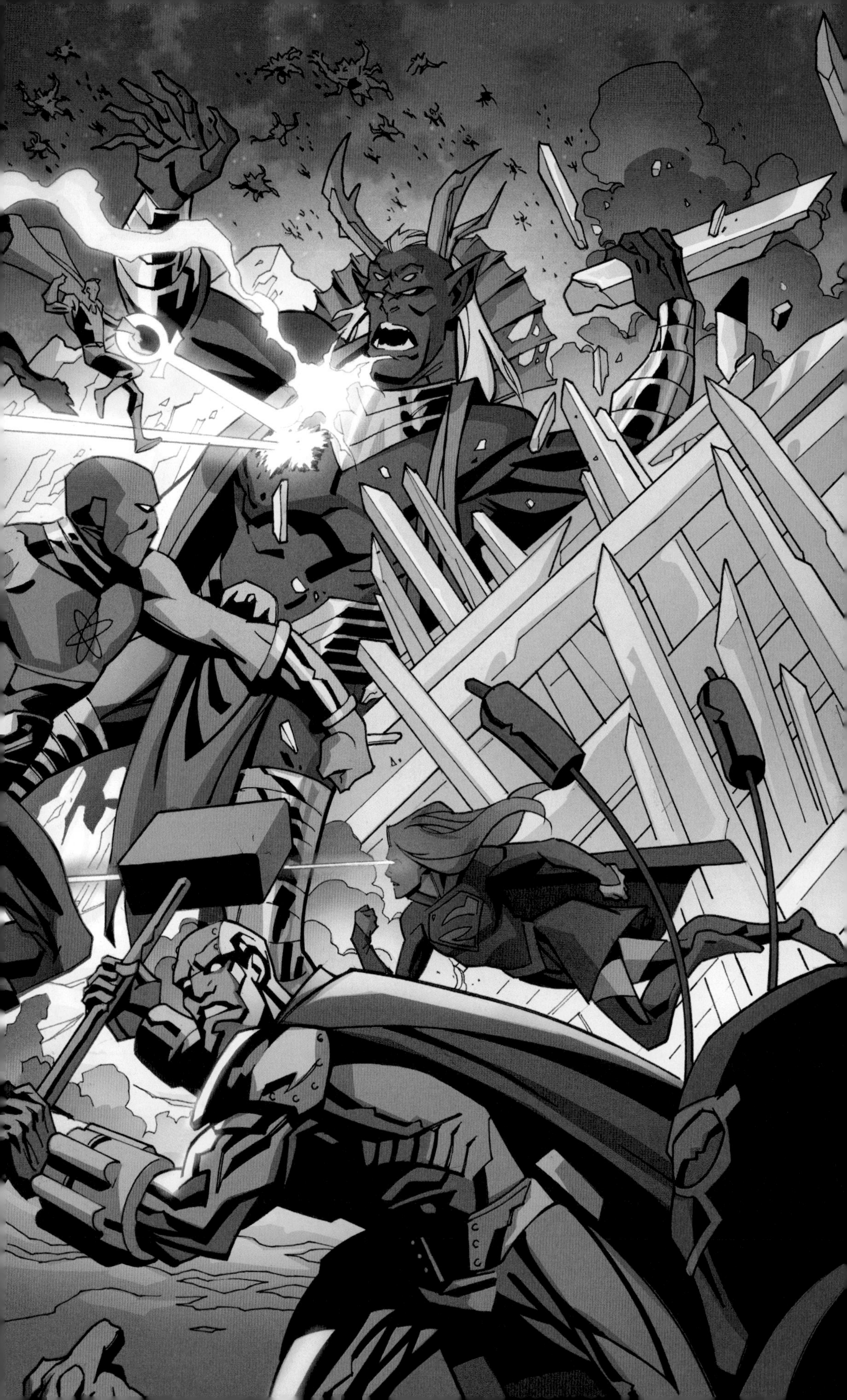

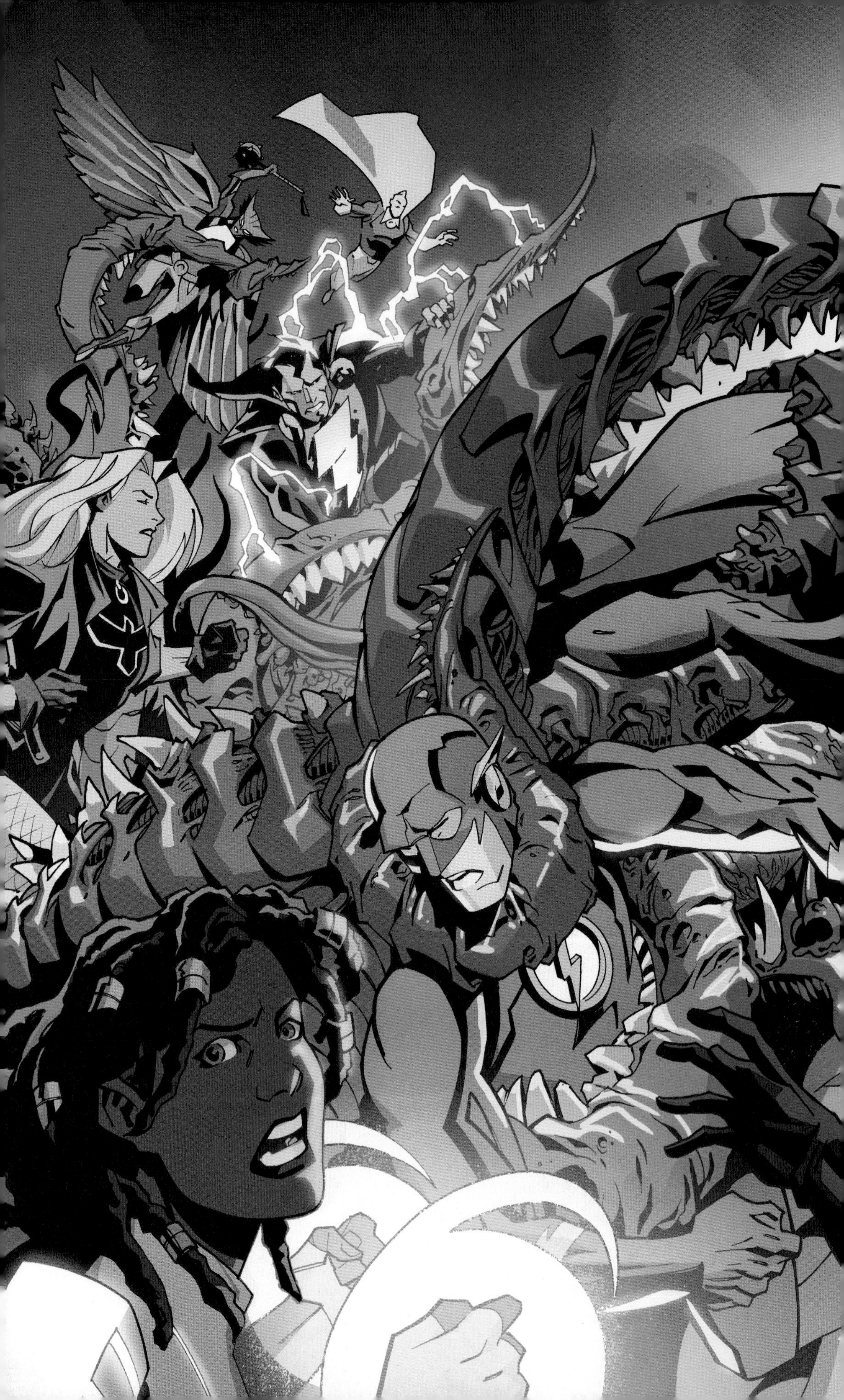

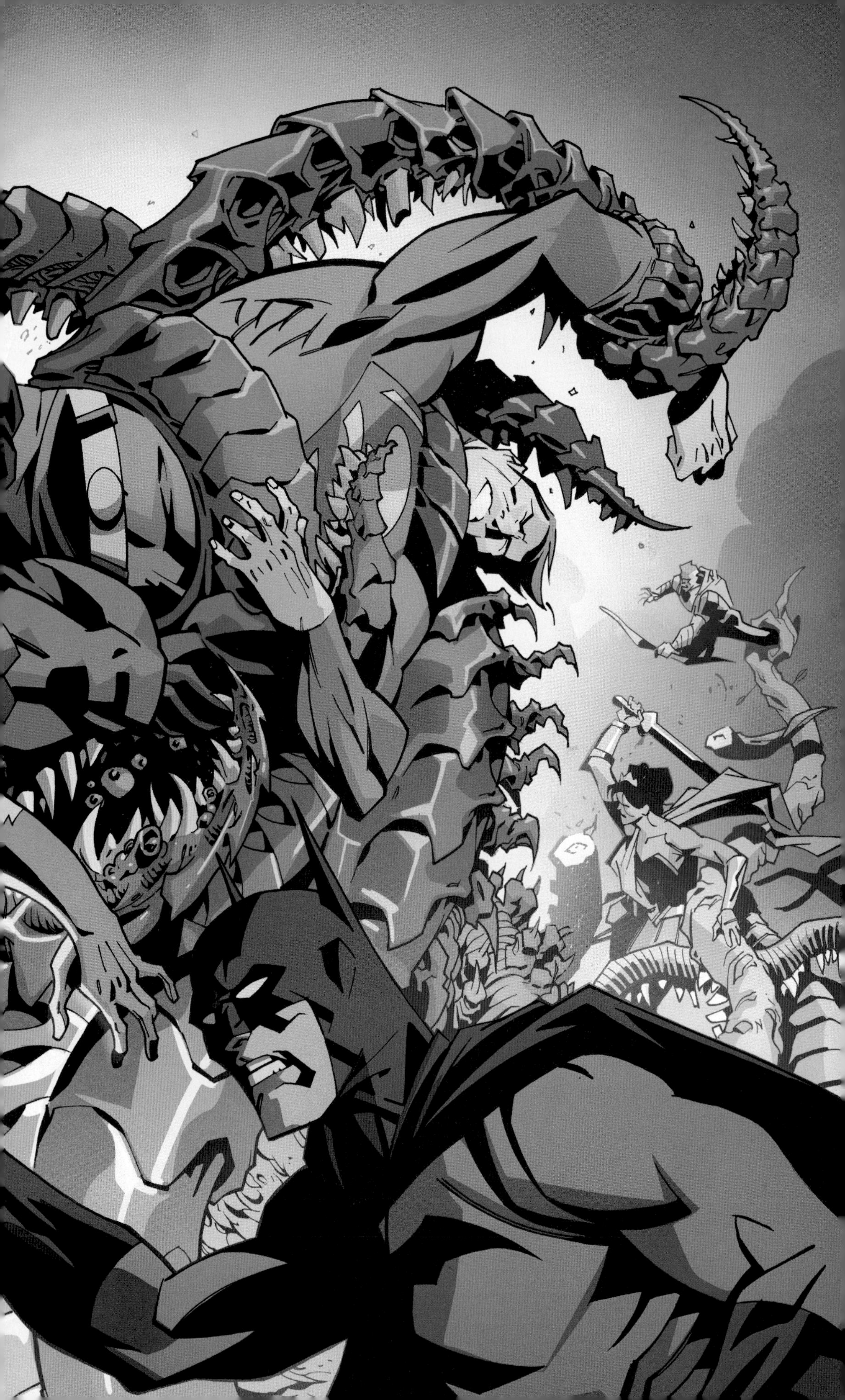

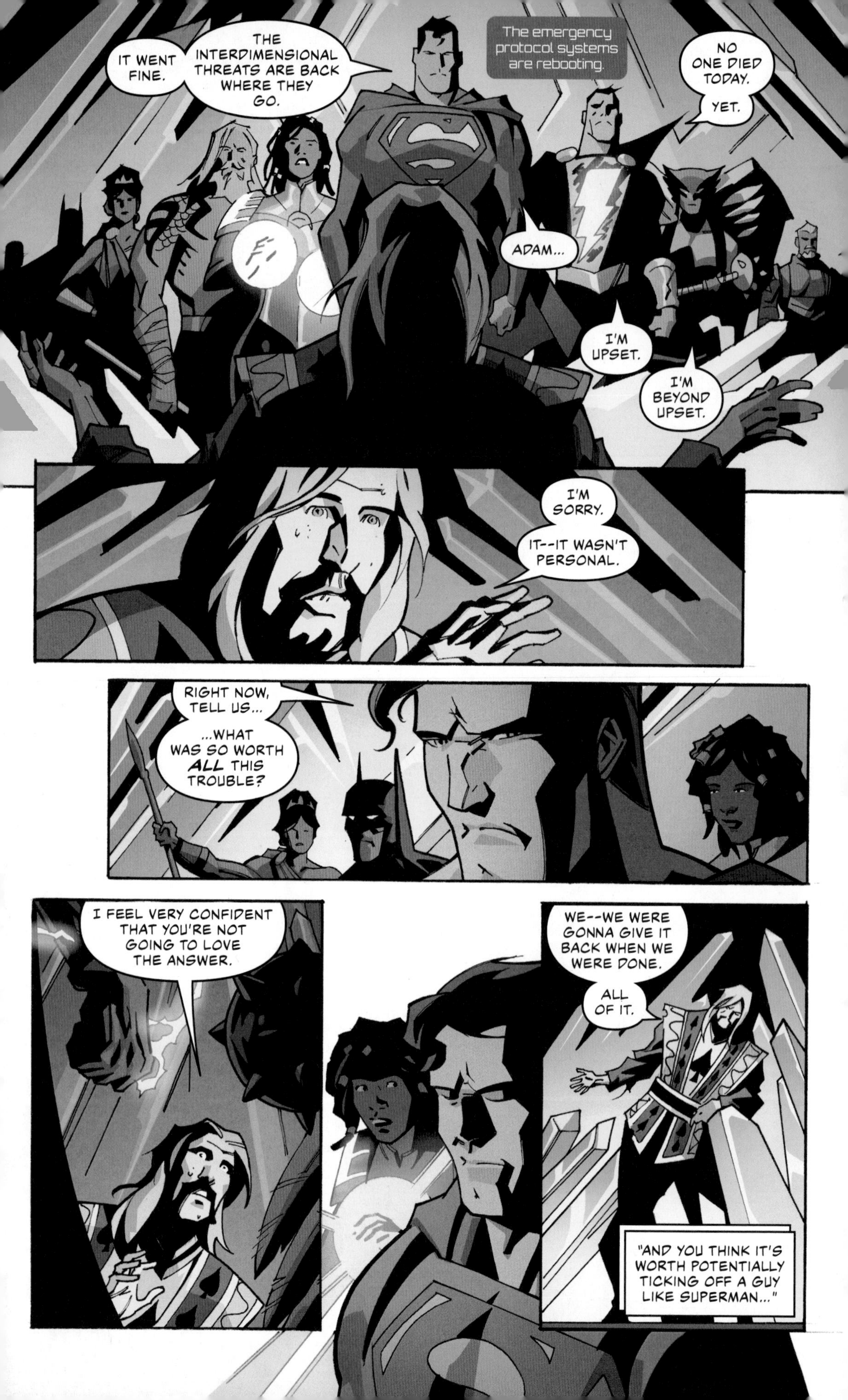
IT WENT FINE.
THE INTERDIMENSIONAL THREATS ARE BACK WHERE THEY GO.
The emergency protocol systems are rebooting.
NO ONE DIED TODAY.
YET.
ADAM...
I'M UPSET.
I'M BEYOND UPSET.
I'M SORRY.
IT--IT WASN'T PERSONAL.
RIGHT NOW, TELL US...
...WHAT WAS SO WORTH ALL THIS TROUBLE?
I FEEL VERY CONFIDENT THAT YOU'RE NOT GOING TO LOVE THE ANSWER.
WE--WE WERE GONNA GIVE IT BACK WHEN WE WERE DONE.
ALL OF IT.
"AND YOU THINK IT'S WORTH POTENTIALLY TICKING OFF A GUY LIKE SUPERMAN..."

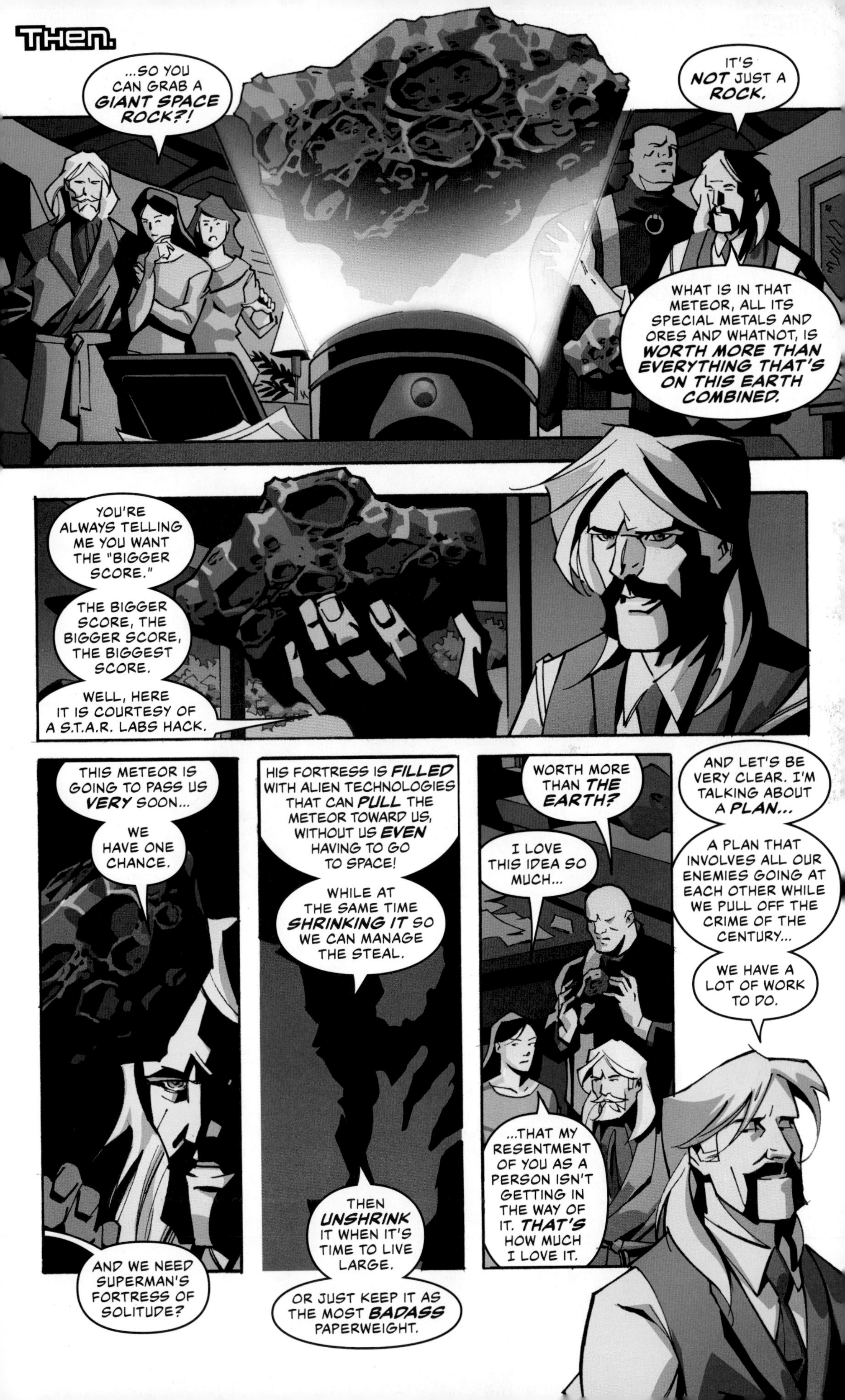
THEN.
...SO YOU CAN GRAB A GIANT SPACE ROCK?!
IT'S NOT JUST A ROCK.
WHAT IS IN THAT METEOR, ALL ITS SPECIAL METALS AND ORES AND WHATNOT, IS WORTH MORE THAN EVERYTHING THAT'S ON THIS EARTH COMBINED.
YOU'RE ALWAYS TELLING ME YOU WANT THE "BIGGER SCORE."
THE BIGGER SCORE, THE BIGGER SCORE, THE BIGGEST SCORE.
WELL, HERE IT IS COURTESY OF A S.T.A.R. LABS HACK.
THIS METEOR IS GOING TO PASS US VERY SOON...
WE HAVE ONE CHANCE.
AND WE NEED SUPERMAN'S FORTRESS OF SOLITUDE?
HIS FORTRESS IS FILLED WITH ALIEN TECHNOLOGIES THAT CAN PULL THE METEOR TOWARD US, WITHOUT US EVEN HAVING TO GO TO SPACE!
WHILE AT THE SAME TIME SHRINKING IT SO WE CAN MANAGE THE STEAL.
THEN UNSHRINK IT WHEN IT'S TIME TO LIVE LARGE.
OR JUST KEEP IT AS THE MOST BADASS PAPERWEIGHT.
WORTH MORE THAN THE EARTH?
I LOVE THIS IDEA SO MUCH...
...THAT MY RESENTMENT OF YOU AS A PERSON ISN'T GETTING IN THE WAY OF IT. THAT'S HOW MUCH I LOVE IT.
AND LET'S BE VERY CLEAR. I'M TALKING ABOUT A PLAN...
A PLAN THAT INVOLVES ALL OUR ENEMIES GOING AT EACH OTHER WHILE WE PULL OFF THE CRIME OF THE CENTURY...
WE HAVE A LOT OF WORK TO DO.

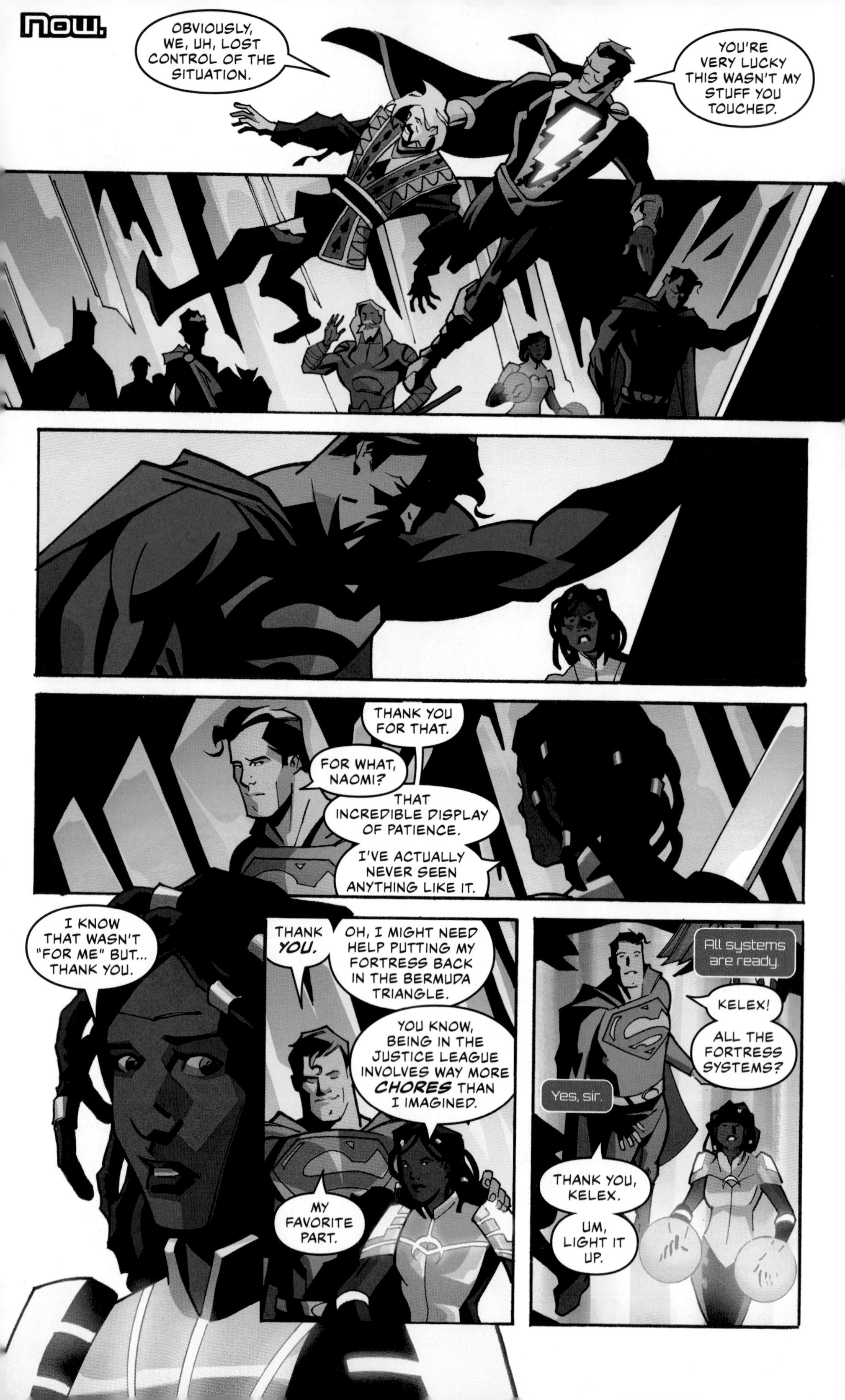
NOW.
OBVIOUSLY, WE, UH, LOST CONTROL OF THE SITUATION.
YOU'RE VERY LUCKY THIS WASN'T MY STUFF YOU TOUCHED.
THANK YOU FOR THAT.
FOR WHAT, NAOMI?
THAT INCREDIBLE DISPLAY OF PATIENCE.
I'VE ACTUALLY NEVER SEEN ANYTHING LIKE IT.
I KNOW THAT WASN'T "FOR ME" BUT... THANK YOU.
THANK YOU.
OH, I MIGHT NEED HELP PUTTING MY FORTRESS BACK IN THE BERMUDA TRIANGLE.
YOU KNOW, BEING IN THE JUSTICE LEAGUE INVOLVES WAY MORE CHORES THAN I IMAGINED.
MY FAVORITE PART.
All systems are ready.
KELEX!
ALL THE FORTRESS SYSTEMS?
Yes, sir.
THANK YOU, KELEX.
UM, LIGHT IT UP.

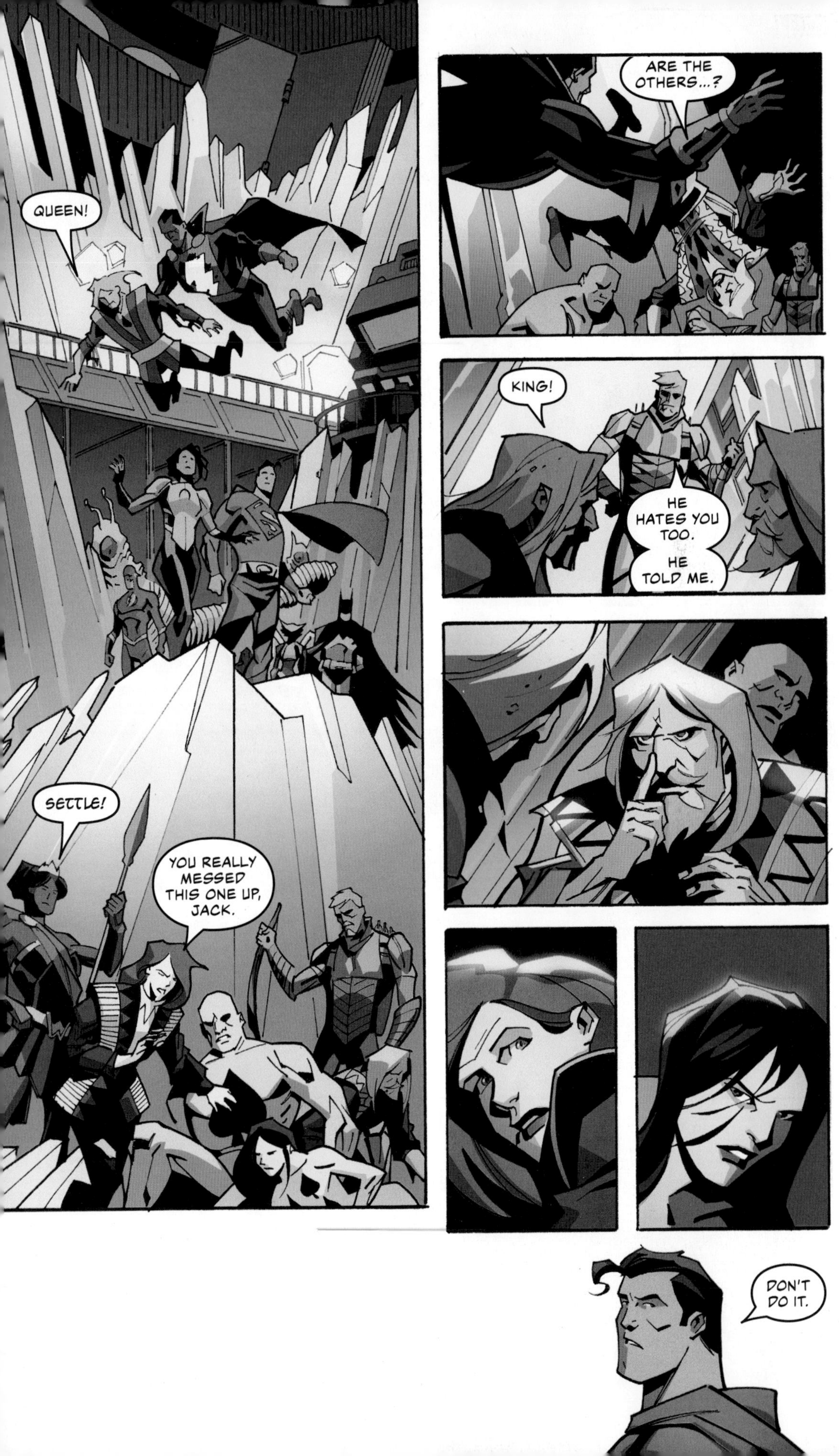
QUEEN!
SETTLE!
YOU REALLY MESSED THIS ONE UP, JACK.
ARE THE OTHERS...?
KING!
HE HATES YOU TOO.
HE TOLD ME.
DON'T DO IT.

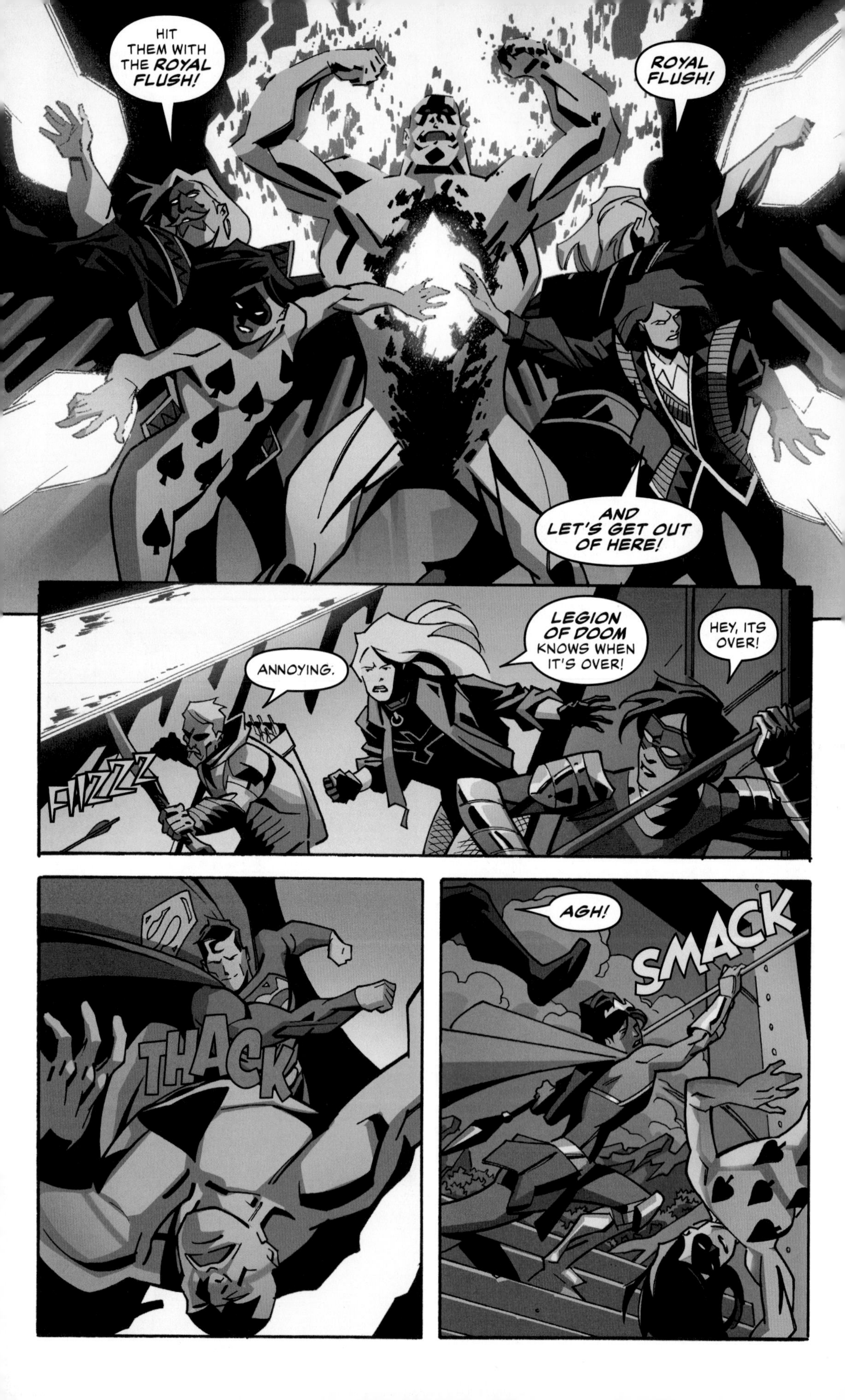
HIT THEM WITH THE ROYAL FLUSH!
ROYAL FLUSH!
AND LET'S GET OUT OF HERE!
ANNOYING.
LEGION OF DOOM KNOWS WHEN IT'S OVER!
HEY, ITS OVER!
FWZZZ
THACK
AGH!
SMACK

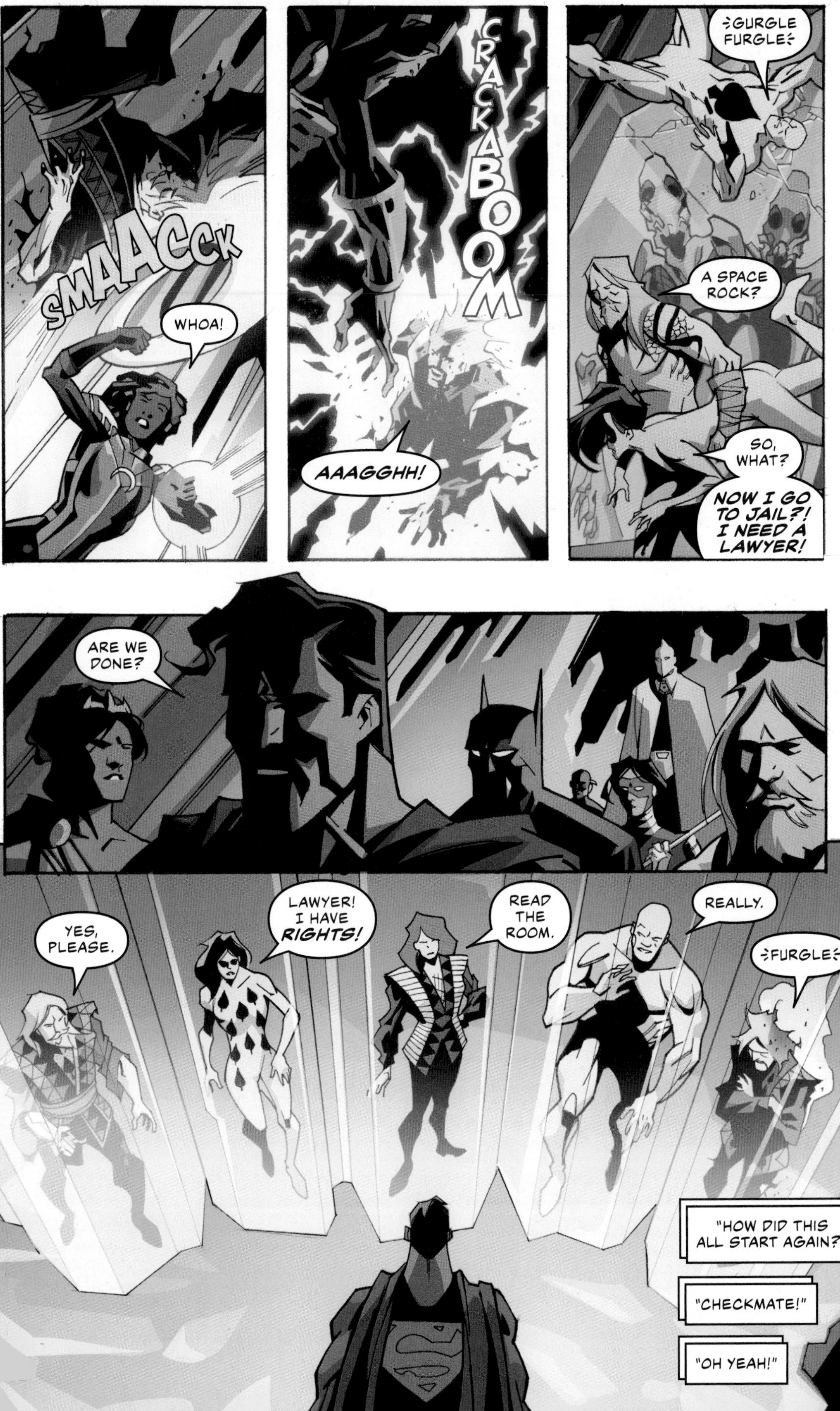

SMAACCK
WHOA!
CRACKABOOM
AAAGGHH!
-GURGLE FURGLE-
A SPACE ROCK?
SO, WHAT?
NOW I GO TO JAIL?! I NEED A LAWYER!
ARE WE DONE?
YES, PLEASE.
LAWYER! I HAVE RIGHTS!
READ THE ROOM.
REALLY.
-FURGLE-
"HOW DID THIS ALL START AGAIN?"
"CHECKMATE!"
"OH YEAH!"

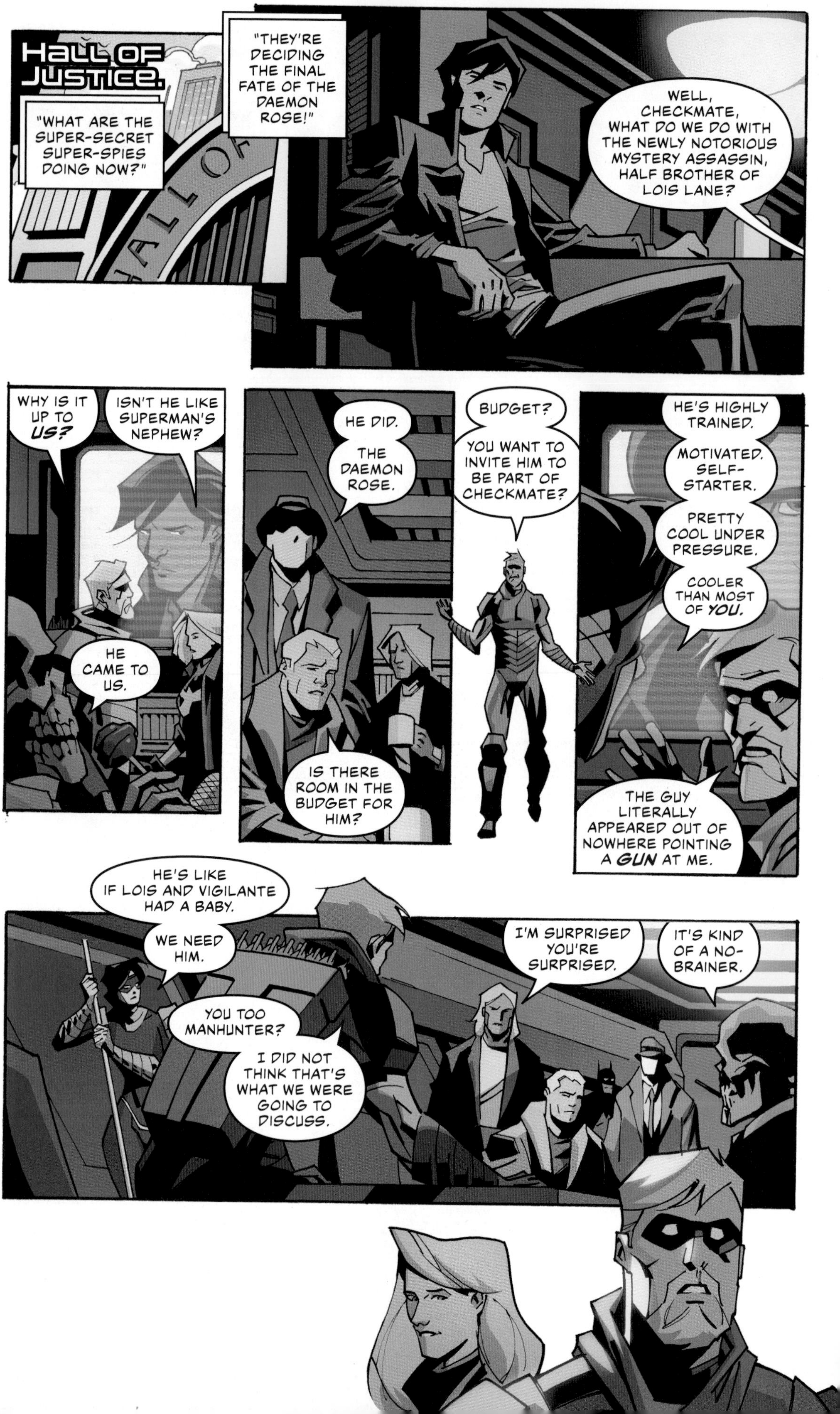
HALL OF JUSTICE.
"WHAT ARE THE SUPER-SECRET SUPER-SPIES DOING NOW?"
"THEY'RE DECIDING THE FINAL FATE OF THE DAEMON ROSE!"
WELL, CHECKMATE, WHAT DO WE DO WITH THE NEWLY NOTORIOUS MYSTERY ASSASSIN, HALF BROTHER OF LOIS LANE?
WHY IS IT UP TO US?
ISN'T HE LIKE SUPERMAN'S NEPHEW?
HE CAME TO US.
HE DID.
THE DAEMON ROSE.
IS THERE ROOM IN THE BUDGET FOR HIM?
BUDGET?
YOU WANT TO INVITE HIM TO BE PART OF CHECKMATE?
HE'S HIGHLY TRAINED.
MOTIVATED. SELF-STARTER.
PRETTY COOL UNDER PRESSURE.
COOLER THAN MOST OF YOU.
THE GUY LITERALLY APPEARED OUT OF NOWHERE POINTING A GUN AT ME.
HE'S LIKE IF LOIS AND VIGILANTE HAD A BABY.
WE NEED HIM.
YOU TOO MANHUNTER?
I DID NOT THINK THAT'S WHAT WE WERE GOING TO DISCUSS.
I'M SURPRISED YOU'RE SURPRISED.
IT'S KIND OF A NO-BRAINER.

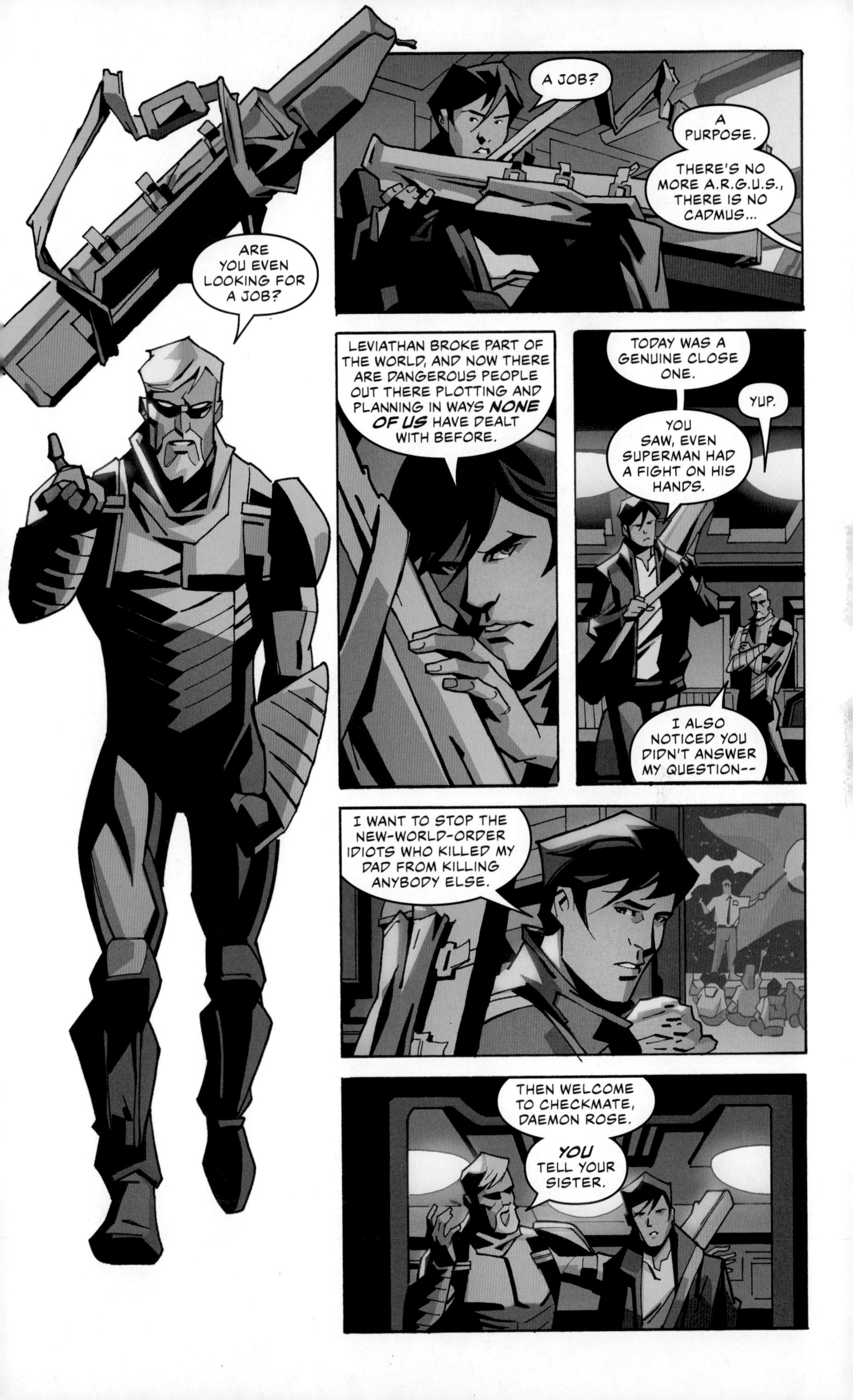
ARE YOU EVEN LOOKING FOR A JOB?
A JOB?
A PURPOSE.
THERE'S NO MORE A.R.G.U.S., THERE IS NO CADMUS...
LEVIATHAN BROKE PART OF THE WORLD, AND NOW THERE ARE DANGEROUS PEOPLE OUT THERE PLOTTING AND PLANNING IN WAYS NONE OF US HAVE DEALT WITH BEFORE.
TODAY WAS A GENUINE CLOSE ONE.
YUP.
YOU SAW, EVEN SUPERMAN HAD A FIGHT ON HIS HANDS.
I ALSO NOTICED YOU DIDN'T ANSWER MY QUESTION--
I WANT TO STOP THE NEW-WORLD-ORDER IDIOTS WHO KILLED MY DAD FROM KILLING ANYBODY ELSE.
THEN WELCOME TO CHECKMATE, DAEMON ROSE.
YOU TELL YOUR SISTER.

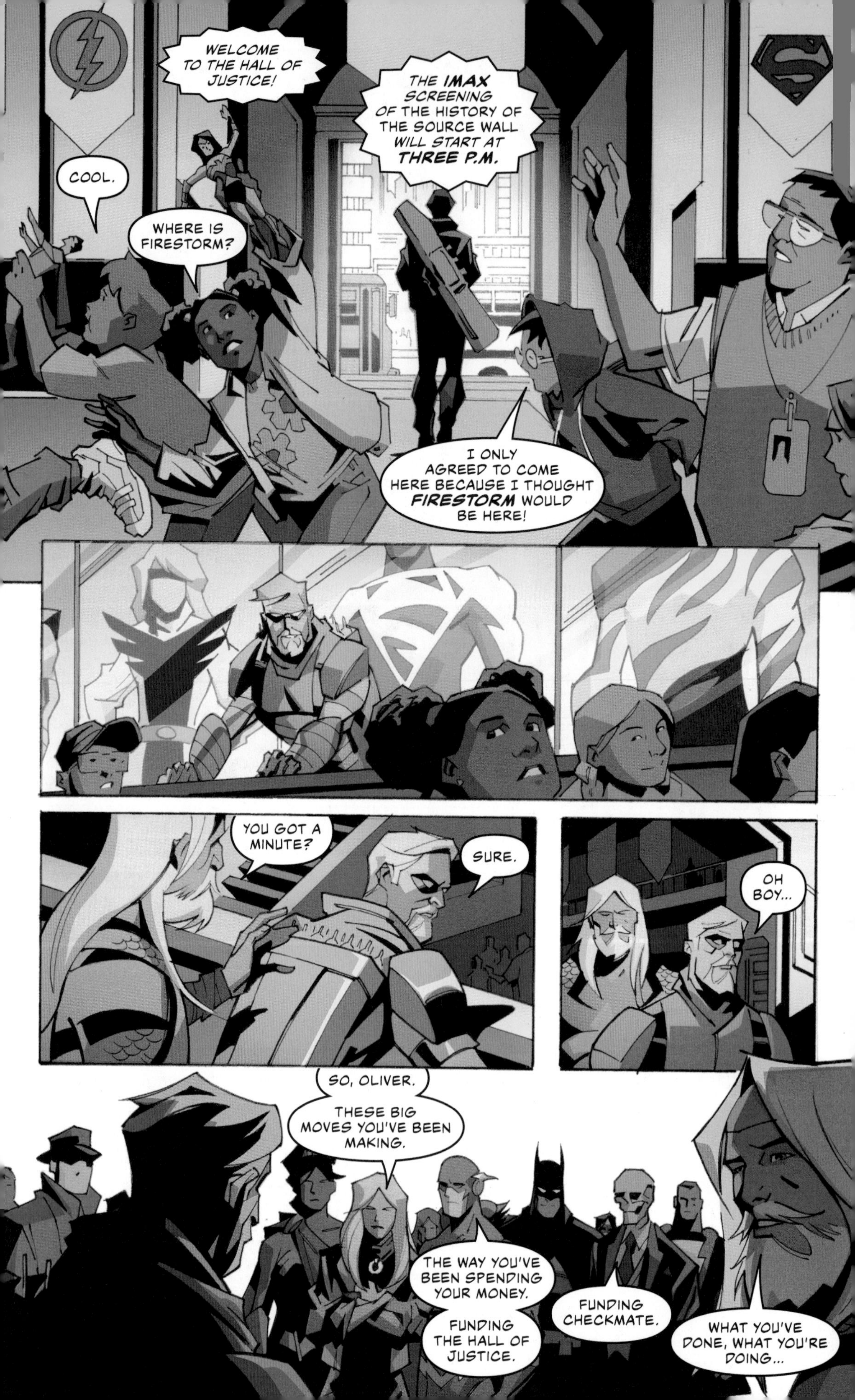
WELCOME TO THE HALL OF JUSTICE!
THE IMAX SCREENING OF THE HISTORY OF THE SOURCE WALL WILL START AT THREE P.M.
COOL.
WHERE IS FIRESTORM?
I ONLY AGREED TO COME HERE BECAUSE I THOUGHT FIRESTORM WOULD BE HERE!
YOU GOT A MINUTE?
SURE.
OH BOY...
SO, OLIVER.
THESE BIG MOVES YOU'VE BEEN MAKING.
THE WAY YOU'VE BEEN SPENDING YOUR MONEY.
FUNDING THE HALL OF JUSTICE.
FUNDING CHECKMATE.
WHAT YOU'VE DONE, WHAT YOU'RE DOING...

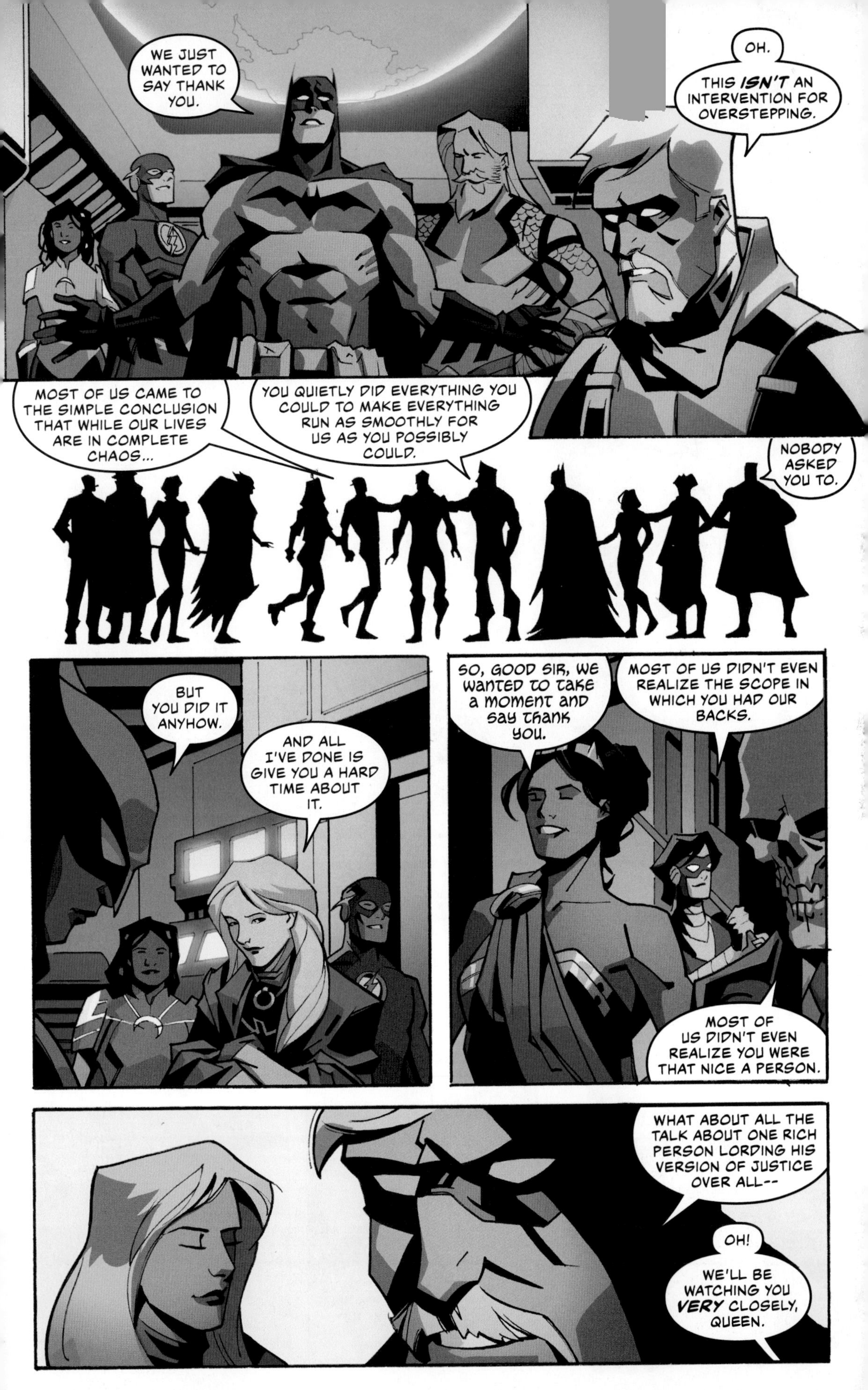

WE JUST WANTED TO SAY THANK YOU.
OH.
THIS ISN'T AN INTERVENTION FOR OVERSTEPPING.
MOST OF US CAME TO THE SIMPLE CONCLUSION THAT WHILE OUR LIVES ARE IN COMPLETE CHAOS...
YOU QUIETLY DID EVERYTHING YOU COULD TO MAKE EVERYTHING RUN AS SMOOTHLY FOR US AS YOU POSSIBLY COULD.
NOBODY ASKED YOU TO.
BUT YOU DID IT ANYHOW.
AND ALL I'VE DONE IS GIVE YOU A HARD TIME ABOUT IT.
SO, GOOD SIR, WE WANTED TO TAKE A MOMENT AND SAY THANK YOU.
MOST OF US DIDN'T EVEN REALIZE THE SCOPE IN WHICH YOU HAD OUR BACKS.
MOST OF US DIDN'T EVEN REALIZE YOU WERE THAT NICE A PERSON.
WHAT ABOUT ALL THE TALK ABOUT ONE RICH PERSON LORDING HIS VERSION OF JUSTICE OVER ALL--
OH!
WE'LL BE WATCHING YOU VERY CLOSELY, QUEEN.

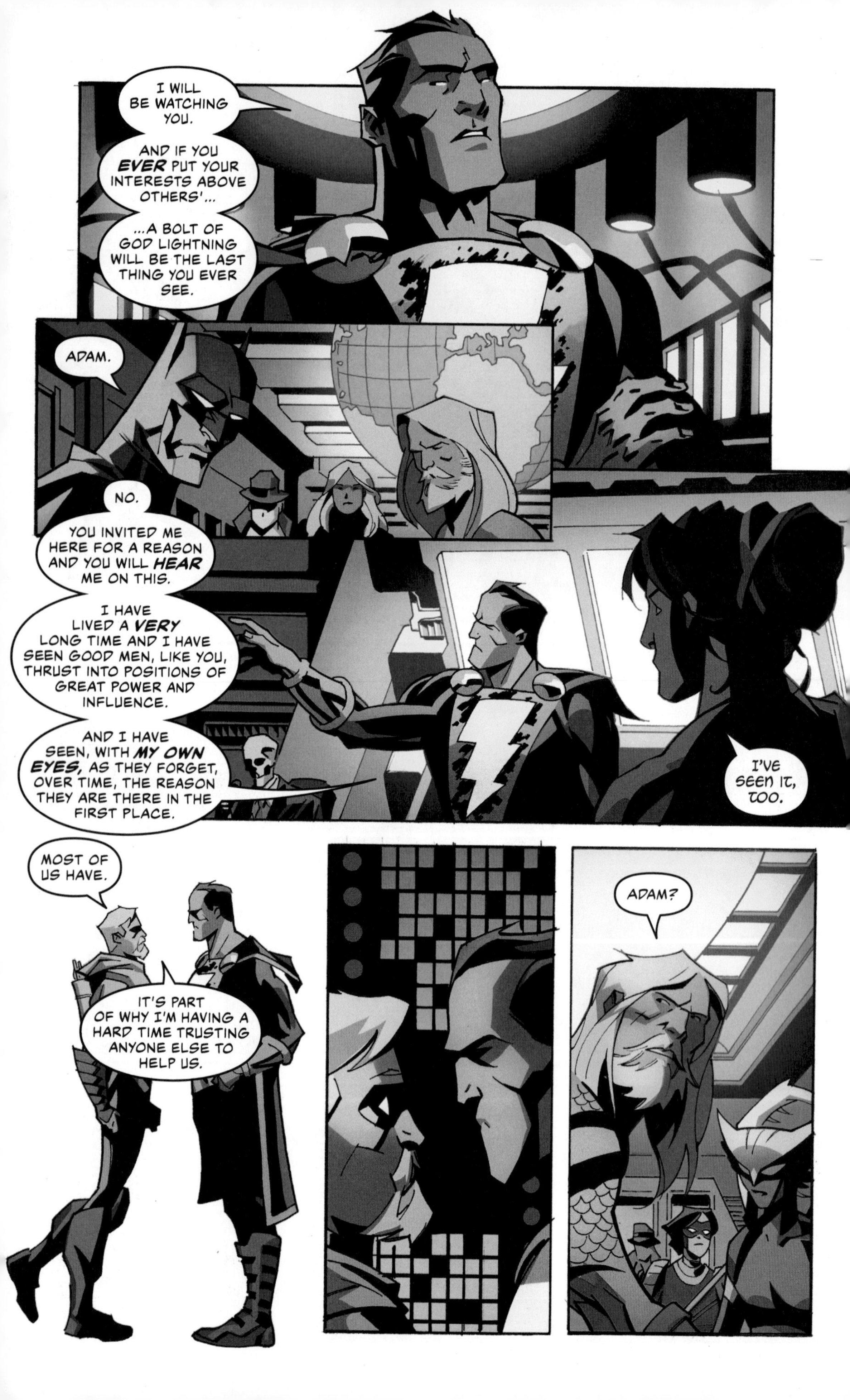

I WILL BE WATCHING YOU.
AND IF YOU EVER PUT YOUR INTERESTS ABOVE OTHERS'...
...A BOLT OF GOD LIGHTNING WILL BE THE LAST THING YOU EVER SEE.
ADAM.
NO.
YOU INVITED ME HERE FOR A REASON AND YOU WILL HEAR ME ON THIS.
I HAVE LIVED A VERY LONG TIME AND I HAVE SEEN GOOD MEN, LIKE YOU, THRUST INTO POSITIONS OF GREAT POWER AND INFLUENCE.
AND I HAVE SEEN, WITH MY OWN EYES, AS THEY FORGET, OVER TIME, THE REASON THEY ARE THERE IN THE FIRST PLACE.
I'VE SEEN IT, TOO.
MOST OF US HAVE.
IT'S PART OF WHY I'M HAVING A HARD TIME TRUSTING ANYONE ELSE TO HELP US.
ADAM?

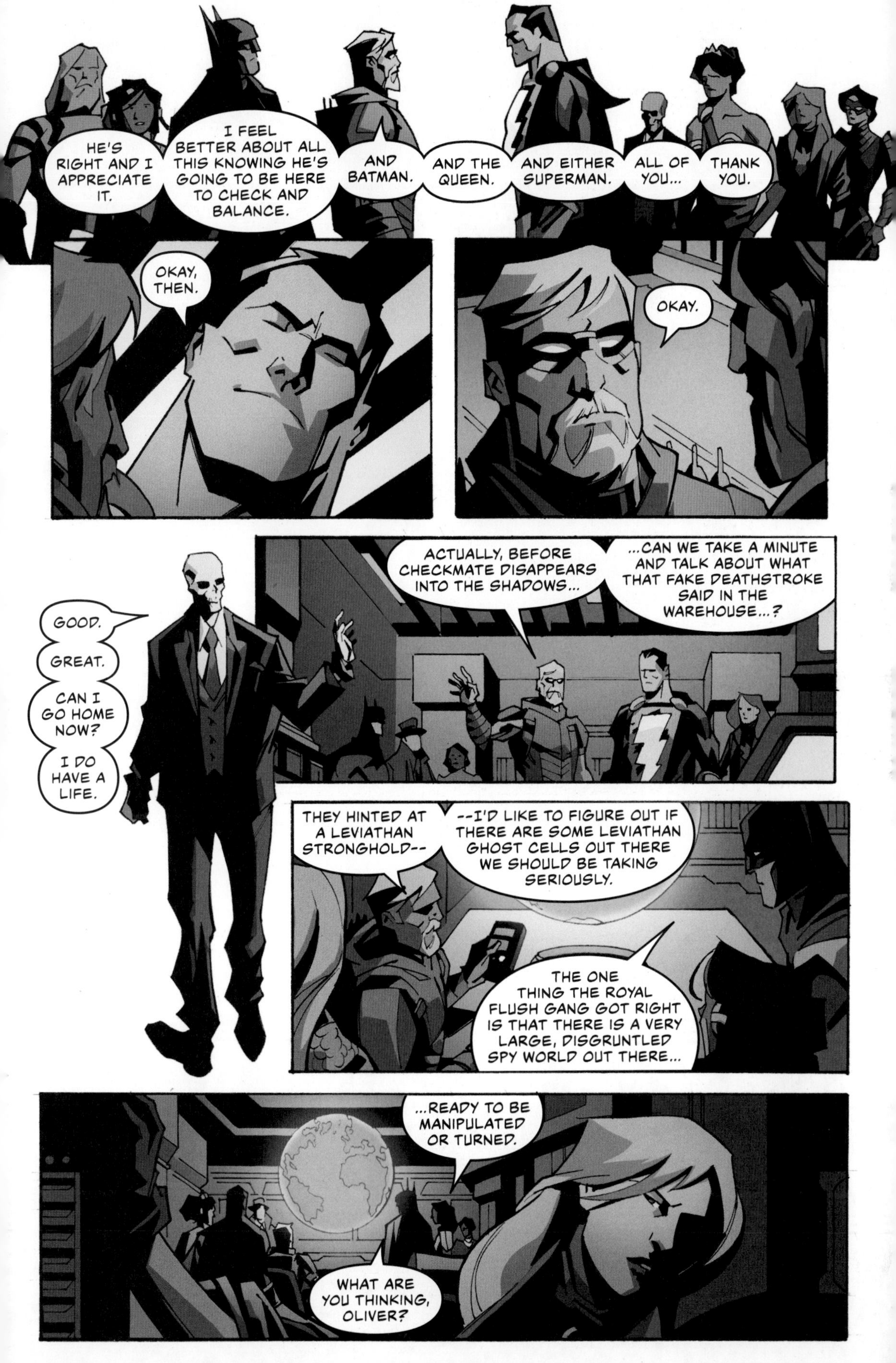
HE'S RIGHT AND I APPRECIATE IT.
I FEEL BETTER ABOUT ALL THIS KNOWING HE'S GOING TO BE HERE TO CHECK AND BALANCE.
AND BATMAN.
AND THE QUEEN.
AND EITHER SUPERMAN.
ALL OF YOU...
THANK YOU.
OKAY, THEN.
OKAY.
GOOD.
GREAT.
CAN I GO HOME NOW?
I DO HAVE A LIFE.
ACTUALLY, BEFORE CHECKMATE DISAPPEARS INTO THE SHADOWS...
...CAN WE TAKE A MINUTE AND TALK ABOUT WHAT THAT FAKE DEATHSTROKE SAID IN THE WAREHOUSE...?
THEY HINTED AT A LEVIATHAN STRONGHOLD--
--I'D LIKE TO FIGURE OUT IF THERE ARE SOME LEVIATHAN GHOST CELLS OUT THERE WE SHOULD BE TAKING SERIOUSLY.
THE ONE THING THE ROYAL FLUSH GANG GOT RIGHT IS THAT THERE IS A VERY LARGE, DISGRUNTLED SPY WORLD OUT THERE...
...READY TO BE MANIPULATED OR TURNED.
WHAT ARE YOU THINKING, OLIVER?

WONDER WOMAN VOL. 1: BLOOD (The New 52)

Hippolyta, queen of the Amazons, has kept a secret from her daughter all her life—and when Wonder Woman learns who her father is, her life will shatter like brittle clay. Super-heroics meet ancient myth as critically acclaimed writer Brian Azzarello teams with Cliff Chiang and Tony Akins to begin a new chapter for the Amazon Princess.

THE NEW YORK TIMES BESTSELLER
THE NEW 52!
WONDER WOMAN
VOLUME 1: BLOOD
BRIAN AZZARELLO CLIFF CHIANG TONY AKINS

Writer: **BRIAN AZZARELLO**
Artist: **CLIFF CHIANG**
Price: **USA $14.99/CAN $17.99**
Format: **TR**
ISBN: **9781401235628**

WONDER WOMAN: EARTH ONE VOL. 1

The most provocative origin of Wonder Woman you've ever seen. Thought-provoking yet reverent, the power and courage of Paradise Island's greatest champion is introduced in this addition to DC's bestselling Earth One original graphic novel series.

WONDER WOMAN
EARTH ONE
VOLUME ONE
GRANT MORRISON
YANICK PAQUETTE
NATHAN FAIRBAIRN
DC COMICS

Writer: **GRANT MORRISON**
Artist: **YANICK PAQUETTE**
Price: **USA $22.99/CAN $27.99**
Format: **HC**
ISBN: **9781401229788**

WONDER WOMAN HISTORIA: THE AMAZONS

Millennia ago, Queen Hera and the goddesses of the Olympian pantheon grew greatly dissatisfied with their male counterparts...and far from their sight, they put a plan into action. A new society was born, one never before seen on Earth, capable of wondrous and terrible things...but their existence could not stay secret for long. When a despairing woman named Hippolyta crossed the Amazons' path, a series of events was set in motion that would lead to an outright war in heaven—and the creation of the Earth's greatest guardian!

WONDER WOMAN
HISTORIA
THE AMAZONS

17+

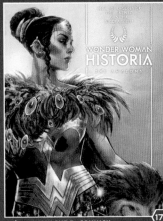

Writer: **KELLY SUE DeCONNICK**
Artists: **PHIL JIMENEZ, GENE HA, and NICOLA SCOTT**
Price: **USA $29.99/CAN $39.99**
Format: **HC**
ISBN: **9781779521354**

NUBIA & THE AMAZONS

After the thrilling events of *Infinite Frontier*, Nubia becomes queen of Themyscira, but the new title also brings challenges. With the unexpected arrival of new Amazons, our hero is forced to reckon with her past and forge a new path forward for her sisters.

NUBIA
& THE AMAZONS
STEPHANIE WILLIAMS
VITA AYALA
ALITHA MARTINEZ
MARK MORALES

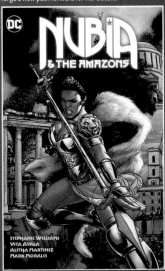

Writers: **VITA AYALA and STEPHANIE WILLIAMS**
Artist: **ALITHA MARTINEZ**
Price: **USA $24.99/CAN $33.99**
Format: **HC**
ISBN: **9781779516671**

TRIAL OF THE AMAZONS

Trial of the Amazons is an epic crossover event where all the Amazonian tribes will collide and compete for leadership. Discover who guides the Amazons into the future and who is trying to destroy them in the process!

TRIAL OF THE
AMAZONS

Writer: **BECKY CLOONAN, MICHAEL CONRAD, STEPHANIE WILLIAMS, and VITA AYALA**
Artist: **JOËLLE JONES**
Price: **USA $29.99/CAN $39.99**
Format: **HC**
ISBN: **9781779516824**

WONDER GIRL: HOMECOMING

This is where the legend of Yara Flor begins! Meet the new Wonder Girl—and the future of Wonder Woman! The story of Yara Flor starts here!

WONDER GIRL
HOMECOMING
JOËLLE JONES
ADRIANA MELO
LEILA DEL DUCA
JORDIE BELLAIRE

Writer: **JOËLLE JONES**
Artist: **JOËLLE JONES**
Price: **USA $39.99/CAN $53.99**
Format: **HC**
ISBN: **9781779516664**

ALL-STAR SUPERMAN

A spectacular reimagining of the Superman mythos, from the Man of Steel's origin to his greatest foes and beyond. This Eisner Award winner goes back to basics to create a new vision of the world's first superhero.

ALL-STAR SUPERMAN
DC
GRANT MORRISON | FRANK QUITELY | JAMIE GRANT

Writer: **GRANT MORRISON**
Artist: **FRANK QUITELY**
Price: **USA $29.99/CAN $39.99**
Format: **TR**
ISBN: **9781401290832**

SUPERMAN: RED SON (New Edition)

A vivid tale of Cold War paranoia that reveals how the ship carrying the infant who would later be known as Superman lands in the 1950s Soviet Union. Raised on a collective farm, the infant grows up and becomes a symbol to the Soviet people, and the world changes drastically from what we know.

DC
"One of the best stories in the history of the Man of Steel." —IGN
SUPERMAN
RED SON
MARK MILLAR DAVE JOHNSON KILIAN PLUNKETT

Writer: **MARK MILLAR**
Artists: **DAVE JOHNSON and KILIAN PLUNKETT**
Price: **USA $17.99/CAN $23.99**
Format: **TR**
ISBN: **9781401247119**

THE DEATH OF SUPERMAN

The event that shocked the world! Doomsday has landed on Earth, causing death and destruction to anything—and anyone—that dares stand in his way. When the beast nears Metropolis, Superman answers the call to stop him. And then the unthinkable happens. The Man of Steel...dies!

DC COMICS
THE DEATH OF
SUPERMAN

Writers: **DAN JURGENS, JERRY ORDWAY, LOUISE SIMONSON, and more**
Artists: **JON BOGDANOVE, TOM GRUMMETT, DAN JURGENS, and more**
Price: **USA $17.99 /CAN $21.99**
Format: **TR**
ISBN: **9781401266653**

SUPERMAN: REIGN OF THE SUPERMEN

Four men return claiming to be the recently deceased Man of Steel—but who is the real Superman? By writer/artist Dan Jurgens, this storyline heralded the return of the one, true Superman!

DC COMICS
REIGN OF THE SUPERMEN
SUPERMAN

Writer: **DAN JURGENS**
Artist: **DAN JURGENS**
Price: **USA $24.99/CAN $29.99**
Format: **TR**
ISBN: **9781401266639**

SUPERMAN: WHATEVER HAPPENED TO THE MAN OF TOMORROW? THE DELUXE EDITION

The acclaimed final adventure of the Man of Steel featuring his last stand against Lex Luthor, Brainiac, and his other foes, from the writer of *Watchmen*, Alan Moore.

DC
NEW YORK TIMES BESTSELLING AUTHOR ALAN MOORE • CURT SWAN
SUPERMAN
WHATEVER HAPPENED TO THE MAN OF TOMORROW?
THE DELUXE EDITION
SEE
The Rampage of BIZARRO!
MEET
The NEW Brainiac Luthor TEAM!
EXPERIENCE
The Return of the FEARSOME FUNSTERS!
SURVIVE
The Daily Planet's LAST STAND!
WITNESS
The Killing of CLARK KENT!
IN MEMORIAM
SUPERMAN
ATTEND
The Legion of Super-Heroes LAST SALUTE!

Writer: **ALAN MOORE**
Artists: **CURT SWAN and DAVE GIBBONS**
Price: **USA $29.99/CAN $39.99**
Format: **HC**
ISBN: **9781779504890**

SUPERMAN: EARTH ONE

Forget everything you know about the Man of Steel and brace yourself for a staggering new take on the world's most popular superhero. Return to Smallville and experience the journey of Earth's favorite adopted son as he grows from boy to Superman like you've never seen before!

SUPERMAN
The #1 New York Times Bestseller
EARTH ONE
VOLUME ONE
J. MICHAEL STRACZYNSKI
SHANE DAVIS
—THE HOLLYWOOD REPORTER
DC

Writer: **J. MICHAEL STRACZYNSKI**
Artist: **SHANE DAVIS**
Price: **USA $14.99/CAN $17.99**
Format: **TR**
ISBN: **9781401224691**

BATMAN VOL. 1: THE COURT OF OWLS (The New 52)

Batman has heard tales of Gotham City's Court of Owls: that the members of this powerful cabal are the true rulers of Gotham. The Dark Knight dismissed the stories as rumors and old wives' tales. Gotham was his city. Until now.

THE #1 NEW YORK TIMES BESTSELLER
THE NEW 52!
BATMAN
VOLUME 1
THE COURT OF OWLS
"SNYDER MIGHT BE THE DEFINING BATMAN WRITER OF OUR GENERATION." – COMPLEX MAGAZINE
SCOTT SNYDER GREG CAPULLO JONATHAN GLAPION

Writer: **SCOTT SNYDER**
Artist: **GREG CAPULLO**
Price: **USA $16.99/CAN $19.99**
Format: **TR**
ISBN: **9781401235420**

BATMAN VOL. 2: THE CITY OF OWLS (The New 52)

For over a century, the Court of Owls has ruled Gotham City in secret—their reach inescapable, their power unstoppable. Until they battled the Batman.

THE #1 NEW YORK TIMES BEST-SELLING SERIES
THE NEW 52!
BATMAN
"ONE OF THE BEST TITLES ON THE MARKET." —THE ONION / AV CLUB
VOLUME 2
THE CITY OF OWLS
SCOTT SNYDER GREG CAPULLO JONATHAN GLAPION JAMES TYNION IV RAFAEL ALBUQUERQUE JASON FABOK

Writer: **SCOTT SNYDER**
Artist: **GREG CAPULLO**
Price: **USA $16.99/CAN $19.99**
Format: **TR**
ISBN: **9781401232597**

BATMAN VOL. 1: THEIR DARK DESIGNS

Deathstroke, the world's greatest mercenary, is back in town under a new contract. As the Caped Crusader draws closer to uncovering the figure pulling the strings, the love of his life, Catwoman, holds the sinister secret in her claws. Can Batman pry it from her without tearing their relationship apart? And will it be enough to stop the coming plot against him?

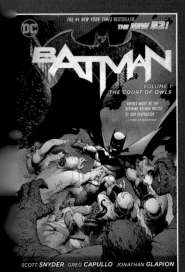

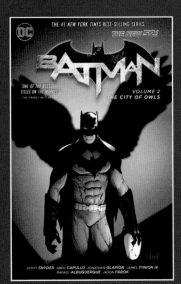

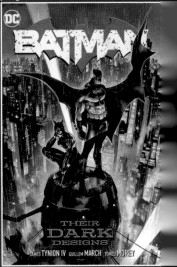

BATMAN
THEIR DARK DESIGNS
JAMES TYNION IV GUILLEM MARCH TOMEU MOREY

Writer: **JAMES TYNION IV**
Artist: **GUILLEM MARCH**
Price: **USA $24.99/CAN $33.99**
Format: **TR**
ISBN: **9781779508010**

BATMAN VOL. 1: I AM GOTHAM (Rebirth)

There are two new heroes in town with the powers of Superman and a devotion to preserving all that is good about this twisted city. But what happens if Gotham's new guardians go bad? What if they blame the Batman for the darkness that threatens to drown their city?

DC UNIVERSE REBIRTH
BATMAN
VOL.1 I AM GOTHAM
TOM KING • DAVID FINCH

BATMAN: DETECTIVE COMICS VOL. 1: THE NEIGHBORHOOD

With the loss of his fortune and manor, the election of Mayor Nakano, and the growing anti-vigilante sentiment in Gotham, Bruce Wayne must rethink how to be Batman...or risk being left behind by his own city.

BATMAN
DETECTIVE COMICS
THE NEIGHBORHOOD
MARIKO TAMAKI DAN MORA VIKTOR BOGDANOVIC JORDIE BELLAIRE

I AM BATMAN VOL. 1

Jace Fox thrusts himself into action when the Magistrate's crackdown on Alleytown begins! With his own Batsuit, Jace hits the streets to inspire and protect...but one Gotham vigilante pays the ultimate price when they're shot down in cold blood.

I AM BATMAN
VOL. 1
JOHN RIDLEY OLIVIER COIPEL TRAVEL FOREMAN STEPHEN SEGOVIA

CATWOMAN VOL. 1: DANGEROUS LIAISONS

t's a new era for Catwoman, with a new creative team and a new target—Gotham City's underworld! Meow, Catwoman is bored of Alleytown and has returned to Gotham City proper for bigger fish to fry and to go back to doing what she does best...stealing crime boss secrets for blackmail and looking damn sexy while doing it, of course.

CATWOMAN
DANGEROUS LIAISONS
TINI HOWARD
NICO LEON
BENGAL
JORDIE BELLAIRE
VERONICA GANDINI
DC

Writer: **TINI HOWARD**
Artists: **NICO LEON and BENGAL**
Price: **USA $16.99/CAN $22.99**
Format: **TR**
ISBN: **9781779517289**

BATGIRL VOL. 1: BATGIRL OF BURNSIDE (The New 52)

The next chapter of *Batgirl* begins with a new creative team and a bold new direction! Barbara Gordon moves across Gotham City to begin the next chapter of her life as Batgirl!

CAMERON STEWART BRENDEN FLETCHER BABS TARR with MARIS WICKS
DC COMICS
BATGIRL
VOLUME 1
BATGIRL OF BURNSIDE
"Smart and chic." ENTERTAINMENT WEEKLY

Writers: **CAMERON STEWART and BRENDEN FLETCHER**
Artists: **BABS TARR and MARIS WICKS**
Price: **USA $14.99/CAN $17.99**
Format: **TR**
ISBN: **9781401257989**

NIGHTWING VOL. 1: LEAPING INTO THE LIGHT

Nightwing is back—and his drive to keep Blüdhaven safe ha never been stronger! But his adoptive city has elected a nev mayor with the last name Zucco. When Nightwing enlists Batgirl's help in investigating the politician bearing the sam name as the man who murdered his parents, she unearths details that will shock and fundamentally change the hero.

DC
TOM TAYLOR
BRUNO REDONDO
NIGHTWING
LEAPING INTO THE LIGHT

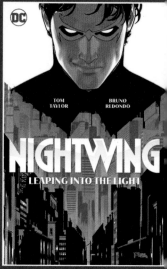

Writer: **TOM TAYLOR**
Artist: **BRUNO REDONDO**
Price: **USA $24.99/CAN $33.99**
Format: **HC**
ISBN: **9781779512789**

ROBIN VOL. 1: THE LAZARUS TOURNAMENT

Damian Wayne will be forced to find his own path as Robin away from both sides of his family—his father, Bruce Wayne, the Dark Knight, and his mother, Talia l Ghul, the daughter of Ra's al Ghul, the ecoterrorist nown as the Demon's Head!

ROBIN
The LAZARUS TOURNAMENT
JOSHUA WILLIAMSON · GLEB MELNIKOV
JORGE CORONA
DC

Writer: **JOSHUA WILLIAMSON**
Artists: **GLEB MELNIKOV and JORGE CORONA**
Price: **USA $19.99/CAN $25.99**
Format: **TR**
ISBN: **9781779514332**

RED HOOD AND THE OUTLAWS VOL. 1: DARK TRINITY (Rebirth)

Red Hood embraces his dark side and looks to take down Gotham with the help of his new Outsiders: Bizarro and Artemis! Red Hood returns with a brand-new series by longtime Red Hood writer Scott Lobdell with art by Dexter Soy (*Mortal Kombat X*)!

DC UNIVERSE REBIRTH
RED HOOD AND THE OUTLAWS
VOL.1 DARK TRINITY
SCOTT LOBDELL • DEXTER SOY • VERONICA GANDINI
DC

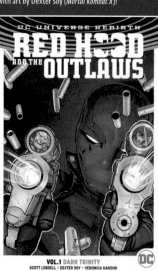

Writer: **SCOTT LOBDELL**
Artists: **DEXTER SOY and VERONICA GANDINI**
Price: **USA $16.99/CAN $22.99**
Format: **TR**
ISBN: **9781401268756**

BATGIRLS VOL. 1: ONE WAY OR ANOTHER

Two Bats are better than one! Cassandra Cain and Stephanie Brown star in the team-up book you've been waiting for—under the mentorship of Barbara Gordon, the original Batgirl!

DC
BATGIRLS
ONE WAY OR ANOTHER
BECKY CLOONAN
MICHAEL W. CONRAD
JORGE CORONA
SARAH STERN

Writers: **BECKY CLOONAN and MICHAEL W. CONRAD**
Artists: **JORGE CORONA and SARAH STERN**
Price: **USA $16.99/CAN $22.99**
Format: **TR**
ISBN: **9781779517067**